Motivating Behavior Change
Among Illicit-Drug Abusers

Motivating Behavior Change Among Illicit-Drug Abusers

Research on Contingency Management Interventions

EDITED BY

Stephen T. Higgins and Kenneth Silverman

AMERICAN PSYCHOLOGICAL ASSOCIATION • WASHINGTON, DC

Published by
American Psychological Association
750 First Street, NE
Washington, DC 20002

Copies may be ordered from
APA Order Department
P.O. Box 92984
Washington, DC 20090-2984

In the U.K., Europe, Africa, and the Middle East, copies may be ordered from
American Psychological Association
3 Henrietta Street
Covent Garden, London
WC2E 8LU England

Typeset in Goudy by EPS Group Inc., Easton, MD

Printer: Data Reproductions Corp., Auburn Hills, MI
Dust jacket designer: Berg Design, Albany, NY
Technical/Production Editor: Amy J. Clarke

Library of Congress Cataloging-in-Publication Data
Motivating behavior change among illicit-drug abusers : research on contingency
    management interventions / edited by Stephen T. Higgins and Kenneth
    Silverman.—1st ed.
        p.   cm.
    Includes bibliographical references and index.
    ISBN 1-55798-570-7 (cloth : acid-free paper)
    1. Drug abuse—Treatment.   2. Behavior modification.   3. Token economy
(Psychology)   I. Higgins, Stephen T.   II. Silverman, Kenneth 1953–
RA564.M58   1999
616.86'30651—dc21   98-47471
                                                                                CIP

British Library Cataloguing-in-Publication Data
A CIP record is available from the British Library.

Printed in the United States of America
First Edition

CONTENTS

CONTRIBUTORS

Leslie Amass, Department of Psychiatry, University of Colorado School of Medicine

Mark A. Belding, Allan Collautt Associates, Inc., Broomall, PA

Warren K. Bickel, Human Behavioral Pharmacology Laboratory, Departments of Psychiatry and Psychology, University of Vermont

George E. Bigelow, Department of Psychiatry and Behavioral Sciences, Johns Hopkins University School of Medicine

Edward J. Cone, National Institute of Drug Abuse Intramural Research Program, Addiction Research Center, Baltimore, MD

Amy L. Copeland, Department of Psychiatry, University of California, San Francisco

Thomas J. Crowley, Department of Psychiatry and Addiction Research and Treatment Service, University of Colorado School of Medicine

Robert Dantona, Human Behavioral Pharmacology Laboratory, Department of Psychiatry and Psychology, University of Vermont

Sandy Dow, Los Angeles (CA) Addiction Treatment Research Center and Friends Research Institute

Thad A. Eckman, Department of Psychiatry and Biobehavioral Sciences, University of California, Los Angeles, School of Medicine and West Los Angeles Veterans Administration Medical Center

Ronith Elk, Women Can Do Great Things, Houston, TX

Dominick L. Frosch, Los Angeles (CA) Addiction Treatment Research Center and Friends Research Institute

Sharon M. Hall, Department of Psychiatry, University of California, San Francisco, and San Francisco Veterans Administration Medical Center

Stephen T. Higgins, Human Behavioral Pharmacology Laboratory, Departments of Psychiatry and Psychology, University of Vermont

Alice Huber, Matrix Center and Friends Research Institute, Los Angeles, CA

Martin Y. Iguchi, RAND Corporation, Santa Monica, CA

Murray E. Jarvik, West Los Angeles Veterans Affairs Medical Center and Department of Psychiatry, University of California, Los Angeles, School of Medicine

Michael Kidorf, Department of Psychiatry, Johns Hopkins University School of Medicine

Kimberly C. Kirby, Department of Psychological Studies in Education, Temple University

Walter Ling, Los Angeles Addiction Treatment Research Center, Friends Research Institute, West Los Angeles Veterans Affairs Medical Center, and Department of Psychiatry, University of California, Los Angeles, School of Medicine

Damian C. Madsen, West Los Angeles Veterans Affairs Medical Center and Department of Psychiatry, University of California, Los Angeles, School of Medicine

Lisa A. Marsch, Human Behavioral Pharmacology Laboratory, Departments of Psychiatry and Psychology, University of Vermont

Carmen L. Masson, Department of Psychiatry, University of California, San Francisco

A. Thomas McLellan, Center for Studies of Addiction, Philadelphia (PA) Veterans Administration Medical Center and University of Pennsylvania School of Medicine

Michael McMann, Matrix Center and Friends Research Institute, Los Angeles, CA

Cecelia L. McNamara, Department of Medicine, University of Alabama at Birmingham School of Medicine

Max Michael, Department of Medicine, University of Alabama at Birmingham School of Medicine and Birmingham Health Care for the Homeless

Jesse B. Milby, Department of Medicine, University of Alabama at Birmingham School of Medicine

Andrew R. Morral, RAND Corporation, Santa Monica, CA

Michael V. Pantalon, Department of Psychiatry and Substance Abuse Center, Yale University School of Medicine

Nancy A. Piotrowski, Alcohol Research Group, Berkeley, CA

Sam Popkin, Birmingham (AL) Veterans Administration Medical Center

Kenzie L. Preston, National Institute of Drug Abuse Intramural Research Program, Addiction Research Center, Baltimore, MD

Richard Rawson, Matrix Center and Friends Research Institute and Department of Psychiatry, University of California, Los Angeles, School of Medicine

Lisa J. Roberts, Addictive Behaviors Research Center, University of Washington

John M. Roll, Department of Psychiatry and Behavioral Neuroscience, University Psychiatry Center, Wayne State University School of Medicine

Richard S. Schottenfeld, Department of Psychiatry and Substance Abuse Center, Yale University School of Medicine

Joseph E. Schumacher, Department of Medicine, University of Alabama at Birmingham School of Medicine

Charles R. Schuster, Department of Psychiatry and Neuroscience, University Psychiatry Center, Wayne State University School of Medicine

Andrew Shaner, Department of Psychiatry and Biobehavioral Sciences, University of California, Los Angeles, School of Medicine and West Los Angeles Veterans Administration Medical Center

Steven Shoptaw, Los Angeles (CA) Addiction Treatment Research Center and Matrix Center and Friends Research Institute

Kenneth Silverman, Department of Psychiatry and Behavioral Sciences, Johns Hopkins University School of Medicine

James L. Sorensen, Department of Psychiatry, University of California, San Francisco

Maxine L. Stitzer, Department of Psychiatry and Behavioral Sciences, Johns Hopkins University School of Medicine

Jennifer W. Tidey, Human Behavioral Pharmacology Laboratory, Departments of Psychiatry and Psychology, University of Vermont

Douglas E. Tucker, Department of Psychiatry and Biobehavioral Sciences, University of California, Los Angeles, School of Medicine and West Los Angeles Veterans Administration Medical Center

Stuart Usdan, Department of Medicine, University of Alabama at Birmingham School of Medicine

Dennis Wallace, Department of Medicine, University of Alabama at Birmingham School of Medicine

Conrad J. Wong, Human Behavioral Pharmacology Laboratory, Departments of Psychiatry and Psychology, University of Vermont

FOREWORD

The demonstration that animals would self-administer many drugs of abuse led to a major reformulation of the conceptual framework of the problem of drug addiction. Today, it is well accepted that drugs of abuse serve as positive reinforcers for the behavior leading to their acquisition and self-administration. Furthermore, it is also recognized that for drugs that produce physical dependence, drug self-administration may also be maintained by the reduction of the aversive withdrawal state, that is, by negative reinforcement. The conceptualization of drugs of abuse within the framework of the principles of behavior analysis pointed to antecedent variables and modulating events that had been shown to be of importance with behaviors maintained by more commonly used reinforcers, such as food, water, or sex, and therefore may be of importance in controlling drug-seeking behaviors. Studies of such antecedent variables as deprivation and satiation as well as schedules of reinforcement have shown that behavior maintained by drug reinforcers follows the same general rules as behavior maintained by other positive reinforcers. More recently, human laboratory research has confirmed and extended the relevance of a behavior analytic approach to understanding the etiology, prevention, and treatment of substance abuse. This volume on contingency management interventions for the treatment of drug abuse represents an outgrowth of this research and is a marvelous example of how basic research can have important clinical applications.

Preeminent researchers in this field, Higgins and Silverman have shown their scholarship in their selection of contributors for this volume and in the comprehensiveness of its coverage. This volume begins with a chapter by Bigelow and Silverman detailing the conceptual and empirical foundations of contingency management approaches illustrated in the remainder of the book. This opening chapter is of great importance because it shows the rich empirical basis for the interventions described in the next

12 chapters. The diversity of settings, drug problems, and people whose lives have been positively affected by the use of contingency management procedures is impressively demonstrated in these chapters. This wealth of information will provide guidance to practitioners interested in the application of specific contingency management interventions. These chapters also will be of value as a teaching tool for illustrating rigorous clinical research. The next two chapters focus on methodological issues. First, Preston et al. describe the basis of using quantitative urinalysis drug testing as a means of reinforcing short-term abstinence that would not be revealed by qualitative urinalysis. This methodology has great potential for guaranteeing the shortest possible temporal interval between a period of abstinence and the delivery of the reinforcer. Second, Pantalon and Schottenfeld outline ways of adapting methods used in other areas of psychotherapy to the contingency management approach to better monitor the global behavioral changes produced by these procedures.

The volume ends with two marvelous chapters. First, Kirby, Amass, and McLellan discuss the vexing problem of how to get effective treatment interventions developed by university-based treatment researchers adopted by community treatment programs. The history of success in this regard can dampen ones ardor for research as a means of improving treatment effectiveness. Kirby et al. provide a practical and insightful discussion of strategies for surmounting many of the challenges involved in disseminating contingency management interventions to community clinics. Finally, one of the pioneers of the contingency management approach to the treatment of drug abuse, Crowley summarizes the clinical implications of the research reviewed and speculates about important research issues for the future. I cannot think of anyone better suited to this task.

In summary, I am honored to have been asked to write the foreword to this volume. I believe that it will be of great importance as a textbook and reference work. I also believe that the truly compassionate side of contingency management approach is apparent in the writings of these dedicated researchers. Far from an Orwellian schema of behavioral control, contingency management approaches offer the greatest hope to those trying to gain control over their disordered lives by offering them the means of understanding how to control their behavior. Higgins, Silverman, and all of the contributors to this volume are to be congratulated on a fine piece of work.

PREFACE

The contributors to this volume review and critique research efforts to use contingency management interventions to motivate behavior change among illicit-drug abusers. They were invited to contribute because of their national and international reputations for research and clinical excellence. Each chapter is intended to be sufficiently detailed and current to be of value to researchers, clinicians, and policymakers alike who are involved in decreasing illicit-drug abuse.

Bringing an edited book to fruition requires a great deal of support from many. Foremost among those to whom we extend our sincere gratitude are the contributors for taking precious time from their already demanding schedules to prepare their chapters. We thank the National Institute on Drug Abuse, especially John Boren and Jack Blaine, for supporting most of the research projects described in this volume and for assisting us in sponsoring a meeting on this same topic in Bethesda, Maryland, on September 14 and 15, 1995. That meeting was an invaluable first step toward organizing this volume. We sincerely thank all the people at the American Psychological Association who were involved in the publication of this volume for their guidance, flexibility, and support, especially our development editor, Ed Meidenbauer. We thank Dale Desranleau for her untiring assistance and technical support in preparing this volume, Finally, I (Higgins) thank Tamra, Tara, and Lucy for their wonderful support, love, and companionship and Mary T. Higgins and Agnes Doran for early inspiration. I (Silverman) wish to thank Ann, Danny, and Jake for their loving support.

Stephen T. Higgins
Burlington, VT

Kenneth Silverman
Baltimore, MD

I

THE BASICS OF
CONTINGENCY
MANAGEMENT

INTRODUCTION

STEPHEN T. HIGGINS

Illicit-drug abuse remains a major U.S. public health problem. Recent national survey data reveal that an estimated 24 million members of U.S. households age 12 years and older report using an illicit drug in the past year and that almost 14 million report use in the past month (Substance Abuse and Mental Health Services Administration [SAMHSA], 1998a, 1998b). Many are heavy drug users. Approximately 6.4 million individuals report using marijuana, and 682,000 report using cocaine on an average of once a week or more in the past year (SAMHSA, 1998a, 1998b). Alarming trends also are evident. For example, from 1993 to 1997, the number of individuals who reported using heroin in the past month increased from 68,000 to 325,000 (SAMHSA, 1995, 1998a, 1998b). As another example, from 1993 to 1997 the number of youths (12–17 years old) who reported using an illicit drug in the past month almost doubled from approximately 1.4 million to 2.6 million.

Illicit-drug abuse contributes to many of the most disturbing individual and societal problems in the United States. Cocaine and heroin abuse are associated with increased crime and incarceration; drug-exposed neonates;

the spread of AIDS, tuberculosis, hepatitis, and other infectious diseases; poverty; trauma; and violence (Konkol & Olsen, 1996; Montoya & Atkinson, 1996; National Institute of Justice, 1997; SAMHSA, 1998; Tardiff et al., 1994). Marijuana abuse—typically considered less harmful than cocaine and heroin abuse—is associated with impairments in memory, attention, motivation, and health; problems in interpersonal relationships and employment; and an increased abuse of other drugs (Halikas, Weller, Morse, & Hoffman, 1983; Jones, 1980; Kandel, 1984; Stephens, Roffman, & Simpson, 1993). Annual costs associated with illicit-drug abuse in the United States are estimated in the billions of dollars, mostly because of the high levels of morbidity, mortality, and lost productivity associated with this problem (Center on Addiction and Substance Abuse, 1994; Rice, Kelman, Miller, & Dunmeyer, 1990). When considered in terms of unrealized potential, ruined families, and emotional–psychological suffering, the costs are incalculable.

Treatment can be effective in helping illicit-drug abusers decrease drug abuse and improve other important areas of functioning (e.g., Higgins & Wong, 1998; Stitzer & Higgins, 1995). Indeed, such improvements are estimated to result in cost savings that well exceed the cost of providing treatment (e.g., Rydell & Everingham, 1994). Unfortunately, the majority of illicit-drug abusers do not seek out formal substance abuse treatment (Regier et al., 1993), and a large proportion of those who do either leave treatment prematurely or continue abusing drugs (Higgins & Wong, 1998). Additionally, chronic relapse among those who show initial treatment improvement, although not unique to substance abusers, certainly is a major problem (Hall, Havassy, & Wasserman, 1990, 1991). Treatment efforts also are complicated by high rates of co-occurring serious psychiatric, legal, vocational, and other problems among illicit-drug abusers that often demand professional intervention (Ball & Ross, 1991; Onken, Blaine, Genser, & Horton, 1997; Regier et al., 1990).

CONTINGENCY MANAGEMENT: A SCIENTIFICALLY BASED TREATMENT APPROACH

Tremendous interest exists among the drug abuse research and treatment communities in developing empirically based and effective interventions to enhance motivation for change among substance abusers, including those with comorbid disorders. Contingency management interventions represent one of several empirically based and effective approaches to enhancing motivation among substance abusers. The chapters in this volume provide compelling evidence that illicit-drug abusers, even those with severe and complicated forms of drug abuse and associated problems, can be motivated to change their behavior through this approach.

One of the most distinguishing features of the contingency management approach is its robust scientific foundation. Contingency management interventions are based on extensive basic-science and clinical research evidence, demonstrating that drug abuse is heavily influenced by learning and conditioning and is quite sensitive to systematically applied environmental consequences (Griffiths, Bigelow, & Henningfield, 1980; Higgins, 1996, 1997; Stitzer & Higgins, 1995). An excellent review of the scientific and theoretical underpinnings of the contingency management approach is provided in chapter 1 of this volume.

Contingency management procedures arrange for the systematic application of behavioral consequences for drug use and abstinence as well as other therapeutic behavior. This volume provides detailed overviews of many of the most innovative and efficacious of the contingency management research projects under way in the United States.

Contingency management interventions almost always involve one or more of the following generic contingencies to motivate increases and decreases in the frequency of a therapeutically desirable and undesirable behavior: (a) Positive reinforcement involves delivery of a desired consequence (e.g., a voucher exchangeable for retail items), contingent on the individual meeting a therapeutic goal (e.g., negative urinalysis test results); (b) negative reinforcement involves removing an aversive or confining circumstance (e.g., intense criminal justice supervision), contingent on meeting a target therapeutic goal (e.g., attending counseling sessions); (c) positive punishment involves delivery of a punishing consequence (e.g., a professional reprimand), contingent on evidence of undesirable behavior (e.g., positive urinalysis test results); and (d) negative punishment involves removal of a positive condition (e.g., the monetary value of a voucher to be earned is reduced), contingent on evidence of the occurrence of an undesirable behavior (e.g., missing a scheduled counseling session).

Reinforcement and punishment contingencies can be effective in motivating change, but the former generally are preferred over the latter by patients and therapists alike (see chapter 16, this volume). A judicious combination of frequent positive reinforcement and infrequent negative punishment can be very effective as is illustrated, for example, by the voucher program described in chapter 2 and elsewhere in this volume. Whether the contingencies involve reinforcement, punishment, or both, to be effective they must be applied systematically and with minimal delay between occurrence of the target response and delivery of the consequence. Also critical to successful contingency management is precise information on the occurrence of the therapeutic target response. With drug abusers, this is usually whether they have used drugs recently and involves some form of objective monitoring of biological products indicative of drug use. Urinalysis testing is the most common monitoring procedure. The chapters in this volume illustrate a rich variety of different ways of effectively implementing these basic tenets of contingency management with illicit-drug abusers. In chapter 14 the important matters about urinalysis and other objective methods of monitoring drug use are discussed, and in chapter 15 the importance of carefully monitoring and studying further the "process" of implementing contingency management interventions is examined.

COCAINE ABUSERS

Although contingency management studies on the treatment of various types of licit- and illicit-drug abuse have been available in the clinical research literature for several decades, a new and more intense interest arose in the 1990s when the appplication of these strategies was shown to be effective in the treatment of cocaine dependence. When cocaine abuse reached epidemic proportions in the United States in the early and mid 1980s, there was virtually nothing in the clinical literature demonstrating how this problem could be effectively treated. Clinical research efforts were launched throughout the United States examining an extensive variety of pharmacological and psychosocial interventions. Within the context of this large clinical research effort, contingency management interventions have proved to be one of the few reliably efficacious treatments for cocaine dependence (see Higgins & Wong, 1998, for a review). Much of the research that spurred this renewed interest in contingency management is reviewed in chapters 2, 3, 4, and 8 of this volume.

SPECIAL POPULATIONS

Illicit-drug abuse always presents a daunting clinical challenge, but when combined with pregnancy, homelessness, serious mental illness, HIV, or other infectious diseases, the clinical challenges are enormous. Efforts are under way at numerous sites throughout the United States to extend contingency management to the treatment of such special populations of drug abusers.

Homeless

The relationship between substance abuse and homelessness is now well documented (Breakey et al., 1989). Contingency management interventions in combination with intensive psychosocial treatment are proving to be effective and promising efforts for decreasing drug abuse and increasing important areas of functioning among homeless crack and other substance abusers. Schumacher, Milby, et al. completed randomized clinical trials demonstrating the efficacy of an intervention that combines housing and employment contingent on drug abstinence with an intensive day hospital treatment (see chapter 4, this volume).

Seriously Mentally Ill

Prevalence of drug abuse among those with serious mental illness is three- to sixfold higher than among the general population (Hughes, Hatsukami, Mitchell, & Dahlgren, 1986; Regier et al., 1990). Unfortunately, little is known about how to effectively treat drug abuse in this special population. To my knowledge, there are no controlled clinical trials reported documenting the efficacy of any treatment for illicit-drug abuse among the seriously mentally ill, so the need for progress in this area is clear. Shaner et al. (chapter 5) provide a detailed overview of the problem of illicit-drug abuse in this population and review studies on relationships between cocaine abuse, increased psychiatric symptomatology, and possible misallocation of disability payments to the purchase of cocaine among persons disabled by serious mental illness. They discuss their initial research efforts to use contingency management to decrease cocaine abuse in this population. Additional research on the use of contingency management for decreasing drug use among persons with schizophrenia is reported in chapter 2.

Other Medical Conditions

With pregnant abusers, toxicity to the fetus can result not only from the direct pharmacological effects of the abused drugs but also from the generally impoverished and neglectful lifestyle of the mother, including poor compliance with prenatal care. Elk and colleagues have been investigating the efficacy of contingency management interventions for increasing attendance at prenatal medical appointments and decreasing drug use among pregnant illicit-drug abusers (Elk, chapter 6, this volume). Preliminary results from their studies are encouraging, especially regarding the potentially important health benefits that may accrue from increasing compliance with prenatal care visits among these expectant mothers. In a programmatic research effort, Elk and colleagues adapted similar procedures for increasing compliance with medication regimens among tuberculosis-infected drug abusers, and the initial evidence from that effort is encouraging as well.

OPIATE ABUSERS

Use of combined pharmacological and behavioral treatments is increasing in the field of substance abuse treatment (Onken, Blaine, &

Boren, 1995). No area better illustrates the efficacy of combining pharmacological and behavioral interventions than the treatment of opiate abuse. Effective pharmacotherapies exist for heroin and other opiate abuse in the form of methadone, buprenorphine, and other medications. However, as mentioned above, behavioral interventions are needed to increase the proportion of opiate abusers who will avail themselves of treatment with these medications. For those who enter treatment, combining these medications with effective behavioral treatments is critical for producing optimal treatment outcomes (McLellan, Arndt, Metzger, Woody, & O'Brien, 1993).

Sorensen, Masson, and Copeland (chapter 7) review the challenge of increasing treatment enrollment among intravenous drug abusers and review results from projects at numerous sites across the United States examining the efficacy of incentives for that purpose. These and other interventions to promote treatment participation among opiate and other illicit-drug abusers who otherwise would not enter treatment are essential if substantial progress is to be made in decreasing illicit-drug abuse.

Ongoing patterns of cocaine abuse are particularly prevalent and problematic among many of those who participate in methadone maintenance treatment (Silverman, Bigelow, & Stitzer, 1998). Methadone is very effective for decreasing opiate use but does little directly to decrease cocaine abuse. Consistent with observations in the larger population of cocaine abusers, cocaine abuse among methadone patients is associated with increased rates of HIV infection, unemployment, criminal activity, and complications during pregnancy (Silverman et al., 1998). Silverman, Preston, Stitzer, and Schuster (chapter 8) describe a programmatic series of clinical trials documenting the efficacy of contingency management interventions for decreasing cocaine and opiate abuse and increasing participation in vocational training among methadone maintenance patients. Piotrowski and Hall (chapter 9) review a related program for effectively and simultaneously increasing abstinence from multiple drugs of abuse among methadone maintenance patients.

One should not forget that illicit-drug abusers are more likely than the general population to abuse licit drugs. Approximately 90% of methadone patients are regular cigarette smokers (Clemmey, Brooner, Chutuape, Kidorf, & Stitzer, 1997). In the past, treating cigarette smoking among those enrolled in treatment for illicit-drug abuse was uncommon. However, as awareness has increased regarding the morbidity and mortality of cigarette smokers, and as drug abuse patients have become interested in smoking cessation, the situation has changed. There now is considerable interest in and progress being made in providing effective smoking cessation interventions to patients enrolled in drug abuse treatment (Clemmey et al., 1997; Irving, Seidner, Burling, Thomas, & Brenner, 1994; Story & Stark, 1991). Shoptaw et al. (chapter 12) report on their efforts to use a contingency management intervention to increase smoking abstinence among maintenance patients.

Opioid detoxification is associated with early attrition and resumption of illicit-opioid abuse (Milby, 1988). Nevertheless, there continues to be demand for opioid detoxification among opioid abusers, and failure at detoxification is sometimes a criterion for admission into methadone maintenance programs (Ball & Ross, 1991). For these reasons, there is interest in improving the efficacy of opioid detoxification (e.g., Reilly et al., 1995). Bickel and Marsch (chapter 13) report on their successful research efforts to improve the efficacy of opioid detoxification by combining it with an intensive behavioral treatment that includes contingency management and the community reinforcement approach.

When treating opioid abusers with methadone and related pharmacotherapies, a number of routine clinic privileges are available for use as incentives in contingency management interventions. An attractive feature of using clinic privileges as incentives is their relatively low cost. Kidorf and Stitzer (chapter 11) provide an excellent overview of the effective use of clinic privileges routinely available in the methadone clinic to reinforce abstinence from illicit-drug use and promote other therapeutic changes in opioid abusers.

The vast majority of the contingency management interventions used to increase abstinence from drug use involves contingencies placed directly on results of some objective marker of recent drug use, usually urinalysis results. An interesting alternative that has not been as thoroughly researched but merits investigation is to place contingencies on compliance with counseling goals to foster lifestyle changes that are inconsistent with drug abuse. Morral et al. (chapter 10) review the research literature on the efficacy of contingency management interventions for improving compliance with treatment regimens; they also review results from a recent project demonstrating the efficacy of a contingency management intervention in increasing compliance with counseling goals for reducing drug abuse among methadone maintenance patients.

The discussion of whether to place contingencies on objective measures of drug use, such as urinalysis, or on engagement in alternative behaviors deemed therapeutic or incompatible with drug abuse raises an interesting question: When the contingencies are placed directly on objective indexes of drug use, what new behaviors do successful patients engage in that allow them to successfully abstain from drug use? Unfortunately, little has been reported on this question. Conducting more "process" research with participants in contingency management interventions may demonstrate more generally how illicit-drug abusers change their behavior while also providing empirically based targets for treatment planning (chapter 15).

INTEGRATING RESEARCH AND PRACTICE

In most areas of drug abuse treatment, the interventions developed and shown to be efficacious in research settings are not those routinely used in community clinics (Miller et al., 1995). Contingency management is no exception. Contingency management has and continues to be an intervention applied largely in research settings. A host of factors contribute to this situation; some are philosophical, others more practical. Kirby, Amass, and McLellan (chapter 16) provide an insightful discussion of these issues, along with suggestions for more effective dissemination. Clearly, the need for improvements in the efficacy of treatments for illicit-drug abuse is too great and the contingency management approach has too much of value to offer for the status quo to continue. In this volume, Silverman and I seek to contribute to the efforts to better disseminate contingency management procedures by bringing together in one source reports from the most accomplished and innovative researchers in the United States on the application of contingency management to the treatment of illicit-drug abuse.

The important scientific and clinical obstacles to be overcome in further developing the contingency management approach to the treatment of illicit-drug abuse are discussed with keen insight and candor by Crowley in chapter 17.

Finally, an array of innovative strategies for addressing some of the most serious challenges involved in treating illicit-drug abusers are reviewed in this volume. Certainly none of these strategies are magic bullets or provide the "answer" to effective drug abuse treatment. However, I strongly suspect and hope that some of these strategies can benefit clinicians, policy makers, and other professionals committed to improving the quality of care provided to illicit-drug abusers.

REFERENCES

Ball, J. C., & Ross, A. (1991). *The effectiveness of methadone maintenance treatment.* New York: Springer-Verlag.

Breakey, W. R., Fischer, P. J., Kramer, M., Nestadt, G., Romanoski, A. J., Ross, A., Royall, R., & Stine, M. (1989). Health and mental health problems of homeless men and women in Baltimore. *Journal of the American Medical Association, 262,* 1352–1357.

Center on Addiction and Substance Abuse. (1994). *The cost of substance abuse to America's health care system: Report 2. Medicare hospital costs.* New York: Columbia University.

Clemmey, P., Brooner, R., Chutuape, M. A., Kidorf, M., & Stitzer, M. L. (1997).

Smoking habits and attitudes in a methadone maintenance treatment population. *Drug and Alcohol Dependence, 44,* 123–132.

Griffiths, R. R., Bigelow, G. E., & Henningfield, J. E. (1980). Similarities in animal and human drug taking behavior. In N. K. Mello (Ed.), *Advances in substance abuse: Behavioral and biological research* (Vol. 1, pp. 1–90). Greenwich, CT: JAI Press.

Halikas, J. A., Weller, R. A., Morse, C. L., & Hoffman, R. G. (1983). Regular marijuana use and its effect on psychosocial variables: A longitudinal study. *Comprehensive Psychiatry, 24,* 229–235.

Hall, S. M., Havassy, B. E., & Wasserman, D. A. (1990). Commitment to abstinence and acute stress in relapse to alcohol, opiate, and nicotine. *Journal of Consulting and Clinical Psychology, 58,* 175–181.

Hall, S. M., Havassy, B. E., & Wasserman, D. A. (1991). Effects of commitment to abstinence, positive moods, stress, and coping on relapse to cocaine use. *Journal of Consulting and Clinical Psychology, 59,* 526–532.

Higgins, S. T. (1996). Some potential contributions of reinforcement and consumer-demand theory to reducing cocaine abuse. *Addictive Behaviors, 21,* 803–816.

Higgins, S. T. (1997). Applying learning and conditioning theory to the treatment of alcohol and cocaine abuse. In B. A. Johnson & J. D. Roache (Eds.), *Drug addiction and its treatment: Nexus of neuroscience and behavior* (pp. 367–385). Philadelphia: Lippincott-Raven.

Higgins, S. T., & Wong, C. J. (1998). Treating cocaine abuse: What does research tell us? In S. T. Higgins & J. L. Katz (Eds.), *Cocaine abuse: Behavior, pharmacology, and clinical applications* (pp. 343–361). San Diego, CA: Academic Press.

Hughes, J. R., Hatsukami, D. K., Mitchell, J. E., & Dahlgren, L. A. (1986). Prevalence of smoking among psychiatric outpatients. *American Journal of Psychiatry, 143,* 993–997.

Irving, L. M., Seidner, A. L., Burling, T. A., Thomas, R. G., & Brenner, G. F. (1994). Drug and alcohol abuse inpatients' attitudes about smoking cessation. *Journal of Substance Abuse Treatment, 6,* 267–278.

Jones, R. T. (1980). Human effects: An overview. In R. C. Peterson (Ed.), *Marijuana research findings* (DHHS Publication No. ADM 80-1001, NIDA Research Monograph 31, pp. 54–80). Washington, DC: U.S. Government Printing Office.

Kandel, D. B. (1984). Marijuana users in young adulthood. *Archives of General Psychiatry, 41,* 200–209.

Konkol, R. J., & Olsen, G. D. (Eds.). (1996). *Prenatal cocaine exposure.* New York: CRC Press.

Milby, J. B. (1988). Methadone maintenance to abstinence: How many make it? *Journal of Nervous and Mental Diseases, 176,* 409–422.

Miller, W. R., Brown, J. M., Simpson, T. L., Handmaker, N. S., Bien, T. H., Luckie, L. F., Montgomery, H. A., Hester, R. K., & Tonigan, J. S. (1995). What works?

A methodological analysis of the alcohol treatment literature. In R. K. Hester & W. R. Miller (Eds.), *Handbook of alcoholism treatment approaches: Effective alternatives* (2nd ed., pp. 12–44). Boston: Allyn & Bacon.

Montoya, I. D., & Atkinson, J. S. (1996). Determinants of HIV seroprevalence rates among sites participating in a community based study of drug use. *Journal of Acquired Immune Deficiency Syndromes and Human Retrovirology, 13*, 169–176.

McLellan, A. T., Arndt, I. O., Metzger, D. S., Woody, G. E., & O'Brien, C. P. (1993). The effects of psychosocial services in substance abuse treatment. *Journal of the American Medical Association, 269*, 1953–1959.

National Institute of Justice. (1997). *1996 drug use forcasting: Annual report on adult and juvenile arrestees*. Rockville, MD: National Institute of Justice Clearinghouse.

Onken, L. S., Blaine, J. D., & Boren, J. J. (Eds.). (1995). *Integrating behavioral therapies with medications in the treatment of drug dependence* (NIH Publication No. 95-3899, NIDA Research Monograph 150). Rockville, MD: National Institute on Drug Abuse.

Onken, L. S., Blaine, J. D., Genser, S., & Horton, A. M. (Eds.). (1997). *Treatment of drug-dependent individuals with comorbid mental disorders* (NIH Publication No. 97-4172, NIDA Research Monograph 172). Rockville, MD: National Institute on Drug Abuse.

Regier, D. A., Farmer, M. E., Rae, D. S., Locke, B., Keith, S. J., Judd, L. L., & Goodwin, F. K. (1990). Comorbidity of mental disorders with alcohol and other drug abuse: Results from the Epidemiological Catchment Area Study. *Journal of the American Medical Association, 264*, 2511–2519.

Regier, D. A., Narrow, W. E., Rae, D. S., Manderscheid, R. W., Locke, B. Z., & Goodwin, F. K. (1993). The de facto US mental and addictive disorders service system: Epidemiologic Catchment Area prospective 1-year prevalence rates of disorders and services. *Archives of General Psychiatry, 50*, 85–94.

Reilly, P. M., Sees, K. L., Shopshire, M. S., Hall, S. M., Delucchi, K. L., Tusel, D. J., Banys, P., Clark, H. W., & Piotrowski, N. A. (1995). Self-efficacy and illicit opioid use in a 180-day methadone detoxification treatment. *Journal of Consulting and Clinical Psychology, 63*, 158–162.

Rice, D. P., Kelman, S., Miller, L. S., & Dunmeyer, S. (1990). *The economic costs of alcohol and drug abuse and mental illness: 1985* (Report submitted to the Office of Financing and Coverage Policy of the Alcohol, Drug Abuse, and Mental Health Administration, U.S. Department of Health and Human Services). San Francisco: University of California, Institute for Health and Aging.

Rydell, C. P., & Everingham, S. S. (1994). *Controlling cocaine: Supply versus demand programs*. Santa Monica, CA: RAND.

Silverman, K., Bigelow, G. E., & Stitzer, M. L. (1998). Treatment of cocaine abuse in methadone maintenance patients. In S. T. Higgins & J. L. Katz (Eds.), *Cocaine abuse: Behavior, pharmacology, and clinical application* (pp. 363–389). San Diego, CA: Academic Press.

Stephens, R. S., Roffman, R. A., & Simpson, E. E. (1993). Adult marijuana users seeking treatment. *Journal of Consulting and Clinical Psychology, 61,* 1100–1104.

Stitzer, M. L., & Higgins, S. T. (1995). Behavioral treatment of drug and alcohol abuse. In F. E. Bloom & D. J. Kupfer (Eds.), *Psychopharmacology: The fourth generation of progress* (pp. 1807–1819). New York: Raven Press.

Story, J., & Stark, M. J. (1991). Treating cigarette smoking in methadone maintenance clients. *Journal of Psychoactive Drugs, 23,* 203–215.

Substance Abuse and Mental Health Services Administration. (1995). *National Household Survey on Drug Abuse: Main findings, 1993* (DHHS Publication No. SMA 95-3020). Rockville, MD: National Clearinghouse for Alcohol and Drug Information.

Substance Abuse and Mental Health Services Administration. (1998a). *National Household Survey on Drug Abuse: Population estimates 1997* (DHHS Publication No. SMA 98-3250). Rockville, MD: National Clearinghouse for Alcohol and Drug Information.

Substance Abuse and Mental Health Services Administration. (1998b). *Preliminary results from the 1997 National Household Survey on Drug Abuse* (DHHS Publication No. SMA 98-3251). Rockville, MD: National Clearinghouse for Alcohol and Drug Information.

Tardiff, K., Marzuk, P. M., Leon, A. C., Hirsch, C. S., Stajie, M., Portera, L., & Hartwell, N. (1994). Homicide in New York City: Cocaine use and firearms. *Journal of the American Medical Association, 272,* 43–46.

1

THEORETICAL AND EMPIRICAL FOUNDATIONS OF CONTINGENCY MANAGEMENT TREATMENTS FOR DRUG ABUSE

GEORGE E. BIGELOW AND KENNETH SILVERMAN

The contingency management approach to drug abuse treatment is derived from an extensive theoretical, laboratory, and clinical history. The other contributors to this volume review the empirical developments regarding contingency management in the field of drug abuse treatment. Our aim in this chapter is to provide a brief overview and historical context of these contributory antecedents.

The historical roots of contingency management treatments for drug abuse lie in two general areas—the more general of these areas is the operant behavior pharmacology conceptualization of drug abuse and drug self-administration; the more specific of these areas is work on the behavioral analysis and treatment of alcoholism. Work in each of these two areas originated relatively independently, with the themes joining only later. The behavioral pharmacology theme developed in the animal laboratory as a

Preparation of this chapter was supported by Grants K05-DA00050, P50-DA05273, P50-DA09258, and R01-DA09426 from the National Institute on Drug Abuse.

basic behavioral science strategy for developing experimental models of substance abuse and dependence. In contrast, the behavior analysis and treatment theme began with the clinical phenomena of alcohol abuse and dependence and applied behavioral science principles to understanding and altering these clinical disorders. It is interesting to note that both approaches derived from the same general theoretical and conceptual orientation of operant psychology, which has viewed substance use disorders as instances of reinforced operant behavior that are amenable to control by environmental consequences (i.e., behavioral contingencies).

An important aspect of contingency management's historical context involves consideration of the success of contingency management interventions in the alcohol abuse and alcoholism field. Approximately 2 to 3 decades ago, substantial work was conducted on contingency management approaches to alcohol abuse and alcoholism. Yet at present in the alcoholism field, contingency management approaches have relatively little prominence or visibility. In a commentary section at the end of this chapter, we speculate on reasons why contingency management therapies apparently failed to take root and grow in the alcoholism field despite clinical trials showing impressive efficacy. Contrasts between the alcoholism and drug abuse fields are discussed that support optimism that the drug abuse field may be a more receptive, fertile, and nourishing environment for contingency management treatment. The empirical contributions in this volume also provide strong support for that optimism.

THEORETICAL FOUNDATIONS

Contingency management approaches to drug abuse derive from the operant behavioral psychology perspective of B. F. Skinner (1938, 1972) and others. The essence of this perspective is the belief that behavior is learned and reinforced by interaction with environmental contingencies. The perspective holds that behavior—even complex human behavior—is orderly and amenable to scientific study and analysis and that an objective scientific approach will yield advances in the understanding, prediction, and control of behavior. The central tenets of this operant behavior conceptualization are that behavior is learned, that similar learning processes occur in animals and humans, that behavior is often controlled by its consequences, and that behavior can be changed by changing its consequences.

In this operant behavior conceptualization, drug self-administration behavior is seen as the behavioral core of drug abuse disorders. Drugs of abuse function as positive reinforcers that strengthen and maintain drug self-administration behavior. Drug use behavior is considered abusive when it becomes excessively controlled by the reinforcing effects of drugs and inadequately controlled by the potential reinforcing effects of other activities and events. In this conceptualization, the ability of drugs of abuse to reinforce behavior is biologically normal, and drug abuse behavior disorders result from inadequacies in the environmental contingencies of reinforcement rather than from defects within the individual. An extensive scientific literature supports the view of drug reinforcement as biologically normal. Major elements of that literature include evidence of widespread vulnerability to drug reinforcement; laboratory experimental models involving drug self-administration by animals; and extensive cross-species commonalities in drugs that are self-administered, patterns of self-administration, and variables influencing self-administration (Griffiths, Bigelow, & Henningfield, 1980). The therapeutic task is seen as that of bringing behavior under the control of other alternative behavioral contingencies that selectively reinforce and promote drug abstinence or other non-drug-related prosocial behaviors (Bigelow, Brooner, & Silverman, 1997).

This operant behavior perspective does not hold that drug reinforcement is the only mechanism involved in the development of drug abuse disorders. It recognizes that vulnerability to drug abuse can be influenced by a broad range of biological, environmental, and behavioral variables (e.g., genetics, social context, personality). However, one of the strengths of this perspective is that it suggests mechanisms for intervention—alteration of behavioral contingencies—that are independent of specific etiologic factors.

LABORATORY FOUNDATIONS

Some of the most direct and compelling support for the operant behavior conceptualization of drug abuse comes from laboratory research showing that drugs can serve as reinforcers to maintain drug seeking and drug self-administration in animal subjects. Initial studies demonstrated that chimpanzees (Spragg, 1940), rats (Headlee, Coppock, & Nichols, 1955; Nichols, Headlee, & Coppock, 1956; Weeks, 1962; Weeks & Collins, 1964), and rhesus monkeys (Thompson & Schuster, 1964) who were physiologically morphine dependent would self-administer morphine, suggesting that morphine could serve as a reinforcer in laboratory animals. Subsequently, Pickens and Harris (1968) and Pickens and Thompson (1968) showed that intravenous injections of cocaine or d-amphetamine served as reinforcers in rats who were not physiologically dependent.

Subsequent laboratory research shows that a wide range of drugs can serve as reinforcers in a diverse range of species (Griffiths, Bigelow, & Henningfield, 1980). Furthermore, this research shows a considerable correspondence between drugs that are abused in society and drugs that serve as reinforcers under controlled laboratory conditions (Griffiths, Bigelow, &

Henningfield, 1980). The consistency of these findings across species and the correspondence between laboratory findings and clinical observation suggest that drug reinforcement is a fundamental biological–behavioral mechanism underlying drug abuse. These observations provide a firm empirical basis for viewing drug abuse as operant behavior.

The identification of drug use as operant behavior serves to link the study and treatment of drug abuse to the extensive and broader science of operant behavior. This science reveals a growing body of principles and procedures that modulate behavior. These principles and procedures have been developed in behavioral laboratories with both animals and humans. Between the 1930s and the 1960s—long before the first published reports of contingency management treatment of drug abuse—reinforcement was shown to be capable of modulating or shaping a wide range of behaviors in a diverse range of organisms, including humans (Dews, 1959; Ferster & Skinner, 1957; Hefferline & Keenan, 1963; Lane, 1961; Molliver, 1963; Myers & Mesker, 1960; Salzinger, Waller, & Jackson, 1962; Schroeder & Holland, 1968; Skinner, 1938). Events that could function as reinforcers were found to vary widely as well and included (although were by no means limited to) food and water (Skinner, 1938), electrical brain stimulation (Sidman, Brady, Boren, Conrad, & Schulman, 1955), and heat (Weiss & Laties, 1960); visual stimulation (Kish, 1966); the opportunity to engage in various behaviors such as exploration (Kish, 1966), grooming (Falk, 1958), or running (Hundt & Premack, 1963); as well as events that acquired reinforcing effects through conditioning (Kelleher, 1966).

Research over several decades shows that reinforcement could exert robust and exquisite control over behavior. Rates and patterns of responding changed abruptly and dramatically as a function of within-session changes in the schedule of reinforcement (Ferster & Skinner, 1957); behavior was found to be extraordinarily sensitive to the rate (Catania, 1966; Herrnstein, 1961), immediacy (e.g., Pierce, Hangford, & Zimmerman, 1972), and magnitude (e.g., Hodos & Kalman, 1963) of reinforcement. Operant behaviors could be reduced or eliminated with relative ease through the contingent application of aversive stimuli (punishment; Azrin & Holz, 1966) by reinforcing alternative incompatible behaviors (Catania, 1966), by simply discontinuing reinforcement (extinction; Ferster & Skinner, 1957), or by combining these variables, only to be thoroughly reestablished by reversing the procedures.

These principles of operant conditioning, shown in the laboratory to be powerful and versatile, were applied with increasing frequency to address clinical problems in a variety of treatment settings. Operant principles and procedures were used effectively to decrease a variety of challenging behavior problems of adults with schizophrenia (Allyon & Azrin, 1965; Allyon & Michael, 1959), developmentally delayed or autistic children (Bostow & Bailey, 1969; Lovaas, Freitag, Gold, & Kassorla, 1965), and delinquent boys (Phillips, 1968). Reinforcement also was shown to be effective in increasing language and social behavior in children (Hart, Reynolds, Baer, Brawley, & Harris, 1968; Hopkins, 1968; Reynolds & Risley, 1968), and in establishing complex responses such as generalized imitation (Baer, Peterson, & Sherman, 1967) and linguistic responses (Guess, Sailor, Rutherford, & Baer, 1968) in developmentally delayed children who fail to acquire those behaviors under normal developmental conditions. These demonstrations extended the generality of the principles of operant conditioning and reinforcement and showed the utility of operant principles and procedures in addressing real social problems.

More recently, research in behavioral pharmacology shows unequivocally that as with behavior maintained by nondrug reinforcers, drug self-administration in nonhuman laboratory subjects can be modulated by manipulating variables that affect other operant behaviors. These studies show that drug self-administration can be diminished by increasing the number of responses required for drug reinforcement, by eliminating or blocking the drug reinforcement (i.e., extinction), by punishing the responses on which drug reinforcement is contingent, or by arranging alternative nondrug reinforcers for incompatible behaviors (Bickel, DeGrandpre, & Higgins, 1993; Carroll, 1993; Goldberg, 1976; Griffiths, Bigelow, & Henningfield, 1980; Higgins, 1997; Pickens, Meisch, & Thompson, 1978).

The power and relevance of the principles of operant conditioning to the understanding and treatment of drug abuse were demonstrated in humans in a seminal series of studies in volunteer alcoholics (Bigelow & Liebson, 1972, 1973; Cohen, Liebson, Faillace, & Allen, 1971; Cohen, Liebson, Faillace, & Speers, 1971). Few studies, before or since, demonstrate more convincingly the potential of reinforcement contingencies to control drug use than one of the first studies in this series (Cohen, Liebson, Faillace, & Allen, 1971). That study involved 5 male alcoholic adults living in a residential research unit. Throughout the study, these volunteers were allowed to drink up to 24 oz (710 ml) of 95-proof ethanol on weekdays. During Weeks 1, 3, and 5, a contingency was arranged in which participants could remain in an "enriched" environmental condition as long as they did not drink more than 5 oz (148 ml) of ethanol in a given day; as soon as their ethanol intake exceeded 5 oz, they were removed from the enriched environment and restricted to an "impoverished" environment. During Weeks 2 and 4, participants remained in the impoverished environment, regardless of their ethanol intake. The enriched environment included access to a variety of privileges, such as use of a recreation room, the opportunity to work in the hospital laundry for pay, access to a preferred regular diet, and the ability to receive visitors. None of these privileges were available in the impoverished environment. This contingency produced remarkable control over drinking. During Weeks 1, 3, and 5, all participants reliably drank 5 oz of ethanol per day or less; in contrast, during Weeks 2 and 4, participants routinely drank considerably more, often reaching the daily maximum of 24 oz. In other studies in this series, drinking was modulated by providing monetary payments contingent on abstaining from drinking (Cohen, Liebson, Faillace, & Speers, 1971), by increasing the cost of alcoholic beverages (Bigelow & Liebson, 1972), or by imposing brief periods of isolation contingent on drinking (Bigelow & Liebson, 1973; Bigelow, Liebson, & Griffiths, 1974; Griffiths, Bigelow, & Liebson, 1974, 1977).

More recent laboratory studies show that human self-administration of drugs other than alcohol can be modulated by operant environmental manipulations. For example, human drug self-administration has been found to be sensitive to the number of responses required for drug reinforcement (Bickel et al., 1993; Griffiths et al., 1980) and the availability of nondrug reinforcers for alternative incompatible responses (Carroll, 1993; Higgins, 1997). Perhaps most relevant to contingency management treatment, laboratory research shows that human drug self-administration can be decreased by arranging reinforcement of alternative incompatible responses with nondrug reinforcers (Carroll, 1993; Higgins, 1997). In a pair of such studies (Higgins, 1997), adult human cocaine users were given repeated choices between doses of intranasal cocaine and money. Two separate studies show that participants' choice of cocaine decreased as the magnitude of the alternative reinforcer (i.e., the amount of money) increased.

Overall, laboratory research in animals and humans provides firm experimental grounds for viewing drug abuse as operant behavior, maintained and modifiable by its consequences. The extensive body of research in operant conditioning suggests a range of environmental manipulations that should modulate drug self-administration. The growing body of laboratory research in behavioral pharmacology shows the power of these environmental manipulations to produce dramatic changes in the self-administration of a range of drugs and in a variety of species, including humans.

CLINICAL FOUNDATIONS

The development of therapeutic contingency management approaches to drug abuse is not derived solely from theory and laboratory studies. Clinical research in the treatment of alcoholism provides practical examples of the potency and potential of the contingency management approach to drug dependence. Several early clinical trials of contingency management approaches in the treatment of alcoholism serve as useful illustrations of the approach.

Chronic Public Drunkenness Offenders

Miller (1975) addressed the problem of chronic public drunkenness offenders. The study was conducted at a time when it was still commonplace for chronic public drunkenness to be treated as a simple criminal offense. As a consequence, arrest records could be used as one convenient objective index of public drunkenness frequency. The study was targeted at individuals with documented high rates of public drunkenness arrests (eight or more in the preceding 12 months), long histories of abusive drinking (5 years or more), unstable housing, and unstable employment—a so-called "skid row" population.

Miller (1975) sought to assess whether a positive reinforcement approach of providing desirable goods and services contingent on sobriety would be more successful than the usual-care procedure of providing resources noncontingently to needy skid row residents. For patients in the positive reinforcement treatment condition, arrangements were made with agencies serving the skid row community to continue to provide their goods and services contingent on sobriety and to discontinue those goods and services for 5 days contingent on any instance of observed intoxication or elevated breath alcohol concentration (indicating greater than 10 mg or 100 ml blood alcohol concentration; breath alcohol recordings were obtained randomly in the community). Goods and services included in the contingency arrangement included housing and meals at a relatively desirable service agency, employment, clothing donations, and Veterans Administration canteen booklets exchangeable for cigarettes, meals, or clothing. For patients in the usual-care treatment condition, the same goods and services were available but were provided noncontingently. Twenty participants were enrolled and randomized equally among the two treatment conditions. Miller compared outcomes for the 2 months before and after study initiation.

The primary outcome variables were number of public drunkenness arrests and hours employed at a job per week. Both variables indicated significant superiority ($p < .01$) of the contingent reinforcement treatment during the period of randomized differential treatment, and both showed significant improvement within the contingent reinforcement group and no change within the usual-care group. Mean public drunkenness arrests fell from 1.7 to 0.3 in the reinforcement group, compared with a relative constancy in the usual-care group (1.4 to 1.3). Mean hours employed per week increased from 3.2 to 12.0 in the reinforcement group, compared with a relative constancy in the usual-care group (4.4 to 3.2). In addition to these primary outcomes, breath alcohol samples available from half of the reinforcement group both before and during the intervention showed a large and significant reduction in mean blood alcohol level from 50 mg% to 0.002 mg% ($p < .001$).

Miller (1975) concluded that behavioral treatment strategies based on the principles of contingency management could have substantial beneficial impact on the drinking behavior, drunkenness arrests, and employment of skid row alcoholics. He noted that the common usual-care procedures for allocating service resources may actually be countertherapeutic, in that they may result in the delivery of more services to alcoholics when they are intoxicated than when they are sober and that such an unintended contingency may actually help maintain inappropriate and abusive drinking patterns. From a cost–benefit perspective, an attractive feature of the therapeutic contingency management therapy was that improved treatment outcomes did not depend on the provision of more or different services but simply on the rearrangement of the contingencies under which existing services were dispensed. Thus, it may be possible to improve outcomes by incorporating appropriate contingencies into existing community agencies.

Alcoholic Methadone Patients

Another useful example of the therapeutic value of introducing behavioral contingencies into settings where reinforcing goods and services are otherwise routinely dispensed noncontingently is provided by clinical research on the treatment of alcoholism among methadone maintenance patients. Methadone is an orally effective and long-acting opioid substitution medication that when administered daily in adequate doses is a very effective treatment for heroin dependence. For many years, concurrent alcoholism was the greatest single reason for failure of patients enrolled in methadone maintenance treatment. Liebson, Tommasello, and Bigelow (1978) focused on this problem and evaluated the efficacy of a contingency management intervention for promoting successful treatment of alcoholism. The alcoholism treatment evaluated was the routine ingestion of disulfiram (Antabuse). If ethanol is consumed, disulfiram blocks its complete metabolism and causes accumulation of the partial metabolic product acetaldehyde; the resultant acetaldehyde poisoning is aversive and deters ethanol consumption. In form this treatment is pharmaceutical, but in function its therapeutic effectiveness is through the mechanism of behavioral avoidance (i.e., abstinence of ethanol consumption avoids the aversive ethanol–disulfiram reaction). Unfortunately, as typically used in medical practice (patients receive a prescription with instructions to purchase the medication and to use it daily), disulfiram shows little or no clinical effectiveness, despite its unquestioned pharmacological efficacy; patients apparently avoid the disulfiram more readily than the ethanol. Liebson et al. relied on the reinforcing efficacy of methadone maintenance treatment to establish a therapeutic behavioral contingency that would reinforce the routine ingestion of disulfiram.

The participants were 25 volunteer alcoholic methadone patients who were about to be or had recently been discharged from local methadone maintenance programs because of behavioral problems related to their alcoholism. All patients were initially treated for alcohol withdrawal as needed, which for most involved a brief hospitalization, and were initially treated for 14 days with supervised disulfiram (administered daily under observation immediately before methadone administration). Two patients (8%) dropped out during this initial detoxification and disulfiram induction. Thereafter, 23 patients were randomly assigned to either of two treatment procedures; both involved continued methadone maintenance and disulfiram, to which all consented. All patients were counseled to stop drinking and about the effects of disulfiram, were instructed to take disulfiram daily as an aid to abstinence, and were cautioned that failure to maintain sobriety could result in their termination from methadone treatment. Patients randomized to the control condition were given a supply of disulfiram weekly and instructed to use it. Patients randomized to the contingent intervention were required to continue taking their disulfiram under a nurse's supervision as a precondition to receiving their daily methadone dose (i.e., methadone treatment was used to reinforce disulfiram ingestion). The intervention duration was 6 months, except that patients in the control condition who relapsed to drinking were transferred to the contingent condition for ethical and compassionate reasons. Outcomes were assessed in terms of relapse rate, amount of drinking, criminal behavior, and illicit-drug use.

The two treatment conditions produced dramatically different outcomes. Of the 13 patients randomized to the contingent treatment condition, 11 (85%) successfully completed the 6-month treatment period without a serious drinking relapse; in the control condition, this occurred in only 1 of 10 (10%). The percentage of days drinking (confirmed by breath alcohol test) was 10 times greater in the control condition than in the contingent condition—21% versus 2%. The arrest rate was eight times greater in the control condition than in the contingent condition—0.8 versus 0.1 per 100 days; in the control condition, 57% of arrests were drinking related, whereas in the contingent condition none were. Urinalysis testing for illicit-drug abuse showed no evidence of symptom substitution in the contingent condition (i.e., no evidence of increased use of drugs other than alcohol); in contrast, the trend—although nonsignificant—was toward a generalization of therapeutic benefit (reduced illicit-drug use).

This study illustrates the therapeutic power of incorporating into contingent reinforcing relationships the dispensing of goods or services that would otherwise be dispensed without constructive utilization of their potential reinforcing effects. Using the behavioral reinforcing potential inherent in such circumstances can enhance therapeutic benefit. The efficacy of disulfiram in reducing drinking when its ingestion was assured is also a powerful demonstration that alcoholic drinking behavior can be controlled by its consequences.

Community Reinforcement Treatment of Alcoholism

A third important illustration of the therapeutic power of contingency management therapies for substance abuse is provided by the community reinforcement approach, originally developed by Hunt and Azrin (1973) as a treatment for alcoholism. The previous illustrations focused on therapeutic use of specific reinforcers already existing within patients' life context. The community reinforcement approach is much more ambitious. Although based on the same contingent reinforcement conceptualization of how behavior is influenced and controlled, it attempts to achieve a much more comprehensive transformation of patients' life circumstances. The community reinforcement approach not only establishes contingent relationships to existing potential reinforcers, it also acts to introduce into a patient's life context a broad range of activities thought to function as effective reinforcers for most individuals—employment, social relationships, recreation, and so forth—and then to establish therapeutic contingent reinforcement relationship involving these activities.

In a random-assignment clinical trial, Hunt and Azrin (1973) compared the outcomes of alcoholics treated with the community reinforcement approach with the outcomes of similar matched patients treated with the usual-care approach emphasizing alcohol education and the 12-step program of Alcoholics Anonymous. Both treatment groups received these usual-care services, but the community reinforcement treatment also involved establishing an array of vocational, family, and social–recreational reinforcers in the patients' lives and arranging that drinking would result in a time-out from these reinforcers. Community reinforcement patients received assistance in gaining rewarding employment, in arranging rewarding marital and family interactions, and in engaging in non-alcohol-related recreational and social activities. Contingent relationships were established, such that access to these reinforcers was contingent on abstinence from alcohol and such that instances of drinking would result in relatively immediate and certain time-out from reinforcement. Participants were diagnosed alcoholics who had drunk to the point of physical dependence and had been admitted to a state hospital for treatment of their alcoholism. Outcomes were assessed over a 6-month posthospitalization period in terms of percentage of days drinking, unemployed, absent from home, or institutionalized.

Outcomes in the two treatment groups were significantly different on all four of the outcome indexes throughout the 6-month comparative assessment period, with the community reinforcement treatment having by far the better outcome. In terms of mean percentage of days, each of the adverse outcome indexes was 4–13 times more frequent in usual-care patients than in community reinforcement patients—drinking, 79% versus 14%; unemployed, 62% versus 5%; absent from home, 66% versus 16%; and institutionalized, 27% versus 2%. These results offer powerful support for the reinforcement conceptualization of alcoholism and of alcoholism treatment.

COMMENTS AND CONCLUSION

The preceding sections present three themes relevant to the historical underpinnings of contingency management approaches to drug abuse treatment.

1. The operant behavioral conceptualization of drug abuse commonly adopted by the field of behavioral pharmacology provides a powerful and integrative theoretical framework that facilitates the understanding of drug abuse disorders and guides the search for effective therapeutic interventions.
2. A strong empirical laboratory science base has been developed that documents the applicability of operant behavioral learning principles to the understanding and modification of drug self-administration behavior.
3. Clinical trial applications and evaluations of contingency management procedures in the treatment of alcoholism show great effectiveness of this approach to clinical therapeutics and argue for the approach's generalizability to treatment of other drug dependencies.

These three themes present an optimistic prospect for the success of contingency management applications to drug abuse treatment. However, it is important to recognize also and to consider a more pessimistic aspect of contingency management's scientific history. This more pessimistic aspect is that contingency management treatments have not prospered and grown in the alcoholism field. The encouraging and successful clinical trials in alcoholism treatment described earlier represent work conducted 20–30 years ago. At present, there is relatively little contingency management work in the alcoholism field. Recent major clinical trials of psychosocial treatments for alcoholism—evaluating what are regarded as the accepted, state-of-the-art effective treatments—focus only on comparing variations of verbal therapies (Project MATCH Research Group, 1997), with no involvement of contingency management procedures. Why has this happened, and does it forebode a similar risk for contingency management treatments of drug abuse?

We believe the limited acceptance of contingency management in the alcoholism field derives from differences in theory. It certainly does not derive from data about efficacy; there is no body of empirical literature contradicting the efficacy of contingency management treatments. Instead, neither clinicians nor researchers in the alcoholism field have embraced and accepted the learning-based theoretical orientation of behavioral pharmacology and behavior analysis from which contingency management treatments derive. The dominant theoretical orientation within the alcoholism field is the disease concept of alcoholism (Jellinek, 1960). Central aspects of this theoretical orientation are the loss-of-control concept and the search for genetic and biological bases for alcoholism. The loss-of-control concept is the view that alcoholics' drinking becomes out of control once initiated and, therefore, that only total abstinence is acceptable or feasible. Simply at a semantic level, the disease concept orientation encounters difficulties with the operant behavioral orientation, where the term *control* is widely used as representing a desirable and achievable feature. But the conflict extends well beyond mere semantics. Behavioral researchers and therapists directly challenged the abstinence-only view of the disease theory by proposing that controlled or moderate drinking could be an achievable and even desirable outcome for alcoholics (Bigelow, Cohen, Liebson, & Faillace, 1972; Sobell & Sobell, 1973). Proponents of the disease theory aggressively attacked such suggestions and, in some cases, the investigators with career-threatening accusations and vilification. From a Kuhnian (1962) perspective, this appears to be a case of new data and theory failing to displace a well-accepted and well-entrenched, established theoretical doctrine. A consequence of these attacks and of this failure of theoretical revolution is that further pursuit of behavioral contingency management approaches to alcoholism has been dramatically curtailed for at least 2 decades.

What does this mean for the prospects of contingency management applications to the treatment of drug abuse? If the above interpretation of the alcoholism history is correct, there is reason to be hopeful of greater and more enduring success in the drug abuse field. There are important differences in circumstances in the two fields. First, no strongly entrenched alternative theoretical view in the drug abuse field must be displaced or overcome by contingency management concepts. Second, there is a strong and broad empirical laboratory research base that is supportive of the applicability to drug abuse of the operant learning theories and principles on which contingency management treatments are based. Third, contingency management treatments of drug abuse embrace abstinence as the therapeutic goal, thus eliminating that as a possible source of conflict. This interpretation supports the optimistic view that although the adoption of contingency management treatments in the alcoholism field has been limited, the drug abuse field appears likely to be much more receptive to contingency management treatments.

In addition to the theory concerns that have just been discussed, the practical issue of the relative ease of implementation is one other potential hindrance to the adoption of contingency management therapies. Within an established therapeutic structure in which delivery of verbal therapy is the norm, varying the nature of the verbal therapy will likely seem more convenient than contingency management. Thus, the limited adoption of contingency management treatment for alcoholism may have resulted, in part, from its being less convenient to implement than talk alone. It is true that contingency management procedures may be more difficult and challenging for the therapist, but limiting the search for effective therapies to those that are convenient is analogous to the often-cited error of limiting a search for lost keys to the area under the street lamp. A challenge for contingency management practitioners and researchers—as well as the contributors to this volume and their successors—may be to change prevailing concepts of what treatment is, of how it is delivered, and of how one searches for optimal treatments. Too often, treatment and the search for optimal treatment have been limited to procedures that fit conveniently within the prevailing process of verbal therapy. A more productive approach may be to break out of these verbal process constraints to find interventions, such as contingency management therapies, that show substantial efficacy. Efficacy can then be the criterion used to establish new norms of practice, as it should be.

REFERENCES

Allyon, T., & Azrin, N. H. (1965). The measurement and reinforcement of behavior of psychotics. *Journal of the Experimental Analysis of Behavior, 8,* 357–383.

Allyon, T., & Michael, J. (1959). The psychiatric nurse as a behavioral engineer. *Journal of the Experimental Analysis of Behavior, 2,* 323–334.

Azrin, N. H., & Holz, W. C. (1966). Punishment. In W. K. Honig (Ed.), *Operant behavior: Areas of research and application* (pp. 380–448). New York: Appleton-Century-Crofts.

Baer, D. M., Peterson, R. F., & Sherman, J. A. (1967). The development of imitation by reinforcing behavioral similarity to a model. *Journal of the Experimental Analysis of Behavior, 10,* 405–416.

Bickel, W. K., DeGrandpre, R. J., & Higgins, S. T. (1993). Behavioral economics: A novel experimental approach to the study of drug dependence. *Drug and Alcohol Dependence, 33,* 173–192.

Bigelow, G. E., Brooner, R. K., & Silverman, K. (1997). Competing motivations: Drug reinforcement vs non-drug reinforcement. *Journal of Psychopharmacology, 12,* 8–14.

Bigelow, G. E., Cohen, M., Liebson, I. A., & Faillace, L. A. (1972). Abstinence or moderation? Choice by alcoholics. *Behavior Research and Therapy, 10,* 209–214.

Bigelow, G., & Liebson, I. (1972). Cost factors controlling alcoholic drinking. *Psychological Record, 22,* 305–314.

Bigelow, G., & Liebson, I. (1973). Behavioral contingencies controlling alcoholics' drinking. *Alcoholism, 9,* 24–28.

Bigelow, G., Liebson, I., & Griffiths, R. R. (1974). Alcoholic drinking: Suppression by a brief time-out procedure. *Behavior Research and Therapy, 12,* 107–115.

Bostow, D. E., & Bailey, J. B. (1969). Modification of severe disruptive and aggressive behavior using brief timeout and reinforcement procedures. *Journal of Applied Behavior Analysis, 2,* 31–37.

Carroll, M. E. (1993). The economic context of drug and non-drug reinforcers affects acquisition and maintenance of drug-reinforced behavior and withdrawal effects. *Drug and Alcohol Dependence, 33,* 201–210.

Catania, A. C. (1966). Concurrent operants. In W. K. Honig (Ed.), *Operant behavior: Areas of research and application* (pp. 213–270). New York: Appleton-Century-Crofts.

Cohen, M., Liebson, I., Faillace, L. A., & Allen, R. P. (1971). Moderate drinking by chronic alcoholics. *Journal of Nervous and Mental Disease, 153,* 434–444.

Cohen, M., Liebson, I. A., Faillace, L. A., & Speers, W. (1971). Alcoholism: Controlled drinking and incentives for abstinence. *Psychological Reports, 28,* 575–580.

Dews, P. B. (1959). Some observations on an operant in the octopus. *Journal of the Experimental Analysis of Behavior, 2,* 57–63.

Falk, J. L. (1958). The grooming of the chimpanzee as a reinforcer. *Journal of the Experimental Analysis of Behavior, 1,* 83–85.

Ferster, C. B., & Skinner, B. F. (1957). *Schedule of reinforcement.* Englewood Cliffs, NJ: Prentice-Hall.

Goldberg, S. R. (1976). The behavioral analysis of drug addiction. In S. D. Glick & J. Goldfarb (Eds.), *Behavioral pharmacology* (pp. 283–316). St. Louis, MO: C. V. Mosby.

Griffiths, R. R., Bigelow, G. E., & Henningfield, J. E. (1980). Similarities in animal and human drug-taking behavior. In N. K. Mello (Ed.), *Advances in substance abuse* (Vol. 1, pp. 1–90). Greenwich, CT: JAI Press.

Griffiths, R. R., Bigelow, G. E., & Liebson, I. (1974). Suppression of ethanol self-administration in alcoholics by contingent time-out from social interactions. *Behavior Research and Therapy, 12,* 327–334.

Griffiths, R. R., Bigelow, G. E., & Liebson, I. (1977). Comparison of social time-out and activity time-out procedures in suppressing ethanol self-administration in alcoholics. *Behavior Research and Therapy, 15,* 329–336.

Guess, D., Sailor, W., Rutherford, G., & Baer, D. M. (1968). An experimental analysis of linguistic development: The productive use of the plural morpheme. *Journal of Applied Behavior Analysis, 1,* 297–306.

Hart, B. M., Reynolds, N. J., Baer, D. M., Brawley, E. R., & Harris, F. R. (1968). Effect of contingent and non-contingent social reinforcement on the cooperative play of a preschool child. *Journal of Applied Behavior Analysis, 1,* 73–76.

Headlee, C. P., Coppock, H. W., & Nichols, J. R. (1955). Apparatus and technique involved in a laboratory method of detecting the aversiveness of drugs. *Journal of the American Pharmaceutical Association* (Science ed.), *44,* 229–231.

Hefferline, R. F., & Keenan, B. (1963). Amplitude-induction gradient of a small-scale (covert) operant. *Journal of the Experimental Analysis of Behavior, 6,* 307–315.

Herrnstein, R. (1961). Relative and absolute strength of response as a function of frequency of reinforcement. *Journal of the Experimental Analysis of Behavior, 4,* 267–272.

Higgins, S. T. (1997). The influence of alternative reinforcers on cocaine use and abuse: A brief review. *Pharmacology, Biochemistry, and Behavior, 57,* 419–427.

Hodos, W., & Kalman, G. (1963). Effects of increment size and reinforcer volume on progressive ratio performance. *Journal of the Experimental Analysis of Behavior, 6,* 387–392.

Hopkins, B. L. (1968). Effects of candy and social reinforcement, instructions, and reinforcement schedule leaning on the modification and maintenance of smiling. *Journal of Applied Behavior Analysis, 1,* 121–129.

Hundt, A. G., & Premack, D. (1963). Running as both a positive and negative reinforcer. *Science, 142,* 1087–1089.

Hunt, G., & Azrin, N. H. (1973). A community-reinforcement approach to alcoholism. *Behaviour Research and Therapy, 11,* 91–104.

Jellinek, E. M. (1960). *The disease concept of alcoholism.* New Brunswick, NJ: Hillhouse Press.

Kelleher, R. T. (1966). Chaining and conditioned reinforcement. In W. K. Honig (Ed.), *Operant behavior: Areas of research and application* (pp. 160–212). New York: Appleton-Century-Crofts.

Kish, G. B. (1966). Studies of sensory reinforcement. In W. K. Honig (Ed.), *Operant behavior: Areas of research and application* (pp. 109–159). New York: Appleton-Century-Crofts.

Kuhn, T. S. (1962). *The structure of scientific revolutions.* Chicago: University of Chicago Press.

Lane, H. (1961). Operant control of vocalization in the chicken. *Journal of the Experimental Analysis of Behavior, 4,* 171–177.

Liebson, I. A., Tommasello, A., & Bigelow, G. E. (1978). A behavioral treatment of alcoholic methadone patients. *Annals of Internal Medicine, 89,* 342–344.

Lovaas, O. I., Freitag, G., Gold, V. J., & Kassorla, I. C. (1965). Experimental studies in childhood schizophrenia: Analysis of self-destructive behavior. *Journal of Experimental Child Psychology, 2,* 67–84.

Miller, P. M. (1975). A behavioral intervention program for chronic public drunkenness offenders. *Archives of General Psychiatry, 32,* 915–918.

Molliver, M. E. (1963). Operant control of vocal behavior in the cat. *Journal of the Experimental Analysis of Behavior, 6*, 197–202.

Myers, R. D., & Mesker, D. C. (1960). Operant responding in a horse under several schedules of reinforcement. *Journal of the Experimental Analysis of Behavior, 3*, 161–164.

Nichols, J. R., Headlee, C. P., & Coppock, H. W. (1956). Drug addiction: I. Addiction by escape training. *Journal of the American Pharmaceutical Association* (Science ed.), *45*, 788–791.

Phillips, E. L. (1968). Achievement place: Token reinforcement procedures in a home-style rehabilitation setting for "pre-delinquent" boys. *Journal of Applied Behavior Analysis, 1*, 212–223.

Pickens, R., & Harris, W. C. (1968). Self-administration of *d*-amphetamine by rats. *Psychopharmacologia, 12*, 158–163.

Pickens, R., & Thompson, T. (1968). Cocaine-reinforced behavior in rats. *Journal of Pharmacology and Experimental Therapeutics, 161*, 122–129.

Pickens, R., Meisch, R. A., & Thompson, T. (1978). Drug self-administration: An analysis of the reinforcing effects of drugs. In L. L. Iversen, S. D. Iversen, & S. H. Snyder (Eds.), *Handbook of psychopharmacology* (Vol. 12, pp. 1–37). New York: Plenum.

Pierce, C. H., Hangford, P. V., & Zimmerman, J. (1972). Effects of different delay of reinforcement procedures on variable interval responding. *Journal of the Experimental Analysis of Behavior, 18*, 141–146.

Project MATCH Research Group. (1997). Matching alcoholism treatments to client heterogeneity: Project MATCH posttreatment drinking outcomes. *Journal of Studies on Alcohol, 58*, 7–29.

Reynolds, N. J., & Risley, T. R. (1968). The role of social and material reinforcers in increasing talking of a disadvantaged preschool child. *Journal of Applied Behavior Analysis, 1*, 253–262.

Salzinger, K., Waller, M. B., & Jackson, R. B. (1962). The operant control of vocalization in the dog. *Journal of the Experimental Analysis of Behavior, 5*, 383–389.

Schroeder, S. R., & Holland J. G. (1968). Operant control of eye movements. *Journal of Applied Behavior Analysis, 1*, 161–166.

Sidman, M., Brady, J. V., Boren, J. J., Conrad, D. G., & Schulman, A. (1955). Reward schedules and behavior maintained by intracranial self-stimulation. *Science, 122*, 830–831.

Skinner, B. F. (1938). *The behavior of organisms: An experimental analysis.* Englewood Cliffs, NJ: Prentice-Hall.

Skinner, B. F. (1972). *Cumulative record: A selection of papers* (3rd ed.). New York: Meredith.

Sobell, M. B., & Sobell, L. C. (1973). Individualized behavior therapy for alcoholics. *Behavior Therapy, 4*, 49–72.

Spragg, S. D. S. (1940). Morphine addiction in chimpanzees. *Comparative psy-*

chology monographs (Vol. 15, pp. 1–172). Baltimore: Johns Hopkins University Press.

Thompson, T., & Schuster, C. R. (1964). Morphine self-administration, food-reinforced and avoidance behaviors in rhesus monkeys. *Psychopharmacologia, 5,* 87–94.

Weeks, J. R. (1962). Experimental morphine addiction: Method for autonomic intravenous injects in unrestrained rats. *Science, 138,* 143–144.

Weeks, J. R., & Collins, R. J. (1964). Factors affecting voluntary morphine intake in self-maintained addicted rats. *Psychopharmacologia, 6,* 267–279.

Weiss, B., & Laties, V. G. (1960). Magnitude of reinforcement as a variable in a thermoregulatory behavior. *Journal of Comparative and Physiological Psychology, 53,* 603–608.

II

TREATMENT OF
COCAINE ABUSERS

2

CLINIC AND LABORATORY STUDIES ON THE USE OF INCENTIVES TO DECREASE COCAINE AND OTHER SUBSTANCE USE

STEPHEN T. HIGGINS, JOHN M. ROLL, CONRAD J. WONG, JENNIFER W. TIDEY, AND ROBERT DANTONA

We have been researching the use of contingency management interventions for the treatment of cocaine dependence for nearly 8 years. During the first several years of that effort, two clinical trials were completed examining the efficacy of a multicomponent behavioral treatment against standard drug abuse counseling (Higgins et al., 1991; Higgins, Budney, Bickel, Hughes, Foerg, & Badger, 1993). One component of the behavioral treatment was a contingency management intervention in which patients earned vouchers exchangeable for retail items contingent on submitting urine specimens that tested negative for cocaine in urinalysis screening. The initial two trials supported the efficacy of the multicomponent treatment but were not designed to examine the efficacy of

Preparation of this chapter was supported, in part, by Grants DA09378, DA08076, and DA07242 from the National Institute on Drug Abuse and General Clinical Research Center Award RR-109 from the National Institutes of Health.

the voucher program. After completion of those two initial trials, much of our research has focused on examining the efficacy of the voucher program and on conducting laboratory studies designed to improve understanding of contingency management interventions. In this chapter, we provide an overview of these clinical and laboratory studies on the use of vouchers and other incentives to increase abstinence from substance use.

VOUCHER-BASED THERAPY DURING OUTPATIENT TREATMENT OF COCAINE DEPENDENCE

Behavioral Treatment With and Without Vouchers

As noted above, the primary contingency management procedure used in our behavioral treatment is one in which patients earned vouchers exchangeable for retail items contingent on documentation through urinalysis testing that they had recently abstained from cocaine. The voucher system was in effect for Weeks 1–12 of treatment, with a $1.00 state lottery ticket awarded for each cocaine-negative urinalysis test during treatment Weeks 13–24. The value of the vouchers increased with each consecutive cocaine-negative specimen delivered, and cocaine-positive specimens reset the value of the vouchers at the initial level. Those who were continuously abstinent (all cocaine-negative urine tests) earned the equivalent of $997.50 during Weeks 1–12 and $24 during Weeks 13–24. Ideally, those who are continuously abstinent from cocaine could earn an average maximum of $6.08 per day; in practice, the average earned was approximately $3.50 per day.

The voucher program is combined with an adaptation of the community reinforcement approach (CRA), which is delivered by professional therapists during twice-weekly therapy sessions of 1 hr 30 min during Weeks 1–12 and once-weekly therapy sessions during Weeks 13–24 (see Higgins, Budney, & Bickel, 1994). All counseling was delivered in individual therapy sessions. The goal of CRA is to systematically alter the drug user's environment, so that reinforcement density from nondrug sources is relatively high during sobriety and low during drug use. The typical components of CRA are (a) disulfiram therapy in conjunction with procedures to support medication compliance for those patients who also abuse alcohol, (b) reciprocity relationship counseling for those who have spouses, (c) a job-finders intervention for unemployed patients or those seeking to change jobs, (d) social skills training, (e) assistance in altering social and recreational practices, and (f) drug refusal and other skills training (also see Higgins, 1997; Meyers & Smith, 1995; and Smith & Meyers, 1995, for more information on CRA).

In our first trial assessing the efficacy of the voucher program, 40 cocaine-dependent patients were randomly assigned to receive CRA with or without vouchers (Higgins, Budney, Bickel, Foerg, Donham, & Badger, 1994). CRA was delivered to patients in both treatment groups throughout the 24 weeks of treatment. Vouchers were in effect only during Weeks 1–12 of treatment. During Weeks 13–24, patients in the two treatment groups were treated identically, with both groups receiving a $1.00 state lottery ticket for each cocaine-negative urinalysis test.

Vouchers significantly improved treatment retention and cocaine abstinence. Seventy-five percent of patients in the group with vouchers completed 24 weeks of treatment versus 40% in the group without vouchers. Average duration of continuous cocaine abstinence that could be documented through urinalysis testing was 11.7 ± 2.0 weeks in the group with vouchers versus 6.0 ± 1.5 weeks in the group without vouchers (Figure 2.1). At the end of the 24-week treatment period, significant decreases from pretreatment scores were observed in both treatment groups on the Addition Severity Index (ASI) family–social and alcohol scales, with no differences between the groups. Both groups' scores also decreased on the ASI drug scale, but the magnitude of change was significantly greater for the voucher group, and only the voucher group showed a significant improvement on the ASI psychiatric scale. Additional follow-up assessments were conducted at 9 and 12 months after treatment entry. No significant differences were observed between the two groups in urinalysis results at those times; however, the magnitude of improvement on the ASI composite drug scale remained significantly larger in the voucher group, and only the voucher group showed significant improvement on the ASI psychiatric scale (Higgins et al., 1995).

The positive outcomes observed in the first trial demonstrated the efficacy of the voucher program in increasing treatment retention and cocaine abstinence. The results also raised a number of empirical questions. Because the study described above was conducted with cocaine abusers living in Burlington, Vermont, one question raised was whether the voucher intervention would have efficacy with an inner-city population of cocaine abusers. Silverman, Higgins, et al. (1996) and Silverman, Wong, et al. (1996) addressed that question in a series of experiments conducted in Baltimore, Maryland (see chapter 8, this volume, for an overview of that research effort). Another question raised is whether the improvements in outcome observed in our voucher versus no-voucher trial were a direct result of the vouchers reinforcing abstinence or an indirect result of vouchers increasing treatment retention and hence the amount of counseling and other services received, which may have been the proximal causes for the improved outcomes.

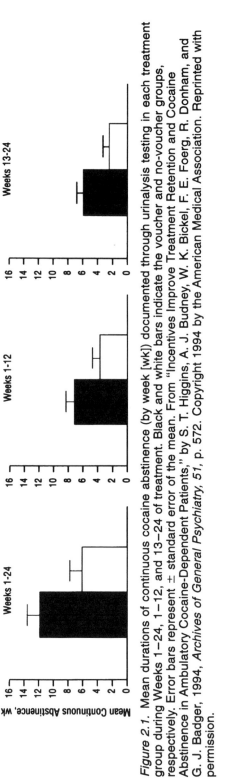

Figure 2.1. Mean durations of continuous cocaine abstinence (by week [wk]) documented through urinalysis testing in each treatment group during Weeks 1–24, 1–12, and 13–24 of treatment. Black and white bars indicate the voucher and no-voucher groups, respectively. Error bars represent ± standard error of the mean. From "Incentives Improve Treatment Retention and Cocaine Abstinence in Ambulatory Cocaine-Dependent Patients," by S. T. Higgins, A. J. Budney, W. K. Bickel, F. E. Foerg, R. Donham, and G. J. Badger, 1994, *Archives of General Psychiatry, 51*, p. 572. Copyright 1994 by the American Medical Association. Reprinted with permission.

Contingent Versus Noncontingent Vouchers

A second trial was conducted to better understand how voucher-based reinforcement of abstinence improved outcomes when treatment retention was comparable between the treatment groups (Higgins, Wong, Budney, English, & Kennedy, 1997). Seventy cocaine-dependent adults were randomly assigned to receive CRA and contingent or noncontingent vouchers. In the contingent group, vouchers were delivered in the same manner as described above. In the noncontingent group, vouchers were delivered independent of urinalysis results, and the schedule of delivery was yoked to the contingent group. This yoking procedure was based on the design used by Silverman, Higgins, et al. (1996) in their seminal study on voucher-based therapy with inner-city cocaine abusers. The purpose of the noncontingent vouchers in the present trial was to equate treatment retention between the two groups. By doing so, it provided an opportunity to assess whether vouchers directly reinforced cocaine abstinence. If they did, then the contingent voucher group would have achieved greater cocaine abstinence.

Results are still preliminary, but the percentage of patients in the contingent group (36%) who achieved 12 weeks or more of continuous cocaine abstinence was threefold greater than the noncontingent group (12%), which is a statistically significant difference. Overall mean duration of continuous abstinence was somewhat greater in the contingent than the noncontingent group (9.1 weeks vs. 6.5 weeks), but that difference was not statistically significant. The failure to detect a statistically significant difference in mean duration of continuous abstinence appeared to be because treatment retention was slightly better in the noncontingent than contingent group. When that difference was controlled for either by entering retention as a covariate or by restricting the analysis to those participants who completed the 12-week voucher program, the contingent group achieved significantly longer durations of mean continuous cocaine abstinence than the noncontingent group.

The results demonstrate that vouchers can directly reinforce cocaine abstinence. The results also indicate that the outcome differences observed in the vouchers versus no-vouchers trial (Higgins, Budney, Bickel, Foerg, Donham, & Badger, 1994) were probably a combination of vouchers directly reinforcing cocaine abstinence and increasing the duration and amount of counseling services received, which also improved outcomes. Future trials are needed to better understand such combined effects. Toward that end, a randomized clinical trial is currently under way in our clinic to empirically assess what CRA contributes to outcomes above and beyond the effects of the contingent voucher program. Patients are being randomly assigned to receive the contingent voucher program alone or in combination with CRA. Preliminary results are not yet available from that trial.

Vouchers and Participants' Confidence in Abstaining From Cocaine Use in Risky Situations

One concern that can be raised regarding the use of contingency management interventions such as vouchers to treat cocaine or other substance abuse is that they may adversely affect patients' self-efficacy by increasing their reliance on external sources of motivation. High ratings of confidence in one's ability to abstain from drugs, or self-efficacy, predict positive outcomes in a variety of substance abuse disorders as well as other health-related problems (e.g., Baer, Holt, Lichtenstein, 1986; Bandura, 1994; Reilly et al., 1995).

To begin to assess this issue, we modified the Situational Confidence Questionnaire (SCQ) short-form (Annis, 1984; Annis & Graham, 1988) for use with a cocaine-dependent population (Wong, Higgins, & Badger, 1997). The SCQ is a commonly used instrument for assessing self-efficacy in problem drinkers. The SCQ contains 42 items that assess patient confidence in the following seven areas that may affect drinking: (a) negative emotional states, (b) negative physical states, (c) positive emotional states, (d) level of personal control, (e) urges and temptations, (f) interpersonal conflict, and (g) social pressure to drink. Individuals are asked to imagine themselves in high-risk situations and indicate on a 6-point scale (0 = *not at all*, 20 = *20% confident*; 40 = *40% confident*; 60 = *60% confident*; 80 = *80% confident*; and 100 = *very confident*) how confident they are that they can resist the urge to drink heavily in each situation. To modify the SCQ for use in this study, the phrase *drinking heavily* was replaced with *use cocaine*, and 11 items were modified by replacing descriptive words associated with cocaine use (e.g., "If I would pass by a liquor store" was changed to "If I would pass by a dealer"). The instrument was administered to the 70 patients who participated in the contingent versus noncontingent vouchers trial described above. Participants completed the instrument at the initiation of treatment and again at 6, 12, and 24 weeks after treatment entry.

Results can be summarized as follows. First, there were no significant differences in confidence between the two groups at baseline. Second, situational confidence increased significantly during the course of treatment, both during the initial 12 weeks when the voucher program was in effect and during Weeks 13–24 after the voucher program was discontinued. There were no treatment group differences in that regard. Third, baseline situational confidence significantly predicted cocaine abstinence during treatment in the contingent group but not the noncontingent group. In the contingent group, greater situational confidence at baseline was associated with a greater duration of continuous cocaine abstinence during the 24 weeks of treatment ($r = .51$, $p < .01$). In the noncontingent group, greater situational confidence at baseline was not associated with greater abstinence ($r = -.09$, ns).

In summary, no evidence was found that vouchers adversely affected a standard measure of self-efficacy. Instead, confidence increased steadily and significantly in both groups throughout the 24 weeks of treatment. Moreover, it was the combination of high baseline confidence and contingent positive reinforcement with vouchers that predicted the greatest duration of cocaine abstinence. Neither high baseline confidence with noncontingent vouchers nor low baseline confidence with contingent vouchers was associated with sustained periods of continuous cocaine abstinence comparable with levels achieved by individuals with high baseline confidence who received contingent positive reinforcement for abstinence.

LABORATORY MODELS

Decreasing Cocaine Use Through a Monetary Incentive

To examine the question of whether vouchers or comparable reinforcers can directly increase cocaine abstinence, we took the question into a laboratory setting, where greater experimental control could be exercised over important variables, and a cocaine self-administration laboratory could be set up.

The first experiment was conducted with 4 healthy individuals who did not meet diagnostic criteria for cocaine dependence or any other form of drug dependence (except nicotine) but who were users of cocaine (Higgins, Bickel, & Hughes, 1994). These individuals were invited to participate in a study in which they could receive cocaine or a number of other stimulant medications. The drug was administered intranasally in 10.0-mg doses of cocaine hydrochloride or a placebo consisting of approximately 0.4 mg cocaine and 9.6 mg lactose. The maximum dose of cocaine allowed per session was 100.0 mg, which is a psychoactive dose. The experiment was conducted in two phases. The first phase consisted of two exposure sessions and one test session. During the two exposure sessions, participants sampled the cocaine and placebo in separate sessions under double-blind conditions, with the compounds labeled Drug A and Drug B. During the test session, participants were permitted to make a maximum of 10 exclusive choices between Drugs A and B. Choices were registered by a completion of 10 responses on either of two concurrently available levers associated with the drug and placebo options. Participants could also forgo either option. Sessions lasted for a maximum of 2 hr. Participants had to choose the cocaine over placebo seven times or more during the double-blind cocaine versus placebo choice session to participate in the next phase of the experiment. Participants were not informed of that criterion. The reason for the criterion was that experimenters wanted to study individuals for whom cocaine functioned as a reinforcer because that is a central feature of cocaine abuse.

During the second phase of the experiment, the placebo option was replaced by an option to earn money. Instead of choosing between cocaine and a placebo, participants now chose between cocaine and varying amounts of money. Cocaine versus money sessions were structured like the cocaine versus placebo session. Participants were informed of monetary values before each cocaine versus money session, and values were varied across sessions. Values varied from $0 to $2 per choice or, in total sums, from $0 to $20 per session. Payment occurred immediately after each session.

All 4 participants exclusively chose the cocaine over the placebo, demonstrating that the drug functioned as a reinforcer and satisfying the eligibility criterion for participation in the second phase of the experiment (data not provided). During sessions comparing cocaine and money, the choice of cocaine decreased as the amount of money available increased, with all participants exclusively choosing money in the $2 per choice condition (Figure 2.2). These results illustrate the malleability of cocaine preference in human cocaine users and demonstrate unequivocally that monetary-based incentives can increase cocaine abstinence independent of any possible influence of counseling or other psychosocial intervention.

Alcohol Use and Incentives to Decrease Cocaine Use

Prevalence of alcohol dependence among cocaine-dependent patients enrolled in treatment is 60% or higher, and as many as 97% of current cocaine users also are current users of alcohol (Carroll, Rounsaville, & Bryant, 1993; Grant & Harford, 1990; Higgins, Budney, Bickel, Foerg, & Badger, 1994). As part of a CRA intervention, we provided disulfiram therapy for those with alcohol abuse or dependence as well as for others who reported that their cocaine use was associated with alcohol use. During the therapy, we observed that participants were more successful in abstaining from cocaine when they were taking disulfiram (drinking less frequently) than when off the medication (drinking more frequently). To begin to assess this observation, Higgins, Budney, Bickel, Hughes, and Foerg (1993) conducted a chart review on 16 cocaine-dependent individuals who received disulfiram therapy. Disulfiram therapy was associated with significant reductions in drinking and cocaine use. For example, the percentage of cocaine-positive specimens during disulfiram therapy was 11% ± 3 versus 25% ± 6 when off the medication. As this was a chart review, no causal inferences can be made regarding the contribution of disulfiram to these effects. However, our hypothesis is that alcohol use increases the

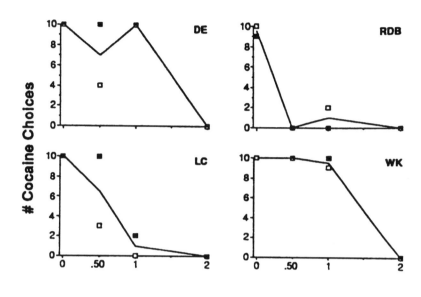

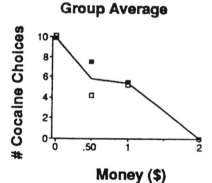

Figure 2.2. Number of cocaine choices are plotted as a function of the value of money available per choice in the monetary option. Participants made a maximum of 10 choices between cocaine and money each session. Data are presented for each of the 4 participants and as a group average. Results from the first and second exposures to the different monetary values are shown separately. DE, RDB, LC, and WK are participant identifiers. From "Influence of an Alternative Reinforcer on Human Cocaine Self-Administration," by S. T. Higgins, W. K. Bickel, and J. R. Hughes, 1994, *Life Science, 55,* p. 185. Copyright 1994 by Elsevier Science Inc. (655 Avenue of the Americas, New York, NY 10010-5107). Reprinted with permission.

relative reinforcing effects of cocaine over that provided by vouchers or other nonpharmacological reinforcers.

In a step toward better understanding the relationship between alcohol and cocaine use, Higgins, Roll, and Bickel (1996) conducted an experiment using the cocaine self-administration arrangement described above. They followed the same procedures as outlined above. Participants were 11 volunteers who used alcohol and cocaine but did not meet diagnostic criteria for abuse or dependence on either substance. Nine participants reliably chose the cocaine over the placebo in the cocaine versus placebo choice session (data not provided), demonstrating that cocaine functioned as a reinforcer and establishing the participants' eligibility for the subsequent cocaine versus money sessions. Two participants who did not meet the eligibility criterion and 2 additional participants who had scheduling conflicts were excluded from the cocaine versus money sessions. As in the prior study, cocaine preference decreased as an orderly function of increasing value in the monetary option (see Figure 2.3, left-most function). Those results provided a replication of the earlier findings. However, this study had an additional feature that distinguished it from the prior study. Prior to each cocaine versus money session, participants were treated with three varying doses of alcohol (placebo, 0.5 g/kg, and 1.0 g/kg). Pretreatment with the active doses of alcohol increased preference for the cocaine over the monetary reinforcer, with the effect being most discernible in the high money condition (see Figure 2.3, middle and right-most functions). It is interesting to note that on average alcohol pretreatment did not eliminate the ability of the monetary reinforcer to effectively compete with cocaine (it did in some individuals), but it diminished that effect in the high money condition.

These results confirm our hypothesis that alcohol use can increase the relative reinforcing effects of cocaine over an alternative monetary reinforcer. Extending those results to the clinical setting, it appears likely that alcohol use can significantly decrease the efficacy of contingency management and probably other therapeutic interventions for cocaine abuse.

Caffeine Use and Incentives to Decrease Cocaine Use

The majority (68%) of cocaine-dependent patients in our clinic reported daily use of caffeinated beverages (Budney, Higgins, Hughes, & Bickel, 1993). Caffeine can increase cocaine self-administration in some laboratory preparations with nonhumans (Comer & Carroll, 1996; Schenk, Valadez, Horger, Snow, & Wellman, 1994). To learn more about the potential relationship between caffeine and cocaine use in humans, Roll, Higgins, and Tidey (1998) conducted an experiment examining the acute

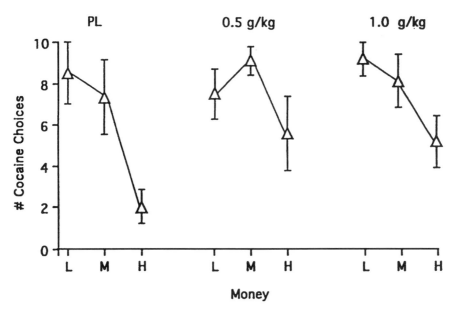

Figure 2.3. Number of cocaine choices during sessions involving alcohol pretreatment is shown as a function of three money conditions [low (L), medium (M), high (H)], with separate functions presented for each of the three alcohol doses [placebo (PL), 0.5 g/kg, 1.0 g/kg]. All data points represent means from the 7 participants who completed the experiment; brackets represent ± standard error of the mean. From "Alcohol Pretreatment Increases Preference for Cocaine Over Monetary Reinforcement," by S. T. Higgins, J. M. Roll, and W. K. Bickel, 1996, *Psychopharmacology, 123*, p. 4. Copyright 1996 by Springer-Verlag. Reprinted with permission.

effects of caffeine (0, 150, and 300 mg/70 kg) on preference for cocaine versus monetary reinforcement. The experiment was conducted in two phases following the methods described above. Seven participants who showed a preference for cocaine over placebo in Phase 1 of the study completed the second phase. During each of nine sessions in the second phase, patients were pretreated with one of the caffeine doses and then given a maximum of 10 choices between a 10-mg dose of cocaine or various amounts of money. Consistent with the prior findings, choice of cocaine decreased significantly as an orderly function of increasing value of the monetary option, but caffeine pretreatment had no discernible influence on that relationship (data not provided).

These negative findings with caffeine demonstrate that although some drugs (e.g., alcohol) may increase the preference for cocaine over alternative nondrug reinforcers, not all commonly used drugs do so. More research is needed to determine which of the commonly used and abused drugs adversely affect efforts to abstain from cocaine.

Other Experimental Models

Variations in the Schedule of Reinforcement for Abstinence

Although experimental studies of cocaine self-administration in humans can be informative regarding some very clinically relevant matters, they also can be relatively cumbersome to conduct in terms of participant recruitment, medical screening, monitoring, and so forth. For this reason, we began developing another model of stimulant drug self-administration that would be less cumbersome to study but would provide us the opportunity to ask questions pertinent to improving our understanding of contingency management interventions. We adapted a procedure initially developed by Stitzer and Bigelow (1982), in which cigarette smokers who are not attempting to quit smoking are recruited into a study and asked to attempt to abstain from smoking for 5 consecutive days or sometimes longer. Abstaining from cigarette smoking for even a few days can be very difficult. For example, in studies of cigarette smokers who attempt to quit on their own, approximately 75% resume smoking within 1 week (Hughes et al., 1992). Thus, the baseline of 5 days provides a great opportunity to examine the influence of incentives or other variables hypothesized to increase smoking abstinence. Because cigarette smoking satisfies all of the cardinal features of drug abuse (e.g., Hughes, 1993), we consider this to be an efficient model for researching questions pertinent to the voucher program and other contingency management interventions.

One question of interest to us was whether the complex schedule of reinforcement used in the voucher program influenced outcomes and whether a simpler reinforcement schedule may be equally efficacious. Recall that we use a schedule in which the value of the vouchers increases with each consecutive cocaine-negative urinalysis test, every three consecutive negative tests results in a bonus, and a positive test resets vouchers to their initial low value.

To address the issue of varying the schedule of reinforcement, Roll, Higgins, and Badger (1996) recruited 60 cigarette smokers from the community who were not trying to quit smoking at the time. Participants were requested to abstain from smoking for 5 consecutive days and then were randomly assigned to one of three groups: (a) progressive rate of reinforcement, (b) fixed rate of reinforcement, and (c) response-independent reinforcement. All participants agreed to visit the laboratory or to be visited by the experimenters at a place convenient for them, three times per day (morning, afternoon, evening), so a sample of expired air could be obtained that would permit the experimenters to assess carbon monoxide (CO) levels. CO level in expired air is a convenient, objective method for measuring recent cigarette smoking. In this study, abstinence from smoking was operationalized as a CO reading ≤ 11 parts per million. Participants in the progressive group earned $3.00 for the first specimen submitted indicating abstinence and that amount increased by $0.50 for each subsequent negative specimen submitted; every third consecutive negative specimen earned a $10.00 bonus. Failure to meet the abstinence criterion reset the value of monetary reinforcement to the initial $3.00 level. Three consecutive negative tests following a reset returned payment level to the amount it was at prior to the reset. Participants in the fixed group received a fixed sum of money ($9.80) each time they submitted a CO specimen that met the abstinence criterion. Bonuses for consecutive negative tests and the reset contingency for positive tests did not apply to this group. The overall amount of money that could be earned in the progressive and fixed reinforcement groups was the same. Finally, participants in the response-independent control group received money independent of CO readings and in amounts and according to a schedule of delivery that was yoked to the schedule of participant payment in the progressive reinforcement group.

The efficacy of contingent reinforcement was demonstrated by the fact that the mean percentage of trials in which CO levels met the abstinence criterion was significantly higher in the progressive and fixed reinforcement groups than in the control group (see Figure 2.4, upper panel). There were no significant differences between the progressive and fixed groups on that measure. The progressive and fixed groups differed in the percentage of participants who resumed smoking during the 5-day trial after having achieved a period of initial abstinence (i.e., three consecutive CO specimens ≤ 11 ppm), which can be thought of as a laboratory measure of relapse. Ninety percent ($n = 18$), 100% ($n = 20$), and 55% ($n = 11$) of patients in the progressive, fixed, and control groups achieved a period of initial abstinence (not shown). However, only 22% of patients ($n = 4$ of 18) in the progressive group who achieved a period of abstinence resumed smoking during the 5-day study period compared with 60% ($n = 12$ of 20) and 82% ($n = 9$ of 11) of patients in the fixed and control groups ($p < .01$; see Figure 2.4, bottom panel).

These results suggest that where the complex schedule of reinforcement is important is not in generating initial abstinence but in sustaining continuous abstinence once an initial period has been achieved. This is only a single study and replications are needed. However, at this point, it appears that the use of a more complex schedule as done in the voucher program is a clinically useful strategy in contingency management interventions.

Use of Incentives to Decrease Drug Use Among the Dually Diagnosed

Substance abuse in all forms is common among adults with schizophrenia and others with serious mental illness, resulting in an array of

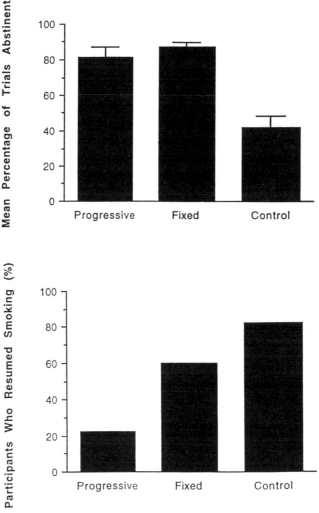

Figure 2.4. Mean percentage of 15 carbon monoxide (CO) test trials on which participants in each group were abstinent (CO ≤ 11 ppm) during the course of the 5-day study period. Error bars represent the standard error of the mean (upper panel). Percentage of participants in each group who obtained three consecutive abstinences and subsequently resumed smoking during the 5-day study period (lower panel). From "An Experimental Comparison of Three Different Schedules of Reinforcement of Drug Abstinence Using Cigarette Smoking as an Exemplar," by J. M. Roll, S. T. Higgins, and G. J. Badger, 1996, *Journal of Applied Behavior Analysis, 29,* p. 499. Copyright 1996 by the *Journal of Applied Behavior Analysis.* Reprinted with permission.

individual and societal adverse effects (Regier et al., 1990; Shaner et al., chapter 5, this volume). Some researchers have suggested that contingency management interventions using monetary incentives may be an effective means of reducing cocaine and other drug abuse in these difficult-to-treat patients (Shaner et al., 1995, and chapter 5, this volume). We concur that contingency management interventions are an important approach to investigate considering the relatively extensive literature demonstrating their efficacy in promoting other forms of behavior change in people with serious mental illnesses (e.g., Corrigan & Liberman, 1994). However, to our knowledge, no controlled studies have been reported addressing the sensitivity of drug use by adults with schizophrenia to contingency management interventions. The only evidence we are aware of is a recent report by Shaner et al. (1997) showing that contingent monetary reinforcement was effective in reducing cocaine use in 2 cocaine abusers with schizophrenia.

In our opinion, the sensitivity of substance use by those with a serious mental illness is an important empirical question that merits careful experimental investigation. Toward that end, Roll, Higgins, Steingard, and McGinley (1998) conducted an experiment with 11 adult outpatients with schizophrenia recruited through a local mental health center. Their purpose was to examine whether a monetary incentive could be used to induce initial abstinence from cigarette smoking in these participants. It is important to note that this experiment was conducted strictly as a feasibility study testing the sensitivity of smoking by patients with schizophrenia to programmed environmental consequences, not a clinical smoking-cessation trial.

The study was conducted in three 5-day (Monday–Friday) phases. The first phase was a baseline condition during which participants smoked in their usual manner. CO readings were obtained once a day during that period. The second phase was the intervention condition. CO specimens were collected three times a day (morning, afternoon, evening) during this period. Participants with readings less than or equal to 11 ppm earned monetary reinforcement according to the same progressive schedule used in the smoking study above. The third phase was a return to baseline during which CO specimens were again collected once a day and participants were free to smoke as they wished. Participants were paid $5 per specimen during each of the baseline conditions independent of CO levels. Participants were also contacted one time after their participation in the 3-week study (at an average of 8 weeks later) for an assessment of smoking status.

Results were analyzed using only afternoon CO readings from the intervention condition, which is consistent with when specimens were collected in the two baseline conditions. The total number of CO specimens less than or equal to 11 ppm was significantly lower in the intervention than baseline conditions, and the total number of consecutive CO specimens less than or equal to 11 ppm was significantly lower during the intervention condition relative to the two baseline conditions (see Figure 2.5). These differences were not an artifact of basing results on the afternoon CO readings from the intervention condition. Comparable results were obtained when the morning or evening CO readings from the intervention condition were used in the analyses.

These results provide empirical evidence from a carefully controlled experimental study demonstrating that abstinence from smoking in patients with schizophrenia can be increased with contingent positive reinforcement. The results are consistent with the preliminary evidence above supporting the utility of incentives for increasing cocaine abstinence in adults with schizophrenia and provide compelling empirical support for going forward with the exploration of contingency management interventions to reduce substance abuse in adults with schizophrenia and other serious mental illnesses.

In addition to the experiment described, Tidey, Higgins, Bickel, and Steingard (in press) completed a laboratory-based experiment further ex-

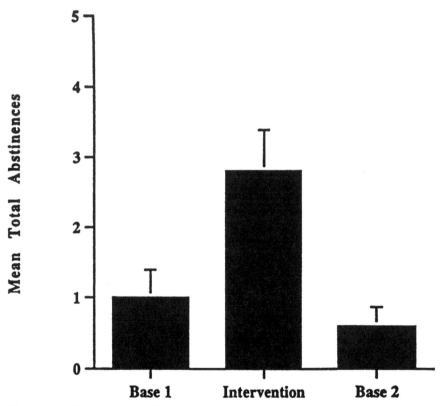

Figure 2.5. Total number of afternoon carbon monoxide specimens less than or equal to 11 ppm during the two baseline and intervention conditions. From "Use of Monetary Reinforcement to Reduce the Cigarette Smoking of Persons With Schizophrenia: A Feasibility Study," by J. M. Roll, S. T. Higgins, S. Steingard, and M. McGinley, 1998, *Experimental and Clinical Psychopharmacology, 6,* p. 159. Copyright 1998 by the American Psychological Association. Reprinted with permission.

amining the sensitivity of cigarette smoking by adults with schizophrenia to monetary incentives. In this experiment, patients abstained from cigarette smoking for a sufficient duration of time (usually about 6 hr) to decrease their baseline CO levels by at least 50%. These smoke-deprived individuals were then given an opportunity during 3-hr experimental sessions to earn puffs (two per episode) on a lit cigarette of their preferred brand by completing a specified number of lever presses. The number of lever presses required per two puffs varied from 50 to 6,400 in random order across separate experimental sessions. Additionally, during designated sessions, an alternative activity was available wherein individuals could earn monetary reinforcement at a fixed rate of $0.25 per 400 responses of a second lever. In this arrangement, variations in the number of responses required per opportunity to smoke can be conceptualized as varying the price of smoking. The variation regarding the presence or absence of money permits one to examine whether the availability of an alternative monetary reinforcer would influence participants' sensitivity to changes in the price of smoking.

Results from a representative participant who completed this experiment are shown in Figure 2.6. It is important to note that as the price for smoking increased, responding increased (upper panel) and smoking decreased (lower panel). That is, the participant's overall response output increased but not enough to prevent a decrease in the overall amount of smoking. More germane to the purpose of this chapter is the observation that total response output and number of puffs earned decreased substantially when the monetary alternative was available compared with when the alternative was not available. In other words, the presence of a monetary alternative increased this participant's sensitivity to the price of smoking.

Although this was not a contingency management intervention per se, the results lend further support to the position that substance use by adults with schizophrenia can be reduced by making monetary alternatives available either contingent on abstinence or contingent on behavior that is incompatible with substance use.

SUMMARY AND CONCLUSION

There are four points we want to underscore regarding this summary of our recent contingency management research. First, there is now a solid empirical base from the above studies and those of others to conclude that the voucher system is efficacious in reducing cocaine and other forms of substance abuse. Certainly more needs to be learned about this intervention, including how it can be modified so that a larger proportion of patients evidence clinically meaningful benefit from it and the durability of

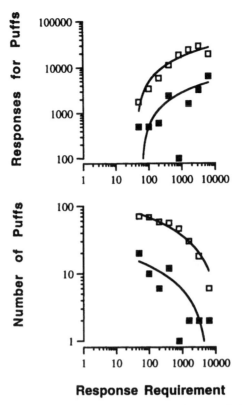

Figure 2.6. Data from a representative participant in a study by Tidey et al. (in press). Total number of responses emitted (upper panel) and number of cigarette puffs earned (lower panel) as a function of fixed-ratio value. Open symbols represent values in the absence of an alternative option; filled symbols represent values when an alternative option to earn monetary reinforcement was present.

effects over time. However, there appears to remain little question that it can significantly reduce drug use through direct reinforcement processes and, probably indirectly as well, through increased treatment retention and compliance.

Second, the available evidence suggests that alcohol use can thwart the efficacy of vouchers and monetary incentives for cocaine abstinence. Whether alcohol use also decreases the efficacy of vouchers or other contingency management interventions in decreasing other forms of drug use (e.g., opioid use) is unknown but an important area for future study. In contrast to alcohol use, caffeine use does not appear to affect the efficacy of monetary incentives for cocaine abstinence. We know of no other experimental data on the effects of other drug use on the efficacy of incentives in increasing cocaine abstinence, but such information is sorely needed. We doubt that alcohol is unique in having deleterious effects on cocaine abstinence; however, the results from the alcohol and caffeine studies illustrate that there are important between-drug differences in this regard. Careful experimental studies are needed to improve the understanding of the influence of multiple drug use and abuse on the efficacy of contingency management and other therapeutic interventions.

Third, the schedule of contingent reinforcement delivery appears to influence the efficacy of monetary incentives in maintaining drug abstinence. We suggest that the progressive and fixed schedules of reinforcement are equiefficacious in generating an initial period of drug abstinence but that the latter is more effective in sustaining periods of continuous abstinence. These conclusions are based on only a single experimental report. Clearly, more studies are needed. Further research on this topic should improve the efficacy of contingency management interventions and improve the understanding of the behavioral processes involved in relapse.

Fourth, although still preliminary, the studies on smokers with schizophrenia suggest that contingency management interventions are an important treatment strategy to evaluate in efforts to develop effective treatments for individuals with drug abuse and concomitant serious mental illness. Finding effective treatments for so-called dually diagnosed patients is an enormously challenging and important area, and we recommend the chapter by Shaner et al. (chapter 5, this volume) for a detailed discussion of this problem.

REFERENCES

Annis, H. M. (1984, August). *Analysis of the Situational Confidence Questionnaire.* Paper presented at the 92nd Annual Convention of the American Psychological Association, Toronto, Ontario, Canada.

Annis, H. M., & Graham, J. M. (1988). *Situational Confidence Questionnaire (SCQ) user's guide.* Toronto, Ontario, Canada: Addiction Research Foundation.

Baer, J. S., Holt, C. S., & Lichtenstein, E. (1986). Self-efficacy and smoking reexamined: Construct validity and clinical utility. *Journal of Consulting and Clinical Psychology, 54,* 846–852.

Bandura, A. (1994). Social cognitive theory and exercise of control over HIV infection. In R. J. DiClemente & J. L. Peterson (Eds.), *Preventing AIDS: Theories and methods of behavioral interventions* (pp. 25–59). New York: Plenum Press.

Budney, A. J., Higgins, S. T., Hughes, J. R., & Bickel, W. K. (1993). Nicotine and caffeine use in cocaine-dependent individuals. *Journal of Substance Abuse, 5,* 117–130.

Carroll, K. M., Rounsaville, B. J., & Bryant, K. J. (1993). Alcoholism in treatment-seeking cocaine abusers: Clinical and prognostic significance. *Journal of Studies on Alcohol, 54,* 199–208.

Comer, S. D., & Carroll, M. E. (1996). Oral caffeine pretreatment produced modest increases in smoked cocaine self-administration in rhesus monkeys. *Psychopharmacology, 126,* 281–285.

Corrigan, P. W., & Liberman, R. P. (Eds.). (1994). *Behavior therapy in psychiatric hospitals.* New York: Springer.

Grant, B. F., & Harford, T. C. (1990). Concurrent and simultaneous use of alcohol with cocaine: Results of national survey. *Drug and Alcohol Dependence, 25,* 97–104.

Higgins, S. T. (1997). Applying learning and conditioning theory to the treatment of alcohol and cocaine abuse. In B. A. Johnson & J. D. Roache (Eds.), *Drug addiction and its treatment: Nexus of neuroscience and behavior* (pp. 367–386). Philadelphia: Lippincott-Raven.

Higgins, S. T., Bickel, W. K., & Hughes, J. R. (1994). Influence of an alternative reinforcer on human cocaine self-administration. *Life Science, 55,* 179–187.

Higgins, S. T., Budney, A. J., & Bickel, W. K. (1994). Applying behavioral concepts and principles to the treatment of cocaine dependence. *Drug and Alcohol Dependence, 34,* 87–97.

Higgins, S. T., Budney, A. J., Bickel, W. K., Foerg, F. E., & Badger, G. J. (1994). Alcohol dependence and simultaneous cocaine and alcohol use in cocaine-dependent patients. *Journal of Addictive Diseases, 13,* 177–189.

Higgins, S. T., Budney, A. J., Bickel, W. K., Foerg, F. E., Donham, R., & Badger, G. J. (1994). Incentives improve treatment retention and cocaine abstinence in ambulatory cocaine-dependent patients. *Archives of General Psychiatry, 51,* 568–576.

Higgins, S. T., Budney, A. J., Bickel, W. K., Foerg, F. E., Ogden, D., & Badger, G. J. (1995). Outpatient behavioral treatment for cocaine dependence: One-year outcome. *Experimental and Clinical Psychopharmacology, 3,* 205–212.

Higgins, S. T., Budney, A. J., Bickel, W. K., Hughes, J. R., & Foerg, F. (1993). Disulfiram therapy in patients abusing cocaine and alcohol. *American Journal of Psychiatry, 150,* 675–676.

Higgins, S. T., Budney, A. J., Bickel, W. K., Hughes, J. R., Foerg, F., & Badger, G. (1993). Achieving cocaine abstinence with a behavioral approach. *American Journal of Psychiatry, 150,* 763–769.

Higgins, S. T., Delaney, D. D., Budney, A. J., Bickel, W. K., Hughes, J. R., Foerg, F., & Fenwick, J. W. (1991). A behavioral approach to achieving initial cocaine abstinence. *American Journal of Psychiatry, 148,* 1218–1224.

Higgins, S. T., Roll, J. M., & Bickel, W. K. (1996). Alcohol pretreatment increases preference for cocaine over monetary reinforcement. *Psychopharmacology, 123,* 1–8.

Higgins, S. T., Wong, C. J., Budney, A. J., English, K. T., & Kennedy, M. H. (1997). Efficacy of incentives during outpatient treatment of cocaine dependence. In L. S. Harris (Ed.), *Problems of drug dependence 1996: Proceedings of the 58th annual scientific meeting, the College on Problems of Drug Dependence* (NIDA Monograph Series 174, p. 75). Washington, DC: U.S. Government Printing Office.

Hughes, J. R. (1993). Smoking is a drug dependence: A reply to Robison and Pritchard. *Psychopharmacology, 13,* 282–283.

Hughes, J. R., Gulliver, S. B., Fenwick, J. W., Valliere, W. A., Cruser, K., Pepper, S., Shea, P., Solomon, L. J., & Flynn, B. S. (1992). Smoking cessation among self-quitters. *Health Psychology, 11,* 331–334.

Meyers, R. J., & Smith, J. E. (1995). *Clinical guide to alcohol treatment: The community reinforcement approach.* New York: Guilford Press.

Regier, D. A., Farmer, M. E., Rae, D. S., Locke, B. Z., Keith, S. J., Judd, L. L., & Goodwin, F. K. (1990). Comorbidity of mental disorders with alcohol and other drug abuse: Results from the Epidemiologic Catchment Area (ECA) Study. *Journal of the American Medical Association, 264,* 2511–2518.

Reilly, P. M., Sees, K. L., Shopshire, M. S., Hall, S. M., Delucchi, K. L., Tusel, D. J., Banys, P., Clark, H. W., & Piotrowski, N. A. (1995). Self-efficacy and illicit opioid use in a 180-day methadone detoxification treatment. *Journal of Consulting and Clinical Psychology, 63,* 158–162.

Roll, J. M., Higgins, S. T., & Badger, G. J. (1996). An experimental comparison of three different schedules of reinforcement of drug abstinence using cigarette smoking as an exemplar. *Journal of Applied Behavior Analysis, 29,* 495–505.

Roll, J. M., Higgins, S. T., Steingard, S., & McGinley, M. (1998). Use of monetary reinforcement to reduce the cigarette smoking of persons with schizophrenia: A feasibility study. *Experimental and Clinical Psychopharmacology, 6,* 157–161.

Roll, J. M., Higgins, S. T., & Tidey, J. (1998). Effects of an alternative reinforcer and caffeine on human cocaine self-administration. In L. S. Harris (Ed.), *Problems of drug dependence 1997: Proceedings of the 59th annual scientific meeting, the College on Problems of Drug Dependence* (NIDA Monograph Series 178, p. 286). Washington, DC: U.S. Government Printing Office.

Schenk, S., Valadez, A., Horger, B. A., Snow, S., & Wellman, P. J. (1994). Interactions between caffeine and cocaine in tests of self-administration. *Behavioural Pharmacology, 5,* 153–158.

Shaner, A., Eckman, T. A., Roberts, L. J., Wilkins, J. N., Tucker, D. E., Tsuang, J. W., & Mintz, J. (1995). Disability income, cocaine use, and repeated hospitalization among schizophrenic cocaine abusers. *New England Journal of Medicine, 12,* 777–783.

Shaner, A., Roberts, L. J., Eckman, T. A., Tucker, D. E., Tsuang, J. W., Wilkins, J. N., & Mintz, J. (1997). Monetary reinforcement of abstinence from cocaine among mentally ill patients with cocaine dependence. *Psychiatric Services, 48,* 807–810.

Silverman, K., Higgins, S. T., Montoya, I. D., Cone, E. J., Schuster, C. R., & Preston, K. L. (1996). Sustained cocaine abstinence in methadone maintenance patients through voucher-based reinforcement therapy. *Archives of General Psychiatry, 53,* 409–415.

Silverman, K., Wong, C. J., Higgins, S. T., Brooner, R. K., Montoya, I. D., Contoreggi, C., Umbricht-Schneiter, A., Schuster, C. R., & Preston, K. L. (1996). Increasing opiate abstinence through voucher-based reinforcement therapy. *Drug and Alcohol Abstinence, 41,* 157–165.

Smith, J. E., & Meyers, R. J. (1995). The community reinforcement approach. In R. K. Hester & W. R. Miller (Eds.), *Handbook of alcoholism treatment approaches: Effective alternatives* (2nd ed., pp. 251–266). Boston: Allyn & Bacon.

Stitzer, M. L., & Bigelow, G. E. (1982). Contingent reinforcement for reduced carbon monoxide levels in cigarette smokers. *Addictive Behaviors, 7*, 403–412.

Tidey, J. W., Higgins, S. T., Bickel, W. K., & Steingard, S. (in press). Effects of response requirement and the availability of an alternative reinforcer on cigarette smoking by schizophrenics. *Psychopharmacology*.

Wong, C. J., Higgins, S. T., & Badger, G. J. (1997). Situational Confidence Questionnaire scores as predictors of outcome in the treatment of cocaine dependence. In L. S. Harris (Ed.), *Problems of drug dependence 1996: Proceedings of the 58th annual scientific meeting, the College on Problems of Drug Dependence* (NIDA Monograph Series 174, p. 276). Washington, DC: U.S. Government Printing Office.

3

CONTINGENCY MANAGEMENT AND RELAPSE PREVENTION AS STIMULANT ABUSE TREATMENT INTERVENTIONS

RICHARD RAWSON, MICHAEL McCANN, ALICE HUBER, AND STEVEN SHOPTAW

The development and evaluation of psychological and behavioral strategies for the treatment of substance abuse disorders are a priority for the National Institute on Drug Abuse (NIDA). Increased importance is given to the expansion and application of these findings for the treatment of stimulant abuse disorders in light of the absence of effective pharmacotherapies for ameliorating cocaine abuse (Meyers, 1992) and methamphetamine abuse disorders (Ling, 1996). Furthermore, there is a substantial accumulation of research supporting the value of these approaches in the treatment of substance abuse disorders (Rawson, 1995; Stitzer & Higgins, 1995).

The authors would like to thank Arthur Corrales, Vikas Gulati, and Ruth deCarteret for their work on this project and Lydia Corrales for her assistance. Preparation of this chapter was supported by Grants DA09419, DA09992, DA11031, and DA10923 from the National Institute on Drug Abuse.

There are two particularly promising psychological–behavioral approaches for the treatment of stimulant abuse disorders. One approach with considerable evidence of support is the use of contingency management techniques (Stitzer, Bigelow, & Gross, 1989). Of all categories of behavioral interventions for substance abuse treatment, contingency management procedures have the most well-established empirical base. Although the systematic application of contingency management within the treatment system has been limited, the tremendous potential value of these procedures is illustrated by the work reported in this volume.

Another set of techniques associated with favorable outcomes are the cognitive–behavioral strategies based on principles of social learning theory (Bandura, 1977, 1981, 1984), collectively referred to as *relapse prevention techniques* (Marlatt & Gordon, 1985). There has been a broad application of relapse prevention techniques across a variety of substance abuse disorders. Data have been reported on the use of these techniques for the treatment of alcoholism (Dimeff & Marlatt, 1995), opiate addiction (McAuliffe, 1990), marijuana use (Roffman, Stephens, Simpson, & Whitaker, 1990), and cigarette smoking (Mermelstein, Karnatz, & Reichmann, 1992). Additionally, in a review, Rawson and colleagues suggested that the relapse prevention approach has been well integrated into the network of substance abuse treatment settings (Rawson, Obert, McCann, & Marinelli-Casey, 1993a, 1993b).

NEED FOR STIMULANT ABUSE TREATMENTS

Cocaine abuse and methamphetamine abuse continue to be major public health problems in the United States. Cocaine abuse is an important factor in drug-related crime and violence (De La Rosa, Lambert, & Gropper, 1990), the spread of infectious diseases (Chaisson, Bacchetti, Brodie, Sande, & Moss, 1989), and prenatal drug exposure (Kain, Kain, & Scarpelli, 1992). Recent surveys on cocaine abuse suggest that the incidence of cocaine-related deaths and emergency room admissions continues to increase (Harrison, 1992) and that cocaine users are a large proportion of drug treatment admissions (Groerer & Brodsky, 1993). Cocaine and crack abuse among methadone maintenance patients is one of the most serious clinical challenges to face clinicians during the 30-year history of methadone maintenance. There is considerable evidence documenting the high levels of cocaine use among methadone patients (Condelli, Fairbank, & Rachel, 1991; Hartel, Schoenbaum, Selwyn, Drucker, & Friedland, 1989; Magura, Siddiqui, Freeman, & Lipton, 1991; U.S. General Accounting Office, 1990), and investigators have found rates of cocaine use among methadone patients as high as 60% in a New York City (Maier, 1989) and 75% in a Virginia (Cushman, 1988) methadone program.

The extent and consequences of methamphetamine use have increased over the past few years, resulting in attention for the first time in the federal national drug control strategy of 1996. Nationally, from 1991 to 1995, the number of methamphetamine-related visits to hospital emergency rooms and the number of methamphetamine-related deaths tripled (Substance Abuse and Mental Health Services Administration [SAMHSA], 1996a, 1996b). Although methamphetamine use was previously viewed as a West Coast phenomenon, there is now concern at the national level about its increasing use in other areas of the country, including Denver, Des Moines, Omaha, St. Louis, Dallas, Atlanta, Philadelphia, and Minneapolis–St. Paul (Office of the National Drug Control Policy, 1996). Of particular concern is the increase in stimulant use by adolescents (e.g., a 40% increase from 1991 to 1994 in the number of 10th-grade students using stimulants; Office of the National Drug Control Policy, 1996).

Currently, there are no medications with demonstrated efficacy for the treatment of stimulant abuse disorders. Although both the contingency management and relapse prevention strategies have the best empirical support as treatment approaches for stimulant-related problems, there is much to be learned about the appropriate application of these strategies as stimulant abuse treatments. The systematic study of contingency management and relapse prevention procedures is likely to provide considerable theoretical and practical knowledge to guide the development of these treatment approaches.

CONTINGENCY MANAGEMENT APPROACH

A detailed review of contingency management is available in other chapters in this volume (i.e., Bigelow & Silverman, chapter 1; Higgins et al., chapter 2). Briefly, contingency management approaches include an array of empirically based interventions for drug abuse treatment. A variety of well-controlled studies support the effectiveness of this approach. Some positive incentive strategies include take-home incentives for methadone maintenance patients (Iguchi, Stitzer, Bigelow, & Liebson, 1988; Magura, Casriel, Goldsmith, Strug, & Lipton, 1988; Milby, Garrett, English, Fritschi, & Clarke, 1978; Stitzer, Bigelow, Liebson, & Hawthorne, 1982; Stitzer, Iguchi, & Felch, 1992), cash incentives for drug-free urine specimens during ambulatory methadone detoxification (Hall, Bass, Hargreaves, & Loeb, 1979; McCaul, Stitzer, Bigelow, & Liebson, 1984), and naturalistic reinforcers in alcoholism treatment using a community reinforcement approach (CRA; Hunt & Azrin, 1973).

In recent years, the CRA procedure developed by Hunt and Azrin (1973) for alcoholism treatment has been combined with explicit contingency management procedures into a strategy for outpatient cocaine abuse treatment (Higgins et al., 1991; also see chapter 2, this volume). Although there are no reports suggesting that contingency management procedures are differentially more or less effective with methamphetamine abusers than cocaine abusers, there are currently no data to assess the issue.

RELAPSE PREVENTION APPROACH

> Relapse Prevention (RP) is a generic term that refers to a wide range of strategies designed to prevent relapse in the area of addictive behavior change. The primary focus of relapse prevention is on the crucial issue of maintenance in the habit-change process. The purpose is twofold: to prevent the occurrence of initial lapses after one has embarked on a program of habit change, and/or to prevent any lapse from escalating into a total relapse. (Marlatt & Gordon, 1985, p. xii)

The techniques used within the designation of the relapse prevention category include the following groups of strategies (Rawson, Obert, McCann, & Marinelli-Casey, 1993a, 1993b).

1. *Psychoeducation.* An important ingredient in relapse prevention models is the use of information and education about a variety of addiction-related topics. Central among the issues taught to substance abusers during the course of treatment are the following: (a) brain chemistry and addiction, (b) conditioned cues and craving, (c) drug and alcohol effects, (d) addiction as a biobehavioral disorder, (e) drug use and AIDS, (f) addiction and the family, and (g) the need for lifestyle change.

2. *Identification of high-risk situations and warning signs for relapse.* Patients are taught that there are behaviors and environments as well as cognitive and affective states that are associated with drug and alcohol use. Through individual and group discussion as well as in homework assignments, patients learn the specific set of conditions that have the greatest association with drug and alcohol use.

3. *Development of coping skills.* Researchers have suggested that substance abusers in high-risk situations have maladaptive coping skills. Much of the relapse prevention "counseling" focuses on teaching and reinforcing alternative coping skills that will not lead to drug and alcohol use.

4. *Development of new lifestyle behaviors.* Once drug and alcohol use has been reduced or stopped, it is important to reinforce the development of alternative activities to serve as intrinsic

reinforcers of abstinence. Group discussions and homework assignments are used to assist drug and alcohol users in acquiring and maintaining new leisure, recreational, and employment activities that support a drug-free lifestyle.

5. *Increased self-efficacy.* Self-efficacy theory (Bandura, 1977, 1981, 1984) proposes that when people enter high-risk situations for drug or alcohol use, they choose each response on the basis of their appraisal of their ability to cope with the situation. If they view themselves as competent, they will abstain from using drugs or alcohol. To facilitate the development of the self-perception of competence, patients are taught new strategies for enhancing self-efficacy in these situations.

6. *Dealing with relapse—Avoiding the abstinence violation effect.* Within relapse prevention models, the reality of relapse is addressed. Patients are taught to view return to drug and alcohol use as "slips" or "lapses" that need not lead back to full-blown relapse and readdiction. This approach in dealing with a return to alcohol and drug use can interrupt the cycle in which a lapse turns into an extended relapse episode.

Extensive use of relapse prevention materials has been made as a central element in an integrated model of outpatient treatment referred to as the *neurobehavioral model*—or more recently as the *Matrix model* (Rawson, Obert, McCann, & Ling, 1991; Rawson, Obert, McCann, Smith, & Ling, 1990). Researchers evaluated the manualized, multicomponent outpatient protocol in trials that (a) compared the Matrix model to an inpatient treatment program (Rawson, Obert, McCann, & Mann, 1985), (b) compared different stimulant-abusing populations (Rawson et al., 1991), (c) evaluated the efficacy of the model with cocaine and methamphetamine users as an HIV-risk reduction strategy (Shoptaw, Reeback, Frosch, & Rawson, 1998), (d) evaluated the model with cocaine-abusing methadone maintenance patients (Magura et al., 1994), and (e) compared the treatment response of cocaine and methamphetamine users (Huber et al., 1997). In all of these evaluations of the Matrix model, a substantial reduction in stimulant use and an increase in positive prosocial behavior were associated with treatment participation (Rawson et al., 1995). Because the Matrix model protocol comprises a number of elements (i.e., relapse prevention techniques, family interventions, self-help involvement, motivational interviewing), it has not been possible to determine the specific contribution of relapse prevention techniques to the clinical impact of the model. A more circumscribed and methodologically uncontaminated program of research is required to assess the efficacy of relapse prevention.

Researchers at Yale University have created a protocol to evaluate the value of relapse prevention techniques for the treatment of cocaine abusers (Carroll, Rounsaville, & Keller, 1991) and have conducted several well-controlled evaluations of relapse prevention protocol for the treatment of cocaine abuse. In another study, Carroll, Rounsaville, and Gawin (1991) evaluated a weekly, 12-session protocol of individual sessions involving the random assignment of 42 participants to either a relapse prevention condition or a similar amount of contact with a therapist using an interpersonal psychotherapy approach (IPT). There were indications that the relapse prevention approach appeared superior to the IPT approach, but because of the relatively small sample size, the group differences did not achieve statistical significance. Two thirds of the relapse prevention group were retained for the 12-week protocol, and 38% of the IPT group completed the protocol. During the course of treatment, there was a very substantial decrease in cocaine use for participants in both groups. Of significant interest is the finding that with a subsample of severely addicted cocaine users, the relapse prevention approach did result in a statistically significantly better treatment outcome on two measures of abstinence at follow-up.

In a later study, Carroll, Rounsaville, Gordon, et al. (1994; see also Carroll, Rounsaville, Nich, et al., 1994) extended these earlier findings on the efficacy of relapse prevention with cocaine abusers. In a study comparing relapse prevention to a case management approach, the during-treatment data did not demonstrate an overall difference between relapse prevention and case management; however, Carroll et al. reported that there was evidence that the more severe cocaine abusers and the more depressed participants showed a superior response to the relapse prevention condition (Carroll, Rounsaville, Gordon, et al., 1994). In addition in a later report at follow-up, the cocaine abstinence rate of the relapse prevention group participants was significantly higher than for the case management group participants. Unfortunately, the follow-up data in this report were from multiple time points, and the highest rate of follow-up interviews was at 3 months posttreatment (67%). Although this rate of follow-up interviews is low and complicates interpretation of study findings, the researchers suggested that the relapse prevention procedures produced a delayed treatment effect (Carroll, Rounsaville, Nich, et al., 1994).

Another research group from Seattle, Washington, reported equivocal results in an evaluation of relapse prevention for cocaine abuse treatment. Wells, Peterson, Gainey, Hawkins, and Catalano (1994) found few meaningful differences in treatment outcome between an outpatient relapse prevention protocol and a 12-step-based protocol approach. Participants in both groups reported a significant decrease in cocaine and other drug and alcohol use from pretreatment to posttreatment and follow-up. Although there was evidence that the participants in the 12-step group returned to alcohol use to a greater degree than did the participants in the relapse prevention condition, there were no differences between the two groups on measures of cocaine use.

Despite the enthusiastic use of relapse prevention techniques in the field of substance abuse treatment, well-controlled experimental research to support the efficacy of the procedures for cocaine abuse treatment is modest. In many of the experimental demonstrations, relapse prevention techniques have been associated with significant reduction in cocaine use, but the amount of reduction has been comparable for participants treated in comparison or control conditions (e.g., Carroll, Rounsaville, Gordon, et al., 1994; Wells et al., 1994). Currently, there are no data on the efficacy of relapse prevention strategies applied to the treatment of methamphetamine abuse disorders.

CURRENT PROGRAM OF CONTINGENCY MANAGEMENT AND RELAPSE PREVENTION RESEARCH AT THE MATRIX CENTER

Evaluations of contingency management and relapse prevention appear to provide some support for the use of these techniques for cocaine abuse treatment with both primary cocaine abusers and cocaine-abusing methadone patients. The program of research established at the Matrix Center in the early 1990s was initiated to provide a set of data on the impact of contingency management and relapse prevention on the drug use and associated behaviors of a number of stimulant-abusing populations. The studies in this program of research have all been designed to (a) use parallel study designs and protocols across study populations to allow for comparisons of study findings across different populations of stimulant abusers; (b) use standardized, manualized relapse prevention and contingency management protocols, properly monitored to ensure the integrity of implementation; (c) use a carefully selected, well-established battery of process and outcome measures and use a common quality-assurance monitoring system of data collection and data management; (d) use an adequate sample size to ensure appropriate statistical power; and (e) direct and monitor the studies using a common research management team to minimize study-to-study and site-to-site variation in study methods. The following NIDA-funded projects are currently under way at facilities operated by the Matrix Center and Matrix Institute on Addictions in southern California.

Behavioral–Cognitive Behavioral Trial for Cocaine Abuse

Study 1: Primary cocaine abusers. One hundred eighty individuals meeting *Diagnostic and Statistic Manual of Mental Disorders* (4th ed.; *DSM-IV*; American Psychiatric Association, 1994) criteria for cocaine abuse dependence are being randomly assigned into one of three 16-week treatment conditions. The conditions are as follows:

- Relapse prevention only: three weekly, 90-min group sessions in which a set of relapse prevention topic worksheets are presented and discussed by a trained master's degree level group leader and group members.
- Contingency management only: three weekly visits to the clinic to provide urine samples analyzed for drugs of abuse. Urine samples negative for benzolecognine earn individuals vouchers that can be traded for goods and services not associated with drug use. Participants in this condition receive no counseling support.
- Relapse prevention and contingency management: three weekly visits in which individuals attend relapse prevention sessions and participate in the contingency management voucher system, as described above.

Baseline measures evaluate psychiatric diagnosis using the Structured Clinical Inventory for *DSM-IV* (SCID), drug use and related behavior using the Addiction Severity Index (ASI), and HIV risk behavior using the Risk Assessment Battery (RAB). All participants provide urine samples three times per week. Treatment process data using the treatment services review are collected weekly; the ASI and RAB are repeated at 90, 180, and 360 days postadmission along with urine samples. The goal of this study is to determine the relative acceptability, efficacy, and durability of effects of contingency management and relapse prevention alone and in combination.

Study 2: Cocaine-abusing methadone-maintained patients. Two-hundred cocaine-abusing methadone maintenance patients are being randomly assigned to one of four 16-week treatment conditions. Three of the conditions are identical to the conditions in Study 1. A fourth condition consists of standard methadone treatment, with three urine samples weekly and data collection as with the other three groups. No cocaine abuse intervention is delivered to participants in the fourth group. The resulting design of this study is (a) relapse prevention only, (b) contingency management only, (c) relapse prevention plus contingency management, and (d) no treatment. All data collection instruments and time points are identical to those in Study 1.

The sample in this project is very different from the sample in Study 1. The methadone-maintained patients have much longer and much more severe drug use histories, much greater involvement in the criminal justice system, poorer education, fewer resources, and much higher levels of psychopathology, as measured at baseline. A particular interest in this project is to compare the findings from Study 1 with those from Study 2.

These data should add greatly to understanding the generalizability and limitations of findings by examining two very different study samples within a concurrent parallel study design. The contingency management of tobacco smoking in opiate addicts is described in detail in chapter 12 (this volume).

Behavior Therapy for Gay Male Methamphetamine Users

This 4-year project uses a study design exactly parallel to Study 1 above. The purpose of the study is to evaluate contingency management and relapse prevention alone and in combination for the treatment of methamphetamine abuse. This study will be the first to evaluate contingency management and relapse prevention with methamphetamine abusers and with a sample of 180 gay and bisexual men. The reason gay and bisexual men have been selected as the study sample is that there is a very high incidence of methamphetamine use among this group, and the sexual behavior that is associated with their methamphetamine use puts them at extremely high risk for HIV transmission. The findings from this study will address the efficacy of contingency management and relapse prevention for reducing methamphetamine use and whether reduction of this drug use is associated with a reduction in HIV risk behavior.

Medication–Behavior Therapy for Methamphetamine Abusers

The overall objective of this 4-year project is to evaluate a pharmacotherapy (Sertraline) and contingency management for methamphetamine abuse and dependence. The study uses a 2 × 2 factorial design, and 220 individuals will be randomly assigned to one of four experimental conditions—(a) Sertraline–contingency management, (b) Sertraline–no contingency management, (c) placebo–contingency management, (d) placebo–no contingency management—and treated for 12 weeks. In addition, individuals will participate in a thrice-weekly, manualized psychosocial program using the relapse prevention protocol from the other studies. In this study, relapse prevention groups serve as a treatment platform on which to evaluate the effects of contingency management and a medication, alone and in combination. Major assessments are conducted at baseline, 4 and 8 weeks after randomization, the conclusion of the intervention (12 weeks), and 6- and 12-month follow-ups after study admission. The study will allow us to evaluate whether these approaches differentially engage and retain participants in treatment as measured by survival analysis, reduce methamphetamine use as measured by urine toxicology and self-report, improve psychosocial functioning as measured by the ASI and other measures, and reduce HIV risk behavior as measured by the RAB.

All of the studies described above are under way. Because "preliminary analyses" or "peeking at" study trends can influence the conduct of ongoing study activities and thereby influence the final study outcomes, no partial study data will be reported until the study is completed. However, this program of research, which addresses some very important theoretical issues and establishes some methodologies for addressing commonly encountered research quandries, will collect information on the practical application of treatment methods.

THEORETICAL ISSUES

The research conducted in this series of studies addresses some conceptually intriguing treatment issues. For example, the relapse prevention approach is grounded in the cognitive behavioral philosophy that maintains that clinically significant behavior change is generated by the delivery of clinically relevant information to patients in a context that reinforces the discontinuation of harmful behavior and the acquisition of health-promoting behavior. The essential treatment experience involves the communication of information from the treatment materials and the group leader to the study participants. The change of the participant's behavior is presumably based on this transfer of information. This treatment paradigm is common to many forms of counseling and psychotherapy.

In contrast, the contingency management approach, a simple positive reinforcement paradigm, makes no assumptions about the need to deliver new information to individuals to promote behavior change. In this model, the methods used by the participants to change their behavior are unknown. The principle underlying the contingency management intervention is that behavior change occurs in response to the proper set of contingencies. Conceptually, the relapse prevention and contingency management procedures have fundamentally different assumptions and approaches to promote and explain behavior change. The addition of a condition that would combine both procedures allows for a determination of whether these two behavior change strategies are complementary. Particular attention will be given to determining if different groups of stimulant abusers respond differently to the different approaches. For example, as a supplementary treatment for methadone maintenance patients, the contingency management procedure may be a sufficient or even preferable treatment to address their cocaine abuse. However, for primary cocaine abusers who may expect treatment to take the form of some type of "therapy," the application of contingency management procedures may be viewed quite differently. Another issue of considerable interest is whether the cognitive impairment that is associated with chronic methamphetamine abuse will affect the impact and efficacy of the cognitively mediated materials in the relapse prevention approach. Data from this program of research may provide some new information on these important conceptual issues.

METHODOLOGICAL CONSIDERATIONS

A number of procedural issues were encountered as this program of research was developed. The following strategies were used to ensure standardization across studies.

Lead-In Group

This is a 2-week, 60-min prerandomization orientation and screening group that potential study participants in all studies attend twice weekly (four sessions total). Individuals are taught basic drug-cessation skills according to a manualized protocol and receive a $5 gift voucher for attending. In this way, all potential participants receive the opportunity to sample the relapse prevention approach (the group discussion of drug-cessation skills) and the contingency management approach (the $5 gift coupon). During the 2-week lead-in period, all study baseline measures are collected. Also if potential participants miss more than one of the four scheduled sessions, they are excluded from the randomization into the study. Individuals may reapply after a 30-day waiting period. Although this screening procedure may limit the generalizability of study findings by eliminating participants who are less compliant, it is comparable with a "wash out" period in medication trials. In our opinion, the lead-in group is extremely useful in establishing an initial common baseline across study conditions.

Safety Screen

One of the concerns of this study was that the contingency management-only condition would not offer a sufficient intervention to provide safe and ethical treatment for participants. Therefore, once a week all participants in all study conditions are administered the Beck Depression Inventory. Scores above 16, or positive responses to the two suicidality questions, trigger an immediate consultation and evaluation by the study clinical supervisor. In addition, all study staff, including the relapse prevention counselor, the contingency management technician, the research assistant, and the lead-in counselor, received training in identifying and addressing patients who are intoxicated and in need of emergency assistance. To date, these procedures appear to be effective in systemically addressing the needs of patients who may be in jeopardy.

Staff Role Segregation and Information Control

With each study, different staff members are assigned to (a) conduct a lead-in group, (b) collect research data, (c) conduct relapse prevention groups, and (d) serve as contingency management technician. This task separation is necessary to ensure the independence of each of the study conditions. Use of the same counselor for the lead-in and relapse prevention groups may serve to differentially encourage or discourage subsequent engagement in the relapse prevention study condition. Similarly, use of the research assistant to serve as the contingency management technician would offer the research assistant a different data source for contingency management participants than is available for the relapse prevention only and no-treatment condition participants. The staff role segregation policy ensures the standardization of staff contact and minimizes differential data access across study conditions.

In a similar manner, a protocol was established to ensure uniformity of information flow. For example, the research assistant collects weekly data on drug use through self-report and urinalysis. On some occasions, these data do not correspond with each other and may not correspond with reports that the same study participant has given to his or her relapse prevention counselor. The research assistant's protocol is to be a collector of information from only two sources of data: the self-report data provided in the weekly data collection session and the urinalysis data. The research assistant does not exchange data about participant performance with other study staff members (e.g., the relapse prevention counselor, contingency management technicians, other study participants). Although all participants are given the results of urine tests and the relapse prevention and contingency management staff also have these results, the self-reports given to the research assistants are not shared with the other staff. The use of these protocols plays an important role in the standardization of data collection and ensures study uniformity.

Relapse Prevention Protocol as a Medication Study Psychosocial "Platform"

The use of the three-times-per-week relapse prevention group condition as a stimulant medication psychosocial platform has now been used in a series of research studies including the medication and behavior therapy for the methamphetamine abuse study described above. This manualized group procedure was proven an excellent model for standardizing the psychosocial material delivered to individuals who are receiving a medication or other experimental noncounseling intervention (e.g., contingency management). As recently discussed by Lavori and Block (1998), the major threat to the validity of medication trials is missing data. Although concern has been expressed that a three-times weekly counseling protocol may provide too much treatment and thereby obscure medication effects, Lavori and Block believe that this concern is outweighed by the concern for excessive dropouts or missing data, or both. The findings from the Sertraline–contingency management trial should provide additional data on the methodological value of this psychosocial platform.

ISSUES INVOLVING THE APPLICATION OF CONTINGENCY MANAGEMENT AND RELAPSE PREVENTION APPROACHES

Acceptability

Cocaine-Using Methadone Maintenance Patients Versus Primary Cocaine Users

On the basis of our previous experience that few methadone-maintained addicts voluntarily enroll in a cocaine treatment program, we offered a 33% reduction in monthly methadone maintenance fees ($120–$180 to $80–$120) during the period of their active study participation. Even with this incentive, which was made noncontingent on treatment success, recruitment was difficult. Clinic urinalysis data indicate that approximately 40–45% of the clinic census ($n = 200$) is using cocaine, and the clinic counselors strongly encourage treatment for anyone with a cocaine-positive urine toxicology result. However, even with the clear indication of problem cocaine use and a substantial financial incentive to participate in the study, recruitment was very difficult ($n = 90$, over 2 years). The cocaine-abusing methadone patient continues to be a difficult-to-treat client.

Based on our earlier difficulty in recruiting methadone-maintained patients into counseling studies, it was our a priori hypothesis that contingency management would be the preferred treatment at the methadone clinic. In contrast, we expected that many of the primary cocaine users would have preconceived beliefs about treatment as therapy counseling. Therefore, we predicted that many primary cocaine addicts would resist receiving contingency management without any other concurrent treatment and that they would prefer the relapse prevention condition. We anticipated that patients might refuse treatment or immediately drop out as a result of nonacceptance or that patients seeking treatment would decline once the possible treatment conditions were described. To date, only 2 participants have immediately dropped out of 200 participants enrolled at both sites, and both were primary cocaine abusers. In both cases, contrary to what we expected, the dropout was randomly assigned to relapse prevention. Our data indicate that both primary cocaine abusers and methadone-maintained cocaine abusers accept contingency management, even in the absence of any other treatment.

Cocaine Versus Methamphetamine Users

In our clinical experience of methamphetamine abusers, there are numerous anecdotal reports and early empirical data (Simon, 1998) that cognitive functioning is significantly impaired for up to 4 months after initial abstinence. Memory functioning, abstract thinking, and decision making are diminished. Therefore, we predict that the early parts of relapse prevention treatment may be less effective with methamphetamine abusers than cocaine abusers, and we suggest that these cognitive impairments may have less impact on the efficacy of contingency management techniques.

Mechanisms of Change Associated With Behavioral Treatments

Behavior Change Associated With Treatment Response

We expect that relapse prevention participants will use skills and techniques presented during the relapse prevention sessions and that the more these techniques are used, the more behavior change will occur and that these changes will correlate with successful treatment outcome. There was no prediction regarding the amount, type, and effect of behavior change among contingency management-only group participants. To assess behavior change, McCann, Hasson, and Rawson (1996) created a treatment activities survey and a participant's rating of treatment components. Early reports of these ratings suggest that the relapse prevention participants do report more behavior change in the direction predicted but that there does not appear to be an association between that behavior change and reduced drug use. Further analysis will not be conducted until the study is completed.

Ethics and Safety

As described above, a protocol was developed in these studies to monitor the safety of participants, especially those in the contingency management-only condition. There is no counseling provided as part of the contingency management protocol, and no suggestions are made about attaining or maintaining abstinence. The behavior technicians have reported that participants do occasionally ask for advice. In these instances, the participant is referred to handouts distributed as part of the 2-week lead-in groups. We were concerned about both the ethical responsibility of providing treatment to those individuals expecting to receive help with their addiction and the necessity of ensuring patient safety in a treatment paradigm that does not include staff trained to recognize and respond to life-threatening situations.

In addition to the safety protocol, any participant can be discontinued from the study and assisted in finding more appropriate treatment, should the need arise. To date, out of 200 participants, only 1 individual has been discontinued from the study (this participant was a primary cocaine addict assigned to relapse prevention), and there has been no evidence that the contingency management-only procedure jeopardizes participants' safety.

CONCLUSION

The development of contingency management and relapse prevention strategies provides the substance abuse treatment field with two potentially valuable approaches for the treatment of stimulant abuse disorders. We hope that our research will generate new information of theoretical importance and practical application.

REFERENCES

American Psychiatric Association. (1994). *Diagnostic statistical manual of mental disorders* (4th ed.). Washington, DC: Author.

Bandura, A. (1977). Self-efficacy: Toward a unifying theory of behavioral change. *Psychological Review, 84*, 191–215.

Bandura, A. (1981). Self-referent thought: A developmental analysis of self-efficacy. In J. A. H. Flavell & L. Ross (Eds.), *Social cognitive development: Frontiers and possible futures* (pp. 147–174). Cambridge, England: Cambridge University Press.

Bandura, A. (1984). Self-efficacy mechanism in human agency. *American Psychologist, 37*, 122–147.

Carroll, K. M., Rounsaville, B. J., & Gawin, F. H. (1991). A comparative trial of psychotherapies for ambulatory cocaine abusers: Relapse prevention and interpersonal psychotherapy. *American Journal of Drug Abuse, 17*, 229–247.

Carroll, K. M., Rounsaville, B. J., Gordon, L. T., Nich, C., Jatlow, P., Bisighini, R. M., & Gawin, F. H. (1994). Psychotherapy and pharmacotherapy for ambulatory cocaine abusers. *Archives of General Psychiatry, 51*, 177–187.

Carroll, K. M., Rounsaville, B. J., & Keller, D. S. (1991). Relapse prevention strategies in the treatment of cocaine abuse. *American Journal of Drug and Alcohol Abuse, 17*, 249–265.

Carroll, K. M., Rounsaville, B. J., Nich, C., Gordon, L. T., Wirtz, P. W., & Gawin, F. H. (1994). One year follow-up of psychotherapy and pharmacotherapy for cocaine dependence: Delayed emergence of psychotherapy effects. *Archives of General Psychiatry, 51*, 989–997.

Chaisson, R. E., Bacchetti, P., Brodie, B., Sande, M. A., & Moss, A. R. (1989). Cocaine use and HIV infection in intravenous drug users in San Francisco. *Journal of the American Medical Association, 261*, 561–565.

Condelli, W. S., Fairbank, M. L., & Rachel, J. V. (1991). Cocaine use by clients in methadone programs: Significance, scope and behavioral interventions. *Journal of Substance Abuse Treatment, 8,* 203–212.

Cushman, P. (1988). Cocaine use in a population of drug abusers on methadone. *Hospital and Community Psychiatry, 39,* 1205–1207.

De La Rosa, M., Lambert, E. Y., & Gropper, B. (Eds.). (1990). *Drugs and violence: Causes, correlates, and consequences* (NIDA Research Monograph 103). Washington, DC: U.S. Government Printing Office.

Dimeff, L. A., & Marlatt, G. A. (1995). Relapse prevention. In R. K. Hester & W. R. Miller (Eds.), *Handbook of alcoholism treatment approaches: Effective alternatives* (2nd ed., pp. 176–194). Boston: Allyn & Bacon.

Groerer, J. C., & Brodsky, M. D. (1993). Frequent cocaine users and their use of treatment. *American Journal of Public Health, 83,* 1149–1154.

Hall, S. M., Bass, A., Hargreaves, W. A., & Loeb, P. (1979). Contingency management and information feedback in outpatient heroin detoxification. *Behavior Therapy, 10,* 443–451.

Harrison, L. D. (1992). Trends in illicit drug use in the United States: Conflicting results from national surveys. *International Journal of Addictions, 27,* 817–847.

Hartel, D. M., Schoenbaum, E. E., Selwyn, P. A., Drucker, E., & Friedland, G. H. (1989, October). *Temporal patterns of cocaine use and AIDS in intravenous drug users in methadone maintenance.* Abstract presented at the Fifth International Conference on AIDS, Montreal, Quebec, Canada.

Higgins, S. T., Delaney, D. D., Budney, A. J., Bickel, W. K., Hughes, J. R., Foerg, F., & Fenwick, J. W. (1991). A behavioral approach to achieving initial cocaine abstinence. *American Journal of Psychiatry, 148,* 1218–1224.

Huber, A., Ling, W., Shoptaw, S., Gulati, V., Brethen, P., & Rawson, R. A. (1997). Integrating treatments for the methamphetamine abuse: A psychosocial perspective. *Journal of Addictive Diseases, 16,* 41–50.

Hunt, G. M., & Azrin, N. (1973). A community reinforcement approach to alcoholism. *Behavior Research and Therapy, 11,* 91–104.

Iguchi, M. Y., Stitzer, M. L., Bigelow, G. E., & Liebson, I. A. (1988). Contingency management in methadone maintenance: Effects of reinforcing and aversive consequences on illicit polydrug use. *American Journal of Drug and Alcohol Dependence, 22,* 1–7.

Kain, Z. N., Kain, T. S., & Scarpelli, E. M. (1992). Cocaine exposure in utero: Perinatal development and neonatal manifestations review. *Clinical Toxicology, 30,* 607–636.

Lavori, P., & Block, D. (1998). *Data analysis for medication development research: A white paper.* Unpublished manuscript, National Institute on Drug Abuse, Medication Development Division.

Ling, P. (1996, November). *Pharmacotherapies for methamphetamine dependence.* Paper presented at the Western Regional Methadone Conference, San Francisco, CA.

Magura, S., Casriel, C., Goldsmith, D. S., Strug, D. L., & Lipton, D. S. (1988). Contingency contracting with polydrug-abusing methadone patients. *Addictive Behaviors, 13,* 113–118.

Magura, S., Rosenblum, A., Lovejoy, M., Handelsman, L., Foote, J., & Stimmel,

B. (1994). Neurobehavioral treatment for cocaine-using methadone patients: A preliminary report. *Journal of Addictive Diseases, 13,* 143–160.

Magura, S., Siddiqui, Q., Freeman, R. C., & Lipton, D. S. (1991). Changes in cocaine use after entry to methadone treatment. *Journal of Addictive Diseases, 10,* 31–45.

Maier, T. J. (1989, June 11). A failing drug treatment. *Newsday,* pp. 32–33.

Marlatt, G. A., & Gordon, J. R. (Eds.). (1985). *Relapse prevention: Maintenance strategies in the treatment of addictive behaviors.* New York: Guilford.

McAuliffe, W. E. (1990). A randomized controlled trial of recovery training and self-help for opioid addicts in New England and Hong Kong. *Journal of Psychoactive Drugs, 22,* 197–210.

McCann, M., Hasson, A., Rawson, R. (1996, June). *Behavior change associated with contingency management and relapse prevention.* Paper presented at the College of Drug Dependence meeting, San Juan, Puerto Rico.

McCaul, M. E., Stitzer, M. L., Bigelow, G. E., & Liebson, I. A. (1984). Contingency management interventions: Effects on treatment outcome during methadone detoxification. *Journal of Applied Behavioral Analysis, 17,* 35–43.

Mermelsten, R. J., Karnatz, T., & Reichmann, S. (1992). Smoking. In P. H. Wilson (Ed.), *Principles and practice of relapse prevention* (pp. 43–68). New York: Guilford.

Meyers, R. E. (1992). New pharmacotherapies for cocaine dependence revisited. *Archives of General Psychiatry, 49,* 900–904.

Milby, J. B., Garrett, C., English, C., Fritschi, O., & Clarke, C. (1978). Take home methadone: Contingency effects on drug seeking and productivity of narcotic addicts. *Addictive Behaviors, 3,* 215–220.

Office of National Drug Control Policy. (1996). *National drug control strategy.* Washington, DC: The White House.

Rawson, R. A. (1995). Is psychotherapy effective for substance abuse. In A. M. Washton (Ed.), *Psychotherapy and substance abuse: A practitioners handbook* (pp. 55–75). New York: Guilford Press.

Rawson, R. A., Obert, J. L., McCann, M. J., & Ling, W. (1991). Psychological approaches to the treatment of cocaine dependency. *Journal of Addictive Diseases, 11,* 97–120.

Rawson, R. A., Obert, J. L., McCann, M. J., & Mann, A. J. (1985). Cocaine treatment outcome: Cocaine use following inpatient, outpatient, and no treatment. *Proceedings of the Committee on Problems of Drug Dependence* (NIDA Research Monograph 67, pp. 271–277). Rockville, MD: National Institute on Drug Abuse.

Rawson, R. A., Obert, J. L., McCann, M. J., & Marinelli-Casey, P. (1993a). Relapse prevention strategies in outpatient substance abuse treatment. *Psychology of Addictive Behaviors, 7,* 85–95.

Rawson, R. A., Obert, J. L., McCann, M. J., & Marinelli-Casey, P. (1993b). Use of relapse prevention strategies in the treatment of substance abuse disorders. *Psychotherapy, 30,* 284–298.

Rawson, R. A., Obert, J. L., McCann, M. J., Smith, D. P., & Ling, W. (1990). Neurobehavioral treatment for cocaine dependency. *Journal of Psychoactive Drugs, 22,* 159–171.

Rawson, R. A., Shoptaw, S. J., Obert, J. L., McCann, M. J., Hasson, A. L., Marinelli-Casey, P. J., Brethen, P. R., & Ling, W. (1995). An intensive outpatient approach for cocaine abuse treatment: The Matrix model. *Journal of Substance Abuse Treatment, 12*, 117–127.

Roffman, R. A., Stephens, R. S., Simpson, E. E., & Whitaker, D. L. (1990). Treatment of marijuana dependencies: Preliminary results. *Journal of Psychoactive Drugs, 22*, 129–137.

Shoptaw, S., Reeback, C., Frosch, D., & Rawson, R. A. (1998). Stimulant abuse treatment as HIV prevention. *Journal of Addictive Disease, 17*, 34–42.

Simon, S. (1998, April). *Neuropsychological functioning of methamphetamine abusers.* Paper presented at the American Society of Addiction Medicine meeting, New Orleans, LA.

Stitzer, M. L., Bigelow, G. E., & Gross, J. (1989). Behavioral treatment of drug abuse. In T. B. Karsu (Ed.), *American Psychiatric Association treatment manual* (pp. 248–280). Washington, DC: American Psychiatric Association Press.

Stitzer, M. L., Bigelow, G. E., Liebson, I. A., & Hawthorne, J. W. (1982). Contingent reinforcement for benzodiazepine-free urines: Evaluation of a drug abuse treatment intervention. *Journal of Applied Behavioral Analysis, 15*, 493–503.

Stitzer, M. L., & Higgins, S. T. (1995). Behavioral treatment of drug and alcohol abuse. In F. E. Bloom & D. J. Kupler (Eds.), *Psychopharmacology: The fourth generation of progress* (pp. 1807–1819). New York: Raven Press.

Stitzer, M. L., Iguchi, M. Y., & Felch, L. J. (1992). Contingent take-home incentive: Effects on drug use of methadone maintenance patients. *Journal of Consulting and Clinical Psychology, 60*, 927–934.

Substance Abuse and Mental Health Services Administration, Office of Applied Studies. (1996a, August). *Historical estimates from the Drug Abuse Warning Network: 1978–94 estimates of drug-related emergency department episodes.* Rockville, MD: National Clearinghouse for Alcohol and Drug Information.

Substance Abuse and Mental Health Services Administration, Office of Applied Studies. (1996b, August). *Preliminary estimates from the Drug Abuse Warning Network.* Rockville, MD: National Clearinghouse for Alcohol and Drug Information.

U.S. General Accounting Office. (1990). *Methadone maintenance: Some treatment programs are not effective; Greater federal oversight needed* (Doc. No. GAO/HRD-90104). Washington, DC: Author.

Wells, E. A., Peterson, P. L., Gainey, R. R., Hawkins, J. D., & Catalano, R. F. (1994). Outpatient treatment for cocaine abuse: A controlled comparison of relapse prevention and twelve-step approaches. *American Journal of Drug and Alcohol Abuse, 20*, 1–17.

III

TREATMENT OF SPECIAL POPULATIONS

4

EFFECTIVE TREATMENT OF HOMELESS SUBSTANCE ABUSERS: THE ROLE OF CONTINGENCY MANAGEMENT

JOSEPH E. SCHUMACHER, JESSE B. MILBY, CECELIA L. McNAMARA,
DENNIS WALLACE, MAX MICHAEL, SAM POPKIN,
AND STUART USDAN

In this chapter, we describe two treatment outcome studies for co-caine dependency among homeless people and present the findings (Milby, Schumacher, McNamara, et al., 1996; Milby, Schumacher, Raczynski, et al., 1996). We also describe how contingency management was used in these studies and discuss the options for technology transfer of contingency management interventions. Before describing the studies, however, we briefly review the relevant literature on homelessness and substance abuse.

The recent prevalence of homelessness in the United States based on national surveys conducted in 1993 is estimated at 3 million people per year, with 600,000 homeless people on any particular night ("Report on

Preparation of this chapter was supported by National Institute on Alcoholism and Alcohol Abuse and National Institute on Drug Abuse Grant AA08819 and National Institute on Drug Abuse Grant DAO8475R01.

homeless," 1994). Deinstitutionalization of mental patients has swelled the homeless population (Bachrach, 1992). Confiscation and sale of low-rent properties and national and local policies that decreased public housing greatly reduce low-cost housing stock (Toro, Trickett, Wall, & Salem, 1991), which contributes to the homeless epidemic.

High prevalence of alcohol abuse, alcoholism, and other substance abuse disorders consistently has been found among homeless people (Breakey et al., 1989; Corrigan & Anderson, 1984; Council on Scientific Affairs, 1989; Drake, Wallach, & Hoffman, 1989; Koegel, Burnam, & Farr, 1988; Rosenheck et al., 1989), especially among homeless people who are mentally ill (Rahav & Link, 1995; Rahav et al., 1995). Prevalence estimates for substance abuse disorders in these studies range from 20% to 63%, with an average estimate of 20% to 35%. Prevalence estimates for alcohol abuse and alcoholism have been consistently higher than rates for other substance abuse disorders (Breakey et al., 1989; Corrigan & Anderson, 1984; Koegel & Burnam, 1988; Rosenheck et al., 1989). The recent emergence of crack cocaine as a major drug of abuse has resulted in increased problems with this drug among homeless people (Raczynski et al., 1993).

In one of the few studies on homelessness that used random sampling from a comparison group of housed poor, Toro et al. (1995) found that homeless people were almost twice as likely to have a lifetime diagnosis of substance abuse as those who have never been homeless. Previously homeless people had a significantly higher rate of substance abuse than those who have never been homeless. In another study, Toro and Wall (1991) found that the first episode of homelessness usually followed the first serious symptoms of substance abuse.

Rosenheck et al. (1989) identified more than 15 variables in a path analysis of homelessness from a large veterans data set. Among variables accounting for variance in prediction of homelessness, substance abuse accounted for the greatest variance. The literature repeatedly indicates the multifaceted nature of substance abuse disorders and the need for a multidimensional treatment approach that coordinates and enhances the use of a range of community services to effectively reach and treat this population (Frances, 1988; Gelberg, Linn, & Leake, 1988; Higgins et al., 1991; Koegel & Burnam, 1988).

The profile of homeless clients we serve in Birmingham, Alabama, is generally consistent with findings from national surveys (La Gory, Ritchey, & Mullis, 1990; LaGory, Ritchey, & Fitzpatrick, 1991; Ritchey, La Gory, Fitzpatrick, & Mullis, 1990). Birmingham's homeless are predominantly native Alabamians (65%), male (77%), and Caucasian (61%), with a mean age of 39.7 years (La Gory et al., 1991). In a randomly selected survey sample of 150 homeless people in Birmingham, interviewers found a majority had diverse and complex social, psychological, and physical problems (Ritchey et al., 1990) and found a significant portion whose homelessness was either preceded or accompanied by stressful life events, most commonly job loss (75%), interpersonal problems (60%), or substance abuse problems (64%). Recently, researchers revealed that crack cocaine and alcohol are the predominant drugs of abuse among homeless people seeking drug treatment at a health care agency for the homeless in the Birmingham metropolitan area (Milby, Schumacher, Raczynski, et al., 1996; Raczynski et al., 1993). Perhaps because of its action at brain centers responsible for reinforcing effects (Wise, 1984), cocaine abuse seems particularly devastating to the beginner user and often turns the regular user into an obsessive cocaine addict whose functional status frequently deteriorates to illegal activity and sometimes homelessness. In both animal models and human studies, researchers suggested that a carefully structured clinical treatment program, which systematically exposes drug abusers to new sources of non-drug-related reinforcers in a non-drug-using social context, may be a viable treatment approach to cocaine dependence (Carroll, Lac, & Nygaard, 1989; Higgins, Budney, Bickel, & Hughes, 1993; Higgins, Budney, Bickel, & Foerg, 1994; Higgins et al., 1991; Silverman, Higgins, Brooner, & Montoya, 1996). This notion led us to develop a day treatment model that included a modest voucher system adapted from Higgins et al. (1991). The program provides exposure to a rich density of non-drug-related recreational and social reinforcers as a therapeutic strategy to initiate abstinence in dually diagnosed, homeless cocaine abusers. This model was developed and tested in two sequential projects, Homeless I and II, which we describe below.

HOMELESS I: COMPARATIVE TREATMENTS FOR SUBSTANCE-ABUSING HOMELESS PEOPLE

In 1991, the Comparative Treatments for Substance-Abusing Homeless Demonstration Project (Homeless I) was designed to develop a day treatment drug program that includes an abstinent-contingent housing and work therapy component (enhanced care) and to compare it to existing drug treatment (usual care) for homeless people in the Birmingham metropolitan area (Raczynski et al., 1993; Milby, Schumacher, Raczynski, et al., 1996). Researchers hypothesized that enhanced care would result in better outcomes for alcohol and cocaine use, employment, and housing than usual care. This was a randomized controlled study with outcomes measured at 2-, 6-, and 12-month follow-up points. Enhanced care consisted of 2 months of day treatment followed by 4 months of abstinent-contingent work and housing therapy. Usual-care clients participated in one to two individual or group counseling sessions per week, with no specified duration. Intent-to-treat statistical analyses were conducted for between-group differences using the Wei Lachin Test and for within-group differences using the paired Wilcoxon Signed Rank Test.

Role of Contingency Management

Contingency management played a critical role in the implementation and outcome of the Homeless I project, particularly in the enhanced-care treatment group. The enhanced-care group had two main components: day treatment and abstinent-contingent housing and work therapy. The innovative abstinent-contingent housing and work therapy component was a strict contingency management operation. After 2 months of psychosocial day treatment focusing on substance abuse problems and recovery, enhanced-care clients were eligible to participate in paid (minimum wage for a maximum of 26 hr a week) work therapy. Clients renovated dilapidated houses to be used as drug-free housing by the clients for modest rent. Participation in the work therapy and housing program was contingent on an initial 2-week period of abstinence and continued abstinence from alcohol and drugs, as measured by weekly random or on-demand urine toxicology tests. If a client obtained urine toxicology test results positive for alcohol or drugs, he or she was told immediately, allowed to request a confirmation test by another procedure, and then restricted from work therapy until two consecutive negative urine toxicologies were obtained. After the second negative toxicology test, the client was able to return to work therapy that day. The contingency management protocol was similar for abstinent-contingent housing. Clients whose drug use was confirmed by random urine toxicology testing were transported to a shelter and locked out of the housing until two consecutive negative urine toxicology test results were obtained. Clients were restricted from work therapy and housing from 4 to 10 weekdays, depending on the urine surveillance schedule. Clients restricted from work therapy and housing were encouraged to attend day treatment meetings as a way to maintain treatment during periods of relapse.

In addition to the concrete rewards of shelter and paid work, less obvious but still important social contingencies were offered in the day treatment program for enhanced-care clients. Daily counseling, positive social interaction, lunch, "good and welfare" (positive statements about a client's behavior given by another client during morning meetings), and a recovery-oriented atmosphere were available to clients who attended day treatment. All clients were encouraged to attend "Club Birmingham," a monthly social event at which clients were reinforced with clapping, cheers, and hugs after reviewing their progress in treatment and in life during stand-up testimonials. Special attention was given to those enhanced- or usual-care clients who had completed different phases of treatment, had the best attendance rates, and completed follow-up assessments.

Club Birmingham was a positive and moving fellowship experience for all clients, staff, and investigators who attended.

Results

The clinical population consisted of 131 homeless people with substance use disorders: 96.2% were African American, 20.6% were female, and the average age was 35.9 years. Follow-up rates were 93 (71.0%) at 2 months, 85 (64.9%) at 6 months, and 89 (67.9%) at 12 months, with no treatment group or assessment point differences. Significant between-group differences in favor of enhanced care were found longitudinally from baseline through 12 months for median reported days of alcohol use in the past 30 days, with enhanced-care clients reporting a greater reduction in alcohol use over the last 30 days than usual-care clients ($p = .026$). Enhanced-care clients reported 8 fewer days of alcohol use in the past 30 days from baseline to 12 months, with no difference in the usual-care group. Reported alcohol use for the enhanced-care group dropped significantly at 2 months and remained stable at 6 and 12 months.

The median proportion of cocaine-positive urine toxicology test results revealed a significant difference between the two treatment groups across all time points ($p = .003$). Enhanced-care clients had 36% fewer positive cocaine toxicology test results at 2 months, 18% fewer at 6 months, and 4% fewer at 12 months than usual-care clients. The greatest reduction in cocaine use for the enhanced-care group was at 2 months and regressed to baseline values at 12 months, with no changes from baseline to 12 months for the usual-care group.

For the median number of days of full-time employment in the past 30 days, the longitudinal difference between groups was not statistically significant across all time points ($p = .504$), but the within-group difference for the enhanced-care group from baseline to the 12-month follow-up point was significant ($p < .01$). The baseline to 12-month within-group difference for the usual-care group was not significantly different. Both groups reported an increase in number of days employed from baseline to 6 months. This improvement was sustained at 12 months by the enhanced-care group, which reported 10 more days employed in the past 30 days from baseline to 12 months, whereas the usual-care group members returned to baseline values.

The median number of days homeless over the last 60 days was significantly different between groups across all time points ($p < .05$). The enhanced-care group reported 52 fewer days homeless in the past 60 days from baseline to 12 months, and the usual-care group showed no change. A large drop in reported days homeless for the enhanced-care group occurred at the 6-month follow-up, after participants moved to the 4-month abstinent-contingent housing and work therapy component. This drop remained stable at 12 months.

In summary, enhanced care proved to be better than usual care on three of the four major outcomes: alcohol use, cocaine use, and number of days homeless. The treatment effect on reduced cocaine use at 2 and 6 months appeared to diminish at 12 months. To our knowledge this was the first controlled outcome study at the time to demonstrate that the homeless population can be retained in a treatment program and effectively treated. The differential role of day treatment versus abstinent-contingent work therapy and housing in treatment outcome, however, could not be established by this study. A follow-up study, Homeless II, described below, was designed to answer this question.

HOMELESS II: INITIATING ABSTINENCE IN DUALLY DIAGNOSED HOMELESS PEOPLE

In 1993, the Initiating Abstinence in Dually Diagnosed Homeless Project (Homeless II) was designed to enhance the day treatment program developed for Homeless I with a behavioral social reinforcement component and to compare this enhanced day treatment program with the same day treatment plus abstinent-contingent housing and work therapy (Milby, Schumacher, McNamara, et al., 1996). In Homeless I, day treatment plus abstinent-contingent housing and work therapy was more effective than traditional drug counseling. However, the differential impact of abstinent-contingent housing and work therapy as compared with day treatment alone was inseparable.

The goal of Homeless II was to determine the benefit of an enhanced Homeless I day treatment program that included immediate abstinent-contingent housing followed by abstinent-contingent housing and work therapy and aftercare (DT+) and to compare it with the modified day treatment only (DT). The researchers also investigated the role of nonpsychotic Axis I mental disorders other than substance use disorders in treatment outcome and the impact of the independent variable on non-drug-related social and recreational activities. Homeless II was a randomized DT+ versus DT controlled study, with outcomes measured at 2-, 6-, and 12-month follow-up points. DT+ consisted of 2 months of behavioral social reinforcement day treatment and immediate abstinent-contingent housing (Phase I), 4 months of aftercare and abstinent-contingent housing for a modest rent and work therapy (Phase II), and then 6 months of aftercare (Phase III). DT consisted of day treatment and aftercare alone, without the housing and work therapy components.

The researchers hypothesized that DT+ would result in better outcomes than DT, DT+ and DT would show increases in non-drug-related social and recreational activities after treatment, and clients without Axis I diagnoses would do better in treatment. We concentrated this review here on the primary outcomes of alcohol and drug use, especially cocaine, employment, and homelessness, similar to Homeless I. Positive results related to the social recreational activities and Axis I diagnoses outcomes can be found in papers presented at the 1996 and 1997 scientific meetings of the College on Problems of Drug Dependence (McNamara et al., 1996; McNamara, Milby, Schumacher, Usdan, & Wallace, 1997).

Role of Contingency Management

Contingency management also played a critical role in both the day treatment and abstinent-contingent housing and work therapy components in Homeless II. However, differences in the design of Homeless I and II affected comparability of the contingency management components, which deserves mention. First, abstinent-contingent and rent-free housing was offered immediately to DT+ participants during the first 2 months of treatment in Homeless II rather than after completion of the day treatment phase as in Homeless I. Abstinent-contingent housing for modest rent was offered after day treatment in the same way as in Homeless I. Second, both treatment groups received the day treatment program, enhanced from Homeless I to include a behavioral social reinforcement component that included voucher reinforcers for social and recreational goal achievement. Third, Club Birmingham added a structured lottery system to reinforce treatment and follow-up compliance.

The abstinent-contingent housing and work therapy contingency management components in Homeless II operated in the same way as in Homeless I; that is, access to housing and participation in work therapy were strictly contingent on abstinence as measured by weekly random urine testing. However, to increase the potency of the housing reinforcer, we offered abstinent-contingent housing for an additional 2 months at start of treatment rather than after completion of day treatments as in Homeless I. During this phase, housing was program provided or rent free because the clients did not have much opportunity to work to pay rent and working during day treatment was discouraged. Drug-free housing was available for up to 6 months. We believe these changes resulted in stronger contingent reinforcement effects for shelter among homeless clients in Homeless II.

The enhancement of the day treatment from Homeless I included the addition of the behavioral social reinforcement (BSR) component. The BSR consisted of an individualized plan for each client, with objectively defined and measurable long- and short-term goals in five major life areas. Once admitted to the Homeless II study, each client met with the clinical psychology fellow to interactively develop a plan with objectively defined goals in areas of addiction, housing, employment, non-drug-related reinforcing social and recreational activities, and mental health. Clients worked on achieving goals and objectives during the course of treatment. Progress, achievement, and barriers to goal accomplishment were reviewed weekly in a goal review group, consisting of a roundtable meeting where clients presented goal progress, peer groups rated achievement or lack thereof, and therapists provided social and voucher reinforcers. In addition, clients could earn tangible incentives if they accomplished their goals and objectives in the area of non-drug-related reinforcing social and recreational activities.

The investigators were interested in increasing the exposure and frequency of involvement in non-drug-related social and recreational activities as an alternative to cocaine use and an intervention for postcocaine use dysphoria. These incentives consist of vouchers worth $8 each; one voucher could be earned by completing at least 75% of the goals for that week, and another could be earned by accomplishing 100% of the goals in the social and recreational activity area. Clients cashed in their vouchers to the recreational therapist for items that would, in turn, facilitate increased exposure and frequency of drug-free social and recreational activities. Sporting equipment, museum passes, cosmetics, and passes to cultural events were a few examples of voucher purchases. The BSR component provided strong social and tangible incentives contingent on successful completion of treatment goals, especially those that increased exposure and frequency of engaging in social and recreational activities as an alternative to the reinforcing effect of cocaine use.

The final enhancement for Homeless II was the development and use of a formalized lottery system. In Homeless I, experimenters observed a powerful effect of the social reinforcement for treatment and follow-up assessment compliance during the Club Birmingham meetings. In Homeless II, treatment and follow-up assessment compliance was formally linked to a monthly lottery. Clients in both treatment groups in Phases II (Months 3–6) and III (Months 7–12) were eligible to participate in the lottery. A lottery ticket was awarded for any defined act of treatment compliance, for example, attending a counseling session or an aftercare meeting, attending a Club Birmingham event, giving a positive or negative urine test, or completing a follow-up assessment. The more lottery tickets earned each month, the greater the chances were of winning a $100 voucher for a goal-related item. In Homeless II, experimenters broadened the use of the voucher for Phase III winners to include rent, transportation to see their family, and legal bills. Clients reported that the lottery provided them with the incentive to participate more actively in treatment and remain more fully engaged in the program.

Results

The clinical population for Homeless II consisted of 141 homeless people with substance use disorders and at least one mental disorder: 82.7% were African American, 23.7% were female, and the average age was 38.2 years. Follow-up rates were 110 (78%) at 2 months and 109 (77%) at 6 months. Results revealed no significant differences in median days reported alcohol use longitudinally from baseline to 6 months between DT and DT+. Within-group analyses showed significant reductions ($ps < .05$) for DT and DT+ in reported alcohol use from baseline to 2 and 6 months. Medians of 9-day (DT+) and 6-day (DT) alcohol use in the past 30 days at baseline were reduced to medians of 0-day use for both groups at 2 and 6 months.

Analyses of cocaine use consistent with Homeless I outcomes consisted of summaries of the proportion of positive cocaine toxicology test results at each of the three assessment points (baseline, 2 months, and 6 months) and cross-sectional assessments of differences in proportions using Mantel Haenszel chi-squared tests for differences in proportions and the Wei Lachin Test for differences at the postbaseline visits. The proportions of positive cocaine toxicology test results at each of three designated assessment points were analyzed with missing values considered randomly missing (as in Homeless I). Chi-square for tests of differences in proportions showed a difference favoring DT+ over DT (11.3% vs. 29.2% positive for cocaine) at 2 months ($p < .05$), with no differences between groups at baseline or 6 months. The Wei Lachin Test provided little evidence of a difference between the two groups at the two postbaseline times ($p = .07$). DT+ appeared to have an effect at 2 months, but it diminished after 6 months. However, there were substantially more participants lost to follow-up in the DT group. To account in part for the adverse impact of differential loss to follow-up found in Homeless II (i.e., a 20% better follow-up rate at 2 and 6 months in the experimental group [DT+]), reanalyses of cocaine use were conducted. For the analyses in which missing data were assigned as positive if a valid reason for missing was unavailable, such as for incarceration or hospitalization, the chi-square tests of differences in proportions again showed a difference favoring DT+ over DT (23.6% vs. 49.2% positive for cocaine) at 2 months ($p < .01$), with no differences between the groups at baseline or 6 months. However, because of the stronger effect at 2 months and some difference between the two groups at 6 months, the Wei Lachin Test revealed a significant difference between the two groups at the two postbaseline times combined ($p < .01$).

Analyses of abstinence from cocaine, marijuana, or alcohol use (any drug) were conducted using weekly random toxicology test results (as measured by one or two weekly random urine toxicology test results) to reflect a more reliable picture of drug and alcohol use over the first 6 months of treatment and aftercare period. Because urine testing at scheduled follow-up points could be anticipated by the clients, could be rescheduled at the clients' convenience, and was perceived by clients to be used to determine housing and work therapy contingencies, investigators believed these conditions had a "sobering" effect on the data. The client-controlled follow-up scheduling procedure allowed clients to briefly stop using cocaine prior to planned follow-up assessments. Also measuring any drug or alcohol use was thought to be a more conservative indicant of abstinence than measuring cocaine use only. For these analyses, there were 110 participants: 84 men (76.3%), 91 (82.7%) African American, and 19 (17.2%) Caucasian, with an average age of 38.2 years.

Weekly random urine toxicology data in Figure 4.1 show that the percentage of DT participants negative for any drug or alcohol use was never greater than the percentage of negative for DT+ participants at any week during the 6-month period. Tests for differences between groups at the 2- and 6-month follow-ups show that after day treatment at 2 months, 75% of the DT+ group were abstinent versus 31% of the DT group, $\chi^2(1)$ = 15.1, $p < .0001$. At 6 months, 50% of the DT+ group were abstinent versus 17% of the DT group, $\chi^2(1) = 4.5$, $p = .034$. Some regression toward baseline occurred in both groups. An estimated average abstinence rate between 12 and 24 weeks of approximately 16% for DT versus 45% for DT+ revealed a difference of 29% favoring DT+, which was almost twice the average percentage of abstinence observed in the DT group.

Figure 4.2 shows a more conservative measure of abstinence for the two treatment groups: mean consecutive weeks of negative (clean) urine toxicology test results. At 2 months, DT+ participants averaged 5.23 (SD = 2.47) consecutive weeks clean out of a maximum 8 weeks, and DT participants averaged 2.9 (SD = 2.67) consecutive weeks clean. At 6 months, DT+ averaged 10.1 (SD = 7.37) consecutive weeks versus DT at 5.45 (SD = 4.37) consecutive weeks out of a maximum of 26 weeks, which for DT+ is almost twice the average consecutive weeks clean of DT. Because the distributions exhibited extreme nonnormality, differences in location of the distributions were examined using the Wilcoxon Rank Sum Test and were significant ($p < .0001$). The data indicate that the difference in mean consecutive clean weeks diverges with the difference favoring DT+, increasing from 2 to 6 months.

A comparison of Homeless I and Homeless II cocaine use data reveals similar effects of the experimental groups at 2 months, diminishing at 6 months. At 2 months, reductions in cocaine use of 32% were found for both Homeless I and Homeless II experimental groups. However, at 2 months, the control group for Homeless I increased cocaine use by 11% and the control group for Homeless II decreased use by 10%. At 6 months, although the differences between groups diminished for both Homeless I and Homeless II, participants in Homeless II were approximately 20% more abstinent overall than participants in Homeless I. Analyses accounting for

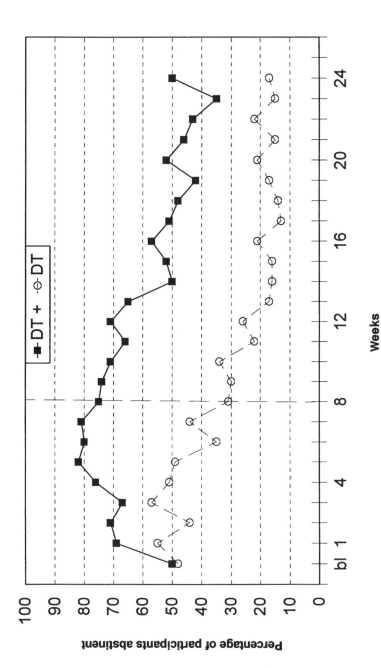

Figure 4.1. Percentage of participants abstinent by week and by treatment group (Comparative Treatments for Substance-Abusing Demonstration Homeless Project II). DT+ = day treatment that included immediate abstinent-contingent housing followed by abstinent-contingent housing and work therapy and aftercare; DT = day treatment only; bl = baseline.

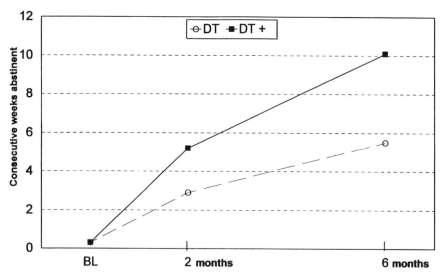

Figure 4.2. Consecutive weeks participants were abstinent by treatment group (Comparative Treatments for Substance-Abusing Demonstration Homeless Project II). DT+ = day treatment that included immediate abstinent-contingent housing followed by abstinent-contingent housing and work therapy and aftercare; DT = day treatment only; BL = baseline.

follow-up attrition in Homeless II reveal patterns and rates of cocaine use in Homeless II more closely resembling Homeless I findings, except for lower overall baseline cocaine use in Homeless I. Analyses of Homeless II drug or alcohol use data using weekly random urine toxicology test results over the 6-month period reflected a more rigorous effect of the experimental condition at 6 months than found using single, nonrandom follow-up measures of cocaine use only.

Finally, it is important to temper the apparent loss of the treatment effect on abstinence from baseline to 6 months in both Homeless I and II by considering a more realistic measure of abstinence at baseline other than urine toxicology results at study entry. Reports from clients at screening and random assignment led investigators to believe that many clients had attempted to terminate their drug use to qualify for free housing. This brief discontinuation of drug use and the short half-life of cocaine may have contributed to an inflated rate of tested abstinence at baseline among a population of admitted recent cocaine users. Although as many as 50% of DT+ and 48% of the DT groups tested negative for alcohol or any drug at baseline, only 2 participants, or 1.4% of the total sample, self-reported to no use of any drug in the past 30 days on the Addiction Severity Index (ASI). Thus, based on ASI data, only 1.4% of the sample was reportedly abstinent the month before seeking treatment. Therefore, treatment effects for abstinence from alcohol or other drug use for the DT+ group reveal an increase in abstinence from 1.4% at baseline, as measured by the ASI, to

75% abstinent at 2 months and 50% abstinent at 6 months, as measured by urine toxicology results. For the DT group, abstinence may have increased to 31% at 2 months and 17% at 6 months, if similarly measured. This reflects substantial within- and between-group differences in improved abstinence outcomes in Homeless II, not apparent in an uninformed examination of abstinence as measured by urine toxicology only.

For employment, nonsignificant differences between DT and DT+ were found longitudinally from baseline to 6 months for median days of full-time employment reported in the past 30 days ($p < .10$). Virtually zero days of employment for the DT+ group at baseline and at 2 months increased to an average of 16 days in the past 30 days for DT+ and 15 days for DT. It appears that day treatment counseling was only as effective in procuring full-time employment. To more fairly indicate employment progress among this homeless population, detailed analyses of employment variables less stringent than full-time employment should be conducted.

For homelessness, significant differences in median days homeless in the past 60 days were found longitudinally between DT and DT+ from baseline to 6 months ($p < .05$). Days homeless was significantly reduced from 60 days at baseline to 20 days at 2 months and to 0 days at 6 months for the DT+ group and from 60 days at baseline to 44.5 days at 2 months and 0 days at 6 months for the DT group. The increase in availability of government-funded shelter plus care housing after 6 months of treatment is believed to be responsible for the reduction in homelessness at 6 months in the DT group.

In conclusion, DT+ showed added positive effect of abstinent-contingent housing and work therapy over DT alone in abstinence and homelessness. Alcohol use was, on the average, reduced to virtually no use at 2 and 6 months for both groups. Employment was increased substantially for both groups. The results based on urinalysis conducted regularly during the course of treatment appeared more sensitive to treatment effects than single follow-up assessments conducted at set time points known to the client and rescheduled at the client's request. On the basis of these findings and given the potential unreliability of self-reported drug use data when contingencies are present (Schumacher et al., 1995), we recommend that investigators use urine toxicology data when practical.

To our knowledge, this was only the second controlled outcome study that demonstrated that a homeless crack cocaine-abusing population can be retained in a treatment program and effectively treated. The differential role of program-provided housing versus abstinent-contingent housing on abstinence and homelessness cannot be established by this study because these potentially independent and potent components were administered together and thus were inseparable for analytic purposes. Future research is needed to answer this question. Difficulty sustaining abstinence suggests the need for improved aftercare effort, also to be investigated in a future study.

SUMMARY AND CONCLUSION

Homeless I and Homeless II show how contingency management can be used in the drug abuse treatment of homeless people. The contingency management approaches successfully implemented in this research consisted of abstinent-contingent housing and work therapy, behavioral social reinforcement, and a treatment and follow-up compliance lottery system. Although the many contingency management approaches in the day treatment component, such as the voucher system and the lottery, were not a direct focus of experimental study, we believe they had a positive impact on the treatment outcomes.

Homeless I was a demonstration project that developed and evaluated the effectiveness of innovative treatment approaches for homeless people with substance use disorders. This innovative contingency management treatment approach that was designed to meet the basic needs of shelter and work for homeless people resulted in improved substance use and homelessness outcomes. Originally conceptualized as a housing and work adjunct to the day treatment component, abstinent-contingent housing and work therapy worked as an intervention for both drug abuse and homelessness. Homeless II increased the potency of the housing contingency by offering clients abstinent-contingent and rent-free housing when they first sought treatment—when it is most needed. Further research is needed to support the belief that offering abstinent-contingent housing early in treatment may result in better treatment retention and outcome indexes than when offered later in treatment.

In Homeless II, more formalized contingency management approaches were added to an existing day treatment program. The day treatment program was enhanced with the BSR component by adding a structured protocol to reinforce treatment goal achievement, particularly non-drug-related social and recreational activities. The use of monetary vouchers facilitated the exposure and frequency of reinforcing activities as an alternative to cocaine use and may have countered the dysphoria experienced with use cessation. Although the BSR component was not the focus of the experimental study in Homeless II, clients in the DT group showed within-group improvements in cocaine use superior to clients in the usual-care group from Homeless I. Many differences in these two studies could account for this finding, suggesting that the impact of adding a BSR component to a traditional outpatient or day treatment program should be explored. Homeless II also demonstrated how a Club Birmingham-type social reinforcement event could adopt a more contingency management orientation by adding a lottery system to reinforce treatment and follow-up assessment compliance. Again the lottery system was not the subject of study in this research, but overall improvements in Homeless II of treatment compliance and follow-up rates of DT+ clients, as compared with Homeless I rates, suggest the potential benefit of this contingency management approach.

Although contingency management approaches demonstrated in this research were successfully implemented and likely contributed to the successful outcomes measured in the areas of drug and alcohol use, housing, and employment of homeless people, the transfer of this technology presents some challenges. The success of any contingency management approach relies on the strict and consistent enforcement of the contingencies. Evicting clients from their homes and suspending them from work as a consequence of relapse is not always a reasonable or practical endeavor for health care providers. It involves regular and accurate monitoring of alcohol and drug use, which requires additional resources. It also involves the open access to shelters for temporary housing and stable drug-free houses or apartments that can financially survive vacancy during periods of relapse. Finally, it requires an ethical compatibility with and philosophical belief in the theory of contingency management and reinforcement principles.

The transfer of contingency management components requires additional funding to support weekly urine testing, vouchers, and lottery awards. Many drug treatment agencies are set up for urine testing, and the additional costs of adding more tests each week may not be that prohibitive. For those agencies not using urine testing, investment in relatively frequent urine testing is essential to implementing any contingency for reduced drug use or abstinence. Random urine testing provides any drug treatment agency with a valid and reliable source of information to measure client progress and program effectiveness. Additionally, random urine testing is a treatment intervention itself. Many clients identified urine surveillance as an important treatment component from Homeless I and II. It is a simple step to develop a contingency management program when urine testing is in place. Monitoring, recognizing, and rewarding clean urine (through positive social or tangible rewards) reinforces initiated and sustained abstinence and counters the negative attention most health care providers give to clients when their urine tests indicate relapse.

Creative means for obtaining rewards from the business community using vouchers and lottery awards can result in a steady flow of pizzas, sporting event and entertainment passes, and bus tokens. Automatically dismissing the use of agency funds for vouchers or lottery awards may be premature. Two $8 vouchers per week for an 8-week treatment program costs $128 per client, or $64 per month per client. A monthly $100 lottery award for 20 clients costs $5 per client per month. To add a contingency management voucher and lottery program would cost less than $70 per month per client. Further cost-effectiveness research is needed to weigh the costs versus the benefits of implementing these approaches; however, considering costs as high as $100 to $500 per day for residential drug treatment and the potential treatment benefits of a contingency management approach, $70 per month per client appears reasonable and defendable.

In conclusion, contingency management approaches are theoretically sound and empirically validated treatment alternatives or enhancements to traditional treatment programs. Employers are interested in a safe work environment and productive drug-free workers, and from our experience, many employers are interested in working together with treatment agencies to make this happen. The Housing and Urban Development Agency is already making rent vouchers contingent on the successful completion of drug treatment programs. Thus, the current climate is consistent with the use of housing and vocational service resources in contingency management approaches to drug treatment, especially in light of the present findings.

The perspective that program- or government-provided housing or vocational rehabilitation services are benefits or resources that can be more efficiently used by people in recovery than those distracted by drug-dependent lifestyles is consistent with a contingency management theoretical approach. As demonstrated in this research, such resources can be effectively used as incentives to initiate and sustain abstinence, not simply to be retracted as a punishment for relapse. Although housing and vocational service resources are inherently connected and can be perceived one way (reward) by the client when successfully achieved and the other way (punishment) when taken away, contingency management is designed to ultimately improve the quality of life for the client.

REFERENCES

Bachrach, L. L. (1992). What we know about homelessness among mentally ill persons: An analytic review and commentary. In H. R. Lamb, L. L. Bachrach, & F. I. Kass (Eds.), *Treating the homeless mentally ill* (pp. 13–40). Washington, DC: American Psychiatric Association.

Breakey, W. R., Fischer, P. J., Kramer, M., Nestadt, G., Romanoski, A. J., Ross, A., Royall, R. M., & Stine, O. C. (1989). Health and mental health problems of homeless men and women in Baltimore. *Journal of the American Medical Association, 262*, 1352–1357.

Carroll, M. E., Lac, S. T., & Nygaard, S. L. (1989). A concurrently available nondrug reinforcer prevents the acquisition or decreases the maintenance of cocaine-reinforced behavior. *Psychopharmacology, 97*, 23–29.

Corrigan, E. M., & Anderson, S. C. (1984). Homeless alcoholic women on skid row. *American Journal of Drug and Alcohol Abuse, 10*, 535–549.

Council on Scientific Affairs. (1989). Health care needs of homeless and runaway youths. *Journal of the American Medical Association, 262,* 1358–1361.

Drake, R. E., Wallach, M. A., & Hoffman, J. S. (1989). Housing instability and homelessness among aftercare patients of an urban state hospital. *Hospital and Community Psychiatry, 40,* 46–51.

Frances, R. J. (1988). Update on alcohol and drug disorder treatment. *Journal of Clinical Psychiatry, 49,* 13–17.

Gelberg, L., Linn, L. S., & Leake, B. D. (1988). Mental health, alcohol and drug use, and criminal history among homeless adults. *American Journal of Psychiatry, 145,* 191–196.

Higgins, S. T., Budney, A. J., Bickel, W. K., & Foerg, F. E. (1994). Incentives improve outcome in outpatient behavioral treatment of cocaine dependence. *Archives of General Psychiatry, 51,* 568–576.

Higgins, S. T., Budney, A. J., Bickel, W. K., & Hughes, J. R. (1993). Achieving cocaine abstinence with a behavioral approach. *American Journal of Psychiatry, 150,* 763–769.

Higgins, S., Delaney, D., Budney, A., Bickel, W. K., Hughes, J. R., Foerg, F., & Fenwick, J. W. (1991). A behavioral approach to achieving initial cocaine abstinence. *American Journal of Psychiatry, 148,* 1218–1224.

Koegel, P., & Burnam, M. A. (1988). Alcoholism among homeless adults in the inner city of Los Angeles. *Archives of General Psychiatry, 51,* 1011–1018.

Koegel, P., Burnam, M. A., & Farr, R. K. (1988). The prevalence of specific psychiatric disorders among homeless individuals in the inner city of Los Angeles. *Archives of General Psychiatry, 45,* 1085–1092.

La Gory, M., Ritchey, F., & Fitzpatrick, K. (1991). Homelessness and affiliation. *Sociological Quarterly, 32,* 201–218.

La Gory, M., Ritchey, F. J., & Mullis, J. (1990). Depression among the homeless. *Journal of Health and Social Behavior, 31,* 87–101.

McNamara, C. L., Milby, J. B., Schumacher, J. E., Popkin, S. J., Wallace, D., McGill, T., & Michael, M. (1996, June). *The role of Axis I diagnosis in substance abuse treatment outcome with homeless cocaine abusers.* Paper presented at the 58th annual scientific meeting of the College on Problems of Drug Dependence, San Juan, Puerto Rico.

McNamara, C. L., Milby, J. B., Schumacher, J. E., Usdan S., & Wallace, D. (1997, June). *Abstinence contingency may positively impact homeless crack addicts' non-drug-related activities.* Poster session presented at the 59th annual scientific meeting of the College on Problems of Drug Dependence, Nashville, TN.

Milby, J. B., Schumacher, J. E., McNamara, C., Wallace, D., McGill, T., Stange, D., & Michael, M. (1996, June). *Abstinence contingent housing enhances day treatment for homeless cocaine abusers.* Paper presented at the 58th annual scientific meeting of the College on Problems of Drug Dependence, San Juan, Puerto Rico.

Milby, J. B., Schumacher, J. E., Raczynski, J. M., Caldwell, E., Engle, M., Michael,

M., & Carr, J. (1996). Sufficient conditions for effective treatment of substance abusing homeless. *Drug and Alcohol Dependence, 43,* 39–47.

Raczynski, J. M., Schumacher, J. E., Milby, J. B., Michael, M., Engle, M., Lerner, M., & Woolley, T. (1993). Comparing two substance abuse treatments for the homeless: The Birmingham project. *Alcohol Treatment Quarterly, 10,* 217–233.

Rahav, M., & Link, B. G. (1995). When social problems converge: Homeless, mentally ill, chemical misusing men in New York City. *International Journal of the Addictions, 30,* 1019–1042.

Rahav, M., Rivera, J. J., Nuttbrock, L., Mg-Mak, D., Sturz, E. L., Link, B. G., Struening, E. L., Pepper, B., & Gross, B. (1995). Characteristics and treatment of homeless, mentally ill, chemical-abusing men. *Journal of Psychoactive Drugs, 27,* 93–103.

Report on homeless in America. (1994, May 9). Washington, DC: Cable News Network.

Ritchey, F. J., La Gory, M., Fitzpatrick, K. M., & Mullis, J. (1990). A comparison of homeless, community-wide, and selected distressed samples on the CES-Depression Scale. *American Journal of Public Health, 80,* 1384–1386.

Rosenheck, R., Leda, C., Astrachan, B., Milstein, R., Leaf, P., Thompson, D., & Errera, P. (1989). Initial assessment data from a 43-site program for homeless chronic mentally ill veterans. *Hospital and Community Psychiatry, 40,* 937–942.

Schumacher, J. E., Milby, J. B., Raczynski, J. R., Caldwell, E., Engle, M., Carr, J., & Michael, M. (1995). Validity of self-reported crack cocaine use among homeless persons in treatment. *Journal of Substance Abuse Treatment, 12,* 335–339.

Silverman, K., Higgins, S. T., Brooner, R. K., & Montoya, I. D. (1996). Sustained cocaine abstinence in methadone maintenance patients through voucher-based reinforcement therapy. *Archives of General Psychiatry, 53,* 409–415.

Toro, P. A. Bellavia, C. W., Daeschler, C. V., Ownes, B. J., Wall, D. D., Passero, J. M., & Thomas, D. M. (1995). Distinguishing homlessness from poverty: A comparative study. *Journal of Consulting and Clinical Psychology, 63,* 280–289.

Toro, P. A., Trickett, E. J., Wall, D. D., & Salem, D. A. (1991). Homelessness in the United States: An ecological perspective. *American Psychologist, 46,* 1208–1218.

Toro, P. A., & Wall, D. D. (1991). Research on homeless persons: Diagnostic comparisons and practice implications. *Professional Psychology: Research and Practice, 22,* 479–488.

Wise, R. A. (1984) *Neural mechanisms of the reinforcing action of cocaine* (NIDA Research Monograph 50, pp. 15–33). Washington, DC: U.S. Government Printing Office.

5

DISABILITY INCOME, COCAINE USE, AND CONTINGENCY MANAGEMENT AMONG PATIENTS WITH COCAINE DEPENDENCE AND SCHIZOPHRENIA

ANDREW SHANER, DOUGLAS E. TUCKER, LISA J. ROBERTS,
AND THAD A. ECKMAN

In this chapter, we review the problem of cocaine abuse among individuals with schizophrenia, including epidemiology, clinical consequences, treatment obstacles, and innovative treatment programs. We then focus on one particular treatment obstacle: the potential for disability income to facilitate cocaine use. Finally, we examine the rationale and empirical support for a potential solution: using disability income in a deliberate program to reinforce abstinence.

EPIDEMIOLOGY

Cocaine abuse is common in both community and treatment samples of individuals with schizophrenia. For example, the prevalence of cocaine abuse in one large-scale epidemiologic survey was 17% (Regier et al.,

1990). In a sample of adults with schizophrenia admitted to a Veterans Affairs psychiatric hospital, 25% abused cocaine (Khalsa, Shaner, Anglin, & Wang, 1991). Cocaine is rarely used alone but is usually part of a larger polysubstance abuse pattern (Cuffel, 1996). Although not as frequent as alcohol and cannabis use, cocaine abuse has become increasingly prevalent (Cuffel, 1996). Until recently, it was thought that people with schizophrenia used stimulants to "self-medicate" negative symptoms or medication side-effects, but it now appears that stimulant and other substance abuse is related to a range of factors, including availability, cost, demographics, and peer influences (Cuffel, 1996; Muesar, Drake, & Wallach, 1998).

CLINICAL CONSEQUENCES

Substance abuse has deleterious consequences for individuals with schizophrenia, including more severe psychiatric symptoms with poorer psychosocial functioning and treatment outcome (Barbee, Clark, Crapanzano, Heintz, & Kehoe, 1989; Benda & Datallo, 1988), higher rates of relapse and rehospitalization (Carpenter, Mulligan, Bader, & Meinzer, 1985), less history of drug or alcohol treatment (Hall, Popkin, Devaul, & Stickney, 1977; Richardson, Craig, & Haugland, 1985), more admissions to emergency rooms, noncompliance with pharmacological and psychosocial treatment (Lyons & McGovern, 1989), increased suicidal and criminal behavior (Safer, 1987; Zitrin, Hardesty, Burdock, & Drossman, 1976), and increased violence (Swanson, Holzer, Ganju, & Jono, 1990; Yesavage & Zarcone, 1983). Individuals with schizophrenia and substance abuse have more trouble obtaining meals, managing finances, and maintaining stable housing; they have higher levels of hostility, depression, violence, and suicide; and they pose more management problems in hospitals, in the community, and at home (Cuffel, 1996). Episodes of substance abuse tend to precede decreases in level of function, rather than the other way around (Shumway, Chouljian, & Hargreaves, 1994). The course of psychiatric treatment is worsened by substance abuse (Chen et al., 1992). These individuals use more emergency and institutional (hospital and jail) services and incur greater costs for these services (Bartels et al., 1993).

Cocaine may be particularly destructive for individuals with schizophrenia because it is dopaminergic; excess dopamine has been associated with the pathophysiology of schizophrenia (Lieberman, Kinon, & Loebel, 1990). Cocaine and similar stimulants can thus exacerbate the course of schizophrenia by worsening psychotic symptoms (Gold & Bowers, 1978; Richard, Liskow, & Perry, 1985) and by causing increased anxiety and depression (Serper et al., 1995; Sevy, Kay, Opler, & Van Pragg, 1990), suicidality (Seibyl et al., 1993), increased aggressiveness (Honer, Gerwitz, & Turey, 1987), and an increased rate of psychiatric hospitalization (Brady et al., 1990). The subgroup of dually diagnosed patients with schizophrenia who use substances other than alcohol and cannabis may be more difficult and expensive to treat in outpatient settings and may have higher rates of violence (Cuffel, Shumway, Chouljian, & MacDonald, 1994).

Substance-abusing individuals with schizophrenia tend to be young men of low socioeconomic status, with fewer prior hospitalizations, more stable premorbid personalities, and more frequent family histories of substance abuse than non-substance-abusing individuals with schizophrenia (Cuffel, 1996). Also substance abuse among patients with schizophrenia may actually be less severe than abuse occurring in the non-mentally ill population, although people with schizophrenia may suffer more social and behavioral consequences (Cuffel, 1996).

TREATMENT OBSTACLES

Patients with schizophrenia and substance abuse are very difficult to treat for several reasons, including poorly integrated treatment, high treatment dropout rate, diagnostic uncertainty, and learning deficits.

Poorly Integrated Treatment

The traditional separation of mental health and substance abuse treatment programs leads to difficulties in integrating treatment, resulting in miscommunications, contradictory recommendations, and noncompliance (Galanter, Castaneda, & Ferman, 1988; Kline, Harris, Bebout, & Drake, 1991; Wallen & Weiner, 1989). Many researchers have reported poor outcomes with sequential, parallel, or otherwise uncoordinated treatment, usually because patients "fall through the cracks" between treatment programs (Mueser & Noordsy, 1996; Ridgely, Goldman, & Willenbring, 1990).

High Dropout (and Drop-In) Rate

Mentally ill substance abusers tend to relapse more often and require more time to achieve abstinence than nonmentally ill substance abusers (Carey & Carey, 1990). This often leads to a "revolving door" pattern of treatment, with emergency visits to general and psychiatric emergency departments (Bassuk, 1980). This pattern has been described as "heavy, discontinuous, and episodic," with more and shorter inpatient admissions and more nontreatment periods (Cohen & Klein, 1974; Richardson, Craig, & Haugland, 1985).

Diagnostic Uncertainty

Cocaine and other stimulants can lead to diagnostic error in two ways. First, they can mimic schizophrenic symptoms in people who do not have schizophrenia (Bell, 1973; Flaum & Schultz, 1996; Satel, Southwick, & Gawin, 1991; Sherer, 1988), and second, these drugs can worsen (or sometimes improve) schizophrenic symptoms in those who already have the disorder (Angrist, Rotrosen, & Gershon, 1980; Dixon, Haas, Weiden, Sweeney, & Frances, 1991; Janowsky & Davis 1976; van Kammen & Boronov, 1988; van Kammen et al., 1982). Such diagnostic errors may lead to inappropriate treatment. On the one hand, the misdiagnosis of schizophrenia in a patient who actually has a substance-induced psychosis may lead to inappropriately prolonged use of antipsychotic medication. On the other hand, missing the diagnosis of schizophrenia may lead to a failure to use antipsychotic medication. Diagnostic uncertainty and inaccuracy may also lead to exclusion from appropriate treatment programs. For example, substance abuse treatment programs often accept patients with transient toxic psychoses but exclude patients with schizophrenia or uncertain diagnoses.

Learning Deficits

As a group, patients with schizophrenia perform poorly on cognitive measures compared with individuals without mental illness (Gold & Harvey, 1993; Green, 1993). The former suffer from impairments in attention (Braff, 1993; Gold, Randolph, Carpenter, Goldberg, & Weinberger, 1992), abstraction (Saykin et al., 1991), learning and memory (Gold et al., 1992; Paulsen et al., 1995), and executive functions (McGrath, 1991; Weinberger, Berman, & Zec, 1986). These learning deficits vary considerably among individuals, and a characteristic cognitive profile has yet to emerge (Green, 1993). Nevertheless, these deficits may contribute to drug-taking behaviors. This is particularly true of deficits in executive function, such as the failure to consider the consequences of one's actions, lack of self-control, and lack of assertiveness. In addition, cognitive deficits may make it difficult for individuals with schizophrenia to benefit from traditional approaches to treating substance abuse. For example, patients with schizophrenia may have trouble remembering the negative consequences of drug use, alternative behaviors to drug use, and how to engage in those alternative behaviors.

COMPREHENSIVE INTEGRATED TREATMENT

Integration

One way to overcome treatment obstacles is through comprehensive integrated treatment (Roberts, Shaner, Eckman, Tucker, & Vaccaro, 1992).

It is now generally accepted that dually diagnosed patients require simultaneous and integrated psychiatric and substance abuse treatment (Bond, McDonel, Miller, & Pensec, 1991; Drake, Yovetich, Bebout, Harris, & McHugo, 1997; Lehman, Myers, Thompson, & Corty, 1993). Ideally, a single team or program should be responsible for a patient's treatment of both schizophrenia and substance abuse throughout all phases of treatment, including acute inpatient care and long-term rehabilitation (Roberts et al., 1992).

Assertive Case Management

Case management, modeled on the Program for Assertive Community Care model (Stein & Test, 1980), has become a standard method for integrating treatments in outpatient settings. For example, nearly all of the 13 National Institute of Mental Health dual diagnosis demonstration programs funded between 1987 and 1990 included some form of case management (Drake & Noordsy, 1994).

Tolerance of Diagnostic Uncertainty

When it is unclear whether severe psychotic symptoms are primary or drug induced, dual diagnosis treatment programs should treat substance abuse and the psychotic symptoms. Furthermore, for a substantial proportion of patients, it may not be possible to resolve diagnostic uncertainty, even after months of treatment (Shaner et al., 1998).

Behavioral Interventions

Treatment programs should use behavioral approaches that compensate for cognitive impairments. Researchers have demonstrated that structured skills training approaches designed to foster sustained attention, problem solving, and goal setting (Liberman & Green, 1992) improve psychosocial outcomes in patients with schizophrenia (Dobson, McDougall, Busheikin, & Aldous, 1995; Eckman et al., 1992). An adaptation designed to teach drug relapse prevention skills to individuals with schizophrenia has shown promising early results (Shaner, Roberts, Eckman, & Wilkins, 1997). Other researchers also are developing behavioral treatments for this population (Bellack & Gearon, 1998; Carey, 1996).

Antipsychotic Medication

Antipsychotic medication is a mainstay of treatment for patients with schizophrenia, regardless of whether they abuse substances. Dose and choice of agent may have to be adjusted for those who abuse substances, however, because of potential drug interactions and altered metabolism (Decker & Ries, 1993; Gastfriend, 1993). Newer antipsychotic medications, often called *serotonin-dopamine antagonists*, may offer some advantages over traditional antipsychotic medications in this population, including superior efficacy and fewer side-effects (Brady & Roberts, 1995; Buckley, Thompson, Way, & Meltzer, 1994; Kosten & Ziedonis, 1997; Wilkins, 1997). In addition, serotonin-dopamine antagonists may improve cognitive deficits, such as impaired memory, in people with schizophrenia (Green et al., 1997). This effect may be especially important because most treatments for substance abuse, particularly cognitive–behavioral treatments, require patients to learn new concepts and skills.

DISABILITY INCOME MAY FACILITATE COCAINE USE

Another obstacle to treating substance abuse among individuals with schizophrenia is that many receive disability income from the Social Security Administration (SSA) or if they are veterans from the Veterans Benefits Administration (VBA). This disability income is intended to pay for the basic needs of people with severe mental illness. The problem is that in these individuals, direct payment of disability income may facilitate the use of drugs and alcohol that exacerbate mental illness, worsen disability, and lead to hunger and homelessness by depleting meager financial resources. In this section, we describe the two major sources of federal disability income and review the evidence that direct payment of disability income creates an obstacle to treatment for individuals with both schizophrenia and substance abuse.

Disability Income for People With Schizophrenia

The symptoms of schizophrenia—hallucinations, delusions, disorganized thoughts, poor concentration, and a markedly impaired ability to experience and express emotion—often prevent afflicted individuals from working in competitive employment. These people, just like those disabled by illnesses such as heart disease, stroke, or epilepsy, are eligible for disability income from SSA. If the illness began during military service, they also may be eligible for disability income from VBA.

There are two separate categories under which an individual may qualify for benefits. The first, Social Security disability insurance (SSDI), provides benefits to those who have been employed and have thereby contributed to Social Security. The second, supplemental security income (SSI), provides benefits to disabled adults who are indigent (Social Security Administration [SSA], 1997). Because schizophrenia usually first appears in late adolescence or early adulthood before the individual has had a chance to contribute to Social Security, SSI is often the only compensation option available.

SSA defines disability as

the inability to engage in any substantial gainful activity by reason of any medically determinable physical or mental impairment(s) which can be expected to result in death or which has lasted or can be expected to last for a continuous period of not less than 12 months. (SSA, 1997, p. 392)

Until recently, this definition applied to substance use disorders. However, a rapid increase in the number of SSI beneficiaries (MacDonald, 1995) and dramatic cases of addicts spending disability income on drugs and alcohol led Congress to restrict and then eliminate SSI for substance use disorders.

The Contract With America Advancement Act of 1996 prohibits SSI and SSDI benefits entirely for individuals whose drug addiction or alcoholism (or both) contributes to the disability. Those with a primary disability (including severe mental illness) who also are addicted or alcoholic still may receive benefits but only if the disability would remain even if the individual were (hypothetically) not using drugs or alcohol. Benefits continue for as long as the beneficiary remains disabled by the primary disabling illness (e.g., schizophrenia). Although beneficiaries must be given appropriate treatment referrals by the state agency, there is no longer any requirement that treatment actually be administered either for the primary illness or for the substance abuse, unless such treatment for the primary illness would be expected to render the beneficiary no longer disabled (M. Greenberg, personal communication, February 1997).

Current regulations require that disability payments be redirected to a representative payee (an individual or institution) if the beneficiary is legally incompetent or found to be mentally or physically incapable of managing benefit payments (SSA, 1997). Traditionally, representative payees have ensured that minimal living needs are consistently met by receiving the monthly check and paying rent; by disbursing funds for food, clothing, and other essentials; and by monitoring discretionary spending.

Treatment programs can establish a representative payee by contacting SSA and describing the impairments that make the individual incapable of managing benefits. Patients who do not spend their money appropriately on basic and future needs (i.e., food, clothing, shelter) for whatever reason, including spending this money on drugs and alcohol, are usually found incapable of managing their own benefits, regardless of the nature of their disability. Patients may voluntarily agree to payee assignment. Programs that serve as payee should maintain a relationship with the local field office (branch or district office) of SSA (M. Greenberg, personal communication, February 1997).

VBA disability compensation rules are similar, in that alcoholism and addictions are not compensated and a fiduciary (payee) can be appointed if the beneficiary is not competent to manage his or her own funds. At the request of family members or clinicians, VBA will investigate the beneficiary's competence and the suitability of the proposed fiduciary. An important restriction is that employees of the Department of Veterans Affairs (VA; including clinical staff) may not serve as the fiduciaries for VBA benefits. Thus, a VA clinical program interested in developing a representative payee program must contract with a community provider of such services if the goal is to manage benefits from both SSA and VBA.

Both the SSA and VBA disability compensation systems attempt to identify appropriate beneficiaries and provide them compensation. One important problem, particularly for many dually diagnosed individuals, is the identification and programmatic response to the beneficiary's incapacity to manage benefits. At present, there is no consistent or systematic method to assess such capacity, and decisions about payee assignment are generally left to families and caregivers to make on an individual basis (Rosenheck, 1997). In addition, although the involvement of a representative payee is theoretically effective, in practice this approach routinely breaks down, and there is some evidence that payeeships may have little effect on dual diagnosis outcomes (Rosenheck, Lam, & Randolph, 1997). Chronically psychotic drug abusers can be extremely difficult to engage and treat effectively, and it is thus often quite challenging to find reliable individuals or programs willing to act as representative payees. In addition, some patients who are already receiving disability payments may avoid treatment rather than risk losing direct control of their income. As a result, many dually diagnosed patients, even those in well-designed treatment programs, do not have effective representative payees. Researchers have found that this often leads to the destructive monthly cycle of patients spending disability income directly on alcohol and drugs, with resultant symptomatic exacerbations, homelessness, and revolving door rehospitalizations (Ries & Comtois, 1997; Satel, Reuter, Hartley, Rosenheck, & Mintz, 1997; Shaner et al., 1995), although this finding has been disputed (Frisman & Rosenheck, 1997).

Disability Income and Cocaine Use Among Schizophrenia Patients

To investigate the consequences of direct disability payments, Shaner et al. (1995) examined data from a study comparing the efficacy of two experimental treatment programs for 105 cocaine-dependent men with schizophrenia at the Veterans Affairs Medical Center in West Los Angeles, California. These patients had severe mental illness and a long-term dependence on cocaine, with repeated admissions to psychiatric hospitals; many were homeless. Case managers and other clinicians in both treatment conditions struggled to obtain representative payees but were unsuccessful.

Data regarding cocaine use, psychiatric symptoms, and psychiatric hospitalizations were collapsed into a single prototypal month by grouping the data into ten 3-day intervals on the basis of calendar day. Data collected on the first 3 days of any month were in the first interval, data from the second 3 days were in the second interval, and so forth.

Cocaine use, psychiatric symptoms, and hospital admissions all peaked during the first three intervals, shortly after the arrival of the disability payment on the 1st day (Figure 5.1). The cyclic pattern of drug use strongly suggests that it was influenced by the receipt of disability payments on the 1st day of the month. The average patient spent nearly half his or her total income on illegal drugs. Because the cost of board-and-care homes in Los Angeles approved by the VA (a minimum of $680 per month) exceeded the patient's median monthly income, one can surmise that cocaine use contributed to homelessness by depleting the funds required for shelter. Psychotic symptoms were more severe on the days when cocaine was present in the urine than on other days. Thus, the increased rate of hospitalization following the peak in cocaine use probably resulted from the deleterious effects of cocaine use in the form of exacerbated psychiatric symptoms and homelessness. The troubling irony is that income intended to compensate for the disabling effects of severe mental illness may have the opposite effect.

An interesting and unexpected finding was that cocaine use, psychiatric symptoms, and hospitalization actually began to increase a few days before the first of the month. This pattern may have been due to a business practice reported by many of the patients. During the last week of the month, local drug dealers extend credit to people who receive monthly disability income. In a perverse sense, the certainty of the monthly payments makes these patients good credit risks.

The finding that direct payment of disability income facilitates cocaine abuse creates a dilemma—how to provide for the needs of disabled individuals without simultaneously facilitating addictions that worsen illness and disability? Simply withdrawing disability income from severely impaired and needy psychiatric patients does not eliminate drug abuse and may exacerbate hunger and homelessness. Part of the solution to this dilemma is to direct disability payments to representative payees who could ensure that minimal living needs are consistently met. However, representative payees cannot prevent drug use paid for by other means, such as panhandling. Therefore, payees must be integrated into comprehensive programs that treat both mental illness and substance abuse through education, case management, and appropriate psychological and medical interventions.

One potential intervention is to provide disability income in a way that reinforces abstinence rather than facilitates continued drug abuse. Disability income can be dispensed contingent on abstinence from drugs. Im-

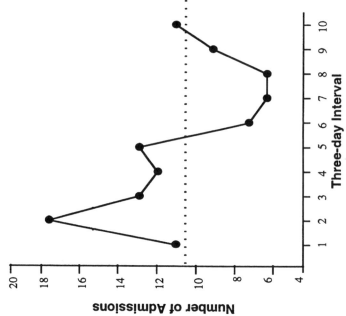

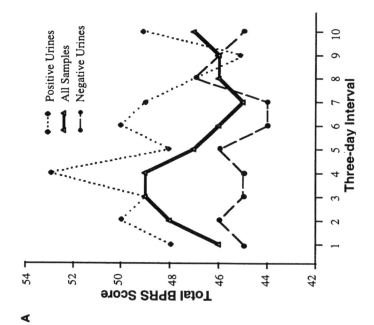

SHANER ET AL.

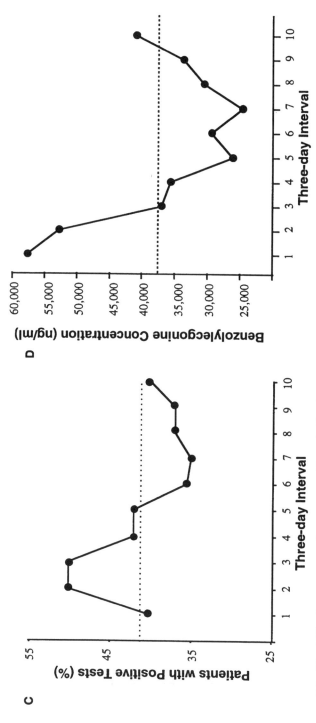

Figure 5.1. Disability, income, cocaine use, and hospitalization among individuals with schizophrenia. A: The severity of psychiatric symptoms, determined on the basis of the overall score on the 24-item Brief Psychiatric Rating Scale (BPRS); a higher score indicates more severe symptoms. B: The mean number of psychiatric admissions; the dotted line indicates the mean value (10.6 admissions) for all 10 intervals. C: The mean percentages of patients with positive tests for cocaine; the dotted line indicates the mean value (41%) for all 10 intervals. D: The mean benzoylecgonine concentrations in positive specimens; the dotted line indicates the mean value (36,852 ng/ml) for all 10 intervals. From "Disability Income, Cocaine Use, and Repeated Hospitalization Among Schizophrenic Cocaine Abusers: A Government-Sponsored Revolving Door?" by A. Shaner, T. A. Eckman, L. J. Roberts, J. N. Wilkins, D. E. Tucker, J. W. Tsuang, and J. Mintz, 1995, *New England Journal of Medicine, 333,* pp. 780 and 781 (Figures 1–4). Copyright 1995 by the *New England Journal of Medicine.* Reprinted with permission.

plementing such a program with disability income itself requires that several significant obstacles be overcome, including (a) locating willing representative payees, (b) establishing a mechanism for providing them with regular drug test results on a timely basis, (c) maintaining patients in comprehensive treatment programs, and (d) not the least, surviving challenges to the legality of controlling entitlements in this way. Despite these difficulties, mental health centers already use representative payees and a form of contingent disbursement of benefits for severely ill and dually diagnosed patients (Ries & Dyck, 1997).

Contingency management is the therapeutic technique of rewarding healthful and appropriate behaviors in hopes of increasing their frequency. Various forms of contingency management have been used successfully to modify the behavior of patients with schizophrenia (Kazdin, 1978; Masters & Rimm, 1987) and substance abusers (Hester, Nirenberg, & Begin, 1990; Sobell, Sobell, Ersner-Hershfield, & Nirenberg, 1982). For example, reinforcement improved daily living skills among chronic outpatients with schizophrenia (Liberman, Fearn, DeRisi, Roberts, & Carmona, 1977). Vouchers contingent on abstinence markedly reduced cocaine use among cocaine abusers (Higgins et al., 1994). Monetary reinforcement was effective in reducing cocaine use among pregnant women and tuberculin-exposed patients (Elk et al., 1995; chapter 6, this volume). Among mentally ill substance abusers, contingency management has been used to increase treatment attendance (Carey & Carey, 1990).

Only in two studies to date have researchers examined the effect of contingency management on substance use itself among severely mentally ill people (Peniston, 1988; Shaner, Roberts, Eckman, Tucker, et al., 1997). In the first study (Peniston, 1988), contingency management (praise, day passes from inpatient status, fines) reduced drinking among 8 male veterans diagnosed with chronic schizophrenia and hospitalized in a psychiatric ward. Alcohol consumption during day passes was reduced during the intervention phase and at 6-month and 1-year follow-ups.

In the second study, Shaner, Roberts, Eckman, Tucker, et al. (1997) investigated whether cocaine abuse by individuals with schizophrenia could be meaningfully altered by monetary reinforcement. They selected 2 treatment refractory patients whom they had struggled unsuccessfully to treat for 4 years in a comprehensive program. Both were actively psychotic, frequent cocaine users who were poorly adherent to treatment and homeless, despite receiving monthly SSI payments. For both patients, persistent drug use combined with frequent exacerbations of psychotic symptoms had resulted in a pattern of repeated psychiatric hospitalizations, followed by elopement and withdrawal from treatment. Typically, they were admitted with acute alcohol and cocaine intoxication, complicated by hallucinations, delusions, depression, and suicidal ideation. Psychotic and mood symptoms improved rapidly, although not completely, with antipsychotic medications. Unfortunately, the patients often eloped from the hospital or dropped out of treatment only to return to the hospital when psychotic symptoms flared coincident with episodes of heavy drug use. The few times that they accepted a referral to an outpatient clinic for treatment, they failed to show up for appointments, withdrew from treatment, and returned to live on the streets. Each month they spent their disability income on drugs rather than on food, clothing, and shelter and financed additional drug use by panhandling and recycling beverage containers. Multiple attempts to establish a representative payee failed.

The intervention consisted of paying both patients $25 daily as long as a rapid qualitative test for the cocaine metabolite benzoylecgonine in the urine was negative. Experimenters determined efficacy by examining the results of quantitative urine toxicologies performed twice weekly throughout the study. The proportion of urine tests positive for benzoylecgonine and the mean concentration of benzoylecgonine among positive specimens were lowest during the intervention for both patients (Figure 5.2). The mean benzoylecgonine concentration fell by 75%.

Although the intervention was successful in reducing cocaine use in these 2 patients, the experimenters' main interest in this small study was to lay the groundwork for future research by systematically gaining experience with how to conduct the intervention and how to measure its effects (Dukes, 1965; Shapiro, 1961). In this respect, several aspects of the study deserve further attention.

1. The effect was restricted to use of cocaine. Indeed, targeting one drug may have encouraged compensatory use of other drugs. One patient used more marijuana, and 2 used more alcohol. From an experimental standpoint, this strongly suggests that it was the contingency that led to reduced cocaine use rather than a related but nonspecific factor that reduced drug use in general. However, from a therapeutic perspective, it means that the typical pattern of multiple substance use disorders among cocaine abusers with schizophrenia requires additional contingency management. Some support for this idea is offered by Budney, Higgins, Delaney, and Kent (1991), who found that the use of multiple substances could be reduced by sequentially adding them to the protocol.

2. These 2 patients were also quite poor, which has two implications. First, the strength of any particular level of monetary reinforcement probably depends on the patient's financial assets. Setting payment levels on an individualized basis might be more effective, but in some programs it may be impractical. Second, after paying for basic necessities, there may be little money remaining to use in a program of contingency

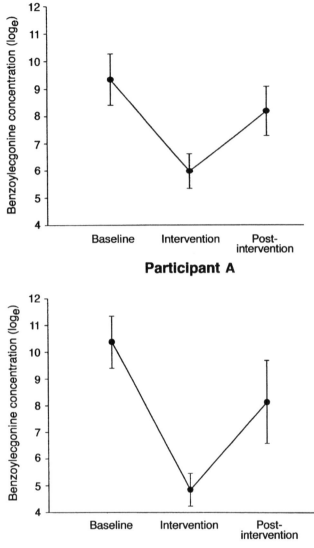

Figure 5.2. Cocaine use by 2 participants during a three-phase contingency management study. Benzoylecgonine, the major metabolite of cocaine, was measured in the participants' urine samples. Results are antilogs of the mean values (and 95% confidence intervals). Note that the mean of the log-transformed distribution is close to the median (50th percentile) of the original distribution. Expressed in terms of the original scale, the confidence intervals around the mean are asymmetrical because the original distribution was skewed. From "Monetary Reinforcement of Abstinence From Cocaine Among Mentally Ill Patients With Cocaine Dependence," by A. Shaner, L. J. Roberts, T. A. Eckman, D. E. Tucker, J. W. Tuang, J. N. Wilkins, and J. Mintz, 1997, *Psychiatric Services, 48,* p. 809. Copyright 1997 by the American Psychiatric Association. Reprinted with permission.

management. Thus, it is important to determine whether lower levels of monetary reinforcement, for example $5 or $10, for a negative urine test would be effective. Similarly, it is important to investigate the effectiveness of different schedules of reinforcement, such as rewarding the third consecutive negative urine toxicology. In clinical practice, determining the optimal intensity and schedule of reinforcement is likely to be a complex process, depending on a number of factors including the relative poverty or wealth of the patient, the phase of recovery, and the severity of psychiatric symptoms.

3. The intervention involved cash rather than vouchers. One possible objection to using cash is the speculation that cash can be used to buy cocaine. However, in this study, receipt of cash was contingent on negative urine specimens. It would have been counterproductive for patients to spend the money on cocaine because the $25 received as reinforcement on Monday to purchase cocaine would cost $75 to $100 in missed opportunities to receive additional money for negative drug tests during the rest of the week. Both patients immediately commented on this dilemma when first told of the contingency. Although cash was practical and effective in this small study, it may be impractical in some settings. For this reason, it is important to experiment with noncash reinforcers of various kinds. Both of the patients immediately began wondering how they might spend the money earned for negative tests. One patient considered buying a laptop computer on which to write poems and short stories because he had enjoyed his college writing courses before psychotic symptoms had forced him to drop out. The other patient bought new clothes and got a haircut. Thus, whether the reinforcer is cash or vouchers, clinical programs should be prepared to help patients decide how to use their new financial resources.

These 2 patients achieved several weeks of abstinence for the first time in several years of almost daily cocaine use. Surprisingly, they remained abstinent even immediately after receiving monthly disability checks. These results suggest that when traditional psychological, behavioral, and pharmacological approaches fail, contingency management may produce abstinence in some patients. Moreover, disability income, which in some circumstances may drive cocaine use, can instead reward abstinence.

TREATMENT MODELS

As mentioned earlier, some programs are already disbursing disability income contingent on patient behavior. For example, at the Harborview Recovery and Rehabilitation Program in Seattle, Washington (Ries & Comtois, 1997), a representative payee ensures that basic needs are met and works closely with case managers and other clinicians to vary the control over the remaining funds. When tight control is not needed, the representative payee pays rent and disburses the remaining funds in cash payments two to four times a month. At the other extreme, funds are electronically transferred to pay rent, and meal tickets (as opposed to cash) are distributed several times a week. Staff lead shopping outings to ensure that funds are used for food, clothing, or other basic necessities. Participants can earn more monetary freedom by demonstrating better treatment participation, decreased substance use, and increased money management skills.

At the VA Medical Center in West Los Angeles, we are developing an approach that integrates representative payee services and clinical care. In this model, the representative payee serves as an accountant and record keeper, managing the disbursement of the patient's funds after receiving input from clinical team members. This approach necessarily requires a close working relationship between the representative payee and the clinicians. The representative payee is ultimately responsible for deciding how each patient's money is spent. However, the payee, who has an office in the same building that houses the clinical program, meets regularly with the patient's clinical team and evaluates the team's recommendations regarding the use of the patient's funds. Working together, the clinical team and representative payee ensure that disability income provides basic necessities and does not facilitate drug and alcohol abuse.

In some cases, merely establishing a representative payee eliminates monthly binges and leads to treatment adherence and abstinence. However, in other cases, patients continue to use drugs and alcohol, purchased with spending money provided by the representative payee or with money obtained from panhandling or recycling containers. In such cases, we have begun disbursing disability income contingent on abstinence in a manner analogous to the pilot study described earlier. This involves providing small amounts of disability income to patients on a daily or nearly daily basis, according to a plan proposed by the clinical team and approved by the payee. The plan allows the clinical team to specify conditions that a patient must meet to obtain the small daily payment, including attending treatment sessions or providing drug-free urine specimens. When this approach is warranted, the clinical team negotiates a contingency contract with the patient stipulating the conditions under which the patient will receive cash allotments. The payee receives regular input from the patient's case manager regarding adherence to other conditions specified in the contract, and the payee disburses the funds when the clinical team verifies that the conditions are met.

LEGAL AND ETHICAL CONCERNS

The contingent disbursement of disability income raises a number of concerns that we have expressed as questions in the following discussion:

1. *Is it legal to withhold disability income until a urine toxicology test result is negative?* In general (Ries & Ellingson, 1990), the law gives the payee substantial discretion in determining how money is disbursed. The payee is expected to make regular payments as necessary and appropriate for current and future basic needs (i.e., food, clothing, shelter, and medical care), including small amounts for "personal comfort" items, such as cigarettes, soda, and candy. There is no legal obstacle to the contingent withholding or disbursement of these discretionary personal comfort moneys for outpatients if it is in accordance with relevant treatment goals, such as abstinence, as measured by urine tests (P. Faff, personal communication, February 1997). This strategy is fully supported by SSA as long as the rationale is to ensure that the patient's money is spent on current and future basic needs. Such conditions and restrictions on benefits are seen ultimately as the most protective of people's dignity because they promote recovery from addiction and prevent unchecked spending of residual benefits on drugs and alcohol. Different field offices may use different criteria in making individual decisions, however, and these should be discussed in advance by the payee or program.

2. *Is contingent monetary reinforcement not a form of coercion?* "Coercion is a process by which an 'agent' exercises certain type of control or power over a 'target.' In short, the agent gets the target to do something he would not otherwise do" (Carroll, 1991, p. 130). In the context of community care, coercion can range from friendly persuasion through interpersonal pressure to control of resources and use of force (Lucksted & Coursey, 1995). Thus, contingent payments are indeed an intermediate form of coercion.

3. *Do individuals not have the right to spend "their" money on whatever they want including drugs?* Although it is possible to consider disability payment as an entitlement used however the

recipient wants, many members of society, including clinical staff, regard it as part of an implicit social contract to provide for the basic necessities of living. This is quite distinct from money earned by work, which spontaneously diminishes or stops if the individual becomes too intoxicated to function (Diamond, 1996). Thus, there is an ethical conflict between the individual value of freedom and the societal goals of health, safety (for the patient and others), and community integration. In practice, treatment goals are often pursued, even against patients' wishes, when these efforts are expected to lead ultimately to greater health, freedom, and choice for the patient.

4. *Why should society pay people extra to do what they should do on their own?* To some degree, there appears to be a societal unwillingness to pay people extra to do what they should do on their own. For example, the use of money as reinforcement, even in the form of vouchers, has not gained wide acceptance in the treatment of non-mentally ill addicts. This is true, despite the success of this treatment strategy in clinical trials (Elk et al., 1995; Higgins et al., 1994) and its modest cost. The advantage of this approach is that it uses the patient's own money as a reinforcer—money that would otherwise facilitate drug use. Another approach, used in some substance abuse programs, is to collect moderate sums on admission and return the money on a contingent basis.

5. *Why should restrictions not be placed on others who receive public assistance?* Should addicts or alcoholics with a primary disabling physical illness (instead of mental illness) receive payments contingent on negative drug tests? Should disability payments to patients with heart or lung disease be made contingent on cessation of tobacco smoking or compliance with exercise programs (Feldman, 1996)? These are interesting and worthwhile questions. If the assistance money itself fuels substance abuse, exacerbates the primary disabling illness, and leads to a diminution of health and autonomy, then restrictions should be appropriately placed on its disbursement.

6. *Is there a risk that patients will turn to crime, prostitution, panhandling, or prescription drug diversion when their drug money is cut off?* This has been reported anecdotally and furthers the argument that representative payees are merely one component of comprehensive care (Geller, 1996). Also, the risk is probably small because these illegal sources of income require organization, determination, effort, and personal risk, as opposed to simply collecting a monthly check. Availability

seems to be a major factor in choice and timing of substance abuse among people with schizophrenia.

CONCLUSION

Our attempt in this chapter to analyze the therapeutic and counter-therapeutic consequences of disability law was an exercise in *therapeutic jurisprudence*, the study of the role of law as a therapeutic agent. This interdisciplinary field views law from a mental health perspective, recognizing the profound effects that law can have on the mental health of citizens for both good and ill. It strives to reduce the countertherapeutic effects while enhancing the therapeutic ones, without sacrificing due process and justice values (Wexler, 1996). Disability policy is an evolving area at the interface of politics, law, and psychiatry that requires a broad range of input, including clinical considerations. Clinicians working on the front lines with mentally disabled, substance-dependent patients have a unique perspective—one that is essential to the current debate.

Rosenheck (1997) outlined five key questions for future research in the area of disability payments and chemical dependence:

1. Does unrestricted disability income exacerbate substance use in vulnerable populations, and do the adverse consequences outweigh the benefits of such funds?
2. Does assignment of representative payees improve outcomes among such beneficiaries?
3. Which money management procedures result in the best outcomes?
4. How can candidates for payeeship or guardianship best be identified?
5. How should effective payees be recruited, trained, and retained?

Clearly, these questions show that much work needs to be done before contingent disbursement of discretionary disability funds can be recommended broadly. The technique should be assessed in controlled trials and in the context of comprehensive treatment programs either employing or acting as representative payees. It is unclear, for example, if the reinforced behavior continues after contingent payments are discontinued. However, effective treatment for severely mentally ill addicts remains elusive, and clinicians must search for innovative psychological, behavioral, and pharmacological approaches to both substance abuse and severe mental illness. The search for treatment should turn to new ways of managing disability income, especially when other approaches have failed and disability income is clearly fueling substance abuse.

The *Social Security Handbook* (SSA, 1993) states that "no restrictions, implied or otherwise, are placed on how people spend their SSI benefit" (p. 389) and that SSI is "paid under conditions that are as protective as possible of people's dignity" (p. 389). For patients with cocaine dependence and schizophrenia, however, these two goals may be incompatible. The failure to place restrictions on how patients spend disability income results in cycles of cocaine use, exacerbated symptoms, homelessness, and psychiatric hospitalizations that ultimately deprive patients of their dignity. This is particularly unfortunate because such poor clinical and social outcomes contrast with the relatively good outcomes reported among patients with substance abuse and schizophrenia who become abstinent. In two studies (Dixon, Haas, Weiden, Sweeney, & Frances, 1991; Zisook et al., 1992), researchers suggested that substance-abusing patients with schizophrenia have better social functioning and a better prognosis than other patients with schizophrenia. During periods of substance abuse, patients with schizophrenia are severely ill and their symptoms are difficult to manage. When abstinent, however, such patients have less severe psychotic symptoms and better social functioning than those who have never abused substances. In other words, these patients would probably have a relatively good prognosis were it not for substance abuse because the schizophrenia itself is relatively mild. This is the "silver lining" behind the cloud of dual disorders.

Clearly, then, an important part of protecting dignity is to impose the necessary restrictions to ensure that disability income provides for basic necessities and promotes recovery from severe mental illness and addiction. The combination of representative payees and contingency management has the potential to achieve this. First, representative payees can ensure that disability income provides for recipients' basic necessities and does not facilitate drug use that worsens the already disabling mental illness. Second, contingency management using disability income as the reinforcer can promote abstinence. As substance abuse remits, patients can be given greater control over disability funds. Eventually it may be possible to restore direct payment of disability income to the now abstinent patient. Thus, the combination of representative payees and contingency management must be viewed not as an end in itself but as an intermediate step toward restoring the patient's health and autonomy.

REFERENCES

Angrist, B., Rotrosen, J., & Gershon, S. (1980). Differential effects of amphetamine and neuroleptics on negative and positive symptoms in schizophrenia. *Psychopharmacology, 72,* 17–19.

Barbee, J. G., Clark, P. D., Crapanzano, M. S., Heintz, G. C., & Kehoe, C. E. (1989). Alcohol and substance abuse among schizophrenic patients presenting to an emergency psychiatric service. *Journal of Nervous and Mental Disease*, *177*, 400–407.

Bartels, S. J., Teague, G. B., Drake, R. E., Clark, R. E., Bush, P. W., & Noordsy, D. L. (1993). Substance abuse in schizophrenia: Service utilization and costs. *Journal of Nervous and Mental Disease*, *181*, 227–232.

Bassuk, E. (1980). The impact of deinstitutionalization on the general psychiatric emergency ward. *Hospital and Community Psychiatry*, *31*, 623–627.

Bell, D. S. (1973). The experimental reproduction of amphetamine psychosis. *Archives of General Psychiatry*, *29*, 35–40.

Bellack, A. S., & Gearon, J. S. (1998). Substance abuse treatment for people with schizophrenia. *Addictive Behaviors*, *23*, 749–766.

Benda, B., & Datallo, P. (1988). Homelessness: Consequence of a crisis or a long-term process? *Hospital and Community Psychiatry*, *39*, 884–886.

Bond, G. R., McDonel, E. C., Miller, L. D., & Pensec, M. (1991). Assertive community treatment and reference groups: An evaluation of their effectiveness for young adults with serious mental illness and substance abuse problems. *Psychosocial Rehabilitation Journal*, *15*, 31–43.

Brady, K., Anton, R., Ballenger, J. C., Lydiard, R. B., Adinoff, B., & Selander, J. (1990). Cocaine abuse among schizophrenic patients. *American Journal of Psychiatry*, *147*, 1164–1167.

Brady, K., & Roberts, J. (1995). The pharmacotherapy of dual diagnosis. *Psychiatric Annals*, *25*, 344–352.

Braff, D. (1993). Information processing and attention dysfunctions in schizophrenia. *Schizophrenia Bulletin*, *19*, 233–259.

Buckley, P., Thompson, P. A., Way, L., & Meltzer, H. Y. (1994). Substance abuse and clozapine treatment. *Journal of Clinical Psychiatry*, *55*, 114–116.

Budney, A. J., Higgins, S. T., Delaney, D. D., & Kent, L. (1991). Contingent reinforcement of abstinence with individuals abusing cocaine and marijuana. *Journal of Applied Behavior Analysis*, *24*, 657–665.

Carey, K. B. (1996). Substance use reduction in the context of outpatient psychiatric treatment: A collaborative, motivational, harm reduction approach. *Community Mental Health Journal*, *32*, 291–306.

Carey, K. B., & Carey, M. P. (1990). Enhancing the treatment attendance of mentally ill chemical abusers. *Journal of Behavior Therapy and Experimental Psychiatry*, *21*, 205–209.

Carpenter, M. D., Mulligan, J. C., Bader, I. A., & Meinzer, A. E. (1985). Multiple admissions to an urban psychiatric center: A comparative study. *Hospital and Community Psychiatry*, *36*, 1305–1308.

Carroll, J. (1991). Consent to mental health treatment: A theoretical analysis of coercion, freedom, and control. *Behavioral Sciences and the Law*, *9*, 129–142.

Chen, C., Balogh, M., Bathija, J., Howanitz, E., Plutchik, R., & Conte, H. R. (1992). Substance abuse among psychiatric inpatients. *Comprehensive Psychiatry*, *33*, 60–64.

Cohen, M., & Klein, D. (1974). Posthospital adjustment of psychiatrically hospitalized drug users. *Archives of General Psychiatry, 31*, 221–227.

Cuffel, B. (1996). Comorbid substance use disorder: Prevalence, patterns of use, and course. *New Directions for Mental Health Services, 70*, 93–105.

Cuffel, B. J., Shumway, M., Chouljian, T. L., & MacDonald, T. (1994). A longitudinal study of substance use and community violence in schizophrenia. *Journal of Nervous and Mental Disease, 182*, 704–708.

Decker, K. P., & Ries, R. K. (1993). Differential diagnosis and psychopharmacology of dual disorders. *Psychiatric Clinics of North America, 16*, 703–718.

Diamond, R. (1996). Coercion and tenacious treatment in the community: Applications to the real world. In D. Dennis & J. Monahan (Eds.), *Coercion and aggressive community treatment: A new frontier in mental health law* (pp. 51–72). New York: Plenum Press.

Dixon, L., Haas, G., Weiden, P. I., Sweeney, J., & Frances, A. J. (1991). Drug abuse in schizophrenic patients: Clinical correlates and reasons for use. *American Journal of Psychiatry, 148*, 224–230.

Dobson, D. J., McDougall, G., Busheikin, J., & Aldous, J. (1995). Effects of social skills training and social milieu treatment on symptoms of schizophrenia. *Psychiatric Services, 46*, 376–380.

Drake, R. E., & Noordsy, D. L. (1994). Case management for people with coexisting severe mental disorder and substance use disorder. *Psychiatric Annals, 24*, 427–431.

Drake, R. E., Yovetich, M. A., Bebout, R. R., Harris, M., & McHugo, G. J. (1997). Integrated treatment for dually diagnosed homeless adults. *Journal of Nervous and Mental Disease, 185*, 298–305.

Dukes, W. (1965). N = 1. *Psychological Bulletin, 64*, 74–79.

Eckman, T. A., Wirshing, W. C., Marder, S. R., Liberman, R. P., Johnston-Cronk, K., Zimmerman, K., & Mintz, J. (1992). Technique for training schizophrenic patients in illness self-management: A controlled trial. *American Journal of Psychiatry, 149*, 1549–1555.

Elk, R., Schmitz, J., Spiga, R., Rhoades, H., Andres, R., & Grabowski, J. (1995). Behavioral treatment of cocaine-dependent pregnant women and TB-exposed patients. *Addictive Behaviors, 20*, 533–542.

Feldman, J. (1996). Disability payments among schizophrenic cocaine abusers [Letter]. *New England Journal of Medicine, 334*, 665.

Flaum, M., & Schultz, S. K. (1996). When does amphetamine-induced psychosis become schizophrenia? *American Journal of Psychiatry, 153*, 812–815.

Frisman, L., & Rosenheck, R. (1997). The relationship of public support payments to substance abuse among homeless veterans with mental illness. *Psychiatric Services, 48*, 792–795.

Galanter, M., Castaneda, R., & Ferman, J. (1988). Substance abuse among general psychiatric patients: Place of presentation, diagnosis, and treatment. *American Journal of Drug Alcohol Abuse, 14*, 211–235.

Gastfriend, D. R. (1993). Pharmacotherapy of psychiatric syndromes with co-morbid chemical dependence. *Journal of Addictive Disorders, 12,* 155–170.

Geller, J. (1996). Disability payments among schizophrenic cocaine abusers [Letter]. *New England Journal of Medicine, 334,* 665.

Gold, M. S., & Bowers, M. B., Jr. (1978). Neurobiological vulnerability to low-dose amphetamine psychosis. *American Journal of Psychiatry, 135,* 1546–1548.

Gold, J. M., & Harvey, P. D. (1993). Cognitive deficits in schizophrenia. *Psychiatric Clinics of North America, 16,* 295–312.

Gold, J. M., Randolph, C., Carpenter, C. J., Goldberg, T. E., & Weinberger, D. R. (1992). Forms of memory failure in schizophrenia. *Journal of Abnormal Psychology, 101,* 487–494.

Green, M. F. (1993). Cognitive remediation in schizophrenia: Is it time yet? *American Journal of Psychiatry, 150,* 178–187.

Green, M. F., Marshall, B. D., Jr., Wirshing, W. C., Ames, D., Marder, S. R., McGurk, S., Dern, R. S., & Mintz, J. (1997). Does Risperidone improve verbal working memory in treatment-resistant schizophrenia? *American Journal of Psychiatry, 154,* 799–804.

Hall, R. C. W., Popkin, M. K., Devaul, R., & Stickney, S. K. (1977). The effect of unrecognized drug abuse on diagnosis and therapeutic outcome. *American Journal of Drug and Alcohol Abuse, 4,* 455–465.

Hellerstein, D. J., & Meehan, B. (1987). Outpatient group therapy for schizo-phrenic substance abusers. *American Journal of Psychiatry, 144,* 1337–1339.

Hester, R. K., Nirenberg, T. D., & Begin, A. M. (1990). Behavioral treatment of alcohol and drug abuse: What do we know and where shall we go? In M. Galanter (Ed.), *Recent advances in alcoholism. Vol. 8: Combined alcohol and other drug dependence: The syndrome, social deviancy, biological issues, clinical issues* (pp. 305–327). New York: Plenum Press.

Higgins, S., Budney, A. J., Bickel, W. K., Foerg, F. E., Donham, R., & Badger, G. J. (1994). Incentives improve outcome in outpatient behavioral treatment of cocaine dependence. *Archives of General Psychiatry, 51,* 568–576.

Honer, W., Gerwitz, G., & Turey, M. (1987, August, 22). Psychosis and violence in cocaine smokers [Letter]. *Lancet, 2,* 451.

Janowsky, D. S., & Davis, J. M. (1976). Methylphenidate, dextroamphetamine, and levamphetamine: Effects on schizophrenic symptoms. *Archives of General Psychiatry, 33,* 304–308.

Kazdin, A. (1978). *History of behavior modification: Experimental foundations of contemporary research.* Baltimore: University Park Press.

Khalsa, H. K., Shaner, A., Anglin, M. D., & Wang, J. C. (1991). Prevalence of substance abuse in a psychiatric evaluation unit. *Drug and Alcohol Dependence, 28,* 215–223.

Kline, J. M., Harris, M., Bebout, R. R., & Drake, R. E. (1991). Contrasting integrated and linkage models of treatment for homeless, dually diagnosed adults. *New Directions for Mental Health Services, 50,* 95–106.

Kosten, T. R., & Ziedonis, D. M. (1997). Substance abuse and schizophrenia: Editors' introduction. *Schizophrenia Bulletin, 23*, 181–186.

Lehman, A. F., Myers, C. P., Thompson, J. W., & Corty, E. (1993). Implications of mental and substance use disorders. A comparison of single and dual diagnosis patients. *Journal of Nervous and Mental Disease, 181*, 365–370.

Liberman, R. P., Fearn, C. H., DeRisi, W., Roberts, J., & Carmona, M. (1977). The credit-incentive system: Motivating the participation of patients in a day hospital. *British Journal of Social Clinical Psychology, 16*, 85–94.

Liberman, R. P., & Green, M. F. (1992). Whither cognitive–behavior therapy for schizophrenia? *Schizophrenia Bulletin, 18*, 27–35.

Lieberman, J. A., Kinon, B. J., & Loebel, A. D. (1990). Dopaminergic mechanisms in idiopathic and drug-induced psychoses. *Schizophrenia Bulletin, 16*, 97–110.

Lucksted, A., & Coursey, R. (1995). Consumer perceptions of pressure and force in psychiatric treatments. *Psychiatric Services, 46*, 146–152.

Lyons, J. S., & McGovern, M. P. (1989). Use of mental health services by dually diagnosed patients. *Hospital and Community Psychiatry, 40*, 1067–1069.

MacDonald, H. (1995, January 20). SSI fosters disabling dependency. *The Wall Street Journal*, p. A12.

Masters, J., & Rimm, D. (1987). *Behavior therapy: Techniques and empirical findings* (3rd ed.). San Diego, CA: Harcourt Brace Jovanovich.

McGrath, J. (1991). Ordering thoughts on thought disorder. *British Journal of Psychiatry, 158*, 307–316.

Mueser, K. T., Drake, R. E., & Wallach, M. A. (1998). Dual diagnosis: A review of etiological theories. *Addictive Behaviors, 23*, 717–734.

Mueser, K., & Noordsy, D. (1996). Group treatment for dually diagnosed clients. *New Directions for Mental Health Services, 70*, 33–51.

Paulsen, J. S., Heaton, R. K., Sadek, J. R., Perry, W., Delis, D. C., Braff, D., Kuck, J., Zisook, S., & Jeste, D. V. (1995). The nature of learning and memory impairments in schizophrenia. *Journal of the International Neuropsychological Society, 1*, 88–99.

Peniston, E. (1988). Evaluation of long-term therapeutic efficacy of behavior modification program with chronic male psychiatric inpatients. *Journal of Behavior Therapy and Experimental Psychiatry, 19*, 95–101.

Regier, D. A., Farmer, M. E., Rae, D. S., Locke, B. Z., Keith, S. J., Judd, L. L., & Goodwin, F. K. (1990). Comorbidity of mental disorders with alcohol and other drug abuse. Results from the Epidemiologic Catchment Area (ECA) Study. *Journal of the American Medical Association, 264*, 2511–2518.

Richard, M. L., Liskow, B. I., & Perry, P. J. (1985). Recent psychostimulant use in hospitalized schizophrenics. *Journal of Clinical Psychiatry, 46*, 79–83.

Richardson, M. A., Craig, T. J., & Haugland, G. (1985). Treatment patterns of young chronic schizophrenic patients in the era of deinstitutionalization. *Psychiatric Quarterly, 57*, 104–110.

Ridgely, M. S., Goldman, H. H., & Willenbring, M. (1990). Barriers to the care of persons with dual diagnoses: Organizational and financing issues. *Schizophrenia Bulletin, 16,* 123–132.

Ries, R. K., & Comtois, K. A. (1997). Managing disability benefits as part of treatment for persons with severe mental illness and comorbid drug/alcohol disorders: A comparative study of payees and non-payee participants. *American Journal on Addictions, 6,* 330–338.

Ries, R., & Dyck, D. (1997). Representative payee practices of community mental health centers in Washington state. *Psychiatric Services, 48,* 811–814.

Ries, R. K., & Ellingson, T. (1990). A pilot assessment at one month of 17 dual diagnosis patients. *Hospital and Community Psychiatry, 41,* 1230–1233.

Roberts, L. J., Shaner, A., Eckman, T. A., Tucker, D. E., & Vaccaro, J. V. (1992). Effectively treating stimulant abusing schizophrenics: Mission impossible? *New Directions in Mental Health Services, 53,* 55–65.

Rosenheck, R. (1997). Disability payments and chemical dependence: Conflicting values and uncertain effects. *Psychiatric Services, 48,* 789–791.

Rosenheck, R., Lam, J., & Randolph, F. (1997). Impact of representative payees on substance use by homeless persons with serious mental illness. *Psychiatric Services, 48,* 800–806.

Safer, D. J. (1987). Substance abuse by young adult chronic patients. *Hospital and Community Psychiatry, 38,* 511–4.

Satel, S., Reuter, P., Hartley, D., Rosenheck, R., & Mintz, J. (1997). Influence on retroactive disability payments on recipients' compliance with substance abuse treatment. *Psychiatric Services, 48,* 796–799.

Satel, S. L., Southwick, S. S., & Gawin, F. H. (1991). Clinical features of cocaine-induced paranoia. *American Journal of Psychiatry, 148,* 495–498.

Saykin, A. J., Gur, R. C., Gur, R. E., Mozley, P. D., Mozley, L. H., Resnick, S. M., Kester, B., & Stafiniak, P. (1991). Neuropsychological function in schizophrenia. *Archives of General Psychiatry, 48,* 618–624.

Seibyl, J. P., Satel, S. L., Anthony, D., Southwick, S. M., Krystal, J. H., & Charney, D. S. (1993). Effects of cocaine on hospital course in schizophrenia. *Journal of Nervous and Mental Disease, 181,* 31–37.

Serper, M. R., Alpert, M., Richardson, N. A., Dickson, S., Allen, M. H., & Werner, A. (1995). Clinical effects of recent cocaine use on patients with acute schizophrenia. *American Journal of Psychiatry, 152,* 1464–1469.

Sevy, S., Kay, S. R., Opler, L. A., & Van Pragg, H. M. (1990). Significance of cocaine history in schizophrenia. *Journal of Nervous and Mental Disease, 178,* 642–648.

Shaner, A., Eckman, T. A., Roberts, L. J., Wilkins, J. N., Tucker, D. E., Tsuang, J. W., & Mintz, J. (1995). Disability income, cocaine use, and repeated hospitalization among schizophrenic cocaine abusers: A government-sponsored revolving door? *New England Journal of Medicine, 333,* 777–783.

Shaner, A., Roberts, L. J., Eckman, T. A., Racenstein, J. M., Tucker, D. E., Tsuang, J., & Mintz, J. (1998). Sources of diagnostic uncertainty for chronically psychotic cocaine abusers. *Psychiatric Services, 49,* 684–690.

Shaner, A., Roberts, L. J., Eckman, T. A., Tucker, D. E., Tsuang, J. W., Wilkins, J. N., & Mintz, J. (1997). Monetary reinforcement of abstinence from cocaine among mentally ill patients with cocaine dependence. *Psychiatric Services, 48,* 807–810.

Shaner, A., Roberts, L. J., Eckman, T. A., & Wilkins, J. N. (1997). *Skills training for substance abusing schizophrenic patients* (NIDA Research Monograph Series 178, p. 256). Washington, DC: U.S. Government Printing Office.

Shapiro, M. (1961). The single case in fundamental clinical psychological research. *British Journal of Medical Psychology, 34,* 255–262.

Sherer, M. A. (1988). Intravenous cocaine: Psychiatric effects, biological mechanisms. *Biological Psychiatry, 24,* 865–885.

Shumway, M., Chouljian, T. L., & Hargreaves, W. A. (1994). Patterns of substance use in schizophrenia: A Markov modeling approach. *Journal of Psychiatric Research, 28,* 277–287.

Sobell, M. B., Sobell, L. C., Ersner-Hershfield, S., & Nirenberg, T. (1982). Alcohol and drug problems. In A. S. Bellack, M. Hersen, & A. E. Kazdin (Eds.), *International handbook of behavior modification and therapy* (pp. 501–533). New York: Plenum Press.

Social Security Administration. (1997). *Social security handbook* (13th ed.; DHHS Pub. No. SSA 65–008). Washington, DC: U.S. Government Printing Office.

Stein, L. I., & Test, M. A. (1980). Alternatives to mental hospital treatment: I. Conceptual model, treatment program, and clinical evaluation. *Archives of General Psychiatry, 37,* 392–397.

Swanson, J. W., Holzer, C. E., Ganju, V. K., & Jono, R. T. (1990). Violence and psychiatric disorder in the community: Evidence from the Epidemiologic Catchment Area Surveys. *Hospital and Community Psychiatry, 41,* 761–770.

van Kammen, D. P., & Boronow, J. J. (1988). Dextro-amphetamine diminishes negative symptoms in schizophrenia. *International Clinical Psychopharmacology, 3,* 111–121.

van Kammen, D. P., Bunney, W. E., Docherty, J. P., Marder, S. R., Ebert, M. H., Rosenblatt, J. E., & Rayner, J. N. (1982). *d*-Amphetamine induced heterogeneous changes in psychotic behavior in schizophrenia. *American Journal of Psychiatry, 139,* 997–999.

Wallen, M. C., & Weiner, H. D. (1989). Impediments to effective treatment of the dually diagnosed patient. *Journal of Psychoactive Drugs, 21,* 161–168.

Weinberger, D. R., Berman, K. F., & Zec, R. F. (1986). Physiological dysfunction of dorsolateral prefrontal cortex in schizophrenia: I. Regional cerebral blood flow evidence. *Archives of General Psychiatry, 43,* 114–124.

Wexler, D. (1996). Therapeutic jurisprudence in clinical practice. *American Journal of Psychiatry, 153,* 453–455.

Wilkins, F. N. (1997). Pharmacology of schizophrenia patients with comorbid substance abuse. *Schizophrenia Bulletin, 23,* 215–228.

Yesavage, J. A., & Zarcone, V. (1983). History of drug abuse and dangerous behavior in inpatient schizophrenics. *Journal of Clinical Psychiatry, 44*, 259–261.

Zisook, S., Heaton, R., Moranville, J., Kuck, J., Jernigan, T., & Braff, D. (1992). Past substance abuse and clinical course of schizophrenia. *American Journal of Psychiatry, 149*, 552–553.

Zitrin, A., Hardesty, A. S., Burdock, E. I., & Drossman, A. K. (1976). Crime and violence among mental patients. *American Journal of Psychiatry, 13*, 142–149.

6

PREGNANT WOMEN AND TUBERCULOSIS-EXPOSED DRUG ABUSERS: REDUCING DRUG USE AND INCREASING TREATMENT COMPLIANCE

RONITH ELK

Cocaine-dependent patients who are health compromised face additional hazards because of their drug dependence as well as health challenges. Treatment interventions that address both the drug use and the specific health risks are required. Two examples of cocaine-dependent populations requiring such specialized interventions are tuberculosis (TB)-exposed patients and pregnant women. In this chapter, I discuss various treatment strategies implemented to simultaneously decrease drug use and enhance compliance with the required medical regimen in these two health-compromised populations.

EXTENT OF THE PROBLEM AND NEED FOR SPECIALIZED TREATMENT INTERVENTIONS

TB Infectivity in Cocaine-Dependent Patients

Cocaine-dependent patients who have been exposed to TB face serious health risks. Continued drug abuse leads to engagement in high-risk behaviors resulting in an increased risk for hepatotoxicity, sexually transmitted diseases, HIV, and AIDS. Progression of infection to clinically active TB is more common among immunocompromised people, such as alcoholics, drug abusers, and HIV and AIDS patients, than among the general population (Curtis et al., 1994; Foley, Ehr, Raza, & Devlin, 1995; Haverkos, 1991; Pust, 1992). Cocaine-dependent patients who have been exposed to TB, particularly those who inject drugs, are at high risk for developing active tuberculin disease. They therefore are a high priority group for preventive therapy (American Thoracic Society, 1992; Bloom & Murray, 1992; Centers for Disease Control [CDC], 1990a, 1990b; Haverkos, 1991; Neville et al., 1994; Perlman et al., 1995; Selwyn et al., 1992). Preventive therapy is designed to keep latent infection from progressing to clinically active disease. When taken as prescribed, preventive treatment (chemoprophylaxis with isoniazid [INH]) has been effective in 90–100% of cases in preventing the disease (American Thoracic Society, 1992, 1994; Bloom & Murray, 1992; Davidson & Quoc Le, 1992). However, it is estimated that between 20% and 80% of all patients in the United States do not comply with the regimen (CDC, 1992; Nazar-Stewart & Nolan, 1992; Novick, 1992). Drug and alcohol abusers have been identified as high risk for noncompliance (Marwick, 1992; Nazar-Stewart & Nolan, 1992). There are data to indicate that drug-abusing patients fail to comply with the TB-treatment regimen primarily because of a return to active use of drugs, particularly cocaine (Selwyn et al., 1992). Noncompliance with the treatment regimen can lead to treatment failure; drug-resistant disease, which is continuing to rise dangerously in the United States (e.g., Bloom & Murray, 1992); continuing transmission of infection; and increasing disability and death (American Thoracic Society, 1992; Snider & Roper, 1992). One of the greatest challenges of TB control is to achieve compliance with the full regimen. Identifying and implementing techniques that enhance compliance is crucial.

Cocaine Abuse and Poor Prenatal Care Among Pregnant Women

Drug abuse among pregnant women is one of the most complex, expensive, and damaging health care problems today (Andres, 1993; McLellan, 1992; Sokol, Ager, & Martier, 1992). The proportion of drug-exposed births and cocaine-positive urine samples among pregnant women vary widely across studies (CDC, 1990c; Chasnoff, Landress, & Barett, 1990; Robins, Mills, Krulewitch, & Herman, 1993). Despite many attempts, it is still difficult to determine how many pregnant women use cocaine during pregnancy or how many babies have been exposed to the drug in utero (Robins et al., 1993). There are data to indicate an association between cocaine use and low birth weight, premature delivery, premature rupture of membranes, and spontaneous abortions (Andres, 1993).

At present, it is unknown to what extent these complications are a direct effect of the drug and to what extent they are effects of lack of prenatal care, poor nutrition, and multiple infections (Robins et al., 1993). Cocaine use also has implications for the health of the woman. It increases the risk of infection, poor diet, and sexually transmitted diseases (Robins et al., 1993). Because many women who are dependent on cocaine engage in prostitution to support their habit, the risks of contracting and spreading AIDS is greatly increased (Elk et al., 1997; Elk, Mangus, Rhoades, Andres, & Grabowski, 1998). From cost-estimate studies, neonatal charges for drug-exposed babies are higher than for non-drug-exposed babies (General Accounting Office [GAO], 1990; Phibbs, Bateman, & Schwartz, 1991). National costs per year have been estimated from $385 million to $3 billion (Chasnoff, 1991; Phibbs et al., 1991). Lack of prenatal care among drug-abusing women is a significant factor in these increased neonatal costs; a large number of women who use drugs receive little or no prenatal care (Brown, 1988; Chavkin, Allen, & Oberman, 1991).

Researchers have demonstrated that by providing prenatal care and drug abuse treatment, pregnancy outcomes can be improved and the incidence of complications such as prematurity and low birth weight reduced (Allen, 1991; Finnegan, Hagan, & Kaltenbach, 1991; Finnegan & Kandall, 1992; Fitzsimmons et al., 1986; Paluzzi, Emerling, Leiva, Gazaway, & Huggins, 1995; Randall, 1991; Robins et al., 1993; Schottenfeld, Forsyth, Ball, Pakes, & Brady, 1995; Suffet & Brotman, 1984). Thus, treatments that promote a cessation of cocaine use while increasing compliance with prenatal care increase the likelihood of preventing adverse perinatal effects in the newborn, promote a healthier outcome for the woman, and decrease the costs of care to the community.

The Need for Specialized Interventions in Both Populations

In both TB-exposed individuals and pregnant women, cessation of cocaine use results in a decrease in high-risk behaviors such as criminality and prostitution, thereby decreasing the risk of sexually transmitted diseases, HIV, and AIDS and increasing prosocial and adaptive behavior (Gerstein & Harwood, 1990; McLellan, Luborsky, Woody, & O'Brien, 1982; Simpson & Savage, 1980). TB-infected patients who comply with the prophylactic TB treatment reduce the risk of developing the active disease. Pregnant women who comply with prenatal care decrease the likelihood of adverse perinatal outcomes for themselves and their baby. Therefore, it is crucial to identify interventions that result in a cessation of cocaine use and enhance compliance with the medical treatment (chemophrophylaxis in the first population, and prenatal care in the second).

As described in many of the chapters in this volume, behavioral interventions such as contingency management are effective in reducing co-caine and other illicit-drug abuse and increasing medication compliance. On the basis of that information, I adopted a treatment that combined cognitive–behavioral counseling and contingency management for the projects described below.

DESCRIPTION OF STUDIES IN TB-INFECTED COCAINE-DEPENDENT PATIENTS

Incentives, including money, have been implemented by several TB treatment centers around the country (American Thoracic Society, 1992). However, TB treatment clinics that use incentives usually do so only with patients with active disease. In addition, these incentives are not used systematically. In this section, I describe three different studies conducted by the Treatment Research Clinic of the Substance Abuse Research Center (SARC) group using different approaches, all designed to simultaneously enhance compliance with the treatment regimen and to decrease cocaine use in TB-infected cocaine-dependent patients. There are several elements common to all three studies, which I describe below.

Screening for TB

All patients in the SARC's clinic are routinely screened for TB at intake. The Mantoux technique is used with a purified protein derivative (5 tuberculin units) cutoff of 10 mm in duration to detect TB. Patients with a positive Mantoux test are referred for a chest X-ray to determine the presence of active pulmonary tuberculosis. If a chest X-ray is positive, sputum cultures also are performed. Patients with active symptoms of the disease are referred elsewhere. Patients who do not have the active disease are evaluated for preventive therapy. Results of the patient's liver function tests are screened to determine the patient's ability to tolerate chemophrophylactic treatment. In view of the high risk factor particularly with intravenous drug use, treatment is indicated in all age groups (CDC, 1990b). Although other drugs also may be effective for preventive therapy, there are currently no data available documenting the clinical efficacy of any drug other than INH, which when taken as prescribed is highly effective (American Thoracic Society, 1992, 1994). Treatment therefore consists of INH, dispensed twice a week (900 mg) by the study nurse at the clinic for a period of 6 months. Vitamin B6 is prescribed as a supplement in this potentially malnourished group because INH increases the excretion of Vitamin B6 and patients with chronic drug use may be predisposed to neuropathy (CDC, 1994). Clinicians monitor side-effects with a twice-weekly questionnaire and a monthly liver function test.

Target Population

In all three studies, participants were TB-positive patients without evidence of active tuberculin disease who required chemoprophylactic treatment with INH. All patients met the criteria of the *Diagnostic and Statistical Manual of Mental Disorders* (3rd ed. rev. [DSM-III-R]; American Psychiatric Association, 1987) for cocaine dependence and had used cocaine in the month prior to treatment entry. HIV-seropositive patients were not included in these studies because of differences in type and length of TB treatment.

Urinalysis Testing

Urine specimens collected under video surveillance were later monitored confidentially by the clinic research assistant on duty. Temperature indicators were used as a secondary means of ensuring sample validity. Specimens were immediately refrigerated after collection. Urine testing was conducted at the Neuro-Analytical Chemistry Laboratory on site. Qualitative testing was achieved with the syva enzyme multiplied immunoassay technique system and the toxi-lab thin-layer chromatographic system. The technique is carried out on syva instrumentation and may be used to test for drugs and metabolites or groups of drugs, such as amphetamines, barbiturates, benzodiazepines, cannabinoids, cocaine, methadone, methaqualone, opiates, phencyclidine, and propoxyphene. The toxi-lab system is used to test for more than 200 drugs of abuse or therapy, such as antipsychotic, antidepressant, anticonvulsant, and over-the-counter agents. These screening procedures are reviewed and discrepancies are clarified using gas and liquid chromatographic techniques. Combinations of these methods typically handle any questionable results: Specimens are split and aliquots are frozen for 1 month for retesting and confirmation.

TB Study 1: Self-Adjustment of Methadone Dose in the Treatment of TB-Positive Chronic Opiate Users

In this study, participants were 9 self-referred chronic opiate users who had applied for methadone maintenance and treatment of cocaine dependence. Three quarters were men, and the mean age was 41 years. Forty-two percent of participants were African American, 33% Hispanic, and 25% Caucasian.

Self-adjustment of methadone dose was used in a contingency management procedure, using a within-subject design. This intervention was 24 weeks long, consisting of a 2-week baseline and a 22-week contingency phase. Throughout the study, methadone was dispensed contingent on INH ingestion. No contingencies were placed on drug use during baseline. During the contingent phase, two sets of contingencies were placed on urine results: (a) Positive reinforcers: When both weekly urine samples were drug free, patients could adjust their methadone dose for the following week (within a range of 50–80 mg, in 5-mg increments); and (b) Punishers: When one or more drug samples was positive, patients receive an automatic dose decrease of 5 mg of methadone for the following week. Drug-positive samples at 40 mg resulted in an automatic discharge from the study. Participants could either elect to be referred to another clinic or begin a detoxification at the SARC clinic. (Samples were considered drug positive if they included cocaine, amphetamines, opiates, benzodiazepines, barbiturates, antipsychotics, antidepressants, and antihistamines. Missed visits, invalid urine results, and the absence of methadone also were considered drug positive.) Patients who missed scheduled visits were able to attend the clinic on another day to receive INH and methadone; however, they were not permitted to select their dose for the following week, even if their urine samples were drug free.

Only 1 patient remained in the study until its completion, and another remained in the study until INH was stopped because of raised liver functions (Week 15). The remaining 7 patients were discharged from the study because of drug-positive screens (the eventual consequence of drug use). Almost all patients complied with INH 100% of the time they remained in the treatment. Mean drug use in baseline and contingency phase for all patients is shown in Table 6.1. The proportion of drug-positive urine screens, including cocaine, decreased significantly during the contingent phase. Drug use patterns over time are illustrated in Figure 6.1. During the initial months of treatment, the rate of drug-positive urine samples decreased in response to contingency.

Compliance with INH was extremely high during the time the pa-

TABLE 6.1
Mean Drug Use in Baseline and Contingent Phase
for All Patients in Tuberculosis Study 1

Urine sample	Baseline	Contingency	t	p (two tailed)
Drug positive	.61	.38	2.470	.0068
Cocaine positive	.52	.31	2.311	.0104
Opiate positive	.33	.21	1.567	.1300
"Other" positive	.00	.08	1.635	.1000

Note. Number samples: baseline, 33; contingency, 198. From "Compliance With Tuberculosis Treatment in Methadone-Maintained Patients: Behavioral Interventions," by R. Elk, J. Grabowski, H. Rhoades, R. Spiga, J. Schmitz, and W. Jennings, 1993, *Journal of Substance Abuse Treatment, 10,* p. 374. Copyright 1993 by Elsevier Science. Reprinted with permission.

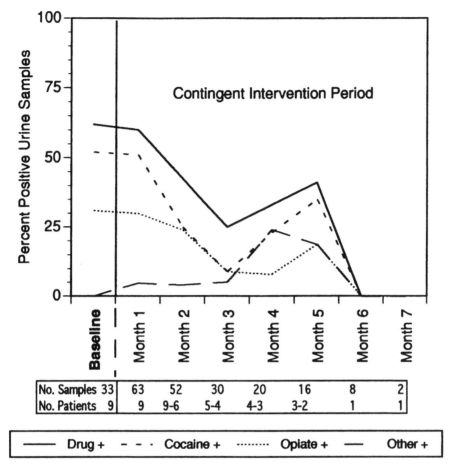

Figure 6.1. Drug use patterns as measured by percentage of drug-positive urine screens over time for patients in Tuberculosis Study 1. From "Compliance With Tuberculosis Treatment in Methadone-Maintained Patients: Behavioral Interventions," by R. Elk, J. Grabowski, H. Rhoades, R. Spiga, J. Schmitz, and W. Jennings, 1993, *Journal of Substance Abuse Treatment, 10,* p. 375. Copyright 1993 by Elsevier Science. Reprinted with permission.

tients remained in the study. However, there was a high rate of supplemental drug use, resulting in dose reductions and discharge from treatment. Despite previous data indicating that aversive contingencies often lead to a greater dropout rate than do positive reinforcers (Iguchi, Stitzer, Bigelow, & Liebson, 1988; Stitzer, Bickel, Bigelow, & Liebson, 1986), I implemented the discharge consequence because of a concern for the risk of hepatotoxicity with concomitant use of illicit drugs and INH. Patients' determination of methadone dose had previously been found effective in decreasing opiate use (e.g., Stitzer et al., 1986). However, the simultaneous implementation of this positive reinforcer with the aversive consequences proved insufficiently effective in decreasing drug use.

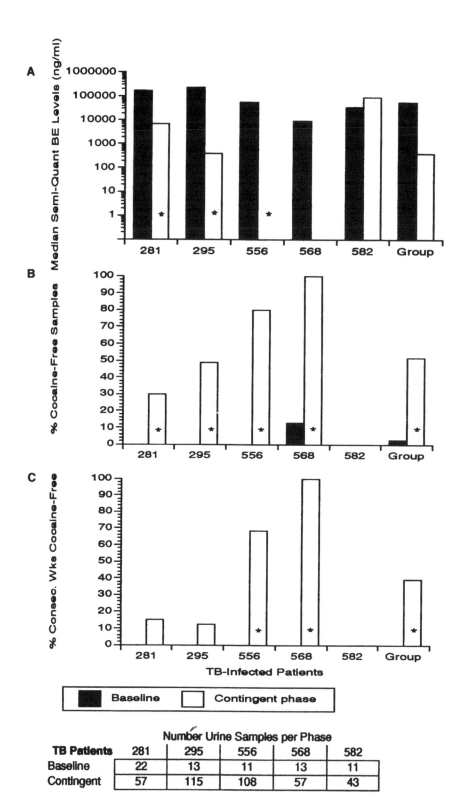

TB Patients	281	295	556	568	582
Baseline	22	13	11	13	11
Contingent	57	115	108	57	43

TB Study 2: Monetary Reinforcers in the Treatment of TB-Positive Chronic Opiate Users

This study was designed to address the unacceptably high discharge rate found in Study 1. It targeted cocaine use only because this was the most frequently abused drug. Participants in this study were 5 self-referred chronic opiate users who were found to be TB-infected during the intake process. They had applied for methadone maintenance and treatment of cocaine dependence.

A multiple baseline across participants (A-B design) consisted of a baseline and contingent intervention period. This design is particularly appropriate when a return to baseline conditions places the participant at risk (Hersen & Barlow, 1976). Patients were required to visit the clinic five times a week throughout the study. During baseline, there were no contingencies on drug use. Length of baseline varied across patients (between 3 and 6 weeks) to control for temporal and situational effects. During the contingent phase, participants received a monetary reinforcer of $12 for each successive decrease in cocaine metabolite level, a reinforcer of $15 for a cocaine-free sample, and a weekly bonus of $20 if all weekly samples per week met the above criteria. Urinalysis results were available immediately. If conditions of the contingency were met, patients were paid at the time of visit, with the bonus paid on the last day of the week. No aversive contingencies were implemented on drug use. Because methadone had already been demonstrated as an effective reinforcer in enhancing compliance with medication (e.g., Liebson, Bigelow, & Flamer, 1973; Liebson, Tommasello, & Bigelow, 1978), it was dispensed contingent on INH ingestion.

Only 1 participant dropped out of the study. There was an extremely high rate of ingestion of INH (97.6%) during the time the participants were in the study. There was a significant decrease in the quantity of cocaine metabolite during the contingent phase in 3 of the patients and a significant increase in the rate of cocaine-free urine samples in 4 patients and in the group as a whole (Figure 6.2).

Despite the small sample size, the data using the shaping procedure and contingencies requiring abstinence from cocaine were encouraging.

Figure 6.2. (*Opposite page*) Cocaine use for tuberculosis (TB)-infected patients in TB Study 2 as measured by (A) cocaine metabolite (benzoylecognine [BE]) levels, (B) percentage of cocaine-free urine samples, and (C) percentage of consecutive weeks (Consec. Wks) of cocaine-free samples. Semi-Quant = quantitative measures that cannot be tested yet. *p < .05. From "Behavior Treatment of Cocaine-Dependent Pregnant Women and TB-Exposed Patients," by R. Elk, J. Schmitz, R. Spiga, H. Rhoades, R. Andres, and J. Grabowski, 1995, *Addictive Behavior, 20,* p. 538. Copyright 1995 by Elsevier Science. Reprinted with permission.

Application of this procedure among a larger sample was planned at this point.

TB Study 3: Monetary Reinforcers in the Treatment of TB-Positive Cocaine-Dependent Patients

This large sample study was designed based on results from the small sample studies described above. Contingency management interventions were found effective in enhancing compliance with the medication regimen and in decreasing cocaine use.

Participants in this ongoing study are TB-infected patients with a primary diagnosis of cocaine dependence or opiate and cocaine dependence entering treatment for drug use ($N = 26$). Forty-six percent of participants are African American, 36% Caucasian, and 18% Hispanic, with a mean age of 39 years. Approximately 71% are skilled or semiskilled workers.

Following stratification on cocaine use at intake (positive or negative for cocaine), participants are randomly assigned to one of three treatment conditions. Patients in all three groups receive the same baseline treatment, including behaviorally based drug counseling twice a week; TB education and treatment, including directly observed therapy of the twice-weekly INH; and HIV pre- and posttest counseling. In addition to the baseline treatment, participants in Group A are reinforced for each urine specimen that is cocaine free ($18). An additional weekly bonus of $20 is earned if all three urine specimens per week are cocaine free. Patients in Group B are reinforced for each urine specimen that is lower in cocaine metabolite levels than that of the previous specimen ($15) and for each urine specimen that is cocaine free ($18). An additional weekly reinforcer of $20 is earned if all three required specimens per week meet the conditions for a decrease or cessation in cocaine use. There are no contingencies on drug use for patients in Group C. This is the control group for the main effects of cocaine intervention. In all groups, randomization to treatment condition follows stratification on drug status at intake.

This study was still ongoing at the time this chapter was prepared; therefore, only preliminary data on 26 participants are available, and data for the two contingent groups are combined and compared with the control group. Significantly more patients in the contingent groups (80%) remained in treatment, compared with the control group (34%; $p = .017$). Patients in the contingent groups had (close to statistically significant) higher rates of cocaine-free urine samples (71%) compared with the control group (45%; $p = .081$; Figure 6.3). Compliance with INH (calculated as the total number of doses ingested over the total prescribed for each patient, usually 48 doses unless INH is stopped temporarily) was significantly

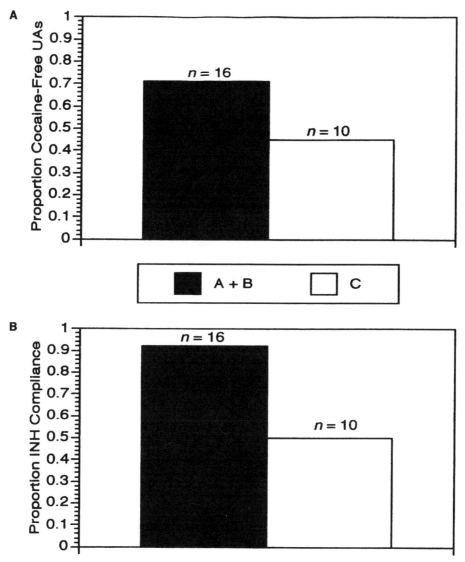

Figure 6.3. (A) Cocaine use as measured by the proportion of cocaine-free urine samples for contingent groups (A + B) versus a control group (C; *p* = .081) and (B) compliance with chemoprophyaxis with isoniazid (INH) treatment (total number of doses ingested over total number prescribed) for the contingent groups (A + B) versus a control group (C; *p* = .003). UAs = urine samples.

higher in the contingent groups (92%) than in the control group (50%; *p* = .003).

Preliminary analyses of data indicate adjunctive contingency management interventions increase compliance with the medication regimen and may increase cocaine abstinence. These studies are nearing completion, and final data will be presented at that time.

DESCRIPTION OF STUDIES WITH PREGNANT COCAINE-DEPENDENT PATIENTS

In this section, I describe three consecutive studies clinicians at SARC conducted as designed to simultaneously enhance compliance with prenatal care and to decrease cocaine use in pregnant cocaine-dependent women. There are several elements common to all studies.

Common Elements

Baseline Treatment

All participants received the baseline treatment, including prenatal care (one visit per week), behaviorally based drug counseling (two individual sessions and one group session per week), prenatal and nutritional education (monthly), and HIV pre- and posttest counseling and testing (every 3 months). In addition, elements essential to the effective recruitment and retention of pregnant drug-dependent women were incorporated (Elk et al., 1997, 1998). This included, for example, a supportive, nonjudgmental atmosphere, free transportation to all required visits, and child care during appointments.

Target Population

In all three studies, participants were pregnant women who met the *DSM-III-R* criteria for cocaine dependence and were currently using cocaine.

Urinalysis Testing

Urinalysis testing was conducted in the same manner as described for the TB studies. Samples were obtained at each of the patient's clinic appointments (three per week).

Pregnancy Study 1: Cocaine-Dependent Pregnant Women

Participants in this study were 7 pregnant cocaine-dependent women, 4 with a primary diagnosis of cocaine dependence, and 3 who met criteria for opiate and cocaine dependence. All participants had more than 50% cocaine-positive urine screens during the baseline period of study. The mean age of the participants was 29 years, with more than half having obtained less than a high school education. Three participants were Caucasian, 3 African American, and 1 Hispanic.

A multiple baseline across participants (A-B) design consisting of a baseline and contingent intervention period was used. Patients were required to visit the clinic three times a week (twice-weekly visits to the drug clinic and weekly visits to the prenatal clinic). During baseline, there were no contingencies on drug use. During the contingent phase, participants received a monetary reinforcer of $10 for each successive decrease in cocaine metabolite level, a reinforcer of $12 for a cocaine-free sample, and a weekly bonus of $15 if all samples per week met the above criteria. Because of staff shortages, patients who met the conditions received reinforcement at their next visit rather than immediately as in the TB studies described above. Time in the study varied depending on the gestational week at intake, with patients remaining in treatment until the end of pregnancy.

All pregnant patients remained in treatment until delivery, with a mean duration in treatment of 16 weeks (range 3–31 weeks). Patients could earn the weekly bonus as a reinforcement for compliance with scheduled prenatal visits and only if all required specimens for the week met criteria. Compliance with prenatal care was defined as the proportion of attendance at scheduled prenatal clinic visits. Attendance was higher during the contingency phase compared with baseline in 4 patients and for the group as a whole (83% in contingency phase vs. 66% in baseline phase). This increase in attendance was statistically significant in 2 patients. Overall compliance with prenatal care throughout the study was high, with a mean rate for the group of 72.5%. There was a decrease in median cocaine metabolite levels in 5 patients and in the group as a whole (statistically significant in 2 patients; Figure 6.4). There was an increase in cocaine-free samples in 6 of the 7 patients and the group of pregnant patients as a whole (significant in 3 patients). Consecutive cocaine-free weeks, a strict criterion for measuring abstinence, were defined as those in which all three samples per week in each of the adjoining weeks were cocaine free. Three of the pregnant patients and the pregnant group as a whole had an increase in consecutive cocaine-free weeks (statistically significant in 1 patient). Because the length of time patients were in the contingent intervention period varied widely, the number of urine samples collected during the contingent intervention period differed greatly, producing some statistically significant individual-patient changes, whereas others that appeared robust were not significant.

Adjunctive contingency management intervention was associated with excellent treatment retention. Additionally, it improved the rate of cocaine abstinence in several of the participants. It is possible the effects were not as strong in this study because of the delay in receipt of the reinforcer.

Pregnancy Study 2: Preventing Relapse to Cocaine Use and Complying With Prenatal Care

This study was designed to determine the effects of adjunctive contingency management intervention on maintaining abstinence from co-

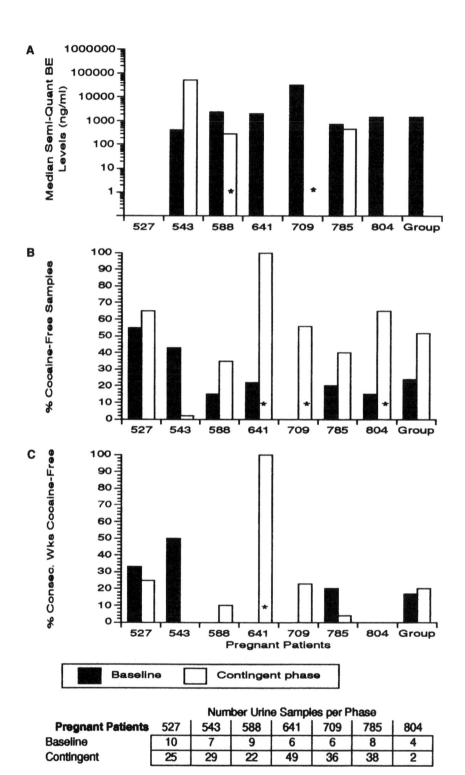

	Number Urine Samples per Phase						
Pregnant Patients	527	543	588	641	709	785	804
Baseline	10	7	9	6	6	8	4
Contingent	25	29	22	49	36	38	2

caine and enhancing prenatal care in cocaine-dependent women who had ceased cocaine use prior to entering treatment. Participants were 12 pregnant women who reported having used cocaine during their current pregnancy but had ceased use of the drug at least 30 days prior to entering the treatment study. Fifty-eight percent of the patients were African American, 8% Hispanic, and 33% Caucasian. Most patients were not married. Although the majority of patients had completed high school, most were currently unemployed. Twenty-five percent were in their third or fourth pregnancy, and 67% had had more than four previous pregnancies. Cocaine was the primary drug of abuse for 92% of the patients. Twenty-five percent of patients had used cocaine regularly (at least three times a week) for 1–5 years, 33% had used cocaine regularly for 6–10 years, and 33% had used it regularly for more than 10 years.

All participants received the baseline treatment as described for Pregnancy Study 1 and were randomly assigned to one of two treatment groups. Participants in Group A received an adjunctive contingency management intervention designed to reinforce both cocaine abstinence and compliance with prenatal care. Participants could earn a monetary reinforcer of $18 for each cocaine-free urine sample and an additional reinforcer of $20 for attending all three sessions each week (including the perinatal visit) and for remaining cocaine free for all three visits, thereby reinforcing for attendance as well as consecutive cocaine-free urine specimens. Participants in Group B received the baseline treatment alone.

The four outcomes measured are shown in Table 6.2. There were high rates of retention in the study (average of 82% of participants in both groups combined) and abstinence from cocaine (average of 99% of samples cocaine free), regardless of group. A nonsignificant trend was found for attendance at prenatal visits, with patients in Group A showing a higher rate of attendance at prenatal visits compared with patients in Group B ($t = 2.22$, $p = 0.77$). None of the patients in Group A experienced adverse perinatal outcomes, compared with 67% of the patients in Group B ($\chi^2 = 5.238$, $p = .022$). Two of the patients in Group A had preterm labor, and 2 other patients delivered preterm (before 37 weeks).

The participants in the current study are of particular interest because they ceased cocaine use independently prior to entering this study. More-

Figure 6.4. (Opposite page) Cocaine use for cocaine-dependent pregnant women in Pregnancy Study 1 as measured by (A) median quantities of cocaine metabolite, (B) percentage of cocaine-free samples, and (C) consecutive weeks (Consec. Wks) cocaine free. Semi-Quant = quantitative measures that cannot be tested yet. *$p < .05$. From "Behavior Treatment of Cocaine-Dependent Pregnant Women and TB-Exposed Patients," by R. Elk, J. Schmitz, R. Spiga, H. Rhoades, R. Andres, and J. Grabowski, 1995, *Addictive Behavior, 20*, p. 539. Copyright 1995 by Elsevier Science. Reprinted with permission.

TABLE 6.2
Clinical Outcomes for Patients in Pregnancy Study 2

Outcome	Group A (n = 6)	Group B (n = 6)	p
No. of patients retained in study	5	4	.210
Proportion cocaine-free urine samples	1.00	.98	.340
Proportion compliant with prenatal visits	1.00	.83	.077
No. of patients experiencing any of the four adverse perinatal outcomes[a]	0	4	.022

Note. From "Cessation of Cocaine Use During Pregnancy: Effects of Contingency Management Interventions on Maintaining Abstinence and Complying With Prenatal Care," by R. Elk, L. Mangus, H. Rhoades, R. Andres, and J. Grabowski, 1998, *Addictive Behavior, 23,* p. 62. Copyright 1998 by Elsevier Science. Reprinted with permission.
[a]Includes preterm delivery, low birth weight, preterm labor, and premature rupture of the membranes.

over, results from this study indicate that maintenance of cocaine abstinence, as well as retention in the treatment program, can be achieved in this population with a behaviorally based baseline treatment, without the need for monetary reinforcers used in more intensive treatment. Adjunctive contingency management intervention increased the rate of compliance with prenatal care, with a concomitant improvement in perinatal outcome. This finding has important implications for cost-effective treatment and the prevention of adverse perinatal outcome. In addition to the obvious health benefits for both woman and child, this finding may have important economic benefits.

Pregnancy Study 3: Monetary Reinforcers in the Treatment of Pregnant Cocaine-Dependent Women

This large sample study was designed based on the preliminary data provided in Pregnancy Studies 1 and 2. Contingency management interventions were found to be effective in enhancing compliance with prenatal visits and in decreasing cocaine use.

Participants were 28 pregnant women who reported having used cocaine during the 30 days prior to entering the treatment study. Fifty-seven percent of the patients were African American, 17% Hispanic, and 26% Caucasian. Twenty-three percent were married at treatment entry, and 46% of the patients had completed high school. Sixty percent of the patients had a pattern of employment in the past 3 years, and 34% were currently employed. Forty percent had been pregnant at least four times.

Two contingency management interventions as adjuncts to baseline treatment were compared with baseline treatment alone. Following stratification on referral source, patients are randomly assigned to one of three groups, all of which received the baseline treatment. In addition, patients in Group A received a reinforcer of $18 for each cocaine-free urine sample

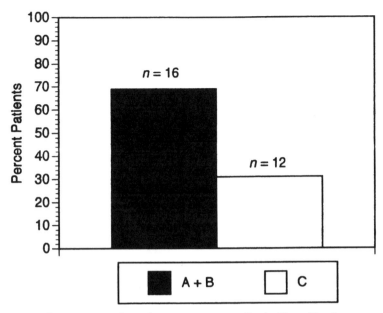

Figure 6.5. Percentage of contingency group patients (A + B) who completed treatment as compared with percentage in control group (C) who completed treatment (*p* = .027).

provided, and an additional $20 if all three urine samples required per week were cocaine free. Patients in Group B were reinforced for each successive decrease in cocaine metabolite ($15) as well as the higher magnitude reinforcer for cocaine abstinence as in Group A ($18). They received an additional reinforcer ($20) if all three urine samples required per week demonstrated a decrease in cocaine metabolite or were cocaine free. Group C received baseline treatment with no contingencies on drug use.

This study is currently under way and therefore only preliminary data are presented. Significantly more patients in the two groups receiving adjunctive contingency management intervention completed treatment (69%) compared with those in the control group (31%; *p* = .027; Figure 6.5). There was a higher rate of abstinence from cocaine in patients in Group A, although this did not reach statistical significance. There was a close to significant difference in the number of patients in Group A (75%) who had none of the four selected risk factors commonly attributed to cocaine use (preterm delivery, low birth weight, preterm labor, premature rupture of the membranes) than the number of patients in Groups B and C combined (27%; *p* = .09).

These strategies are critical because patients receiving adjunctive contingency-management intervention had improved rates of retention in treatment, which in turn is associated with improved outcome (higher rates of compliance with prenatal care and improved perinatal outcome). This study is near completion, and final data will be available at that time.

CONCLUSION

Data from these studies indicate that adjunctive contingency management intervention is effective in simultaneously decreasing drug use and increasing compliance with a medical regimen in drug-dependent populations who have concomitant medical problems. Similar trends were found in two divergent groups of cocaine-dependent patients—pregnant women and TB-infected men and women. These interventions are currently being investigated in other drug-dependent populations who require treatment with medications (e.g., HIV-infected women who are placed on combination antriretroviral therapy to slow the clinical progression of the disease).

These findings have important implications for cost-effective treatment of drug abuse as well as the prevention of adverse medical consequences, such as minimizing perinatal risk, preventing onset of tuberculosis, and slowing the progression of HIV disease (Elk et al., 1995). In addition to the obvious health benefits for the patient, there are obvious health and economic benefits to the community.

In designing contingency management interventions, several important factors need to be considered. First, the baseline treatment provided to the study population should be determined. For example, in treating drug-dependent pregnant women, elements essential to the effective recruitment and retention must be incorporated, such as a woman-sensitive treatment program, provision of transportation and child care, and prenatal care (Elk et al., 1997, 1998). Second, the adjunctive contingency management interventions can and should be directed at the behaviors requiring adjustment. For example, for pregnant cocaine-dependent women who ceased using cocaine prior to entering treatment, contingency management interventions were effective in increasing compliance with prenatal care, resulting in a decrease in adverse perinatal outcomes. Thus, in certain populations, it is necessary to target multiple problem behaviors, whereas in other populations, targeting one specific behavior is needed to provide optimal treatment outcome. Systematic study of such interventions is needed, building both on findings in the literature and on the specific needs of the population. Promising interventions can result not only in a decrease in drug use but also in an increase in other health-related behaviors.

REFERENCES

Allen, M. (1991, May). *Perinatal outcome after intense prenatal care for chemically dependent women.* Paper presented at the annual meeting of the American College of Obstetricians and Gynecologists, New Orleans, LA.

American Psychiatric Association. (1987). *Diagnostic and statistical manual of mental disorders* (3rd ed., rev.). Washington, DC: Author

American Thoracic Society. (1992). Control of tuberculosis in the United States. *American Review of Respiratory Diseases, 146,* 1623–1633.

American Thoracic Society. (1994). Treatment of tuberculosis infection in adults and children. *American Journal of Respiratory and Critical Care Medicine, 149,* 1359–1374.

Andres, R. (1993). Social and illicit drug use in pregnancy. In R. K. Creasy & R. Resnick (Eds.), *Maternal–fetal medicine* (4th ed., pp. 145–164). Philadelphia: Saunders.

Bloom, B. R., & Murray, C. J. (1992). Tuberculosis: Commentary on a reemergent killer. *Science, 257,* 1055–1064.

Brown, S. S. (Ed.). (1988). *Prenatal care: Reaching mothers, reaching infant.* Washington, DC: National Academy Press.

Centers for Disease Control. (1990a). Guidelines for preventing the transmission of tuberculosis in health-care settings, with special focus on HIV-related issues. *Morbidity and Mortality Weekly Report, 39,* 153–156.

Centers for Disease Control. (1990b). Screening for tuberculosis and tuberculosis infection in high-risk populations and the use of preventive therapy for tuberculosis infection in the United States: Recommendation of the Advisory Committee for Elimination of Tuberculosis (ACET). *Morbidity and Mortality Weekly Report, 39,* 1–12.

Centers for Disease Control. (1990c). Current trends: Statewide prevalence of illegal drug use by pregnant women—Rhode Island. *Morbidity and Mortality Weekly Report, 39,* 225–227.

Centers for Disease Control. (1992). Meeting the challenge of multidrug-resistant tuberculosis. Summary of a conference. *Morbidity and Mortality Weekly Report, 41,* 51–57.

Centers for Disease Control. (1994). *TB care guide: Highlights from core curriculum on tuberculosis.* Atlanta, GA: U.S. Department of Health and Human Services.

Chasnoff, I. J. (1991). Drugs, alcohol, pregnancy and the neonate. Pay now or pay later. *Journal of the American Medical Association, 266,* 1567–1568.

Chasnoff, I. J., Landress, H. J., & Barett, M. E. (1990). The prevalence of illegal drug use or alcohol use during pregnancy and discrepancies in mandatory reporting in Pinellas County, Florida. *New England Journal of Medicine, 322,* 1202–1206.

Chavkin, W., Allen, M. H., & Oberman, M. (1991). Drug abuse and pregnancy: Some questions on public policy, clinical management and maternal and fetal rights. *Birth, 18,* 107–112.

Curtis, R., Friedman, S. R., Neaigus, A., Jose, B., Goldstein, M., & Des Jarlais, D. C. (1994). Implications of directly observed therapy in tuberculosis control measures among IDUs. *Public Health Reports, 109,* 319–327.

Davidson, P. T., & Quoc Le, H. (1992). Drug treatment of tuberculosis. *Drugs, 43,* 651–673.

Elk, R., Grabowski, J., Rhoades, H., Spiga, R., Schmitz, J., & Jennings, W. (1993). Compliance with tuberculosis treatment in methadone-maintained patients: Behavioral interventions. *Journal of Substance Abuse Treatment, 10,* 371–382.

Elk, R., Mangus, L. G., LaSoya, R. J., Rhoades, H. M., Andres, R. L., & Grabowski, J. (1997). Behavioral interventions: Effective and adaptable for the treatment of pregnant cocaine-dependent women. *Journal of Drug Issues, 27,* 625–658.

Elk, R., Mangus, L., Rhoades, H., Andres, R., & Grabowski, J. (1998). Cessation of cocaine use during pregnancy: Effects of contingency management interventions on maintaining abstinence and complying with prenatal care. *Addictive Behaviors, 23,* 57–64.

Elk, R., Schmitz, J., Spiga, R., Rhoades, H., Andres, R., & Grabowski, J. (1995). Behavioral treatment of cocaine-dependent pregnant women and TB-exposed patients. *Addictive Behaviors, 20,* 533–542.

Finnegan, L. P., Hagan, T., & Kaltenbach, K. L. (1991). Scientific foundation of clinical practice: Opiate use in pregnant women. *Bulletin of the New York Academy of Medicine, 67,* 223–239.

Finnegan, L. P., & Kandall, S. R. (1992). Maternal and neonatal effects of alcohol and drugs. In J. H. Lowinson, P. Ruiz, R. B. Millman, & A. E. J. G. Langford (Eds.), *Substance abuse: A comprehensive textbook* (2nd ed., pp. 628–656). Baltimore: Williams & Wilkins.

Fitzsimmons, J., Tunis, S., Webster, D., Ezes, J., Wapner, R., & Finnegan, L. P. (1986). Pregnancy in a drug-abusing population. *American Journal of Drug and Alcohol Abuse, 12,* 247–255.

Foley, M. E., Ehr, A. P., Raza, B., & Devlin, C. J. (1995). Tuberculosis surveillance in a therapeutic community. *Journal of Addictive Diseases, 14,* 55–65.

General Accounting Office. (1990). *Drug-exposed infants: A generation at risk* (Pub. No. GAOHRD-90-138). Washington, DC: U.S. Government Printing Office.

Gerstein, D., & Harwood, H. (Eds.). (1990). *Treating drug problems* (Vol. 1). Washington, DC: National Academy Press.

Haverkos, H. W. (1991). Infectious diseases and drug abuse: Prevention and treatment in the drug abuse treatment system. *Journal of Substance Abuse Treatment, 8,* 269–275.

Hersen, M. Z., & Barlow, D. H. (1976). *Single-case experimental designs: Strategies for studying behavior change.* Oxford, England: Pergamon Press.

Iguchi, M., Stitzer, M. L., Bigelow, G. E., & Liebson, I. A. (1988). Contingency management in methadone-maintenance: Effects of reinforcing and aversive consequences on illicit polydrug use. *Drug and Alcohol Dependence, 22,* 1–7.

Liebson, I. A., Bigelow, G., & Flamer, R. (1973). Alcoholism among methadone patients: A specific treatment method. *American Journal of Psychiatry, 130,* 483–485.

Liebson, I. A., Tommasello, A., & Bigelow, G. E. (1978). A behavioral treatment of alcoholic methadone patients. *Annals of Internal Medicine, 89,* 342–344.

Marwick, C. (1992). Do worldwide outbreaks mean tuberculosis once again becomes 'captain of all these men of death'? *Journal of the American Medical Association, 267*, 1174–1175.

McLellan, A. T. (1992). Measurement issues in the evaluation of experimental treatment intervention. In M. M. Kilbey & K. Asghar (Eds.), *Methodological issues in epidemiological, prevention, and treatment research on drug-exposed women and their children* (NIH Research Monograph 117, DHHS Pub. No. ADM 92-1881, pp. 18–30). Washington, DC: U.S. Government Printing Office.

McLellan, A. T., Luborsky, L., Woody, G. E., & O'Brien, C. P. (1982). Is treatment for substance abuse effective? *Journal of the American Medical Association, 247*, 1423–1427.

Nazar-Stewart, V., & Nolan, C. M. (1992). Results of a directly observed intermittent isoniazid preventive therapy program in a shelter for homeless men. *American Review of Respiratory Disease, 146*(1), 57–60.

Neville, K., Bromberg, A., Bromberg, R., Bonk, S., Hanna, B. A., & Rom, W. N. (1994). The third epidemic-multidrug-resistant tuberculosis. *Chest, 105*, 45–48.

Novick, L. F. (1992). Tuberculosis in New York: Rapid rise of a preventable disease. *New York State Journal of Medicine, 92*, 293–294.

Paluzzi, P. A., Emerling, J., Leiva, J., Gazaway, P., & Huggins, G. (1995). Impact of an enhanced model of prenatal care for substance abusers in a comprehensive treatment program. In L. S. Harris (Ed.), *Problems of drug dependence, 1994: Proceedings of the 56th annual scientific meeting, the College on Problems of Drug Dependence. Vol. 2: Abstracts* (NIDA Research Monograph 153, p. 181). Washington, DC: U.S. Government Printing Office.

Perlman, D. C., Salomon, N., Perkins, M. P., Yancovitz, S., Paone, D., & Des Jarlias, D. C. (1995). Tuberculosis in drug users. *Clinical Infectious Diseases, 21*, 1253–1264.

Phibbs, C. S., Bateman, D. A., & Schwartz, R. M. (1991). The neonatal cost of maternal cocaine use. *Journal of the American Medical Association, 266*, 1567–1568.

Pust, R. E. (1992). Tuberculosis in the 1990's: Resurgence, regimens, and resources. *Southern Medical Journal, 85*, 584–593.

Randall, T. (1991). Intensive prenatal care may deliver healthy babies to pregnant drug abusers. *Journal of the American Medical Association, 265*, 2773–2774.

Robins, L. N., Mills, J. L., Krulewitch, C., & Herman, A. A. (1993). Effects of in utero exposure to street drugs. *American Journal of Public Health, 83*(Suppl.), 3–31.

Schottenfeld, R. S., Forsyth, B., Ball, S., Pakes, J., & Brady, C. (1995). Primary care interventions for cocaine abusing pregnant women. In L. S. Harris (Ed)., *Problems of drug dependence, 1994: Proceedings of the 56th annual scientific meeting, the College on Problems of Drug Dependence* (NIDA Research Monograph 153, p. 176). Washington, DC: U.S. Government Printing Office.

Selwyn, P. A., Sckell, B. M., Alcabes, P., Friedland, G. H., Klein, R. S., & Schoenbaum, E. E. (1992). High risk active tuberculosis in HIV-infected drug users with cutaneous anergy. *Journal of the American Medical Association, 268,* 504–509.

Simpson, D., & Savage, L. (1980). Drug abuse treatment remission and outcomes. *Archives of General Psychiatry, 42,* 1043–1049.

Snider, D. E., & Roper, W. L. (1992). The new tuberculosis. *New England Journal of Medicine, 326,* 703–705.

Sokol, R. J., Ager, J. W., & Martier, S. (1992). Methodological issues in obtaining and managing substance abuse information from prenatal patients. In M. M. Kilbey & K. Asghar (Eds.), *Methodological issues in epidemiological, prevention, and treatment research on drug-exposed women and their children* (pp. 80–97). Washington, DC: U.S. Government Printing Office.

Stitzer, M., Bickel, W. K., Bigelow, G. E., & Liebson, I. (1986). Effects of methadone dose contingencies on urinalysis test results of poly-abusing methadone maintenance patients. *Drug and Alcohol Dependence, 18,* 341–348.

Suffet, F., & Brotman, R. (1984). A comprehensive care program for pregnant addicts: Obstetrical, neonatal, and child development outcomes. *International Journal of the Addictions, 19,* 199–219.

IV

TREATMENT OF OPIOID ABUSERS

7

COUPONS–VOUCHERS AS A STRATEGY FOR INCREASING TREATMENT ENTRY FOR OPIATE-DEPENDENT INJECTION DRUG USERS

JAMES L. SORENSEN, CARMEN L. MASSON, AND AMY L. COPELAND

One consistent finding in the epidemiological literature is that only a small percentage of injection drug users (IDUs) find their way into drug abuse treatment programs. Estimates are that only 15–20% of all drug abusers are enrolled in drug abuse treatment at any given time (Schuster, 1988). In the National AIDS Demonstration Research Project, researchers found that more than 40% of the 20,000 IDUs they contacted reported never having participated in drug abuse treatment (Liebman, Knezek, Coughey, & Hua, 1993).

In recent years, the responsibility of drug abuse treatment programs

We appreciate the assistance of Martin Iguchi and Wendee Wechsberg, whose editorial suggestions greatly improved this chapter and who provided copies of the coupons used in their studies. We also are grateful for the assistance of Loreen Nichols and Dennis R. Wong, who provided copies of the coupons used in their study in Oregon. Preparation of this chapter was supported in part by Grants R18DA06097, R01DA08753, P50DA09235, and T32DA07250 from the National Institute on Drug Abuse and by Grant R95-SF-076 from the California University-Wide AIDS Research Program.

for IDUs has expanded to include actively seeking out and motivating potential clients rather than only attending to those who present to drug abuse treatment programs (Ashery, Davis, Davis, & Ross, 1993). The emergence of HIV, tuberculosis, and other communicable diseases among IDUs has increased their visibility to public health officials, who have turned to drug abuse treatment programs for part of the solution. Drug abuse treatment programs have increasingly become less isolated as they have needed to build linkages with health programs (Levin, Trumble, Edmunds, Statman, & Petersen, 1993). Furthermore, the concept of *harm reduction* (e.g., Marlatt & Tapert, 1993) has brought to substance abuse treatment programs more sensitivity to the needs of their clients. Together, these forces have brought a new attitude to drug abuse treatment programs that emphasizes finding ways to reach out to potential clients and attract them into treatment.

In this chapter, we review the use of contingency management approaches, particularly coupon-based incentive programs, to increase IDUs' treatment-seeking behavior and actual entry into drug abuse treatment programs. We first review the use of contingency management procedures as recruitment efforts in health programs generally and then how these procedures have been applied in drug abuse treatment programs. We then focus on the use of coupons–vouchers as a way to attract clients to treatment and as a platform on which to build applied research.

CONTINGENCY MANAGEMENT RECRUITMENT STRATEGIES IN HEALTH PROGRAMS

Contingency management approaches are used to increase participation in a variety of health programs. These innovative recruitment approaches developed from a need to lower the traditional barriers to obtaining medical treatment for populations at risk for health problems. Contingencies are used to attract patients to treatment, promote healthy behaviors, and increase help seeking in a variety of health and community settings with high-risk populations.

A number of programs have used vouchers–coupons as incentives. A *voucher* is any document that provides proof that the terms of a transaction have been met, for example, a contract or a receipt (Soukhanov & Ellis, 1994). The term *coupon* refers more narrowly to a negotiable certificate that entitles the bearer to specific benefits. (Figure 7.1 provides an example of a coupon used in this context.) Coupons were exchanged for free outpatient medical visits, gifts, and prizes to increase participation and compliance with health programs. For example, Steen, Soliman, Bucyana, and Dallabetta (1996) encouraged patients exposed to sexually transmitted diseases to refer their sexual partners to medical treatment by providing cou-

FRONT

IMMEDIATE FREE HEROIN DETOXIFICATION
SAN FRANCISCO GENERAL HOSPITAL

This coupon entitles the bearer to an immediate free 21-day heroin detox at the Outpatient Heroin Detoxification Unit, San Francisco General Hospital, Building 90, Ward 92, 2460 22nd St., San Francisco, CA 94110. The coupon must be presented during the period shown below, Monday through Thursday only, except holidays, between 8:00 and 9:00 A.M. The bearer may receive free counseling/information about AIDS prevention.

*Valid for :*_____*, 198 .*
*Name:*_____*. Coupon #*___

BACK

To be eligible for the immediate, free detox,
the bearer of this coupon:

(1) must be a San Francisco resident; (2) must present the coupon with valid identification at the Outpatient Detoxification Clinic between 8:00 and 9:00 A.M., Monday through Thursday, except holidays, during the dates shown on the front of the coupon; (3) must not have been in methadone (detox or maintenance) treatment during the previous year; and (4) must present themselves for treatment with symptoms of withdrawal from heroin.

For further information call 641-0466.

Figure 7.1. From "Coupons Attract High-Risk Untreated Heroin Users Into Detoxification," by J. L. Sorensen, M. F. Costantini, T. L. Wall, and D. R. Gibson, 1993, *Drug and Alcohol Dependence, 31,* p. 248. Copyright 1993 by Elsevier Science. Reprinted with permission.

pons that could be exchanged for free medical services. Coupons redeemable for food, gifts, and discounts were also used to motivate women to seek prenatal care (Ingram, Rawls, & Moberly, 1993) and increase compliance with postpartum appointments (Smith, Weinman, Johnson, & Wait, 1990), to recruit drug-using men for screening of sexually transmitted diseases (Seidman, Sterk-Elifson, & Aral, 1994), and to increase immunization rates of young children whose families were participating in a supplemental food program (Birkhead et al., 1995). Vouchers redeemable for treatment were also used as an incentive to encourage migrant farm workers to use outpatient medical services (Slesinger & Ofstead, 1996).

In addition to vouchers or coupons, other tangible incentives have been used to encourage individuals to enroll in health programs. Incentives included gifts (Bertera, 1990; Emont & Cummings, 1992; Jeffery, Forster, Baxter, French, & Kelder, 1993; Kronenfeld et al., 1987; Stevens-Simon, O'Connor, & Bassford, 1994; Wilbur, 1983), money (Deren, Stephens, Davis, Feucht, & Tortu, 1994; Jason, Jayaraj, Blitz, Michaels, & Klett, 1990), free work-site health promotion programs (Bly, Jones, & Richardson, 1986; Breslow, Fielding, Herrman, & Wilbur, 1990; Shipley, Orleans, Wilbur, Piserchia, & McFadden, 1988), and free medical treatment (Geringer & Hinton, 1993). These incentives were effective in increasing compliance with postpartum appointments (Stevens-Simon et al., 1994) and enrolling individuals in a blood donation program (Jason, Jackson, & Obradovic, 1987), AIDS risk reduction program (Deren et al., 1994), work-site smoking cessation program (Jason et al., 1990), and a syphilis screening program for a high-risk population (Geringer & Hinton, 1993).

Although recruitment strategies differed across health or institutional settings, most were successful in attracting patients to health programs. Many of these programs developed recruitment strategies that combine incentives with other innovative approaches for increasing participation in health programs. For example, Birkhead et al. (1995) examined the effectiveness of three different interventions (escort, voucher incentives, and passive referral) on immunization rates of young children. The authors found that both escort and voucher incentive models resulted in more children immunized more rapidly than passive referral. However, because of the ease of administration, Birkhead et al. concluded that voucher incentives may be a more suitable intervention for use in institutional settings (with the addition of an escort where feasible). The findings of Birkhead et al. demonstrate that incentive approaches show promise as a method for increasing recruitment and participation in health programs.

VOUCHER–COUPON INCENTIVES TO ATTRACT DRUG ABUSERS INTO TREATMENT

Although behavioral incentives have been used to modify IDUs' behavior once in drug abuse treatment (e.g., Higgins et al., 1991; Stitzer, Iguchi, & Felch, 1992), only recently have such strategies been used to attract IDUs into treatment initially. To our knowledge, it was not until 1989 (Jackson, Rotkiewicz, Quinones, & Passannante) that researchers used coupons to attract out-of-treatment IDUs into detoxification and subsequent drug abuse treatment.

Coupon incentives have several desirable aspects. They improve recruitment rates by removing barriers to entering treatment or providing treatment that otherwise would not be available; they increase motivation to seek treatment and facilitate referrals for difficult-to-reach populations; and they are relatively easy to incorporate into existing drug abuse treatment programs.

Coupon incentive approaches circumvent common impediments to treatment entry, such as financial limitations and long waiting lists, which can interfere with a client's motivation to seek and follow through with treatment. For example, economic changes in New Jersey drug abuse treatment services in the early 1980s made it difficult for clients to enter treatment and most likely accounted for subsequent drastic reductions in detoxification admissions (Jackson et al., 1989). Indeed, many IDUs may be unwilling or unable to pay for treatment; even when cost is not an issue, most programs have long waiting lists that may discourage those seeking treatment.

Many IDUs may fear the consequences of revealing their injection drug use because of the stigma associated with needle use, especially certain subpopulations of IDUs (e.g., pregnant women). The distribution of coupons–vouchers by outreach workers to such subpopulations may serve to circumvent this problem. Outreach workers can engage participants by entering the user's world rather than requiring the user to take the first step, as described elsewhere (Brown & Needle, 1994).

Recently, several groups have used coupon incentives to recruit IDUs into drug abuse treatment programs. In five published studies and several other unpublished works (e.g., Velten et al., 1994; Lurie et al., 1993; Sibthorpe et al., 1991), researchers have cited the successful use of coupon incentives. In each of these studies, outreach workers distributed coupons for free detoxification or drug abuse treatment in areas of prevalent drug use and examined what factors predicted coupon redemption. Researchers also examined what factors predicted continuation in treatment. The five published studies are reviewed below.

Detoxification for Heroin Addiction

Jackson et al. (1989) conducted a study sponsored by the New Jersey State Department of Health to attract heroin abusers into the treatment system by offering timely free detoxification and subsequent drug abuse treatment. Trained ex-addict community health educators distributed 970 coupons for free detoxification in areas of New Jersey where drug use was prevalent. Inclusion criteria were current heroin use and noninvolvement with drug abuse treatment within the last year. Eighty-four percent of the coupons were redeemed (see Table 7.1 for a summary of all the studies discussed in this chapter). Those IDUs who redeemed the coupons tended to be African American and male. A sizable number of the IDUs who redeemed the coupons had never been in treatment before; of those who had been in treatment, 55% had one or more treatment attempts.

Approximately one fourth of the IDUs continued in treatment after the detoxification (defined as additional detoxification attempts or methadone maintenance). Older IDUs were more likely to remain in treatment, and women were more likely than men to remain in treatment. Hispanic ethnicity negatively predicted treatment retention.

Drug Abuse Treatment for IDUs

Wechsberg, Smith, and Harris-Adeeyo (1992) distributed coupons for drug abuse treatment as part of a communitywide educational effort to reduce the risk of HIV infection in IDUs and their sexual partners. Indigenous recovering outreach workers targeted inner-city, public housing areas of North Carolina that were 80–90% African American. The coupon included the logo, address, and phone number where the coupon was to be redeemed; telephone numbers for both the treatment program and the AIDS hotline; and an expiration date (allowing for control of the flow of coupon redeemers). The coupon resembled money in look and size, giving a clear message that there was value to the coupon. Two hundred coupons were given out each year over a 2-year period with 92 and 108 coupons redeemed for treatment in the 2 years of the study, averaging 50% redemption. Coupons had a 30-day expiration date to enter treatment. The majority of coupon redeemers were IDUs, African American, male, and first-time treatment clients, and the mean age was 33 years. The average length of stay in treatment was approximately 2 months.

Heroin Detoxification for IDUs at Risk for HIV

Sorensen, Costantini, Wall, and Gibson (1993) sought to determine how effective coupon distribution was in reaching IDUs at risk for HIV and how the coupon recipients fared in treatment relative to other drug abuse treatment participants. In areas of San Francisco, California, known to be high in drug use, outreach workers distributed approximately 400 coupons redeemable for immediate, free, 21-day heroin detoxification at the San Francisco General Hospital Outpatient Detoxification Clinic. Those recruited into the study met the following inclusion criteria: current heroin use, San Francisco residency, and no drug abuse treatment in the last year. The coupon had several desirable features that differed from the Wechsberg et al. (1992) study coupon, including the following: (a) The title "immediate free heroin detoxification" provided a clear message about

TABLE 7.1

Summary of Studies Using Coupon Incentives

Study	Purpose	Coupon value	Distribution method	No. distributed	Redemption rate	Redeemer characteristics	Treatment retention
Jackson et al. (1989)	Attract heroin IDUs into detoxification, retain IDUs in treatment, AIDS education	Free 21-day detoxification	Male community health educators distributed in areas of high drug use in New Jersey to heroin IDUs	970	84.0%	79% men, 66% African American, 45% no prior treatment	28% remained in treatment, older age, women more likely, Hispanics less likely, two program sites more likely
Wechsberg et al. (1992)	Reduce risk of HIV infection with treatment coupons and communitywide education	Free drug abuse treatment	Minority, indigenous outreach workers distributed in public housing neighborhoods	400	50.0%	Year 1: 83% IDUs, 74% men, 80% African American Year 2: 64% IDUs, 57% men, 67% African American	Average length of stay in treatment approximately 2 months (range = 1 week to 7 months)
Sorensen et al. (1993)	Reach drug users at high risk for HIV: How do coupon recipients perform in treatment?	Free 21-day detoxification	Outreach workers distributed in areas of high drug use in San Francisco (CA) to heroin IDUs	≈400	59.5%	72% men, 69% non-White, 28% no prior treatment, 39% recently shared needles	43% returned for treatment at a later date
Bux et al. (1993)	Identify what IDUs would redeem a coupon, determine whether 21-day or 90-day detox is preferable	Free 21-day or 90-day detoxification to be redeemed in 7–30 days	Outreach works recruited IDUs in areas of high drug use, interviewed in field office, and offered coupons	4,390	Total: 58.5% 21 day: 56.9% 90 day: 59.9%	77% men, 44% no prior treatment, 45% HIV+, 65% African American, 26% Hispanic, 78% daily heroin injection, 54% no previous detoxification, 46% no previous drug abuse treatment	(not stated)
Sibthorpe et al. (1996)	Reach cohort of out-of-treatment IDUs	Free outpatient drug treatment to be redeemed within 30 days	Outreach workers, word of mouth, and clinic and social service referrals in Portland (OR)	225	29.0%	84% Caucasian, 79% more likely to have expressed interest in treatment of initial interview	14% remained in treatment for 6 months

Note. IDUs = injection drug users; HIV+ = HIV positive.

COUPONS–VOUCHERS AND TREATMENT ENTRY   153

what the coupon could be redeemed for; (b) clear instructions were given about how to redeem the coupon and who was eligible to redeem it; and (c) the actual size of the coupon was 2.5 × 4.5 in. (6.35 × 11.43 cm), small enough to fit easily into a wallet, pocket, or purse (see Figure 7.1).

Of the approximate 400 coupons that were distributed, 238 (59.5%) were redeemed. The coupon recipients were significantly older (40 years vs. 37 years), more likely to be male, and more likely to be ethnic minorities when compared with 1,129 clients referred to treatment from other sources in the community. A greater percentage of the coupon recipients had never been in treatment and were more likely to have shared needles in the previous 30 days. There were no significant differences between the groups on mean days in treatment (coupon group: $M = 15.6$, $SD = 5.5$ vs. noncoupon group: $M = 15.7$, $SD = 6.6$) or in discharge status (coupon group = 44.5% completed treatment vs. noncoupon group = 49% completed treatment). Forty-three percent of the coupon recipients returned for later treatment.

Detoxification for New Jersey IDUs

Bux, Iguchi, Lidz, Baxter, and Platt (1993) sought to determine what characteristics predicted whether coupons would be redeemed for free detoxification, and whether coupons for a 90-day detoxification would be redeemed at higher rates than those for a 21-day detoxification. IDUs were recruited by community-based outreach workers in areas in Newark and Jersey City, New Jersey, identified as having a high prevalence of drug use. Inclusion criteria were current injection drug use and noninvolvement with treatment programs for the previous 6 months. The participants were given a coupon for free, immediate, 21-day or 90-day (randomly determined) outpatient detoxification following a research interview and optional HIV test for which they were paid.

Some desirable features unique to this coupon were (a) a serial number that provided a chance to carefully track the distribution and redemption patterns of coupons; (b) warnings that explained the coupon did not guarantee treatment and was not transferable; and (c) a space for both program staff and participant to sign the coupon. Of the 4,840 IDUs recruited, 4,390 accepted coupons and 2,570 (58.5%) proceeded to redeem the coupons for treatment. As researchers predicted, the 90-day coupons were redeemed at a significantly higher rate (59.9%) than the 21-day coupons (56.9%).

The study was successful in recruiting into treatment a number of IDUs who had never been in treatment (43.6% of those who redeemed coupons). The group of IDUs that redeemed the coupons had a significantly higher percentage of Hispanics and significantly fewer African Americans as compared with the nonredeemers. There were no differences between the two groups in gender or age, although women were relatively underrepresented in recruitment (24% of the total sample). Nonredeemers reported homosexual behavior significantly more often than did coupon redeemers.

Coupon redeemers had higher rates of HIV seroprevalence (44.9%) than nonredeemers (36.9%) and had a significantly longer history of injection drug use (M = 13.9 years, SD = 8.5 vs. M = 13 years, SD = 8.6). Most nonredeemers had never received methadone maintenance, and more than half had no previous detoxification treatment. Coupon redeemers were more likely to have had previous treatment, reported more frequent drug injections and more heroin use, but were less likely to use cocaine alone. In addition, they were more likely to engage in AIDS prevention behaviors, such as not sharing needles and using bleach to clean needles.

Drug Abuse Treatment for Oregon IDUs

Sibthorpe, Fleming, Tesselaar, Gould, and Nichols (1996) provided coupons for free, outpatient drug abuse treatment to IDUs in Portland, Oregon. IDUs were recruited by outreach workers and through a referral from health department clinics and local social service agencies. To be included in the study, IDUs must have injected drugs in the last 6 months and not have been in drug treatment in the last 30 days. Additional desirable features of this coupon included (a) instructions on what to say to be given priority for immediate treatment, (b) the telephone numbers of several help lines, and (c) instructions to the redeeming agencies. Although 824 IDUs participated in the study, only 225 (27%) accepted coupons. Twenty-nine percent of those who accepted coupons redeemed them, and 14% of these individuals remained in treatment for 6 months. Coupon redeemers were more likely to be Caucasian and more likely to express interest in drug abuse treatment at the time of the initial interview than nonredeemers.

Cross-Study Comparisons

These studies help us understand individual differences in IDUs that determine whether they respond to voucher- or coupon-based incentives or not. With the exception of Sibthorpe et al. (1996), researchers using coupon incentives were successful in reaching a significant proportion of IDUs who had never been in treatment. The challenge remains, however, to retain IDUs in treatment subsequent to initial detoxification when there is a shortage of longer term treatment slots available. Perhaps, as Sorensen et al. (1993) stated, coupon incentive strategies may be particularly effective in recruiting IDUs when an area acquires new treatment slots.

Overall redemption rates for the Wechsberg et al. (1992), Sorensen et al. (1993), Bux et al. (1993), and Sibthorpe et al. (1996) studies were substantially lower than that of the Jackson et al. (1989) study. One explanation for this difference is that the study by Jackson et al. had fewer restrictions. To accommodate for program restrictions, Sorensen et al. distributed coupons with expiration dates that made them invalid within 1 week. Similarly, the coupons in the Wechsberg et al. and Sibthorpe et al. studies were valid for only 30 days following receipt. The careful tracking procedure used by Bux et al. precluded anyone but the original recipient from redeeming his or her coupon. Other explanations are that the number of participants initially recruited in the Bux et al. study may have been inflated by those who were only interested in payment for the research interview. Finally, at the time Jackson et al. conducted their study, the area of New Jersey had been without free treatment for many years.

Women were underrepresented in distribution and redemption in each of the studies. For example, in the Jackson et al. (1989) study, women were underrepresented in redemption as compared with the proportion of women admitted to the state's drug programs. Outreach workers noted that they encountered female IDUs less frequently on the streets, suggesting that greater efforts must be made to find the places unique to female IDUs and actively encourage them to seek drug abuse treatment. The fact that the majority of outreach workers in these studies were men suggests the need for trained female outreach workers to whom female IDUs may respond more favorably.

Overall, the studies using coupon incentives were successful in recruiting ethnic minorities: Jackson et al. (1989) recruited 66% African American IDUs, Wechsberg et al. (1992) recruited 80% African Americans, Sorensen et al. (1993) recruited 69% ethnic minorities, and Bux et al. (1993) was successful in recruiting a sizable number of Hispanics. In contrast, Sibthorpe et al. (1996) were less successful in their efforts to recruit ethnic minorities. However, the studies varied on which ethnic minority groups responded favorably to coupon incentives (e.g., Hispanics were less likely to remain in treatment in the Jackson et al. study but were more likely to redeem coupons in the Bux et al. study). These findings suggest the need to develop ethnically and culturally sensitive programs to attract and better serve IDUs. The field staff of Bux et al., for example, reported that some clinics were reputed to be especially accessible to Hispanic clients. This suggests that clinics' reputations in the community are an important source of information to those seeking treatment. Outreach work should similarly be developed to include workers of various ethnic backgrounds and language capabilities.

The findings from the Bux et al. (1993) study indicate that treatment length is an important factor. IDUs redeemed the coupons for the 90-day detoxification at a higher rate than the more standard 21-day coupon, indicating a preference for a longer, more gradual detoxification. The fact that a longer stay in detoxification tended to predict return for later treatment in the Sorensen et al. (1993) study lends support to the notion of a longer stay being perceived as a more positive treatment experience—one that tends to increase the probability of future attempts. Perhaps increasing the standard 7–21-day heroin detoxification treatment episodes would successfully retain more IDUs in treatment.

In each of the studies, the majority of coupon redeemers had previous experience in treatment, suggesting that familiarity with treatment may be a predictor of coupon redemption. In fact, in the Bux et al. (1993) study previous detoxification experience significantly predicted redemption, and in the Sibthorpe et al. (1996) study those IDUs with previous treatment experience were more likely to be interested in treatment. This information combined with the misconceptions expressed by IDUs in the Watters (1987) report suggests that outreach education regarding drug abuse treatment programs may be very effective in increasing IDUs' motivation to enter treatment.

Finally, the coupon redeemers in the Bux et al. (1993) study were more concerned about needle hygiene and other HIV-prevention behaviors. Service providers can capitalize on the tendency for coupon redeemers to be conscious of HIV-prevention behaviors, for example, by touting drug abuse treatment as a viable method for reducing the risk for HIV. Findings from the Bux et al. study suggest that IDUs would be receptive to such efforts, especially those who frequent needle exchanges. Future efforts should focus on effectively conveying this message to IDUs.

CONCLUSION

The use of voucher–coupon incentives is an innovative recruitment strategy for increasing treatment entry of drug abusers at high risk for HIV infection and other groups targeted for treatment. Increasing access to drug abuse treatment is pivotal during the current AIDS epidemic because treatment is effective in reducing HIV risk behaviors (Ball, Lange, Myers, & Friedman, 1988). Interventions such as coupon incentives can be easily integrated into existing programs and complement other contingency management approaches used in drug abuse treatment programs.

Based on the research reviewed in this chapter, incentive programs appear effective in increasing treatment entry of opiate-dependent IDUs; however, research is needed to answer many questions about how to use incentives more effectively. There is a paucity of well-controlled studies by researchers attempting to develop and evaluate methods for increasing treatment entry for drug abusers. Incentive programs may be differentially acceptable to people with various personal characteristics (e.g., gender, age, employment, education, living situation, motivation, and cultural differences in meaning of gifts and incentives). Likewise, the organizational and social context in which the incentive program is implemented will have an impact on outcomes, as will the type of incentive program.

It is important to systematically evaluate incentives for increasing treatment entry to identify those most useful for reaching targeted groups. In addition, it is important to evaluate variables specific to program recruiters that may influence the outcome of recruitment efforts, such as demographic characteristics and recruitment activities. It would be useful to integrate incentive programs within community-based settings that work with drug abusers, including public assistance programs, health care programs, homeless shelters, food distribution sites, and needle exchange programs. In addition, alternatives to institutionally based outreach strategies are needed. In fact, street outreach is an often neglected component of health programs directed at drug abusers who do not or cannot readily access health information and services (Wiebel, Biernacki, Mulia, & Levin, 1993). These outreach methods, combined with contingency management programs, can attract those who have never been in drug abuse treatment and can reduce the number of individuals who fail to complete a referral to drug abuse treatment.

REFERENCES

Ashery, R. S., Davis, H., Davis, W. H., & Ross, R. L. (1993). Entry into treatment of IDUs based on the association of outreach workers with treatment programs. In B. S. Brown & G. M. Beschner (Eds.), *Handbook on risk of AIDS: Injection drug users and sexual partners* (pp. 386–395). Westport, CT: Greenwood Press.

Ball, J. C., Lange, W. R., Myers, C. P., & Friedman, S. R. (1988). Reducing the risk of AIDS through methadone maintenance treatment. *Journal of Health and Social Behavior, 29,* 214–226.

Bertera, R. L. (1990). Planning and implementing health promotion in the workplace: A case study of the Du Pont Company experience. *Health Education Quarterly, 17,* 307–327.

Birkhead, G. S., LeBaron, C. W., Parson, P., Grabau, J. C., Barr-Gale, L., Fuhrman, J., Brooks, S., Rosenthal, J., Hadler, S. C., & Morse, D. L. (1995). The immunization of children enrolled in the Special Supplemental Food Program for Women, Infants, and Children (WIC): The impact of different strategies. *Journal of the American Medical Association, 274,* 312–316.

Bly, J. L., Jones, R. C., & Richardson, J. E. (1986). Impact of worksite health promotion on health care costs and utilization: Evaluation of Johnson & Johnson's Live for Life Program. *Journal of the American Medical Association, 256,* 3235–3240.

Breslow, L., Fielding, J., Herrman, A. A., & Wilbur, C. S. (1990). Worksite health promotion: Its evolution and the Johnson & Johnson experience. *Preventive Medicine, 19*, 13–21.

Brown, B. S., & Needle, R. H. (1994). Modifying the process of treatment to meet the threat of AIDS. *International Journal of the Addictions, 29*, 1739–1752.

Bux, D. A., Iguchi, M. Y., Lidz, V., Baxter, R. C., & Platt, J. J. (1993). Participation in an outreach-based coupon distribution program for the free methadone detoxification. *Hospital and Community Psychiatry, 44*, 1066–1072.

Deren, S., Stephens, R., Davis, W. R., Feucht, T. E., & Tortu, S. (1994). The impact of providing incentives for attendance at AIDS prevention session. *Public Health Reports, 109*, 548–554.

Emont, S. L., & Cummings, K. M. (1992). Using a low-cost, prize-drawing incentive to improve recruitment rate at a work-site smoking cessation clinic. *Journal of Occupational Medicine, 34*, 771–774.

Geringer, W. M., & Hinton, M. (1993). Three models to promote syphilis screening and treatment in a high risk population. *Journal of Community Health, 18*, 137–151.

Higgins, S. T., Delaney, D. D., Budney, A. J., Bickel, W. K., Hughes, J. R., Foerg, F., & Fenwick, J. W. (1991). A behavioral approach to achieving initial cocaine abstinence. *American Journal of Psychiatry, 148*, 1218–1224.

Ingram, J., Rawls, R. G., & Moberly, H. D. (1993). Using incentives to motivate women to seek prenatal care: An effective outreach strategy. *Journal of Health and Social Policy, 5*, 23–32.

Jackson, J. F., Rotkiewicz, L. G., Quinones, M. A., & Passannante, M. R. (1989). A coupon program—Drug treatment and AIDS education. *International Journal of the Addictions, 24*, 1035–1051.

Jason, L. A., Jackson, K., & Obradovic, J. L. (1987). Behavioral approaches in increasing blood donations. *Evaluation of the Health Professions, 9*, 439–448.

Jason, L. A., Jayaraj, S., Blitz, C. C., Michaels, M. H., & Klett, L. E. (1990). Incentives and competition in a worksite smoking cessation intervention. *American Journal of Public Health, 80*, 205–206.

Jeffery, R. W., Forster, J. L., Baxter, J. E., French, S. A., & Kelder, S. H. (1993). An empirical evaluation of the effectiveness of tangible incentives in increasing participation and behavior change in a worksite health promotion program. *American Journal of Health Promotion, 8*, 98–100.

Kronenfeld, J. J., Jackson, K., Blair, S. N., Davis, K., Gimarc, J. D., Salisbury, Z., Maysey, D., & McGee, J. G. (1987). Evaluating health promotion: A longitudinal quasi-experimental design. *Health Education Quarterly, 14*, 123–139.

Levin, S. M., Trumble, J. G., Edmunds, M., Statman, J. M., & Petersen, R. C. (1993). Perspectives on linkage of primary health care and substance abuse treatment [Editorial]. *Journal of Addictive Diseases, 12*, 1–8.

Liebman, J., Knezek, L. D., Coughey, K., & Hua, S. (1993). Injection drug users, drug treatment, and HIV risk behavior. In B. S. Brown & G. M. Beschner (Eds.), *Handbook on risk of AIDS: Injection drug users and sexual partners* (pp. 355–373). Westport, CT: Greenwood Press.

Lurie, P., Reingold, A. L., Bowser, B., Chen, D., Foley, J., Guydish, J., Kahn, J. G., Lane, S., & Sorensen, J. (1993). *The public health impact of needle exchange programs in the United States and abroad.* Unpublished manuscript, University of California, San Francisco.

Marlatt, G. A., & Tapert, S. F. (1993). Harm reduction: Reducing the risks of addictive behaviors. In J. S. Baer, G. A. Marlatt, & R. J. McMahon (Eds.), *Addictive behaviors across the lifespan: Prevention, treatment, and policy issues* (pp. 243–273). Newbury Park, CA: Sage.

Schuster, C. R. (1988). Intravenous drug use and AIDS prevention. *Public Health Reports, 103*, 261–266.

Seidman, S. N., Sterk-Elifson, C., & Aral, S. O. (1994). High-risk sexual behavior among drug-using men. *Sexually Transmitted Diseases, 21*, 173–180.

Shipley, R. H., Orleans, C. T., Wilbur, C. S., Piserchia, P. V., & McFadden, D. W. (1988). Effect of the Johnson & Johnson Live for Life Program on employee smoking. *Preventive Medicine, 17*, 25–34.

Sibthorpe, B., Fleming, D., Tesselaar, H., Gould, J., & Nichols, L. (1996). The response of injection drug users to free treatment on demand: Implications for HIV control. *American Journal of Drug and Alcohol Abuse, 22*, 203–213.

Sibthorpe, B., Nichols, L., Tesselaar, H., Roggenburg, L., Gould, J., & Fleming, D. (1991, November). *Intravenous drug users who are not in treatment: Is it from choice or constraint?* Paper presented at the 119th annual meeting of the American Public Health Association, Atlanta, GA.

Slesinger, D. P., & Ofstead, C. (1996). Using a voucher system to extend health services to migrant farm workers. *Public Health Reports, 111*, 57–62.

Smith, P. B., Weinman, M. L., Johnson, T. C., & Wait, R. B. (1990). Incentives and their influence on appointment compliance in a teenage family-planning clinic. *Journal of Adolescent Health Care, 11*, 445–448.

Sorensen, J. L., Costantini, M. F., Wall, T. L., & Gibson, D. R. (1993). Coupons attract high-risk untreated heroin users into detoxification. *Drug and Alcohol Dependence, 31*, 247–252.

Soukhanov, A. H., & Ellis, K. (Eds.). (1994). *Webster's II new Riverside University dictionary.* Boston: Houghton Mifflin.

Steen, R., Soliman, C., Bucyana, S., & Dallabetta, G. (1996). Partner referral as a component of integrated sexually transmitted disease services in two Rwandan towns. *Genitourinary Medicine, 72*(1), 56–59.

Stevens-Simon, C., O'Connor, P., & Bassford, K. (1994). Incentives enhance postpartum compliance among adolescent prenatal patients. *Journal of Adolescent Health, 15*, 396–399.

Stitzer, M. L., Iguchi, M. Y., & Felch, L. (1992). Contingent take-home: Effects on drug use of methadone maintenance patients. *Journal of Consulting and Clinical Psychology, 60*, 927–934.

Velten, E., Kletter, R., Kletter, J., Wolf, B., Roche, O., Han, D., Clark, G., Wirengard, Y., & Aguaya-Garcia, F. (1994, March). *Utilization of treatment vouch-*

ers by heroin addicts exchanging needles on the streets of San Francisco. Paper presented at the National AIDS Update, San Francisco, CA.

Watters, J. K. (1987). A street-based outreach model of AIDS prevention for intravenous IDUs: Preliminary evaluation. *Contemporary Drug Problems, 14,* 411–423.

Wechsberg, W. M., Smith, F. J., & Harris-Adeeyo, T. (1992). AIDS education and outreach to injecting drug users and the community in public housing. *Psychology of Addictive Behaviors* (Special Series: AIDS and HIV Prevention), 6, 107–113.

Wiebel, W. W., Biernacki, P., Mulia, N., & Levin, L. (1993). Outreach to IDUs not in treatment. In B. S. Brown & G. M. Beschner (Eds.), *Handbook on risk of AIDS: Injection drug users and sexual partners* (pp. 437–444). Westport, CT: Greenwood Press.

Wilbur, C. S. (1983). The Johnson & Johnson Program. *Preventive Medicine, 12,* 672–681.

8

EFFICACY AND VERSATILITY OF VOUCHER-BASED REINFORCEMENT IN DRUG ABUSE TREATMENT

KENNETH SILVERMAN, KENZIE L. PRESTON, MAXINE L. STITZER, AND CHARLES R. SCHUSTER

The extensive body of research reviewed in this volume shows clearly that contingency management interventions can be effective. However, there remains a need for more effective and versatile interventions. No type of drug abuse treatment, including contingency management interventions, has been shown to be universally effective. The proportion of patients who respond to contingency management interventions, the magnitude of the effects achieved by those who do respond, and the duration of the effects can be improved in virtually all applications. It is important to note that contingency management procedures have two characteristics, not shared by many drug abuse treatment interventions, that allow for their improvement through systematic and controlled research. First, contingency management procedures are objective and quantitative, so they can be systematically and parametrically manipulated in search of optimal pa-

Preparation of this chapter was suported by Grants R01 DA09426 and P50 DA09258 from the National Institute on Drug Abuse.

rameters of efficiency and effectiveness. Second, contingency management investigations can be guided by the extensive body of laboratory and clinical research on operant conditioning and reinforcement from which the procedures derive. Both laboratory and applied research in operant conditioning provide direction as to how contingency management procedures can be modified to improve effectiveness and utility. Where particular programs are not maximally effective, parameters such as the magnitude of reinforcement, the schedule of reinforcement, or the nature of the reinforcer can be changed until acceptable outcomes are achieved.

However, contingency management procedures vary in their flexibility. For example, not all reinforcers can be easily varied in magnitude or frequency of presentation—dimensions that have been shown to be critical to reinforcer effectiveness (Ferster & Skinner, 1957; Vuchinich & Tucker, 1983; Zeiler, 1977). Consider one of the most widely studied and generally useful contingency management interventions, the contingent presentation of methadone "take-home" doses to opiate-dependent patients in methadone maintenance treatment. (See Kidorf & Stitzer, chapter 11, this volume, for a discussion of take-home methadone doses as reinforcers.) Methadone treatment is an effective pharmacotherapy for opiate dependence, but it can also be inconvenient in that methadone must be ingested once a day, requiring patients to travel to a treatment clinic on a daily basis. For patients who live some distance from the clinic, this requirement represents a substantial cost. To ease this burden, on some visits patients can be given take-home doses of methadone, so that they can ingest some of their doses at home. Some of the earliest contingency management studies identified take-home methadone doses as reinforcers for many methadone patients (Milby, Garrett, English, Fritschi, & Clarke, 1978; Stitzer et al., 1977). In typical contingency management studies using take-home methadone doses, patients attend the clinic on Monday, Wednesday, and Friday of each week to provide urine samples and receive that day's methadone dose. On days that their urine sample is drug free, they receive a take-home methadone dose for the following day (i.e., Tuesday, Thursday, and Saturday). Although this type of intervention has been very effective, some patients do not achieve abstinence when exposed to this intervention (e.g., Stitzer, Iguchi, & Felch, 1992). Unfortunately, there are only a limited number of ways in which this contingency can be improved. For example, take-home doses as reinforcers, it is difficult to increase the magnitude of reinforcement. To continuously screen for new instances of drug use, clinics may require patients to provide urine samples three times per week. Given that limitation, patients can earn only between one and four take-home doses per week—a relatively small range in reinforcement magnitude. Take-home methadone does also have the obvious limitation of being useful only with patients in methadone treatment.

By many standards, money is an ideal reinforcer for use in contingency management procedures (see Elk, chapter 6, this volume, for an additional discussion of monetary reinforcement): Magnitude can be varied continuously over an almost limitless range of values; the risk of satiation are relatively low; money can be given according to a wide range of schedules; and because money is a generalized reinforcer, it is effective with most people. In fact, money has been used effectively in a number of contingency management programs (e.g., Hall, Bass, Hargreaves, & Loeb, 1979; Stitzer & Bigelow, 1983, 1984). Although the utility of money as a reinforcer in contingency management procedures has not been thoroughly explored, it has one characteristic that limits its appeal: Money earned under a contingency management intervention may be used to purchase drugs. It is not at all clear that this concern is warranted, but the concern is not without some basis. First, it is widely assumed among clinicians that having money in hand frequently leads to drug use in many drug abusers, and reports from drug abusers themselves provide some support for this assumption (Kirby, Lamb, Iguchi, Husband, & Platt, 1995). Additional evidence that having money may lead to continued drug use comes from a descriptive study of the relationship between the increase in availability of money and cocaine use in cocaine-dependent patients with schizophrenia (Shaner et al., 1995; see Shaner et al., chapter 5, this volume, for a further discussion of this issue).

VOUCHER-BASED REINFORCEMENT

As described in chapter 2 of this volume, Higgins et al. developed a contingency management intervention that uses the aspects of a monetary reinforcer critical to its reinforcing effectiveness while attempting to control the potential adverse consequences of giving drug abusers money (Higgins et al., 1991); the intervention used was voucher-based reinforcement. Under this intervention, patients received vouchers contingent on emitting the target response. The vouchers had monetary value and were exchangeable for goods and services approved and purchased for the patients by the treatment staff. Patients never received cash. Using vouchers with monetary value, the magnitude of the voucher reinforcer could be varied continuously over an almost limitless range of values, the risks of satiation were relatively low, and it could be given according to a range of schedules. Giving vouchers instead of cash reduced the risk that patients would use their earnings to purchase drugs. In this program, patients received vouchers for providing cocaine-free urine samples. Urine samples were collected three times per week, which was frequent enough to detect most instances of cocaine use. The use of monetary vouchers, which could be varied continuously and widely in magnitude and given frequently, allowed Higgins et al. to design and use a unique reinforcement schedule in which the monetary value of the vouchers increased as the number of consecutive cocaine-free urine samples increased; cocaine-positive urine samples reset the voucher value to the initial low value. This schedule of escalating reinforcement for sustained abstinence appears to be a valuable feature of the voucher system (Roll, Higgins, & Badger, 1996; see Higgins et al., chapter 2, this volume, for a detailed description of this research).

As discussed in several chapters in this volume, applications of this basic voucher system in laboratories across the country are showing that the voucher system is both effective and versatile, producing clinically useful outcomes in diverse patient populations and in a variety of target behaviors (see Bickel & Marsch, chapter 13; Higgins et al., chapter 2; Piotrowski & Hall, chapter 9; Rawson et al., chapter 3; and Shoptaw et al., chapter 12, this volume). In this chapter, we review a series of studies conducted at the intramural research program of the National Institute on Drug Abuse's (NIDA) Addiction Research Center and at Johns Hopkins University School of Medicine that illustrate both the effectiveness and versatility of voucher-based reinforcement interventions.

VOUCHER-BASED REINFORCEMENT OF DRUG ABSTINENCE IN METHADONE PATIENTS

Cocaine

Initial Application

Cocaine abuse is a widespread clinical problem in methadone programs, and few treatments have been shown to be effective in addressing this problem (Silverman, Bigelow, & Stitzer, 1998). A series of studies were conducted evaluating the effectiveness of voucher-based reinforcement of cocaine abstinence in addressing this problem. The first study was conducted at the treatment research clinic of NIDA's Addiction Research Center and included 52 consecutively admitted intravenous heroin abusers in methadone maintenance treatment (Silverman, Higgins, et al., 1996). Patients with heavy cocaine use during the first 5 weeks of methadone treatment participated ($n = 37$). After the 5-week baseline, patients were randomly assigned to an abstinence reinforcement or yoked control group and then participated in a 12-week intervention period.

On Monday, Wednesday, and Friday of each week of the voucher period, abstinence reinforcement patients received vouchers for providing cocaine-free urine samples according to two independent schedules for 12 weeks (Higgins et al., 1991). Under the main schedule, patients received a voucher for each cocaine-free urine sample. The first cocaine-free urine sample earned a voucher worth $2.50; thereafter, vouchers increased in value by $1.50 for each consecutive cocaine-free urine sample. If the patient provided a cocaine-positive urine sample or failed to provide a scheduled urine, the patient did not receive a voucher and the value of the next earned voucher was reset to $2.50; vouchers then increased in value in increments of $1.50 for each consecutive cocaine-free urine sample. If the patient provided six consecutive cocaine-free urine samples, the value of the voucher for the sixth urine sample increased to the highest value that the patient had achieved previously. This schedule provided an escalating reinforcement for sustained abstinence and was designed to promote long periods of sustained abstinence. Under a supplemental schedule, patients received a $10 bonus for every three consecutive cocaine-free urine samples. A patient who remained continuously abstinent for 12 consecutive weeks would earn a total of $1,155 in vouchers. Control patients received noncontingent vouchers that were yoked (matched) in pattern and amount to the vouchers received by patients in the abstinence reinforcement group. The vouchers were exchangeable for goods and services considered consistent with the patient's treatment goals; this was broadly defined and could include living necessities and educational or recreational items and activities. To exchange vouchers, patients made written requests to the staff, and staff went into the community to make requested purchases.

Figure 8.1 shows the longest duration of sustained cocaine abstinence that patients achieved during the 12-week intervention evaluation. On average, abstinence reinforcement patients achieved significantly longer durations of sustained abstinence than did control patients. Furthermore, a significantly greater proportion of patients in the abstinence reinforcement group achieved sustained abstinence (i.e., equal to or more than 5 weeks) than did those in the control group. Nine abstinence reinforcement patients (47%) achieved between 7 and 12 weeks of sustained cocaine abstinence. In contrast, only 1 yoked control patient (6%) achieved more than 2 weeks.

Figure 8.2 shows the effect of the voucher intervention across the weeks of the study. Very few patients in either group were abstinent during any of the baseline weeks, but the percentage of reinforcement patients that were cocaine abstinent increased progressively during the voucher period to a level significantly above that observed in the control group. Rates of abstinence in the abstinence reinforcement patients decreased when the voucher intervention was discontinued in the postintervention period.

Silverman, Higgins, et al. (1996) showed that the voucher-based reinforcement of cocaine abstinence can produce sustained cocaine abstinence in a substantial proportion of cocaine-abusing methadone patients, extending the generality of the voucher intervention to a new population and treatment setting. In addition, researchers showed that the contingency between cocaine use and voucher presentation was critical in achieving the abstinence outcome. Both groups of patients in this study received

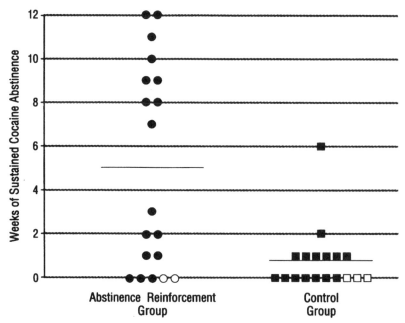

Figure 8.1. Weeks of sustained cocaine abstinence achieved during the 12-week voucher condition. Each point represents data for an individual patient, and the lines represent group means. Open symbols represent patients who dropped out of the study early. From "Sustained Cocaine Abstinence in Methadone Maintenance Patients Through Voucher-Based Reinforcement Therapy," by K. Silverman, S. T. Higgins, R. K. Brooner, I. D. Montoya, E. J. Cone, C. R. Schuster, and K. L. Preston, 1996, *Archives of General Psychiatry, 53*, p. 413. Copyright 1996 by the American Medical Association. Reprinted with permission.

vouchers in approximately equal amounts; however, only the group that received vouchers contingent on cocaine-free urine samples achieved sustained cocaine abstinence.

Broad Beneficial Effects of Abstinence Reinforcement

In the study by Silverman, Higgins, et al. (1996), the voucher intervention was clearly effective in promoting cocaine abstinence in about half of the patients, whereas the other half of the patients appeared relatively resistant to the intervention and failed to achieve sustained abstinence (see Figure 8.1). A second study (Silverman, Wong, et al., 1998) was conducted in part to determine whether the effectiveness of the voucher intervention could be improved by modifying the reinforcement schedule. The reinforcement schedule has been shown to be an important determinant of operant behavior (Ferster & Skinner, 1957; Morse & Kelleher, 1977; Roll et al., 1996; Zeiler 1977). In this study, Silverman et al. evaluated the effects of providing large start-up bonus vouchers for cocaine-free urine samples early in treatment in addition to the escalating reinforcement

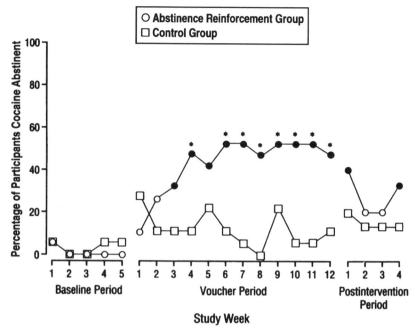

Figure 8.2. Percentage of patients abstinent during 21 successive study weeks. Circles represent data from the abstinence reinforcement group, and squares represent the control group. A patient was considered cocaine abstinent for a given week if all three urine samples for that week were negative for cocaine. Filled points and asterisks indicate the weeks on which the abstinence reinforcement group value differed significantly from the control group value according to planned comparisons based on a repeated-measures analysis of variance ($p \leq .05$ and $p \leq .01$, respectively). Data for the 4-week postintervention period are based on the urinalysis results from patients who completed the postintervention period (i.e., 15 control and 15 abstinence reinforcement patients). From "Sustained Cocaine Abstinence in Methadone Maintenance Patients Through Voucher-Based Reinforcement Therapy," by K. Silverman, S. T. Higgins, R. K. Brooner, I. D. Montoya, E. J. Cone, C. R. Schuster, and K. L. Preston, 1996, *Archives of General Psychiatry, 53,* p. 413. Copyright 1996 by the American Medical Association. Reprinted with permission.

schedule. A second purpose of the study was to document additional beneficial effects of the voucher-based reinforcement of cocaine abstinence suggested by data and patient interviews in the study by Silverman, Higgins, et al. (1996), including increases in opiate abstinence and decreases in patients' reports of their desire to use cocaine.

In the Silverman, Wong, et al. (1998) study, methadone patients who used cocaine during the first 5 weeks of methadone treatment were randomly assigned to receive vouchers for cocaine-free urine samples under one of two schedules of reinforcement or to receive vouchers on a noncontingent basis (control condition). Patients assigned to both abstinence reinforcement interventions received vouchers for providing cocaine-free urine samples under a schedule of escalating reinforcement for sustained abstinence. In addition, patients in one of those groups received large start-up bonus vouchers worth $50 each for cocaine-free urine sample provided early in the voucher period. The total amount in voucher earnings available in the two abstinence reinforcement conditions was held constant by adjusting the total amount of money available under the escalating reinforcement schedules. Patients in the control group received vouchers on a noncontingent basis, yoked in pattern and amount to patients in the escalating reinforcement plus start-up bonus group.

Both voucher-based abstinence reinforcement interventions significantly increased patients' longest duration of sustained cocaine abstinence relative to the control condition. As in the Silverman, Higgins, et al. (1996) study, about half of the patients exposed to the two abstinence reinforcement interventions achieved sustained cocaine abstinence and half did not. Unexpectedly, adding start-up bonuses did not improve abstinence outcomes and may have had an adverse effect (Silverman, Wong, et al., 1998).

Perhaps the most interesting aspect of the Silverman, Wong, et al. (1998) study were the clear effects produced on responses not directly targeted by the voucher intervention. Both abstinence reinforcement interventions significantly increased the percentage of patients abstinent (measured by urinalysis) from opiates, even though patients did not have to provide opiate-free urine samples to earn vouchers. The voucher intervention also affected patient reports of their desire to use cocaine. To characterize the effects of the voucher interventions on self-reports of patients' desire to use cocaine, each week they were asked to rate how much they wanted cocaine in the past week on a 5-point scale from 0 (*not at all*) to 4 (*extremely*). The study showed that both reinforcement interventions significantly decreased patients' ratings of their desire for cocaine relative to the control condition. Overall, this study replicated the effectiveness of the voucher intervention in promoting long periods of sustained cocaine abstinence and extended the results of the Silverman, Higgins, et al. (1996) study by showing that voucher-based reinforcement of cocaine abstinence can have broader beneficial effects beyond its effects on cocaine use.

Effects of Reinforcement Magnitude

The Silverman, Wong, et al. (1998) study confirmed both the effectiveness and limitations of the voucher intervention in addressing cocaine abuse in methadone patients. Although the voucher intervention promoted abstinence in a substantial proportion of patients, researchers confirmed that many patients appeared relatively resistant to the intervention and failed to achieve sustained abstinence. A third study was conducted to determine if sustained cocaine abstinence could be promoted in treatment-resistant patients by increasing the magnitude of voucher reinforcement (Silverman, Chutuape, Bigelow, & Stitzer, 1997). A large body of research in operant conditioning in animals and humans shows that magnitude is an important determinant of reinforcer efficacy (e.g., Hodos, 1963; Kliner, Lemaire, & Meisch, 1988; Neuringer, 1967; Pliskoff & Hawkins, 1967; Stitzer & Bigelow, 1983, 1984; Vuchinich & Tucker, 1983).

In this study, Silverman et al. (1997) included only patients who had failed to achieve 4 weeks or more of sustained cocaine abstinence when exposed to a voucher intervention in which they could earn up to $1,155 in vouchers for providing cocaine-free urine samples. Each treatment-resistant patient in this study was exposed to three 9-week voucher conditions, each followed by a 4-week baseline period. In all three voucher conditions, patients could earn vouchers for providing urine samples negative for cocaine. The three voucher conditions differed in the magnitude of voucher reinforcement available. Patients were exposed to zero, low, and high magnitude voucher interventions in counterbalanced order. In the zero magnitude condition, vouchers had no monetary value. In the low magnitude condition, patients could earn a maximum of $380 in vouchers in the 9-week period; in the high magnitude condition, they could earn a maximum of $3,400 in vouchers.

Twenty-three patients were exposed to each of the three voucher conditions. No patient achieved more than 2 weeks of sustained abstinence in the zero magnitude condition. Patients achieved slightly longer periods of abstinence in the low magnitude condition, but still only 2 patients achieved more than 2 weeks of sustained cocaine abstinence. Abstinence was greatest in the high magnitude condition; half of the patients achieved more than 4 weeks of sustained cocaine abstinence, and several patients achieved between 6 and 8 weeks. These between-group differences were statistically significant. This study shows that sustained abstinence can be promoted, even in extremely treatment-resistant patients, by using relatively high voucher magnitudes.

Opiates

Although methadone is widely used and is a very effective medication for the treatment of opiate dependence, heroin use typically persists in some portion of methadone patients, even with the proper use of methadone (Hartel et al., 1995) and state-of-the-art psychosocial services (McLellan, Arndt, Metzger, Woody, & O'Brien, 1993). Silverman, Wong, et al. (1996) used a within-subject reversal design to assess the effectiveness of voucher-based abstinence reinforcement in reducing opiate use in patients receiving methadone maintenance treatment in an inner-city program. Throughout the study, patients received standard methadone maintenance treatment involving methadone, counseling, and urine monitoring (three times per week). Thirteen patients who continued to use opiates regularly during the first 5 weeks of methadone treatment (baseline) were exposed to a 12-week voucher program in which they could earn vouchers for providing opiate-free urine samples under escalating reinforcement and bonus schedules similar to the ones used by Higgins et al. (1991) and Silverman, Higgins, et al. (1996). Patients continued receiving standard methadone maintenance for 8 weeks after discontinuation of the voucher program (return to baseline). As shown in Figure 8.3, the percentage of urine specimens that were positive for opiates decreased significantly when the voucher program was instituted and increased significantly when the voucher program was discontinued during the return-to-baseline condition. Rates of opiate-positive urine samples in the return-to-baseline condition

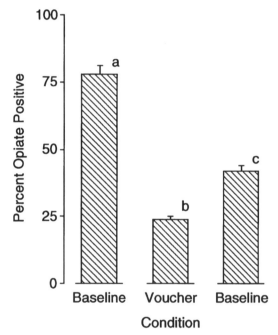

Figure 8.3. Mean percentage of opiate-positive urine samples during the baseline, voucher, and return-to-baseline conditions. Bars represent means based on the percentage of opiate-positive urine samples for all patients averaged across all of the urine collection days of each condition; brackets represent a positive standard error of measurement. Missing urine samples were considered positive. Letters above the bars represent the results of Tukey's honestly significant differences posthoc contrasts; bars that do not have a letter in common are significantly different from each other ($p \leq .01$). From "Increasing Opiate Abstinence Through Voucher-Based Reinforcement Therapy," by K. Silverman, C. J. Wong, S. T. Higgins, R. K. Brooner, I. D. Montoya, C. Contoreggi, A. Umbritch-Schneiter, C. R. Schuster, and K. L. Preston, 1996, *Drug and Alcohol Dependence, 41*, p. 161. Copyright 1996 by Elsevier Science. Reprinted with permission.

remained significantly below the rates observed in the initial baseline period. Overall, Silverman, Wong, et al. showed that voucher-based reinforcement contingencies decrease opiate use in heroin-dependent patients receiving methadone maintenance treatment.

VOUCHER-BASED REINFORCEMENT OF MEDICATION COMPLIANCE

As discussed elsewhere in this volume (see Bigelow & Silverman, chapter 1, this volume, and Elk chapter 6, this volume), contingency management interventions have been used effectively to improve medication compliance. In a study on the use of voucher-based reinforcement to improve medication compliance in opiate abusers, Preston et al. (1997) used a voucher-based reinforcement intervention to promote compliance with naltrexone treatment. The study included patients who met the *Diagnostic and Statistical Manual of Mental Disorders* (3rd ed. [*DSM-III*]; American Psychiatric Association, 1980) diagnosis for opiate dependence within the 60 days prior to study participation. Most patients had recently completed an inpatient opiate detoxification. Patients were randomly assigned to one of three 12-week conditions: contingent on naltrexone ingestion, on a noncontingent basis, or a no-voucher control condition. All patients were offered weekly counseling and naltrexone treatment, and urine samples were collected three times per week. For all patients, naltrexone administrations were scheduled three times per week (Monday, Wednesday, and Friday), which was judged frequent enough to provide adequate opioid blockade even on nonmedication days.

Patients in the contingent voucher condition received a voucher for each dose of naltrexone ingested. The schedule of voucher presentation used for this group of patients was similar to the schedule used in other studies. For the first dose of naltrexone ingestion, a patient earned a voucher worth $2.50. The value of the vouchers increased by $1.50 for each consecutive dose of naltrexone ingested; missed naltrexone doses reset the voucher value to $2.50. In addition, patients earned a $10.00 bonus voucher for every three consecutive naltrexone doses ingested. In total, patients in this group could earn up to $1,155 in vouchers in the 12-week condition. Patients in the noncontingent voucher group received vouchers independent of whether they ingested naltrexone; their vouchers were yoked (matched) to vouchers received by patients in the contingent voucher condition using a procedure similar to the one used by Silverman, Higgins, et al. (1996). Patients in the no-voucher condition did not receive vouchers.

Patients in the no-voucher group dropped out of treatment soon after enrollment, which is consistent with typical clinical experience. Vouchers, whether contingent or noncontingent, significantly improved treatment retention and naltrexone ingestion relative to the no-voucher condition. The best treatment outcomes were achieved by arranging vouchers contingent on naltrexone ingestion. Sustained naltrexone ingestion was greatest in the contingent condition relative to the noncontingent condition. More than half of the patients in the contingent voucher condition maintained 6 weeks or more of sustained naltrexone ingestion. In contrast, only 16% of patients in the noncontingent voucher condition maintained 6 weeks or more of sustained naltrexone ingestion, and no patients in the no-voucher control condition maintained more than 4 weeks of sustained ingestion. Unfortunately, assessment of the effects of the voucher intervention on opiate use based on urinalysis was obscured by the differential dropout across groups. This study clearly shows that voucher-based reinforcement of naltrexone ingestion can have robust effects both on treatment retention and compliance with naltrexone treatment.

VOUCHER-BASED REINFORCEMENT OF VOCATIONAL TRAINING PARTICIPATION

Unemployment is a common and troubling problem among many drug abusers and is associated with continued drug use, poor treatment outcome, and criminal activity (Platt, 1995). Unfortunately, many drug abusers lack the basic academic and job skills that they need to obtain and maintain stable employment; they may require extensive training programs designed to build those skills (Brewington, Arella, Deren, & Randell, 1987; Dennis, Karuntzos, McDougal, French, & Hubbard, 1993; Silverman, Chutuape, Svikis, Bigelow, & Stitzer, 1995). Standard drug abuse treatment services appear to have only small effects on employment (French, Zarkin, Hubbard, & Rachal, 1991). Educational and job training programs are available in many communities; however, relatively few chronically unemployed drug abusers use those resources without specially designed interventions to promote use (Brewington et al., 1987; Dennis et al., 1993).

Silverman, Chutuape, Bigelow, and Stitzer (1996) conducted a study to evaluate the effectiveness of voucher-based reinforcement in promoting attendance of unemployed methadone patients in a job-skills training program. Participants in this study received vouchers for attending daily 2-hr computer data-entry training sessions. Participants were taught to enter numbers on a 10-key pad to high levels of speed and accuracy. Training was scheduled 5 days per week for 16 weeks. The study used a within-patient reversal design to evaluate the effects of vouchers on attendance in the training program. For all participants, the voucher pay amounts varied in three sequential experimental conditions; a high pay condition (Weeks 1–6), a decreasing pay condition (Weeks 7–12), and a return to a high pay condition (Weeks 13–16). During the high pay condition (Weeks 1–6), participants could earn vouchers according to a schedule of escalating pay for sustained attendance. The initial value of daily vouchers, $8, increased by $0.90 for every consecutive day of attendance to a maximum of $34.10; patients did not receive a voucher when they missed class, and the value of their next voucher was reset to the initial low value of $8. During the decreasing pay condition, voucher pay was gradually decreased over time; voucher values decreased each day by 20% of each individual's earnings on the previous day. During the return to a high pay condition, the highest pay level previously achieved by each individual was reinstated and stayed at that level for the remainder of the condition, except that voucher values were reset to $8 following any missed section.

Seven methadone patients were enrolled in the study, 2 dropped out during the first 6 weeks, and 5 completed the entire study. For 4 of the 5 patients who completed the study, training session attendance was clearly related to the magnitude of the vouchers. As shown in Figure 8.4, 4 of the 5 participants (S1, S2, S6, and S7) attended the workplace regularly during the first high pay condition, abruptly stopped attending soon after the decreasing pay condition began, and then resumed regular attendance when the high pay condition was reinstated. Those participants stopped attending the workplace when the daily voucher pay fell to $8.94, $7.04, $6.96, and $6.02, respectively. Only 1 participant (S3) maintained fairly regular attendance throughout most of the decreasing pay condition, but even her attendance became sporadic toward the end of that condition. Mean percentage of work days attended was significantly higher during the two high pay conditions than during the decreasing pay conditions. All participants acquired data-entry skills, and participants reliably rated the work experience as "interesting," "enjoyable," "challenging," and "helpful." Mean ratings for these adjectives obtained on all days attended were significantly higher than ratings of the experience as "frustrating," "boring," or "a waste of time."

CONCLUSION

This series of studies illustrates both the effectiveness of versatility of voucher-based reinforcement in drug abuse treatment. Voucher-based reinforcement has been effective in increasing a range of target behaviors in both methadone- and nonmethadone-maintained patients. It has been effective in promoting abstinence from cocaine and from opiates in methadone patients. In nonmethadone-maintained opiate abusers, it has been effective in increasing treatment retention and in sustaining naltrexone ingestion. Finally, a voucher intervention was shown to be effective in maintaining participation by unemployed methadone patients in a job-

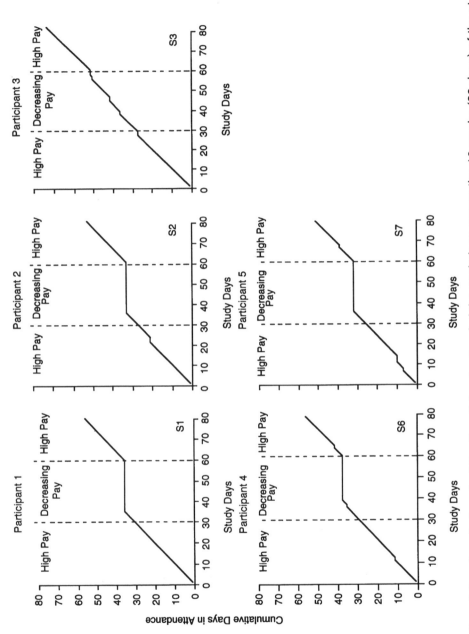

Figure 8.4. Cumulative days that each of the 5 participants attended the workplace across the 16 weeks (80 days) of the study. Vertical dashed lines indicate voucher condition changes. Each panel represents data from a different participant. Numerals in the lower right corner of each panel are participant identifiers (S1, S2, S3, S6, S7). Straight diagonal lines represent continuous attendance; flat horizontal lines indicate nonattendance. From "Voucher-Based Reinforcement of Attendance by Unemployed Methadone Patients in a Job Skills Training Program," by K. Silverman, M. A. Chutuape, G. E. Bigelow, and M. L. Stitzer, 1996, *Drug and Alcohol Dependence, 41*, p. 203. Copyright 1996 by Elsevier Science. Reprinted with permission.

skills training program. Addressing each of these problems—drug abstinence, medication compliance, and participation in training programs—is
critical in drug abuse treatment, and each problem has been resistant to
many conventional treatment approaches. The robust effects achieved in
addressing such a range of difficult problems suggest that voucher-based
reinforcement is a useful tool in drug abuse treatment.

Although the robust effects produced in these studies illustrate the
strength of the intervention, they also serve, by way of contrast, to accen-
tuate the interventions' limitations. Two limitations are common and obvious across all of the applications: Voucher-based reinforcement interventions are not effective in all patients, and their effects do not fully persist
after the intervention is discontinued. The limitations are illustrated in the
first study described on voucher-based reinforcement of cocaine abstinence
(Silverman, Higgins, et al., 1996). Figure 8.1 shows that almost half of the
participants exposed to the voucher-based abstinence reinforcement intervention achieved between 7 and 12 weeks of sustained abstinence—sur-
passing by a substantial margin all control patients but one. In marked
contrast, half of the abstinence reinforcement patients failed to achieve
any substantial periods of sustained abstinence and appeared very similar
to control patients who were not exposed to the intervention. Similarly,
in each of the studies described above, a group of patients appeared relatively resistant to the voucher intervention and failed to emit substantial
amounts of the target behavior. Furthermore, as with virtually all drug
abuse treatments evaluated in controlled trials, the effects of voucher interventions do not reliably persist after the interventions are discontinued
(e.g., see Figure 8.2).

It is important to note that there is good reason to expect that
voucher-based reinforcement interventions can be improved through systematic and controlled research. This expectation is based in part on the
fact, as noted above, that much is known about the conditions that determine the effectiveness of reinforcement in general. Voucher-based reinforcement procedures derive from an extensive body of controlled research in operant conditioning that not only serve as a basis for the initial
development of the procedures but also serve and can continue to serve as
a rich source of information to guide the improvement of these procedures.
Where the procedures prove incomplete in effectiveness, it should be possible to improve them through the systematic application of principles dis-
covered in research on operant conditioning.

A substantial number of studies in operant conditioning show that
reinforcement magnitude is an important determinant of reinforcing effectiveness. Silverman et al. (1997) applied that research and found that the
effectiveness of the voucher intervention could be improved by increasing
voucher magnitude.

This study illustrates a second, related point worth noting. The flexibility of the voucher intervention made it possible to vary the reinforcement magnitude over a range of values. Because of the nature of the reinforcer used in this intervention (i.e., vouchers), the key parameter of reinforcer magnitude could be varied over a range of values and without limiting another key parameter of operant conditioning, the frequency of reinforcer presentations (i.e., presenting a high magnitude voucher on one day does not preclude presenting another high magnitude voucher 2 days later). The literature on operant conditioning is replete with information that may be used to further improve the effectiveness of voucher interventions.

Although voucher-based reinforcement interventions hold promise in the treatment of drug abuse, their utility is clearly limited by their substantial costs. Perhaps the greatest challenge in developing this technology is to create practical applications that use existing sources of funding. Viable applications can take many forms, and creative efforts will be needed to design and evaluate them. For example, at Johns Hopkins University researchers are attempting to integrate voucher-based abstinence reinforcement contingencies into an employment setting. The intent of this program is to use a voucher-based salary that drug abusers earn for work to reinforce drug abstinence (Silverman, Svikis, Robles, Stitzer, & Bigelow, in press). To develop and evaluate this application, researchers established a model work program in which drug abuse patients are hired and paid each day to perform data entry and word-processing jobs. Participants are required to provide a drug-free urine sample to gain access to the workplace each day. Thus, participants can work and receive salary only when they are abstinent from drugs. It is important to note that the intervention retains the high magnitude reinforcement needed to produce the most robust effects in the greatest proportion of patients. A key feature of this intervention is that the drug abuse patients themselves can generate the funds to support the voucher-based reinforcement intervention by working and producing some valued product, thereby making it more practical and potentially available for use on a large scale. This represents only one of many potential practical applications of the voucher-based reinforcement technology. The usefulness to society of this effective and versatile technology will most likely depend on the extent to which researchers establish practical applications that harness existing resources and make it accessible and affordable on a large scale.

REFERENCES

American Psychiatric Association. (1980). *Diagnostic and statistical manual of mental disorders* (3rd ed.). Washington, DC: Author.

Brewington, V., Arella, L., Deren, S., & Randell, J. (1987). Obstacles to the utilization of vocational services: An analysis of the literature. *International Journal of the Addictions, 22*, 1091–1118.

Dennis, M. L., Karuntzos, G. T., McDougal, G. L., French, M. T., & Hubbard, R. L. (1993). Developing training and employment programs to meet the needs of methadone treatment clients. *Evaluation Program Planning, 16*, 73–86.

Ferster, C. B., & Skinner, B. F. (1957). *Schedules of reinforcement.* Englewood Cliffs, NJ: Prentice-Hall.

French, M. T., Zarkin, G. A., Hubbard, R. L., & Rachal, J. V. (1991). The impact of time in treatment on the employment and earnings of drug abusers. *American Journal of Public Health, 81*, 904–907.

Hall, S. M., Bass, A., Hargreaves, W. A., & Loeb, P. (1979). Contingency management and information feedback in outpatient heroin detoxification. *Behavior Therapy, 10*, 443–451.

Hartel, D. M., Schoenbaum, E. E., Selwyn, P. A., Kline, J., Davenny, K., Klein, R. S., & Friedland, G. H. (1995). Heroin use during methadone maintenance treatment: The importance of methadone dose and cocaine use. *American Journal of Public Health, 85*, 83–88.

Higgins, S. T., Delaney, D. D., Budney, A. J., Bickel, W. K., Hughes, J. R., Feorg, F., & Fenwick, J. W. (1991). A behavioral approach to achieving initial cocaine abstinence. *American Journal of Psychiatry, 148*, 1218–1224.

Hodos, W. (1963). Effects of increment size and reinforcer volume on progressive ratio performance. *Journal of the Experimental Analysis of Behavior, 6*, 387–392.

Kirby, K. C., Lamb, R. J., Iguchi, M. Y., Husband, S. D., & Platt, J. J. (1995). Situations occasioning cocaine use and cocaine abstinence strategies. *Addiction, 90*, 1241–1252.

Kliner, D. J., Lemaire, G. A., & Meisch, R. A. (1988). Interactive effects of fixed-ratio size and number of food pellets per fixed ratio on rats' food-reinforced behavior. *Psychological Record, 38*, 121–143.

McLellan, A. T., Arndt, I. O., Metzger, D. S., Woody, G. E., & O'Brien, C. P. (1993). The effects of psychosocial services in substance abuse treatment. *Journal of American Medical Association, 269*, 1953–1959.

Milby, J. B., Garrett, C., English, C., Fritschi, O., & Clarke, C. (1978). Take-home methadone: Contingency effects on drug seeking and productivity of narcotic addicts. *Addictive Behaviors, 3*, 215–220.

Morse, W. H., & Kelleher, R. T. (1977). Determinants of reinforcement and punishment. In W. K. Honig & J. E. R. Staddon (Eds.), *Handbook of operant behavior* (pp. 174–200). Englewood Cliffs, NJ: Prentice-Hall.

Neuringer, A. J. (1967). Effects of reinforcement magnitude on choice and rate of responding. *Journal of the Experimental Analysis of Behavior, 10*, 417–424.

Pliskoff, S. S., & Hawkins, T. D. (1967). A method for increasing the reinforcement magnitude of intracranial stimulation. *Journal of the Experimental Analysis of Behavior, 10*, 281–289.

Platt, J. J. (1995). Vocational rehabilitation of drug abusers. *Psychological Bulletin, 117*, 416–433.

Preston, K. L., Silverman, K. L., Umbricht-Schneiter, A., DeJesus, A., Montoya, I. D., & Schuster, C. R. (1997). Improvement in naltrexone treatment compliance with contingency management. In L. S. Harris (Ed.), *Problems of drug dependence, 1996: Proceedings of 58th annual scientific meeting, the College on Problems of Drug Dependence* (NIDA Research Monograph 174, NIH Pub. No. 97-4236, p. 303.) Washington, DC: U.S. Government Printing Office.

Roll, J. M., Higgins, S. T., & Badger, G. J. (1996). An experimental comparison of three different schedules of reinforcement of drug abstinence using cigarette smoking as an exemplar. *Journal of Applied Behavior Analysis, 29*, 495–505.

Shaner, A. E., Eckman, T. T., Roberts, L. J., Wilkins, J. N., Tucker, D. E., Tsuang, J. W., & Mintz, J. J. (1995). Disability income, cocaine use, and repeated hospitalization among schizophrenic cocaine abusers. *New England Journal of Medicine, 333*, 777–783.

Silverman, K., Bigelow, G. E., & Stitzer, M. L. (1998). Treatment of cocaine abuse in methadone patients. In S. T. Higgins & J. L. Katz (Eds.), *Cocaine abuse research: Behavior, pharmacology, and clinical applications* (pp. 363–388). San Diego, CA: Academic Press.

Silverman, K., Chutuape, M. A., Bigelow, G. E., & Stitzer, M. L. (1996). Voucher-based reinforcement of attendance by unemployed methadone patients in a job skills training program. *Drug and Alcohol Dependence, 41*, 197–207.

Silverman, K., Chutuape, M. A. D., Bigelow, G. E., & Stitzer, M. L. (1997). Reinforcement of cocaine abstinence in treatment resistant patients: Effects of reinforcer magnitude. In L. S. Harris (Ed.), *Problems of drug dependence, 1996: Proceedings of the 58th annual scientific meeting, the College on Drug Dependence* (NIDA Research Monograph 174, NIH Pub. No. 97-4236, p. 74). Washington, DC: U.S. Government Printing Office.

Silverman, K., Chutuape, M. A., Svikis, D. S., Bigelow, G. E., & Stitzer, M. L. (1995). Incongruity between occupational interests and academic skills in drug abusing women. *Drug and Alcohol Dependence, 40*, 115–123.

Silverman, K., Higgins, S. T., Brooner, R. K., Montoya, I. D., Cone, E. J., Schuster, C. R., & Preston, K. L. (1996). Sustained cocaine abstinence in methadone maintenance patients through voucher-based reinforcement therapy. *Archives of General Psychiatry, 53*, 409–415.

Silverman, K., Svikis, D., Robles, E., Stitzer, M. L., & Bigelow, G. E. (in press). A reinforcement-based therapeutic workplace for drug abusers. In L. S. Harris (Ed.), *Problems of drug dependence 1998: Proceedings of the 60th annual scientific meeting, the College on Drug Dependence* (NIDA Research Monograph). Washington, DC: U.S. Government Printing Office.

Silverman, K., Wong, C. J., Higgins, S. T., Brooner, R. K., Montoya, I. D., Contoreggi, C., Umbritch-Schneiter, A., Schuster, C. R., & Preston, K. L. (1996). Increasing opiate abstinence through voucher-based reinforcement therapy. *Drug and Alcohol Dependence, 41*, 157–165.

Silverman, K., Wong, C. J., Umbritch-Schneiter, A., Montoya, I. D., Schuster,

C. R., & Preston, K. L. (1998). Broad beneficial effects of reinforcement of cocaine abstinence in methadone patients. *Journal of Consulting and Clinical Psychology, 66*, 811–824.

Stitzer, M. L., & Bigelow, G. E. (1983). Contingent payment for carbon monoxide reduction: Effects of pay amount. *Behavior Therapy, 14*, 647–656.

Stitzer, M. L., & Bigelow, G. E. (1984). Contingent reinforcement for carbon monoxide reduction: Within-subject effects of pay amount. *Journal of Applied Behavior Analysis, 17*, 477–483.

Stitzer, M. L., Bigelow, G., Lawrence, C., Cohen, J., D'Lugoff, B., & Hawthorne, J. (1977). Medication take-home as a reinforcer in a methadone maintenance program. *Addictive Behaviors, 2*, 9–14.

Stitzer, M. L., Iguchi, M. Y., & Felch, L. J. (1992). Contingent take-home incentive: Effects on drug use of methadone maintenance patients. *Journal of Consulting and Clinical Psychology, 60*, 927–934.

Vuchinich, R. E., & Tucker, J. A. (1983). Behavioral theories of choice as a framework for studying drinking behavior. *Journal of Abnormal Psychology, 92*, 408–416.

Zeiler, M. (1977). Schedule of reinforcement: The controlling variables. In W. K. Honig & J. E. R. Staddon (Eds.), *Handbook of operant behavior* (pp. 201–232). Englewood Cliffs, NJ: Prentice-Hall.

9

TREATMENT OF MULTIPLE DRUG ABUSE IN THE METHADONE CLINIC

NANCY A. PIOTROWSKI AND SHARON M. HALL

Drug abuse in methadone treatment populations is not limited to cocaine. This chapter discusses the use of positive contingencies for treating opioid dependence complicated by the abuse of other drugs. The problem of relapse is also reviewed, and options for maintaining and improving treatment gains are discussed.

Methadone maintenance treatment (MMT) is often successful in helping patients stop or decrease illicit-opioid use (Ball & Ross, 1991). Other drug and alcohol use, however, often persists (Kosten, Rounsaville, & Kleber, 1987; Stitzer, Iguchi, & Felch, 1992; Ward, Darke, Hall, & Mattick, 1992). Drugs commonly used by MMT patients include alcohol, amphetamines, barbiturates, benzodiazepines, cocaine, marijuana, and nicotine (Kosten, 1991; Stitzer et al., 1992; Stitzer & Kirby, 1991).

MMT patients who abuse other drugs are considered at an increased risk for relapse to illicit-opioid use until other drug use has ceased. Opioid users entering treatment using multiple drugs, for instance, are more likely to have less time abstinent in the year following treatment and are more

Preparation of this chapter was supported by National Institute on Drug Abuse Grants 1-R18-DA06097 and T32-07250.

likely to share needles (Sheehan, Oppenheimer, & Taylor, 1993). Similarly, use of cocaine, benzodiazepines, and marijuana predicts relapse to opioid abuse (Wasserman, Weinstein, Havassy, & Hall, 1998). The effects of drug-induced disinhibition, conditioned responses to using certain drugs in combination, and exposure to drug culture are all seen as contributors to this increased relapse risk (Havassy, Hall, & Wasserman, 1991; Unnithan, Gossop, & Strang, 1992; Weddington, 1990). The seriousness of relapse is further highlighted in MMT populations because the needle use associated with opioid dependence carries with it an increased risk for AIDS acquisition and transmission (Darke, Baker, Dixon, Wodak, & Heather, 1992; Ward et al., 1992). Comprehensive treatment approaches addressing multiple drug use are critically important in reaching the goal of improving methadone treatment and in slowing the spread of AIDS.

Contingency management is shown to be an effective strategy for curtailing other drug use in methadone treatment populations, as was discussed in a number of the chapters in this volume (see Bickel & Marsch, chapter 13; Kidorf & Stitzer, chapter 11; Morral, Iguchi, & Belding, chapter 10; Silverman, Preston, Stitzer, & Schuster, chapter 8). Typical strategies for treating opioid addiction with methadone substitution include using methadone administration, take-home privileges, dosage levels, and discharge to shape drug-using behavior (Stitzer, Bickel, Bigelow, & Liebson, 1986). Recent work demonstrates that aside from methadone, reinforcers such as vouchers can be used to decrease the use of drugs such as cocaine (Higgins et al., 1991; Silverman et al., 1996). Studies using voucher-based financial contingencies, however, do not concentrate on achieving complete abstinence from illicit-drug and alcohol use. Instead, these studies are largely limited to investigating the use of monetary reinforcers with cocaine users (Higgins et al., 1991) or opioid users with a secondary cocaine problem (Silverman et al., 1996). Although such work demonstrates efficacious ways of meeting these more limited goals, it does not address the broader problem of multiple drug use as a specific treatment goal.

RATIONALE FOR MULTIPLE DRUG TARGETS

Considering Drug Use Topography and Relapse

Relapse is usually defined as a return to drug use following a significant period of abstinence (Hall, Wasserman, & Havassy, 1991). The significance of any abstinence period typically varies with the drug used and the individual pattern of use under study (Piotrowski, 1995). A 24-hr abstinence period, for instance, is meaningful for a smoker but may not be meaningful for a cocaine abuser who uses the drug in binge patterns. Similarly, great contrast exists in the meaning of a week of abstinence for an alcohol-dependent daily drinker versus a bimonthly binge drinker. Clearly, the meaning of the abstinence period depends on the use pattern and the drug itself. In the case of an MMT patient using multiple drugs, this may be key in terms of modifying a problematic behavior chain. The strength of the behavior pattern, the motivation to change it, and the skills required to make the change are all likely to vary depending on the combination of drugs used and the topography of use (Piotrowski, 1995).

Because the MMT patient is maintained on an opioid agonist, *relapse* is defined as the return to the use of illicit opioids (Weddington, 1990). It is more difficult, however, to address the situation in which a patient avoids illicit opioids but does not stop using other illicit drugs and alcohol. The question becomes "Has the patient relapsed?" Without an explicit goal of treatment being abstinence from these other drugs, presenting this use as a relapse to the patient is difficult. As such, a case must be made for why one would target alcohol and all illicit-drug use, instead of just illicit opioids, as a treatment goal.

Historically, both conditioning and cognitive–behavioral models have provided the means for such arguments, focusing on variables such as commitment and motivation, coping skills, social support, negative affect, cue reactivity, stress, and unproductive thinking strategies (Hall, Wasserman, & Havassy, 1991). First, conditioning may be important. For instance, if a patient always uses drugs in combination or succession, the use of one or more of these drugs may cue the use of the drug of choice. If alcohol frequently precedes opioid injection, for example, alcohol use while the patient is on methadone may cue illicit-opioid cravings, thereby increasing the odds of illicit-opioid use.

Similarly, the route of administration is relevant in conditioning. Although the drug effects are different, the behaviors that comprise smoking, injecting, or inhaling one drug may be similar to the experience of using another. Consider the similarities among smoking tobacco, marijuana, and opium; smoking a pipe of tobacco, marijuana, or "crack"; injecting opioids, amphetamine, or steroids; and snorting cocaine versus amphetamines. In all cases, the shared cues based on the route of administration may contribute to increased cravings for the drug of choice.

From the cognitive–behavioral perspective, other drug use may increase the probability of relapse through disinhibition, as may occur with a state of intoxication, or through drug-related expectancies. The use of drugs may directly and indirectly affect the users' judgments and subsequent behavior. Other drug use may, for instance, promote entry into drug-related environments before adequate skills and self-efficacy are developed to allow successful management of such high-risk situations (Marlatt & Gordon, 1985). Similarly, continued association with drug-using social contacts or poor decisions regarding the selection of coping strategies for dealing with stressors may increase temptations or cravings to use the drug of choice.

Finally, poor thinking strategies that may accompany other drug use, such as the abstinence violation effect (Marlatt & Gordon, 1985), may lead the methadone patient to discount the benefits of refraining from use of illicit opioids and, instead, use them without restraint.

Together, these factors suggest that reducing or eliminating the use of other illicit drugs and alcohol may directly or indirectly reduce the risk of relapse to illicit-opioid use in the patients who use multiple drugs. In addition, evidence generally suggests MMT patients' functioning does improve following the elimination or reduction of other illicit-drug use (Platt, 1995). As such, the goal of complete abstinence from alcohol and all illicit drugs has many potential benefits for methadone patients.

Setting Treatment Goals: Considerations Regarding Social Climate and Policy

In addition to the assertions above, one must consider the more public debate over what is a socially acceptable goal for drug abuse treatment, how treatment is funded, and whether treatment is delivered in a public or private setting (Alonzo, 1993; Dayhoff, Pipe, & Huber, 1994; Humphreys & Rappaport, 1993). Treatment goals, such as controlled use, harm reduction, and abstinence, are very different targets for change, championed by diverse supporters who often move in opposition (Goldstein & Engwall, 1992; Heather, 1995; Humphreys, Noke, & Moos, 1996; Marlatt, Larimer, Baer, & Quigley, 1993; Neuhaus, 1993; Shaffer, 1985; Swindle, Peterson, Paradise, & Moos, 1995; Warburton, 1990). Because alcohol and drug-related problems often have carried social connotations of moral weakness and disease (Hall, Clark, & Sees, 1995; Marlatt & Gordon, 1985), any use—particularly by someone who has had a diagnosed problem—is likely to be viewed skeptically and may be interpreted as a sign of continued moral or disease-related problems. Furthermore, even from a harm-reduction perspective, abstinence is considered the ideal treatment goal (Marlatt, 1996). The potential impact of such social factors on the support and perceived value of treatment goals that do not advocate complete abstinence for alcohol and other drugs of abuse cannot be minimized. As such, public programs that do not promote abstinence from all drugs and alcohol may be at risk. As a point of reference, 12-step groups such as Alcohol Anonymous and Narcotics Anonymous historically have not supported the use of prescribed or licit drugs for their members on the basis of the belief about addiction as a disease (Penick et al., 1990; Weddington, 1990), which create problems for methadone patients. Similarly, the use of psychotropic drugs to aid in the treatment of accompanying major clinical syndromes, such as in the case of dual diagnosis, often stirs controversy and leads to patients' rejection from treatment programs and self-help groups alike (Penick et al., 1990).

Although continued public and patient education regarding the value of agonist therapy and psychotropic medications for addiction and its related psychiatric disorders is obviously needed, these issues underscore the need for the development of strategies promoting abstinence. Strategies promoting abstinence would be particularly valuable to patients who have long-standing problems with opioid addiction or are severely dependent on opioids, who have a history of multiple drug use related to relapse, or who have had little success with treatment programs that do not promote a goal of abstinence from all drugs. It also may be particularly beneficial for the 50% of all drug-abusing patients who are dually diagnosed and already at an elevated risk for relapse (Penick et al., 1990). Not all patients will select this goal or even enter treatment if it is required. Social and financial pressure, however, may force this to be the case when it comes to public programs. Therefore, the treatment research community needs to explore the practical question of how to improve treatments to meet this challenge.

NEW APPROACHES TOWARD ABSTINENCE IN METHADONE TREATMENT

Methadone transition treatment (MTT) is an example of a new approach to the treatment of opioid dependence (Reilly et al., 1995) that has a stated goal of eventual abstinence from all opioids. In contrast to 21-day detoxification programs, MTT provides opioid-dependent individuals with a stable dose of methadone for a 100-day period, during which patients receive psychosocial treatments before an 80-day tapering phase. The rationale behind this approach is that the stabilization phase of methadone dosing combined with psychosocial interventions enables patients to achieve greater success with the cessation of illicit-opioid use. With more time, patients are able to focus on addiction-related issues before detoxification and to learn how to control feelings of withdrawal more effectively. Although MTT demonstrates efficacy for increasing patients' level of functioning and opioid-related treatment outcomes (Reilly et al., 1995), no specific effects on decreasing the other drug use have been reported. Other researchers have attempted to improve on MTT by studying the effects of using different levels of methadone (Banys, Tusel, Sees, Reilly, & Delucchi, 1994) and varying intensities of the psychosocial intervention (Sees, Tusel, Banys, Reilly, Clark, & Delucchi, 1994) during the stabilization phase of MTT. Unfortunately, although these efforts resulted in promising findings regarding the general goal of reducing illicit-opioid use, researchers were unable to show effects on alcohol or other illicit-drug use.

Contingency contracting strategies are a potentially useful means of addressing multiple drug use in an MTT context. As such, we conducted a clinical trial examining the efficacy of contingency contracting for promoting abstinence from all drugs in an ongoing MTT program. We explored the treatment outcome differences between participants receiving MTT with and without contingency contracting for continuous abstinence from alcohol and six illicit drugs. Individuals receiving treatment with contingency contracting were expected to demonstrate longer periods of continuous abstinence from illicit drugs and alcohol by the end of the contracting period as compared with individuals not receiving contingency contracting.

Participants in this trial were individuals from the San Francisco Bay Area (California) who applied for methadone detoxification at the San Francisco Veterans Affairs Medical Center. Individuals did not need to be veterans to participate. Individuals were screened by phone for basic eligibility and then in a face-to-face interview for a detailed review of inclusion and exclusion criteria. Those meeting the eligibility criteria and consenting to participate completed psychosocial assessments and received a third medical screen (e.g., a brief exam and interview, a blood draw, and collection of a urine specimen). Eligible individuals entered MTT at the beginning of the following week. Individuals were randomly assigned to one of the two experimental conditions (i.e., contingency contracting and performance feedback vs. performance feedback alone) immediately before receiving their initial methadone dose. Following methadone administration, participants began other treatment activities.

Men and nonpregnant, nonnursing women between 18 and 65 years of age who were competent to give written informed consent were included. Participants were current opioid abusers, with an initial urine toxicology screen positive for an opioid other than methadone. They met the *Diagnostic and Statistical Manual of Mental Disorders* (3rd ed. rev. [DSM-III-R]; American Psychiatric Association, 1987) criteria for opioid dependence but did not require immediate detoxification from alcohol or barbiturates. Individuals were excluded if they had medical contraindications to methadone treatment or inaccessible veins for venipuncture, which prevented the monitoring of methadone trough levels. Individuals also were excluded if they had participated in a related research protocol in the 6 months prior to intake, were in treatment elsewhere for opioid dependence, were in methadone treatment within the past 7 days, had an initial urine toxicology screen positive for methadone, or had life circumstances making it unreasonable to expect them to remain available for the study's duration. Individuals who met all criteria except for a urine toxicology screen negative for methadone were allowed to return 1 week later to participate if they could meet that criterion. Individuals presenting with additional dependence on alcohol or barbiturates also were allowed to participate at a later date, following detoxification for those drugs.

After the screening, 102 individuals were recruited; 51 were randomly assigned to each treatment condition. Between the treatment conditions, participants did not differ on any intake demographic, psychopathology, or current historical drug use variables. The majority were male (71%), and the average age was 40.5 years (age range 23–60 years). The sample was predominantly Caucasian American (39%) and African American (34%), followed by Hispanic American (15%) and others (12%). Most were unemployed (74.5%); the remainder were employed either full time (6.9%) or part time (8.8%) or retired–disabled (9.8%). Most reported their marital status as single (40%), followed by divorced or separated (36%), married or living with a partner (17%), and widowed (7%). In terms of *DSM-III-R* lifetime diagnostic criteria, at least 36% met the criteria for one major non-substance-related clinical syndrome in addition to opioid dependence. Average modified Addiction Severity Index composite scores (McLellan, 1988) were low for family (.03) and alcohol problems (.07); moderate for legal (.20), psychiatric (.21), and medical problems; and high for drug (.35) and employment problems (.81). Finally, in the 6 months prior to intake, the modal individual had used at least three commonly abused drugs (alcohol, amphetamine, barbiturates, benzodiazepines, cocaine, marijuana, or illicit opioids). In his or her lifetime, the modal participant had experimented with at least 11 drugs.

Participants were interviewed at intake, completing descriptive and other measures (e.g., Addiction Severity Index, Computerized Diagnostic Interview Schedule–Revised; Robins, Cottler, & Keating, 1989; lifetime and recent drug and alcohol use) in addition to submitting urine and breath samples. These measures were readministered monthly thereafter for the 6 months of the program. Urine samples were collected randomly on a twice-weekly basis and once per month on a random schedule; breath samples were collected once per week on a random schedule for the 6 months of treatment. The once-per-month random urine sample provided a measure of whether use was underestimated by the twice-weekly random testing. Contrasts of these samples revealed no differences, suggesting the twice-weekly tests were adequate in detecting use for this study's purposes.

Two biological measures, the presence or absence of drugs in urine and breath samples, served as the dependent measures for the study. Qualitative urine toxicology screening was used to determine the presence or absence of numerous drugs: amphetamine, barbiturates, benzodiazepines, cocaine, heroin, marijuana, and methadone. The enzyme multiplied immunoassay technique used in this study is described elsewhere (Banys et al., 1994). All urine samples were collected under observation by trained monitors. Similarly, a Breathalyzer was used to assess the presence and level of alcohol. Samples showing no evidence of use were recorded as drug free; samples showing use were recorded as drug positive. Failure to submit either type of specimen resulted in an automatic drug-positive test result for performance purposes, unless clinical circumstances warranted other arrangements, such as a make-up test the next day.[1]

The study contrasted two treatment conditions. One was MTT with performance feedback about urine toxicology and breath analysis results. The second was identical to the first with the addition of a contingency contracting component. Participation in treatment-related activities was kept constant between the two conditions through behavioral contracts for attendance. Individuals regularly missing therapeutic activities were put on a behavioral contract. Those failing to attend at least 60% of their therapeutic activities were required to attend 100% for a 7-day contract period or face immediate transition to a 30-day detoxification and expulsion from the study.

Methadone Regimen

Methadone was administered during a 180-day program involving an induction, stabilization, and tapering phase. The induction phase was initiated on the 1st day of study participation with a maximum dose of 30 mg. Doses were increased every 1–3 days to a maximum of 80 mg, unless side-effects developed and necessitated adjustments. Participants were maintained on this dose through the end of the 4th month of treatment. During the 5th and 6th months, doses were tapered down using a steady taper.

Psychosocial Intervention

Psychosocial intervention consisted of four orientation classes, educational classes once weekly for 14 weeks, and twice-weekly group and once-weekly individual therapy for 6 months. Orientation and educational classes are discussed elsewhere in more detail (Reilly et al., 1995). The group component used two cotherapists for each group of 3–10 participants. Groups were 1 hr in duration, focused on drug-abuse-related issues, and accepted new members as space permitted. They were heterogeneous with regard to the patient's gender and treatment condition. Therapists included four master's-level counselors, one doctoral-level clinical psychologist, several psychiatry residents, and one psychiatrist, all of whom had some specialty training for the treatment of chemical dependency. The therapeutic approach of these groups was eclectic, combining aspects of

---

[1]For analytic purposes, the results of breath and urine samples were combined once during each weekly testing period.

supportive, process-oriented, and 12-step approaches. Although drug use and progress in treatment were discussed in the group settings, formal discussion of specific contingency contracting issues was limited to individual therapy. Weekly individual counselor sessions were at least 30–60 min long. Detailed discussion of contingency contracting took place in these sessions as did crisis intervention and individual treatment management.

Contingency Contracting

The contingency hierarchy implemented was unique in its attempts to address four treatment issues. First, the contract specified continuous abstinence from alcohol and six illicit drugs as the target behavior: illicit opioids, amphetamine, barbiturates, benzodiazepines, cocaine, and marijuana. Nicotine was not a target because the treatment staff thought this would make the treatment goals too difficult and because no smoking cessation treatments were also offered.

Second, different drug use was targeted at different times during the course of treatment because illicit opioids and cocaine were seen as most problematic for opioid users (Darke et al., 1992), necessitating immediate intervention. At the same time, however, some of the drugs targeted for abstinence in this study were likely to show up in urine samples for relatively lengthy periods of time, even after new use had stopped (e.g., barbiturates, marijuana). As such, patients were contracted to abstain from illicit opioids and cocaine during the 1st month of treatment, without losing the ability to earn reinforcers during the 1st month of treatment for submitting urine and breath samples indicating alcohol, amphetamine, barbiturate, benzodiazepine, or marijuana use. Participants were reminded, instead, of the need to cease use of these drugs so as not to jeopardize their progress during the subsequent 3 months. In contrast, during Months 2–4, contingencies were based on abstinence from illicit opioids and cocaine as well as alcohol, amphetamine, barbiturate, benzodiazepine, and marijuana.

Third, the hierarchy incorporated a two-tier structure to facilitate both short- and long-term goal setting. Table 9.1 presents these two tiers in detail. In general, the positive contingencies were ordered hierarchically, increasing in value as the number of consecutive drug-free breath and urine samples increased. For each drug-free sample, patients ascended the two-tier hierarchy.

To encourage short-term goal setting and regular reinforcement for progress, patients earned cash credits along the first tier of the contingency hierarchy for each drug-free sample submitted. Each drug-free sample earned $0.35 multiplied by the number of consecutive drug-free samples achieved. A participant's first drug-free sample earned $0.35; two consecutive drug-free samples earned $0.70; three consecutive, $1.05; and so

TABLE 9.1
Monetary Reinforcement Schedule for Drug-Free Urine and Breath Samples

No. of consecutive drug-free samples	Short-term amount earned (in $)	Long-term goal	No. of consecutive drug-free samples	Short-term amount earned (in $)	Long-term goal
1	0.35		20	7.00	
2	0.70	Plateau 1 (1 week, bonus = $10–$15)	21	7.35	
3	1.05		22	7.70	
4	1.40		23	8.05	
5	1.75		24	8.40	
6	2.10		25	8.75	
7	2.45		26	9.10	
8	2.80		27	9.45	Plateau 4 (3 months, bonus = $125–$150)
9	3.15	Plateau 2 (1 month, bonus = $25–$35)	28	9.80	
10	3.50		29	10.15	
11	3.85		30	10.50	
12	4.20		31	10.85	
13	4.55		32	11.20	
14	4.90		33	11.55	
15	5.25		34	11.90	
16	5.60		35	12.25	
17	5.95		36	12.60	Plateau 5 (4 months, bonus = $225–$250)
18	6.30	Plateau 3 (2 months, bonus = $65–$75)	37	12.95	
19	6.65		38	13.30	

Note. Short-term goals are earned for each drug-free sample. Both short- and long-term goals are based on 38 consecutive drug-free specimens over 4 months of contingency contracting. For each plateau of the contingency hierarchy, participants designated a particular item as a reward for meeting the specified long-term abstinence goal.

forth. Once earned, cash credits could be redeemed at any point in the treatment process for items selected by the participant and approved by his or her counselor.

For the long-term goal of achieving lengthy periods of continuous abstinence, participants built a second tier of reinforcements into the hierarchy with their individual counselors. One item was selected for each plateau reached while progressing through the hierarchy. Plateaus were defined as achieving consecutive drug-free sample results for 1 week and 1, 2, 3, and 4 months. Once a plateau was reached, participants received their chosen reinforcer without trading in any cash credits. Such performance achievements were reinforced once for each plateau. The monetary value of each plateau reinforcer increased steadily (see Table 9.1) from $10–$15 worth of items for 1 drug-free week to $225–$250 worth of items for 4 drug-free months.

The fourth unique feature of this hierarchy was that plateaus were used to encourage continuous abstinence while giving patients the message that a drug-positive sample was a slip, not a total relapse. This was done to reinforce the relapse prevention (Marlatt & Gordon, 1985) skills and information taught in the enhanced psychosocial intervention. This contrasts with earlier work using monetary reinforcers (Higgins et al., 1991; Silverman et al., 1996) in which any use immediately reset the value of the next performance specimen to the baseline level. In this study, rather than resetting the value of the next specimen to baseline (e.g., $0.35), a single drug-positive specimen reset the potential value of the next sample to the bottom of the last plateau achieved. A second consecutive drug-positive specimen reset the value of the next specimen to the value of the bottom of the next lowest plateau. Finally, after three consecutive drug-positive samples (indicating over 1 week of use), the potential value of the next specimen was reset to baseline. In each case, drug-positive samples did not earn cash credits. For example, if a participant achieved 34 consecutive drug-free samples (see Table 9.1), the value of sample 35 if drug free would be $12.25. If sample 34 were drug positive, however, the potential value for sample 35 would be reset to the bottom of that plateau or $9.80. If sample 35 were drug positive, the potential value of sample 36 would be reset to $6.65. Finally, if sample 36 were drug positive, the potential value of sample 37 would be reset to the $0.35 baseline.

In the experimental condition, individuals were required to enter into a written contract with their counselor at treatment initiation. The contract covered the first 4 months (17 weeks) of treatment. Reinforcer selection was decided by both the patient and the counselor. In all cases, the reinforcers selected had to be related to fostering an addiction-free lifestyle, not simply meeting basic needs, such as paying rent, bills, and so on. By combining the maximum value of each plateau reinforcer and the running total of cash credits earned for 38 consecutive drug-free specimens collected

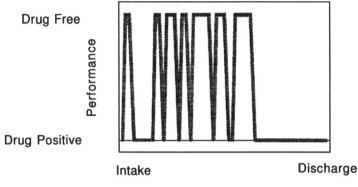

Figure 9.1. An example of a participant performance feedback sheet; results of urine and breath tests (drug free vs. drug positive) plotted for each of 54 consecutive specimens.

in this period, participants could earn a maximum of approximately $755 during the 4 months of contracting. On average, participants in the contingency condition earned $145.

Performance Feedback

Patients in both experimental conditions received graphic feedback of the combined results of their urine and breath analyses. The feedback was given in a dichotomous format (drug free or drug positive) to whether patients were meeting the treatment goals. Figure 9.1 provides an example of one individual's feedback chart over the course of treatment. For each random urine or breath specimen submitted, the participant received feedback on the test results. Over the total course of MTT, there were 54 occasions for each participant, 38 of which were subject to contingency contracting for the contingency group. In addition, patients in the contingency group received feedback of when and which performance plateaus were reached and which cash credits value they had earned and spent.

CLINICAL OUTCOMES

Wilcoxon Rank Score Tests and *t* tests were used for the analyses. Participants receiving treatment with contingency contracting demonstrated longer periods of continuous abstinence from illicit drugs and alcohol after 4 months of treatment (e.g., the end of Week 17 of treatment), as compared with patients not receiving the contingency contracting. Specifically, participants in the contingency condition had longer periods of continuous abstinence as represented by drug-free samples (7.59 vs. 3.53,

$p < .03$). This translated into periods of complete abstinence of 3.5 weeks versus 1.5 weeks. In the 4th month of treatment alone, this effect was quite evident: Patients in the contingency group achieved abstinence periods nearly three times as long as those in the other group (2.9 vs. 1.1 drug-free samples, $p < .0069$).

These findings are accounted for mostly by outliers (e.g., those with exceptionally long periods of abstinence) in the contingency condition. Nearly half of the participants were never able to meet the treatment goals of abstinence by presenting even one drug-free sample. Overall, by the end of the 4th month of treatment, the percentage of drug-free specimens submitted from patients in the contingency group was 34% compared with 17% ($p < .035$) in the noncontingency group. At no other time before the end of the 4th month or after the contingency condition stopped during the methadone tapering did the groups differ. Also when examining these results in more detail, we found no clear interactions (e.g., treatment condition by another specific variable) that indicated better outcomes for individuals in either condition based on the amount of historical or recent drug use experience, Addiction Severity Index symptom severity, the presence of other major psychiatric syndromes, or specific other drug or alcohol use. A trend ($p < .07$) was noted, however, for patients who had a history of using benzodiazepines in the 6 months prior to treatment: When these patients were in the contingency condition, they had a more favorable response than when in the noncontingency condition. These findings suggest that contingency contracting may provide a therapeutic benefit facilitating an overall reduction of illicit-drug and alcohol use by the end of the stabilization phase of MTT. Further refinements to this method seem warranted to maintain treatment gains. A more detailed discussion of the methodological and analytical results of this trial is reported elsewhere (Piotrowski, Tusel, Meek, et al., 1995; Piotrowski, Tusel, Sees, et al., in press; Tusel et al., 1995).

FUTURE DIRECTIONS: INCREASING AND MAINTAINING TREATMENT GAINS

The results of this trial are promising in light of three key facts. First, this trial sought to address a stringent treatment goal: combined continuous abstinence from alcohol and six illicit drugs in MTT patients. Second, these participants were opioid-dependent individuals who had not been subject to baseline stabilization prior to the intake into the trial and the selection effects associated with it. This is in contrast to other contingency management studies (Higgins, Stitzer, Bigelow, & Liebson, 1986; Iguchi, Stitzer, Bigelow, & Liebson, 1988; Silverman et al., 1996; Stitzer, Iguchi, & Felch, 1992) in which participants went through lengthy baseline periods prior to formal study intake. Clients who survive baseline periods of 3 to 12 weeks may necessarily be different from those who do not. Those who survive such lengthy baseline periods may be more motivated to be in treatment or different in terms of impairment. Third, treatment was approached with a less expensive contingency contracting program than implemented in other studies (e.g., Silverman et al., 1996). Whereas participants in this trial received $0.35 for their initial drug-free specimen and up to $755 during the course of the 4-month treatment, participants in the study by Silverman et al. (1996) received $2.50 for their initial drug-free specimen and up to $1,150 during the course of a 12-week trial. Such differences may account for the contrast between these and earlier strong findings in populations not subject to baseline selection effects and receiving more expensive treatments for more limited treatment goals. To address the needs of these patients and to build on this work, we suggest several strategic improvements.

Intervention Effects and Timing

The Induction Phase

No differences were observed between the two treatment conditions after 1 month of the contracting. It may be that the implementation of the contracts at treatment entry, rather than after the induction phase of MTT, made abstinence more difficult. Presumably, because the participants were not at a full blocking dose of methadone until later in the 1st month, the cost–benefit balance of avoiding drug use to earn the minimal, initial rewards of the contingency contract may simply have favored drug use. Thus, it may be best to implement such contracts after a patient has been stabilized on a blocking dose of methadone or to initially use reinforcers of greater value. Another possibility is the effects of a contingency contracting procedure were not yet "believable" to the participants and thus not "real." Contingency contracting was a new treatment strategy for both the patients and the counselors. As such, the rewards may not have been sufficiently salient until some of the larger value rewards were dispensed to those participants achieving longer periods of continuous abstinence.

The Stabilization Phase

The differences between the experimental groups dissipated with the removal of the contingencies after the end of Month 4, although qualitatively they still favored the contingency group. This was expected because the removal of a behavioral reinforcement for new behavior normally leads to decreases in the new behavior. This is a simple demonstration of the process of extinction. Additionally, the contracting intervention ended at the same time the methadone tapering was initiated. This is a time when drug use is known to increase because of withdrawal symptoms and fears surrounding the process of detoxification (Gentile & Milby, 1992; Milby, 1988; Milby, Garrett, English, Fritschi, & Clark, 1978; Raczynski, Wiebe, Milby, & Gurwitch, 1988; Schumacher, Milby, Fishman, & Huggins, 1992). Again, it may be that the qualitatively better performance exhibited by the contingency group would have been more robust had the contracts built in stronger incentives (e.g., higher value cash credits) during the last month of the stabilization phase.

The Tapering Phase

By the end of the tapering phase, patients in the two treatment conditions did not differ in terms of their ability to maintain continuous abstinence. This was expected because of the absence of contingencies to maintain the behavior. It may be necessary during this phase to continue contracting for abstinence to bolster gains made during stabilization and to tilt the cost–benefit balance of succumbing to withdrawal and withdrawal anxiety in favor of maintained abstinence. Furthermore, because it is unrealistic to expect any treatment program to continue cash credit reinforcers beyond the termination of treatment, this may be a good point at which to bring in more community-based reinforcers, including community institutions, families, and workplaces (Hall, Wasserman, & Harvassy, 1991).

Tailoring Treatment to Encourage Response

Nearly half the participants never achieved the goal of abstinence for even one testing occasion, leading one to conclude that continuous abstinence from all drug use was too challenging a goal for this population. This is not an uncommon finding, however, relative to other work previously cited (e.g., Iguchi et al., 1988; Silverman et al., 1996; Stitzer et al., 1992). Thus, we suggest that this goal, although stringent, is not unreasonable to consider. Alternatively, the goal may not have been stringent enough because it did not include nicotine as a drug to avoid. Nicotine may have increased relapse risk by bringing some individuals into drug-using environments. In addition, more than 80% of the participants had some involvement with cocaine, primarily crack cocaine. The similarities between cues associated with cigarette, crack, and opioid smoking may have contributed to the participants' difficulties in achieving abstinence. Further work should clarify aspects of tailoring contingency management around drug use involving such parallel behaviors.

A trend suggests that opioid-dependent individuals who use benzodiazepines (alone or in combination with other drugs), relative to those who are not using benzodiazepines, may be more responsive to voucher-based financial contingencies targeting abstinence from all drug use (Piotrowski et al., 1995). In this sample, there was a tendency for benzodiazepine users who received contingency contracting to have periods of abstinence nearly twice as long as those not receiving them. It may be that some pharmacological or psychological aspects to benzodiazepine use make it more susceptible to this behavioral intervention. For instance, in contrast to cocaine and amphetamine, benzodiazepines have a sedating, anxiolytic effect rather than an excitatory effect. Differences in the pharmacological effects, routes of administration of those drugs, and the psychological make-up of individuals who select such drugs are open for exploration in this regard. It also may be that the acquisition of adaptive behaviors to achieve such anxiety-reducing effects is easier to learn or is better addressed in current treatment approaches than the acquisition of adaptive behaviors to achieve similar excitatory effects.

We suggest that contingency contracting may be a more suitable intervention for specific subpopulations of opioid-dependent individuals entering MTT; studies to determine what types of individuals respond to this intervention are needed. Such work might begin by investigating static, historical, or state-related variables relevant to drug use (e.g., drug-use history, drug choice, and personality and other individual variables, such as psychiatric disorders) as potential indicators of greater or lesser readiness to change or to respond to contingency contracting.

Shaping Outcomes on the Individual Level

Future studies also might investigate outcomes in a more detailed manner, particularly for patients who may be identified early on as potential nonresponders. For instance, we used qualitative urine toxicology screens to assess treatment performance; for potential nonresponders, quantitative screens might be optimal. Although quantitative urine toxicology analyses are considerably more expensive, they might demonstrate treatment effects such as reductions in drug use rather than absolute abstinence. In this way, contingencies could be arranged to shape the behavior of patients who have more difficulty with quitting and to take advantage of small gains in an effort to promote treatment progress.

REFERENCES

Alonzo, A. A. (1993). Health behavior: Issues, contradictions and dilemmas. *Social Science and Medicine, 37,* 1019–1034.

American Psychiatric Association. (1987). *Diagnostic and statistical manual of mental disorders* (3rd ed., rev.). Washington, DC: Author.

Ball, J. C., & Ross, A. (1991). *The effectiveness of methadone maintenance treatment.* New York: Springer-Verlag.

Banys, P., Tusel, D. J., Sees, K. L., Reilly, P. M., & Delucchi, K. L. (1994). Low- (40 mg) versus high- (80 mg) dose methadone in a 180-day heroin detoxification program. *Journal of Substance Abuse Treatment, 11,* 225–232.

Darke, S., Baker, A., Dixon, J., Wodak, A., & Heather, N. (1992). Drug use and HIV risk-taking behavior among clients in methadone treatment. *Drug and Alcohol Dependence, 29,* 263–268.

Dayhoff, D. A., Pope, G. C., & Huber, J. H. (1994). State variations in public and private alcoholism treatment at specialty substance abuse treatment facilities. *Journal of Studies on Alcohol, 55,* 549–560.

Gentile, M. A., & Milby, J. B. (1992). Methadone maintenance detoxification fear: A study of its components. *Journal of Clinical Psychology, 48,* 797–807.

Goldstein, M. B., & Engwall, D. B. (1992). The politics of prevention: Changing definitions of substance use/abuse. *Journal of Health & Social Policy, 3,* 69–83.

Hall, S. M., Clark, H. W., & Sees, K. L. (1995). Drug abuse, drug treatment, and public policy. In W. K. Bickel & R. J. De Grandpre (Eds.), *Drug policy and human nature: Psychological perspectives on the control, prevention, and treatment of illicit drug use* (pp. 77–98). New York: Plenum.

Hall, S. M., Wasserman, D. A., & Havassy, B. E. (1991). Relapse prevention. In R. W. Pickens, C. G. Leukefeld, & C. R. Schuster (Eds.), *Improving drug abuse treatment* (NIDA Research Monograph 106, pp. 279–292). Washington, DC: U.S. Government Printing Office.

Havassy, B. E., Hall, S. M., & Wasserman, D. A. (1991). Social support and relapse: Commonalities among alcoholics, opiate users, and cigarette smokers. *Addictive Behaviors, 16,* 235–246.

Heather, N. (1995). Groundwork for a research programme on harm reduction in alcohol and drug treatment [Special issue]. *Drug and Alcohol Review, 14,* 331–336.

Higgins, S. T., Delaney, D. D., Budney, A. J., Bickel, W. K., Hughes, J. R., Foerg, B. A., & Fenwick, J. W. (1991). A behavioral approach to achieving initial cocaine abstinence. *American Journal of Psychiatry, 148,* 1218–1224.

Higgins, S. T., Stitzer, M. L., Bigelow, G. E., & Liebson, I. A. (1986). Contingent methadone delivery: Effects on illicit-opiate use. *Drug and Alcohol Dependence, 17,* 311–312.

Humphreys, K., Noke, J. M., & Moos, R. H. (1996). Recovering substance abuse staff members' beliefs about addiction. *Journal of Substance Abuse Treatment, 13,* 75–78.

Humphreys, K., & Rappaport, J. (1993). From the community mental health movement to the war on drugs: A study in the definition of social problems. *American Psychologist, 48,* 892–901.

Iguchi, M. Y., Stitzer, M. L., Bigelow, G. E., & Liebson, I. A. (1988). Contingency management in methadone maintenance: Effects of reinforcing and aversive consequences on illicit polydrug use. *Drug and Alcohol Dependence, 22,* 1–7.

Kosten, T. R. (1991). Client issues in drug abuse treatment: Addressing multiple drug abuse. In R. W. Pickens, C. G. Leukefeld, & C. R. Schuster (Eds.), *Improving drug abuse treatment* (NIDA Research Monograph 106, pp. 136–151). Washington, DC: U.S. Government Printing Office.

Kosten, T. R., Rounsaville, B. J., & Kleber, H. D. (1987). A 2.5 year follow-up of cocaine abuse among treated opioid addicts: Have our treatments helped? *Archives of General Psychiatry, 44,* 281–285.

Marlatt, G. A. (1996). Harm reduction: Come as you are. *Addictive Behaviors, 21,* 779–788.

Marlatt, G. A., & Gordon, J. (1985). *Relapse prevention.* New York: Guilford Press.

Marlatt, G. A., Larimer, M. E., Baer, J. S., & Quigley, L. A. (1993). Harm reduction for alcohol problems: Moving beyond the controlled drinking controversy. *Behavior Therapy, 24,* 461–503.

McLellan, A. T. (1988). Addiction Severity Index. In M. Hersen & A. S. Bellack (Eds.), *Dictionary of behavior assessment techniques* (pp. 7–8). New York: Pergamon Press.

Milby, J. B. (1988). Methadone maintenance to abstinence: How many make it? *Journal of Nervous and Mental Disease, 176,* 409–422.

Milby, J. B., Garrett, C., English, C., Fritschi, O., & Clark, C. (1978). Take-home methadone: Contingency effects on drug-seeking and productivity of narcotic addicts. *Addictive Behaviors, 3,* 215–220.

Neuhaus, C. (1993). The disease controversy revisited: An ontologic perspective. *Journal of Drug Issues, 23,* 463–478.

Penick, E. C., Nickel, E. J., Cantrell, P. F., Powell, B. J., Read, M. R., & Thomas, M. M. (1990). The emerging concept of dual diagnosis: An overview and implications. *Journal of Chemical Dependency Treatment, 3,* 1–54.

Piotrowski, N. A. (1995, April). *Methodological and assessment issues in measuring stage of change in new populations.* Paper presented at the Society of Public Health Educators Northern California Conference, Oakland.

Piotrowski, N. A., Tusel, D. J., Meek, P. M., Sees, K. L., Banys, P., Delucchi, K. L., & Hall, S. M. (1995). Positive contingency contracting for abstinence from alcohol and illicit drug abuse in subgroups of polysubstance-abusing opioid addicts. *Alcoholism: Clinical & Experimental Research, 19* (Suppl. A), 624.

Piotrowski, N. A., Tusel, D. J., Sees, K. L., Reilly, P. M., Banys, P., Meek, P., & Hall, S. M. (in press). Contingency contracting for drug and alcohol abstinence in a methadone program. *Experimental and Clinical Psychopharmacology.*

Platt, J. J. (1995). *Heroin addiction: Theory, research, and treatment. Vol. 3: Treatment advances and AIDS.* Malabar, FL: Krieger.

Raczynski, J. M., Wiebe, D. J., Milby, J. B., & Gurwitch, R. H. (1988). Behavioral assessment of narcotic detoxification fear. *Addictive Behaviors, 13,* 165–169.

Reilly, P. M., Banys, P., Tusel, D. J., Sees, K. L., Krumenaker, C. L., & Shopshire,

M. S. (1995). Methadone transition treatment: A treatment model for 180-day methadone detoxification. *International Journal of the Addictions, 30,* 387–402.

Robins, L., Cottler, L., & Keating, S. (1989). *NIMH diagnostic schedule, version III revised.* Ottawa, Ontario, Canada: CDIS Management Group.

Schumacher, J. E., Milby, J. B., Fishman, B. E., & Huggins, N. (1992). Relation of detoxification fear to methadone maintenance outcome: 5-year follow-up. *Psychology of Addictive Behaviors, 6,* 41–46.

Sees, K., Tusel, D., Banys, P., Reilly, P., Clark, H. W., & Delucchi, K. (1994). High- versus low-intensity substance abuse treatment. In L. S. Harris (Ed.), *Problems on drug dependence 1993: Proceedings of the 55th annual scientific meeting, the College on Problems of Drug Dependence* (NIDA Research Monograph 141, p. 365). Washington, DC: U.S. Government Printing Office.

Shaffer, H. J. (1985). The disease controversy: Of metaphors, maps and menus. *Journal of Psychoactive Drugs, 17,* 65–76.

Sheehan, M., Oppenheimer, E., & Taylor, C. (1993). Opiate users and the first year after treatment: Outcome analyses of the proportion of follow-up time spent in abstinence. *Addiction, 88,* 1679–1689.

Silverman, K., Higgins, S. T., Brooner, R. K., Montoya, I. D., Cone, E. J., Schuster, C. R., & Preston, K. L. (1996). Sustained cocaine abstinence in methadone maintenance patients through voucher-based reinforcement therapy. *Archives of General Psychiatry, 53,* 409–415.

Stitzer, M. L., Bickel, W. K., Bigelow, G. E., & Liebson, I. A. (1986). Effect of methadone dose contingencies on urinalysis test results of polydrug-abusing methadone-maintenance patients. *Drug and Alcohol Dependence, 18,* 341–348.

Stitzer, M. L., Iguchi, M. Y., & Felch, L. J. (1992). Contingent take-home incentive: Effects on drug use of methadone maintenance patients. *Journal of Consulting and Clinical Psychology, 60,* 927–934.

Stitzer, M. L., & Kirby, K. C. (1991). Reducing illicit drug use among methadone patients. In R. W. Pickens, C. G. Leukefeld, & C. R. Schuster (Eds.), *Improving drug abuse treatment* (NIDA Research Monograph 106, pp. 178–203). Washington, DC: U.S. Government Printing Office.

Swindle, R. W., Peterson, K. A., Paradise, M. J., & Moos, R. H. (1995). Measuring substance abuse program treatment orientations: The drug and alcohol program treatment inventory [Special issue]. *Journal of Substance Abuse, 7,* 61–78.

Tusel, D. J., Piotrowski, N. A., Sees, K. L., Reilly, P. M., Banys, P., Meek, P., & Hall, S. M. (1995). Contingency contracting for illicit drug use with opioid addicts in methadone treatment. In L. S. Harris (Ed.), *Problems on drug dependence 1994: Proceedings of the 56th annual scientific meeting, the College on Problems of Drug Dependence* (Vol. 2, NIDA Research Monograph 153, NIH Pub. No. 95-3883, p. 155). Washington, DC: U.S. Government Printing Office.

Unnithan, S., Gossop, M., & Strang, J. (1992). Factors associated with relapse among opiate addicts in an outpatient detoxification programme. *British Journal of Psychiatry, 161,* 654–657.

Warburton, D. M. (1990). *Addiction controversies.* London: Harwood Academic.

Ward, J., Darke, S., Hall, W., & Mattick, R. (1992). Methadone maintenance and the human immunodeficiency virus: Current issues in treatment and research. *British Journal of Addiction, 87,* 447–453.

Wasserman, D. A., Weinstein, M., Havassy, B. E., & Hall, S. M. (1998). *Factors associated with lapses to heroin use during methadone maintenance.* Manuscript in preparation, University of California, San Francisco.

Weddington, W. W. (1990). Towards a rehabilitation of methadone maintenance: Integration of relapse prevention and aftercare [Special issue]. *International Journal of the Addictions, 25,* 1201–1224.

10

REDUCING DRUG USE
BY ENCOURAGING
ALTERNATIVE BEHAVIORS

ANDREW R. MORRAL, MARTIN Y. IGUCHI, AND MARK A. BELDING

Abstaining from illicit drugs deprives chronic drug users of powerfully reinforcing events. At the same time, abstinence provides the opportunity to encounter alternative rewards available to those engaged in a drug-free lifestyle, such as finding contact with family and friends more gratifying, holding jobs more easily, and having more time and money to pursue non-drug interests. When natural rewards such as these are encountered, behaviors leading up to the reward are likely to be reinforced, including those contributing to the individual's abstinence. Conversely, if reinforcing events are not encountered, abstinence will not endure. Thus, contact with new natural rewards should diminish drug-maintained behavior, such as drug use (Vuchinich & Tucker, 1988). In this chapter we review evidence from the methadone maintenance treatment literature bearing on this hypothesis.

As described in several chapters in this volume, contingency man-

Preparation of this chapter was supported by National Institute on Drug Abuse Grant R01-DA06096.

agement interventions provide incentives that effectively reduce illicit-drug use by methadone maintenance clients (see Bickel & Marsch, chapter 13, Kidorf & Stitzer, chapter 11, Piotrowski & Hall, chapter 9, and Silverman, Preston, Stitzer, & Schuster, chapter 8). Typically, these interventions involve the delivery of such rewards as money or program privileges when clients demonstrate a period of abstinence by submitting a urine sample testing negative for illicit drugs (a drug-free urine). Ideally, contingency management interventions diminish drug use and increase clients' exposure to the naturally available rewards that will maintain their abstinence, even after the "artificial" or programmatically delivered incentives are eliminated. Unfortunately, this rarely occurs. Although abstinence contingencies often result in reduced drug use, these reductions prove to be highly dependent on the availability of the artificial contingencies. When the programmatically administered contingencies are eliminated, most investigators have reported a rapid relapse to high rates of drug use (Silverman, Wong, et al., 1996; Stitzer, Bigelow, & Liebson, 1980; Stitzer, Bigelow, Liebson, & Hawthorne, 1982).

High relapse rates in extant studies do not prove that abstinence contingencies cannot promote durable abstinence. Possibly, however, abstinence contingencies promote behaviors that are unlikely to endure. That is, drug use may resume because abstinence is achieved by promoting behaviors not reinforced by clients' natural environments. Many different sequences of behavior result in the submission of a drug-free urine sample. One client may stay at home and watch TV to avoid friends and situations associated with drug use, and another may seek out friends and situations not associated with drug use. When these clients are subsequently reinforced for submitting a drug-free urine sample, these strategies or sequences of behavior resulting in abstinence are also reinforced. Nevertheless, the two strategies may not be equally valuable for constructing a sustainable drug-free lifestyle. Watching TV is unlikely to introduce the first client to naturally available rewards for abstinence. As such, this client's abstinence remains dependent on the artificial rewards provided through the contingency management intervention. The second client, by contrast, is more likely to have his or her strategy reinforced by events that are independent of the clinical intervention. As such, the component behaviors of this strategy are strengthened, making abstinence more likely to survive the elimination of artificial reinforcement.

In addition to encouraging abstinence, treatment providers traditionally recommend other behavior changes consistent with a treatment plan that addresses a range of biopsychosocial problems (e.g., improving family life, economic functioning, physical health). Often, too, specific behaviors are described as short-term goals designed to facilitate the achievement of the larger treatment plan goals. For instance, a client with the goal of better anger management may have as a short-term goal using learned anger management techniques at least three times during the next month. We refer to these presumptively therapeutic behaviors as *treatment plan behaviors*. Among the ways treatment plan behaviors may advance the goals of drug treatment, two are conspicuous. First, many are incompatible with drug use. Maintaining employment, repairing marriages, and meeting the conditions of one's prison parole are improbable for many clients who continue to use drugs. Second, treatment plan behaviors may introduce clients to rewards that compete effectively with those available from drug use. Many treatment plan goals correspond to very basic improvements in a client's quality of life. As life becomes more satisfying, the relative value of illicit drugs is or may be diminished.

In this chapter, we review methadone maintenance studies in which behaviors other than the submission of a drug-free urine sample are reinforced that may diminish drug use and bring clients in contact with the natural reinforcement of abstinence that sustains abstinence beyond the availability of artificial, programmatically arranged incentives. This reinforcement strategy, similar to differential reinforcement of alternative behaviors, has been used successfully to treat a variety of aberrant behaviors other than drug use (Marcus & Vollmer, 1996).

REINFORCING TREATMENT PLAN BEHAVIORS

Several lines of evidence suggest that treatment plan behaviors other than abstinence can be experimentally reinforced and can indirectly affect illicit-drug use and other areas of client functioning. Moreover, there is some evidence that providing programmatic or artificial reinforcement for treatment plan behaviors changes behavior in ways that survive the elimination of artificial rewards. In one of the earliest demonstrations with methadone maintenance clients, Hall, Cooper, Burmaster, and Polk (1977) appeared to promote treatment plan behaviors by rewarding them with home delivery of methadone doses, tickets for restaurant dinners, and other privileges. The study consisted of six single case experiments, in which performance of target behaviors was observed before, during, and after implementation of experimental contingencies. Target behaviors were selected in accordance with treatment plan goals and included on-time attendance at work or the clinic and changes in body weight. The results were impressive. Implementation of the contingent rewards was followed by behavior change in the planned direction among all 6 participants, with 3 participants making substantial changes. Moreover, these therapeutic changes appeared to continue for at least 6 to 8 months beyond the thinning and eventual elimination of programmed contingencies.

Hall et al. (1977) observed a variety of therapeutic changes other than reductions in drug consumption after implementing their contingency management interventions, but they did not document the effects on drug use of reinforcing treatment plan behaviors. Similarly, other studies suggest that contingency management interventions reinforce treatment plan behaviors, such as counseling attendance (Stitzer, Bigelow, & Lawrence, 1977); fee payment (Magura, Casriel, Goldsmith, Strug, & Lipton, 1988; Stitzer & Bigelow, 1984); reductions in clients' requests for supplemental benzodiazepine medications (Stitzer et al., 1979); participation in classes, exercise, and self-care on an inpatient methadone treatment ward (Melin, Andersson, & Götestam, 1976); compliance with tuberculosis treatment (Elk et al., 1993); and a variety of prosocial behaviors on inpatient narcotic treatment wards (Glicksman, Ottomanelli, & Cutler, 1971; O'Brien, Raynes, & Patch, 1971). In each of these studies, the target behaviors were the reinforced treatment plan behaviors themselves, not participants' illicit-drug use, which went unreported. Therefore, these studies document the feasibility of using operant principles to promote treatment plan behaviors, but they do not clarify whether promoting such behaviors reduces drug use.

REINFORCING TREATMENT PLAN BEHAVIORS AND ABSTINENCE

In several studies, researchers have reported the effects on drug use of reinforcing multiple behaviors, including abstinence from illicit drugs and treatment plan behaviors such as program rule compliance and attendance at the clinic or scheduled counseling sessions (Baldridge, McCormack, Thompson, Zarrow, & Primm, 1974; Elk et al., 1993; Milby, Garrett, English, Fritschi, & Clark, 1978; Stanton, Todd, Steier, Van Deusen, Cook, 1982). Milby et al., for instance, provided take-home doses of medication to clients engaged in full-time productive activity who submitted drug-free urine samples for 7 consecutive weeks. In comparison with control participants randomly assigned to receive routine methadone maintenance at the clinic, experimental participants demonstrated significantly greater gains in productive activity. Experimental participants also submitted more consecutive drug-free urine samples than control participants, although their overall rate of abstinence was not superior to controls.

Milby et al. (1978) used a complex, time-consuming, and presumably difficult response requirement for reinforcement: 7 consecutive weeks of abstinence and full-time productive activity. Impressively, 40% of the experimental group succeeded in meeting the drug-use portion of the response criteria. Fewer, undoubtedly, met the full criteria to receive a single reward. Other investigators increased the probability of reinforcement by rewarding any of a predetermined set of behaviors that included abstinence and prosocial or therapeutic behaviors (e.g., Beatty, 1978; Rowan-Szal, Joe, Chatham, & Simpson, 1994). For instance, Rowan-Szal et al. established a token economy at a methadone maintenance clinic in which clients earned publicly displayed stars by attending group or individual counseling sessions or by submitting drug-free urine samples. In addition to the reward of public recognition for success, participants could use their stars to obtain small gifts like coffee mugs and T-shirts according to their experimental condition: High-reward participants could choose a gift for every four stars they earned, low-reward participants needed eight stars per gift, and delayed-reward participants were ineligible to receive gifts for their stars until completion of the 3-month intervention. These interventions produced greater group therapy attendance during the 3-month intervention than during the 3-month periods before and after the intervention. Differences in the number of drug-free urine samples submitted during each 3-month interval approached significance (p = .07), with abstinence greatest during the intervention. Finally, high-reward participants made significant reductions in illicit-drug use during and after the intervention.

Data on the density of reinforcement were not provided for the entire sample. Presumably, however, by reinforcing multiple behaviors and each specified behavior rather than requiring a response consisting of multiple successful behaviors, Rowan-Szal et al. (1994) succeeded in establishing a comparatively high density of reinforcement contacted by clients. Nevertheless, the success of their intervention in reducing illicit-drug use cannot be attributed exclusively to the reinforcement of counseling attendance because it was also likely a result of the contemporaneous reinforcement of drug-free urine sample submissions.

EFFECTS ON DRUG USE OF REINFORCING TREATMENT PLAN BEHAVIORS

Several studies indicate that drug use can be reduced by reinforcing treatment plan behaviors designed to compete directly with substance use. The earliest studies documenting this effect with methadone maintenance clients were presented by Liebson, Bigelow, and colleagues (Liebson, Bigelow, & Flamer, 1973; Liebson, Tommasello, & Bigelow, 1978). Alcoholic methadone maintenance clients could choose to ingest disulfiram with their methadone or immediately begin a methadone detoxification leading to program discharge. Ingesting disulfiram (Antabuse) competes specifically with alcohol use by making the effects of alcohol aversive. In addition to reducing their alcohol consumption, however, participants in the experimental condition submitted fewer urine samples with evidence of illicit-drug use than did controls (9% vs. 13%), they were arrested less often, and they maintained employment for a greater percentage of their treatment. In this study, most observed differences were nonsignificant, possibly because of small sample sizes and inadequate statistical power. Nevertheless, the results of this study and a subsequent study by Bickel et al. (1989) suggest that reinforcing a treatment plan behavior other than abstinence from illicit drugs (ingestion of disulfiram) has an indirect, positive effect on a range of clients' ongoing behaviors, including their illicit-drug use.

Although disulfiram ingestion qualifies as a treatment plan behavior as we defined them, the effects on substance use of behaviors that are not as narrowly focused on reducing substance use may present a more interesting question. Kidorf, Stitzer, Brooner, and Goldberg (1994), for instance, offered adjunctive cognitive psychotherapy designed to ameliorate clients' drug craving, negative affect, and weak drug-refusal skills. Intermittently during this 12-week intervention, clients were notified that their attendance of psychotherapy sessions would be rewarded with take-home doses of methadone for the following 3 weeks. As predicted, attendance improved significantly when rewards were available. Drug use, however, was not lower during intervals when therapy attendance was reinforced. Nevertheless, the within-subject reversal design of the study may have obscured the true effects on drug use of reinforcing counseling attendance. Three-week periods during which attendance was rewarded were usually followed by 3-week periods when no reward was available. If psychotherapy takes a few weeks before it is likely to influence drug-using behaviors (and longer before these changes are detectable by urinalysis), the effects on drug use of these short periods of reinforced counseling attendance may have peaked after the reward period concluded, possibly during a subsequent nonreward period. Thus, it may not be possible to detect the positive effects of the intervention on drug use in this study.

We conducted a series of experiments examining whether drug use would be reduced by reinforcing treatment plan behaviors. In the first experiment, 66 methadone clients who completed a 3-month baseline period were randomly assigned to receive rewards for the submission of drug-free urine samples or for attending a problem-solving skills group (Iguchi et al., 1996). As participants attended more groups or submitted more drug-free urine samples, they were provided increasing numbers of take-home doses of methadone, up to four doses per week. As expected, participants receiving urinalysis-contingent reinforcement showed significant reductions in drug use across the 6-month intervention compared with participants reinforced for group attendance. In contrast, participants receiving attendance-contingent reinforcement attended more than 50% of group sessions in comparison with participants not reinforced for group attendance who, on average, attended fewer than 1% of available sessions, $t(64) = 7.35$, $p < .0001$. Thus, although incentives increased group attendance, drug use continued at high rates. Apparently, the treatment plan behavior of group attendance, at least as it was implemented in this study, was not incompatible with continued drug use. Indeed, participants in the skills training program were significantly more likely than urinalysis-contingent patients to have deteriorating urinalysis results during the intervention (Morral, Iguchi, Belding, & Lamb, 1997).

The treatment plan behavior reinforced in the Iguchi et al. (1996) study was the same for all clients: attendance at the skills training group. Using a "one size fits all" response such as group attendance or the submission of a drug-free urine sample offers the advantage of a standardized criterion for reinforcement. Unfortunately, it also constrains studies examining the effect of encouraging treatment plan behaviors because each client's treatment needs differ. Skills deficits, for instance, may not be an equally serious problem for all clients.

In a follow-up study, we examined whether shaping the attainment of individualized treatment plan goals would produce behaviors that were incompatible with drug use (Iguchi et al., 1997). We provided clients with vouchers worth up to $15 per week for objectively documenting their performance of treatment plan tasks devised each week with their counselors in consultation with the investigators. Tasks were designed to provide successive approximations to the behaviors required for treatment plan goal attainment. Thus, response requirements were individualized and used to shape increasingly ambitious new behaviors and continuous improvement.

Shaping the attainment of treatment plan goals is a technically demanding intervention because new operants and measurement strategies to determine task completion must be devised continuously for each client. As with all shaping interventions, there is an art to knowing how difficult (or easy) to make each successive operant. Assigned tasks should neither be so difficult that the client is unlikely to accomplish them nor so easy that making programmatic rewards contingent on them is gratuitous. Consequently, special training and close supervision were required to implement this study.

Task formulation was guided by three principles. First, tasks should ensure that positive change is reinforced, however small these changes may be at first. For instance, a client with poor attendance was assigned the task of attending his next counseling session; he did not. Therefore, the next week's task was simplified to either attending the next counseling session or calling to cancel and reschedule the appointment. This time he did perform the task successfully. The unit of reinforced behavior was systematically simplified until success and voucher delivery were achieved.

The second, related principle is that the counselor and client must agree that there is a reasonably good chance that the client will perform the planned task. This principle shifts emphasis from what a client can or should be able to do to what the client is likely to do. Whether a female client is able to go to her Alcoholics Anonymous (AA) meeting each day is usually irrelevant and unknowable. Undue attention to this question risks provoking fruitless power struggles or resentment between client and counselor who view each other, respectively, as a "hard ass" and an "un-motivated" or "resistant" client. By emphasizing the client's likelihood of completing a task, the apparent simplicity of the task became irrelevant. Whether she could go to her AA meeting or not, both client and counselor were able to agree that she probably would not go every day. Thus, in keeping with the second principle, a more appropriate task was to attend one AA meeting in the next week. This approach reduced the client's tendency to blame herself or feel blamed by her counselor for failing to complete the task. Failures can be attributed to poor task selection rather than to poor motivation or other client inadequacies. Additionally, by working with the client to establish achievable tasks rather than dictating ideal response criteria, the counselor focused on reinforcing successes rather than punishing failures.

The third basic principle is that tasks must be objectively verifiable, with the criteria for determining task completion agreed on in writing at the time the task is planned. Each week when tasks were planned, the task and the criteria for objectively documenting its completion were written on the voucher that the client would earn for successfully completing the task. The counselor and client reviewed these criteria as they were re-corded. For instance, a client with the goal of improving his relationship with his son agreed to a series of tasks requiring him to spend time with his son engaged in mutually agreeable activities. One week, the counselor and client recorded on a voucher that task performance could be docu-mented by bringing in two payment stubs from a trip to the zoo. In the next session, however, the client offered a restaurant bill in lieu of the payment stubs, saying that because it was raining on Saturday he took his son out to dinner. In this case, the counselor provided encouragement for the positive activity that the client reported but not vouchers because the planned documentation was not provided. This rule helped reduce conflicts over what constituted adequate documentation.

Counselors' training emphasized each of these principles and included examples and role-play of task development. The principles also assisted with the researchers' efforts to supervise counselors during weekly team meetings, although they often found it useful to make more epigrammatic suggestions. The following formulations appeared most useful for the coun-selors: (a) Let your clients win—let them experience success by making the tasks simpler; (b) plan tasks that your client is likely to achieve, not tasks you would like them to achieve, or start where your client is, not where you'd like them to be; (c) don't dwell on failures—focus on what can be accomplished, not what wasn't; (d) build on success—challenge clients to do more only after they've experienced some success; and (e) be objective—document and review.

To evaluate the effectiveness of these procedures, we randomly as-signed 103 new methadone maintenance treatment clients who completed a 6-week baseline period to one of three treatment conditions: (a) a control treatment consisting of standard treatment at the methadone clinic (standard group), (b) standard treatment plus up to $15 per week in vouchers for submitting drug-free urine specimens (urinalysis-contingent group), or (c) standard treatment plus up to $15 per week in vouchers for completing treatment plan tasks (treatment plan group). Treatment plan participants could not earn vouchers for submitting drug-free urine specimens. Vouchers had an exchange value of $0.50 but could only be redeemed for expenses determined by the treatment team to be consistent with the goals of treatment. All participants received regularly scheduled individual counseling sessions and were subject to the clinic's system of privilege levels of determining eligibility for take-home bottles of methadone.

As seen in Figure 10.1, treatment plan participants reduced illicit-drug use during this 12-week intervention in comparison with those receiving the standard and urinalysis-contingent treatments (Iguchi, Belding, Morral, Lamb, & Husband, 1997). A repeated-measures analysis of variance revealed a significant Treatment Condition $\times$ Time interaction, $F(6, 196) = 2.27$, $p < .05$. Simple effects tests confirmed that although there were no significant group mean differences at the four time points, only

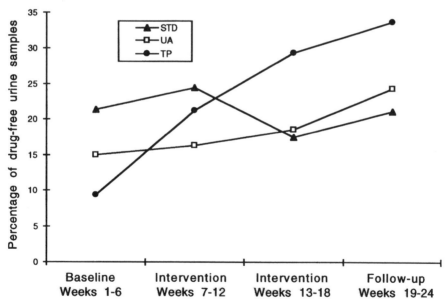

Figure 10.1. Drug-free urine samples submitted by participants receiving standard (STD; $n = 35$), urinalysis contingencies (UA; $n = 27$), and treatment plan contingencies (TP; $n = 41$) treatments. From "Reinforcing Operants Other Than Abstinence in Drug Abuse Treatment: An Effective Alternative for Reducing Drug Use," by M. Y. Iguchi, M. A. Belding, A. R. Morral, R. J. Lamb, and S. D. Husband, 1997, *Journal of Consulting and Clinical Psychology, 65,* p. 425. Copyright 1997 by the American Psychological Association. Reprinted with permission.

the treatment plan condition demonstrated significant changes over time. The magnitude of the treatment plan effects on drug use was clearer when we examined only those 91 participants (of the total sample of 103) who were still consistently failing to submit drug-free urine samples when the experimental treatments began at the end of the 6-week baseline observation period. Among this subsample, participants assigned to the treatment plan condition were far more likely to exhibit large, clinically significant reductions in their use of illicit drugs than were participants assigned to the standard or urinalysis-contingent conditions. Indeed, 13 of the 18 participants who demonstrated this marked reduction in drug use were in the treatment plan condition, $\chi^2(1, N = 91) = 7.95$, $p < .005$ (Morral et al., 1997).

Another striking finding from this study concerned participants' urinalysis performance during the 6 weeks after cessation of the experimental contingencies. In contrast to findings typical of urinalysis-contingency interventions, reductions in drug use observed for the treatment plan group appeared to be maintained, with a trend toward even greater improvement during the 6 weeks following the discontinuation of the contingencies. A univariate analysis of variance for this group between the final 6 weeks of the intervention and the 6-week postintervention follow-up period revealed a time effect that approached significance, $F(1, 40) = 4.23$, $p = .05$. Thus, behavior changes produced by the intervention appeared to survive the elimination of the artificial reinforcement provided.

The failure of urinalysis contingencies to significantly reduce drug use—a departure from previous results—surprised us. Many studies support the efficacy of reinforcing abstinence among methadone maintenance clients (e.g., Glosser, 1983; Hall et al., 1977; Silverman, Higgins, et al., 1996; Stitzer et al., 1982). Indeed, we previously found significantly higher rates of abstinence after implementation of urinalysis-based contingencies (Iguchi et al., 1996). However, these studies generally provided either larger monetary incentives (Stitzer, Bigelow, & Liebson, 1980; Stitzer et al., 1982) or different incentives such as take-home doses of methadone (Iguchi et al., 1988, 1996; Stitzer et al., 1980; Stitzer, Iguchi, & Felch, 1992) for the provision of drug-free urine samples. In selecting the value for the reinforcer in the present study ($5 per drug-free specimen), we equated the value of the reinforcers available each week to participants in the treatment plan and urinalysis-contingencies conditions (Iguchi et al., 1997). Nevertheless, the failure of the urinalysis-contingencies intervention to produce significant improvement over baseline suggests that $5 per drug-free urine sample may have been too low to effectively reinforce abstinence.

It is important to note that participants in all conditions (including the standard group) had some contingencies placed on their urinalysis results because all received the clinic's standard treatment that included a system of privilege levels determining take-home medication eligibility based in part on the submission of drug-free urine samples. The failure of the urinalysis-contingencies treatment to produce better results than the standard treatment may therefore be due to insufficient differentiation of the two interventions. Moreover, because this privilege system applied to participants in the treatment plan condition as well, the degree to which the treatment plan intervention would have been effective in its absence could not be assessed.

CONCLUSION

The studies reviewed above demonstrate that a variety of treatment plan behaviors (other than the submission of drug-free urine samples) can be effectively reinforced among clients in methadone maintenance treatment. Moreover, even when reinforced responses do not appear directly related to the use of target drugs, this reinforcement strategy has resulted in reductions in target drug use. Whereas reinforcing clinic-based psychotherapy attendance or psychoeducational group attendance does not facilitate behaviors incompatible with drug use, at least in the two extant studies examining this effect (Iguchi et al., 1996; Kidorf, Stitzer, Brooner, & Goldberg, 1994), two other types of treatment plan behaviors do appear to have an indirect effect on the use of target drugs. First, reinforcing treatment plan behaviors designed to compete with alcohol consumption can reduce target drug consumption (e.g., Bickel et al., 1989; Liebson et al., 1973, 1978). Second, and perhaps more surprisingly, reinforcing clearly defined behavioral tasks shaping the achievement of clients' individual long-term treatment goals (other than those directly concerning drug use) also appears to result in less drug use (Iguchi et al., 1997; Morral et al., 1997).

Reinforcing treatment plan behaviors may therefore provide a good alternative or adjunct to traditional urinalysis-contingent reinforcement. Moreover, there is some evidence that it reduces drug use among a population of drug users who are typically the most difficult to treat: those who continue to submit few drug-free urine sample after entering methadone treatment. Other studies suggest that even when very desirable rewards are contingent on the submission of drug-free urine samples, a large number of clients, perhaps a majority, never succeed in increasing their submission of drug-free urine samples. Stitzer and Bigelow (1978) showed that methadone maintenance clients preferred take-home doses of their medication to many other potential rewards, including $30 per week, self-selection of methadone doses, the opportunity to submit fewer urine samples, and even the opportunity to avoid counseling. Nevertheless, when offered as many as four take-home medications per week for remaining abstinent from illicit drugs, between 54% and 58% of clients failed to show noteworthy reductions in their illicit-drug use (Iguchi et al., 1996; Stitzer et al., 1992). Other investigators using different procedures and criteria for improvement have reported similar percentages (48–72%) of clients who failed to show clear benefits from contingency management interventions (Dolan, Black, Penk, Robinowitz, & DeFord, 1985; Kidorf & Stitzer, 1993, 1996; Morral et al., 1997; Silverman, Higgins, et al., 1996).

Thus, although urinalysis-contingent reinforcement is a highly effective treatment intervention, there continue to be many clients for whom current protocols do not produce improvements. If the desirability of available consequences of abstinence were substantially greater—perhaps $100 or $1,000 per week—then possibly even the most difficult-to-treat client would respond well to abstinence-contingent reinforcement. However, this type of modification to current protocols is obviously impractical financially (and politically). A more practical alternative, which has been incorporated into our treatment plan intervention, is to reduce the complexity or difficulty of the response requirement for receiving the reward.

The submission of drug-free urine samples is a rare event for many clients and may appear out of reach for those with the most entrenched drug use. Interventions making incentives contingent on abstinence may therefore work best for clients with less severe drug problems. Indeed, of the 13 participants who improved following exposure to abstinence contingencies in a study of contingent versus noncontingent reward (Stitzer et al., 1992), all were submitting at least 30% of drug-free urine samples, even before the onset of the contingency management intervention. In contrast, fewer than one third of the 28 participants who failed to improve were submitting 30% or more drug-free urine samples during this same period. Thus, the participants who benefited from treatment were already abstaining from illicit drugs more often prior to the intervention. Similar results have been reported by others (Dolan et al., 1985; Kidorf, Stitzer, & Brooner, 1994; Saxon, Calsyn, Kivlahan, & Roszell, 1993; Silverman, Higgins, et al., 1996).

These findings suggest that abstinence contingency programs may not modify the behaviors of all participants because many never emit the behavior targeted for reinforcement—the submission of a drug-free urine sample. Thus, they never contact the planned reward. If contacted contingencies shape behavior better than planned contingencies, as would seem likely, it is hardly surprising that urinalysis-contingent reinforcement works best with clients who are already submitting drug-free urine samples. To ensure that the greatest number of clients actually contact planned reinforcement, more effective contingency management interventions may need to reinforce a range of responses, from modest responses within the behavioral repertoires of even the most chronic drug user to more ambitious responses attainable by clients with less severe drug use patterns. For drug users who never submitt drug-free urine samples, for instance, abstinence contingency protocols could reinforce behaviors that are simpler than the submission of a drug-free urine, such as the submission of a urine demonstrating reduced drug use or providing evidence that fewer classes of illicit drugs were used.

Our treatment plan intervention was designed to maximize opportunities for all participants to encounter reinforcement for positive changes in their behavior, even if high rates of drug use continued. We speculated that this approach could be more effective with the hard-to-treat clients. Morral et al. (1997) examined whether the treatment plan intervention successfully modified drug use among these client by analyzing outcomes of those 91 participants with consistently poor urinalysis performance throughout the preintervention baseline period. As expected, receipt of the treatment plan intervention was a significant predictor of improvement among this subsample, even when controlling for a range of demographic and drug-use history variables. Indeed, the odds of these clients improving during the intervention were more than 11 times greater than for those assigned to standard treatment (the 95% confidence interval for this odds ratio ranged from 1.66 to 84.20). Of the three interventions, therefore, the treatment plan intervention was the most effective for modifying the drug use of clients who were submitting the highest percentages of drug-positive urine samples during the baseline period.

The success of the treatment plan intervention is probably attributable to several factors. First, for clients who did not initially provide drug-free urine specimens, the treatment plan intervention offered reinforcement for simpler steps toward abstinence, with each successive step building on prior successes. Second, by promoting behaviors incompatible with drug use (or at least uncommon among clients continuing to use drugs), the treatment plan intervention brought clients in contact with reinforcement available to them in their natural or nonexperimental environments, including, presumably, nonexperimental reinforcement available through the methadone clinic such as the praise and encouragement provided by counselors. Third, our counselors reported that the treatment plan intervention improved the quality of their interactions with clients. Instead of falling into frequent power struggles over counseling attendance, drug use, or other problem behaviors (and perhaps inadvertently reinforcing these behaviors), counselors described a more collaborative treatment relationship developing. Instead of threatening clients with the suspension of privileges, they worked with clients to plan ways they could earn desirable rewards.

Although the treatment plan intervention was successful at reducing average rates of drug use in an enduring way for the group receiving this treatment, these averages are somewhat deceptive. More than 60% of these clients did not make clinically significant improvements in their drug use. Thus, although the treatment plan intervention appears promising as a treatment that could be used in place of or along with abstinence contingent reinforcement, further refinements are required to increase its effectiveness with a larger percentage of clients.

On the basis of the arguments presented above, two procedures in our original treatment plan intervention should be improved. First, in our study (Iguchi et al., 1997), we were not selective about which treatment plan goals should be shaped, except that we prohibited programmatic reinforcement of abstinence itself. We did not not attempt to reinforce attainment of only those goals that seemed most likely to compete with drug use or to bring clients in contact with natural reinforcement. Instead, counselors and clients planned tasks-shaping goals that in their opinion, required the most immediate attention. A more effective treatment plan intervention would target the treatment plan behaviors most likely to reduce drug use. We hope that future research will clarify what these behaviors might be.

The second area in which our treatment plan intervention might benefit from improvement is in the selection of tasks ensuring that clients contact natural reinforcement for their new behaviors. In our study, no effort was made to ensure that such contact occurred. Instead, we assumed that progress toward or achievement of long-term personal goals would be likely to meet with naturally available reinforcement. For some of the clients, our assumption was apparently correct because drug use did not resume after the intervention ended, at least during the 6 weeks we followed their progress. An appealing alternative to this laissez-faire approach to establishing contact with natural reinforcers was originally introduced by Hunt and Azrin (1973) for the treatment of alcoholics and has been further developed by Higgins and colleagues for cocaine treatment (e.g., Higgins et al., 1991). In this community reinforcement approach (CRA), clients' environments are actively modified to increase the efficacy of nondrug reinforcement of target behaviors. For instance, as one part of their CRA, Hunt and Azrin set up an alcohol-free social club in a converted tavern. Abstinent clients and others not using alcohol could pay a fee entitling them to come to the social club to dance, socialize, and play card games or bingo on Saturday nights. Thus, they constructed a new social environment for clients in which abstinence was reinforced. Similarly, as one part of the CRA developed by Higgins et al., arrangements were made with a nonabusing spouse, friend, or colleague to engage with the client in some desirable activity, agreed on in advance, when clients' urinalysis results demonstrated abstinence from cocaine. Use of interventions designed to actively ensure clients contact reinforcement outside of the clinic would likely increase the effectiveness of our treatment plan intervention.

In summary, urinalysis-contingent reinforcement effectively reduces illicit-drug use among a portion of methadone maintenance clients, although these changes rarely persist beyond the availability of artificial, clinic-provided rewards for abstinence. Clearly, therefore, there is a need for new interventions that could be used in conjunction with or as an alternative to urinalysis-contingent reinforcement. We describe one such alternative intervention: reinforcing presumptively therapeutic behaviors such as those formulated in clients' treatment plans. This reinforcement strategy is designed to encourage behaviors that compete with drug use and can be sustained by sources of reinforcement outside of the methadone clinic. Data on the reinforcement of non-drug-use treatment plan behaviors demonstrate that they can be successfully reinforced in the context of methadone maintenance treatment. There is also evidence that reinforcing treatment plan behaviors designed to shape attainment of individualized treatment plan goals indirectly reduces illicit-drug use (e.g., Iguchi et al., 1997). Furthermore, we noted two additional advantages over results typically found in contingency interventions that reinforce abstinence directly. First, reductions in drug use not only survived the cessation of artificial reinforcement but actually strengthened during the first 6 weeks following the intervention, although the significance of this effect, $p = .05$, fell slightly short of the planned significance criterion. Second, the treatment plan intervention was associated with the greatest likelihood of improvement, even among the group of clients usually found most difficult to treat, those with more chronic patterns of drug use (Morral et al., 1997). We conclude that reinforcing behaviors that shape the attainment of treatment plan goals leads to behavior change that competes with drug use and might succeed in bringing clients in contact with natural sources of reinforcement that can sustain these new behaviors.

REFERENCES

Baldridge, P., McCormack, B. S., Thompson, L., Zarrow, A., & Primm, B. J. (1974). Providing incentives to successful methadone patients: Experimental program. *New York State Journal of Medicine, 74*, 111–114.

Beatty, D. (1978). Contingency contracting with heroin addicts. *International Journal of the Addictions, 13*, 509–527.

Bickel, W., Rizzuto, P., Zielony, R. D., Klobas, J., Pangiosonlis, P., Mernit, R., & Knight, W. F. (1989). Combined behavioral and pharmacological treatment of alcoholic methadone patients. *Journal of Substance Abuse, 1*, 161–171.

Dolan, M. P., Black, J. L., Penk, W. E., Robinowitz, R., & DeFord, H. A. (1985). Contracting for treatment termination to reduce illicit drug use among methadone maintenance treatment failures. *Journal of Consulting and Clinical Psychology, 53*, 549–551.

Elk, R., Grabowski, J., Rhoades, H., Spiga, R., Schmitz, J., & Jennings, W. (1993). Compliance with tuberculosis treatment in methadone-maintained patients: Behavioral interventions. *Journal of Substance Abuse Treatment, 10*, 371–382.

Glicksman, M., Ottomanelli, G., & Cutler, R. (1971). The earn-your-way credit system: Use of a token economy in narcotic rehabilitation. *International Journal of the Addictions, 6,* 525–531.

Glosser, D. S. (1983). The use of a token economy to reduce illicit drug use among methadone maintenance clients. *Addictive Behaviors, 8,* 93–104.

Hall, S. M., Cooper, J. L., Burmaster, S., & Polk, A. (1977). Contingency contracting as a therapeutic tool with methadone maintenance clients: Six single subject studies. *Behavior Research and Therapy, 15,* 438–441.

Higgins, S. T., Delaney, D. D., Budney, A. J., Bickel, W. K., Hughes, J. R., Foerg, F., & Fenwick, J. W. (1991). A behavioral approach to achieving initial cocaine abstinence. *American Journal of Psychiatry, 148,* 1218–1224.

Hunt, G. M., & Azrin, N. H. (1973). A community-reinforcement approach to alcoholism. *Behavioral Research and Therapy, 11,* 91–104.

Iguchi, M. Y., Belding, M. A., Morral, A. R., Lamb, R. J., & Husband, S. D. (1997). Reinforcing operants other than abstinence in drug abuse treatment: An effective alternative for reducing drug use. *Journal of Consulting and Clinical Psychology, 65,* 421–428.

Iguchi, M. Y., Lamb, R. J., Belding, M. A., Platt, J. J., Husband, S. D., & Morral, A. R. (1996). Contingent reinforcement of group participation versus abstinence in a methadone maintenance program. *Experimental and Clinical Psychopharmacology, 4,* 315–321.

Iguchi, M. Y., Stitzer, M. L., Bigelow, G. E., & Liebson, I. A. (1988). Contingency management in methadone maintenance: Effects of reinforcing and aversive consequences on illicit polydrug use. *Drug and Alcohol Dependence, 22,* 1–7.

Kidorf, M., & Stitzer, M. L. (1993). Contingent access to methadone maintenance treatment: Effects on cocaine use of mixed opiate-cocaine abusers. *Experimental and Clinical Psychopharmacology, 1,* 200–206.

Kidorf, M., & Stitzer, M. L. (1996). Contingent use of take-homes and split-dosing to reduce illicit drug use of methadone patients. *Behavior Therapy, 27,* 41–51.

Kidorf, M., Stitzer, M. L., & Brooner, R. K. (1994). Contingent methadone take-home doses reinforce adjunct attendance of methadone maintenance patients. *Behavior Therapy, 25,* 109–121.

Kidorf, M., Stitzer, M. L., Brooner, R. K., & Goldberg, J. (1994). Contingent methadone take-home doses reinforce adjunct therapy attendance of methadone maintenance patients. *Drug and Alcohol Dependence, 36,* 221–226.

Liebson, I., Bigelow, G., & Flamer, R. (1973). Alcoholism among methadone patients: A specific treatment method. *American Journal of Psychiatry, 130,* 483–485.

Liebson, I., Tommasello, A., & Bigelow, G. E. (1978). A behavioral treatment of alcoholic methadone patients. *Annals of Internal Medicine, 89,* 342–344.

Magura, S., Casriel, C., Goldsmith, D., Strug, D. L., & Lipton, D. S. (1988). Contingency contracting with polydrug-abusing methadone patients. *Addictive Behaviors, 13,* 113–118.

Marcus, B. A., & Vollmer, T. R. (1996). Combining noncontingent reinforcement and differential reinforcement schedules as treatment for aberrant behavior. *Journal of Applied Behavior Analysis, 29*, 43–51.

Melin, L., Andersson, E., & Götestam, K. G. (1976). Contingency management in a methadone maintenance treatment program. *Addictive Behaviors, 1*, 151–158.

Milby, J. B., Garrett, C., English, C., Fritschi, O., & Clarke, C. (1978). Take-home methadone: Contingency effects on drug seeking and productivity of narcotic addicts. *Addictive Behaviors, 3*, 215–220.

Morral, A. R., Iguchi, M. Y., Belding, M. A., & Lamb, R. J. (1997). Natural classes of treatment response. *Journal of Consulting and Clinical Psychology, 65*, 673–685.

O'Brien, J. S., Raynes, A. E., & Patch, V. D. (1971). An operant reinforcement system to improve ward behavior in in-patient drug addicts. *Journal of Behavior Therapy and Experimental Psychology, 2*, 239–242.

Rowan-Szal, G., Joe, G. W., Chatham, L. R., & Simpson, D. D. (1994). A simple reinforcement system for methadone clients in a community-based treatment program. *Journal of Substance Abuse Treatment, 11*, 217–223.

Saxon, A. J., Calsyn, D. A., Kivlahan, D. R., & Roszell, D. K. (1993). Outcome of contingency contracting for illicit drug use in a methadone maintenance program. *Drug and Alcohol Dependence, 31*, 205–214.

Silverman, K., Higgins, S. T., Brooner, R. K., Montoya, I., Cone, E. J., Schuster, C. R., & Preston, K. L. (1996). Sustained cocaine abstinence in methadone maintained patients through voucher-based reinforcement therapy. *Archives of General Psychiatry, 53*, 409–415.

Silverman, K., Wong, C. J., Higgins, S. T., Brooner, R. K., Montoya, I., Contoreggi, C., Umbricht-Schneiter, A., Schuster, C. R., & Preston, K. L. (1996). Increasing opiate abstinence through voucher-based reinforcement therapy. *Drug and Alcohol Dependence, 41*, 157–165.

Stanton, M. D., Todd, T. C., Steier, F., Van Deusen, J. M., & Cook, L. (1982). Treatment outcome. In M. D. Stanton, T. C. Todd, & Associates (Eds.), *The family therapy of drug abuse and addiction* (pp. 403–421). New York: Guilford Press.

Stitzer, M. L., & Bigelow, G. E. (1978). Contingency management in a methadone maintenance program: Availability of reinforcers. *International Journal of the Addictions, 13*, 737–746.

Stitzer, M. L., & Bigelow, G. E. (1984). Contingent and methadone take-home privileges: Effects on compliance with fee payment schedules. *Drug and Alcohol Dependence, 13*, 395–399.

Stitzer, M. L., Bigelow, G. E., Lawrence, C., Cohen, J., D'Lugoff, B., & Hawthorne, J. W. (1977). Medication take-home as a reinforcer in a methadone maintenance program. *Addictive Behaviors, 2*, 9–14.

Stitzer, M. L., Bigelow, G. E., & Liebson, I. (1979). Reducing benzodiazepine self-administration with contingent reinforcement. *Addictive Behaviors, 5*, 333–340.

Stitzer, M. L., Bigelow, G. E., & Liebson, I. (1980). Reducing drug use among methadone maintenance clients: Contingent reinforcement for morphine-free urines. *Addictive Behaviors, 4*, 245–252.

Stitzer, M. L., Bigelow, G. L., Liebson, I. A., & Hawthorne, J. W. (1982). Contingent reinforcement for benzodiazepine-free urines: Evaluation of a drug abuse treatment intervention. *Journal of Applied Behavior Analysis, 15*, 493–503.

Stitzer, M. L., Iguchi, M. Y., & Felch, L. J. (1992). Contingent take-home incentive: Effects on drug use of methadone maintenance patients. *Journal of Consulting and Clinical Psychology, 60*, 927–934.

Vuchinich, R. E., & Tucker, J. A. (1988). Contributions from behavioral theories of choice to an analysis of alcohol abuse. *Journal of Abnormal Psychology, 97*, 181–195.

11

CONTINGENT ACCESS TO CLINIC PRIVILEGES REDUCES DRUG ABUSE IN METHADONE MAINTENANCE PATIENTS

MICHAEL KIDORF AND MAXINE L. STITZER

Opioid dependence is a substance use disorder characterized by frequent relapse, persistent medical and legal complications, poor social adjustment, and reduced life expectancy (Vaillant, 1992). New admissions to methadone programs exhibit on average at least one additional drug dependence diagnosis, including cocaine, sedative, alcohol, and cannabis dependence (Brooner, King, Kidorf, Schmidt, & Bigelow, 1997; Kidorf, Brooner, King, Stoller, & Wertz, 1998). Comorbid psychiatric disorder also is prevalent, with major depression and antisocial personality disorder as the most prominent Axis I and II diagnoses, respectively (Brooner et al., 1997; Rounsaville, Weissman, Crits-Christoph, Wilber, & Kleber, 1982). In addition to these difficulties, there is the usual spectrum of medical, legal, occupational, social, and familial concerns, which can easily cause one to be pessimistic regarding the prospects of behavior change for this population.

It should be mentioned at the outset that methadone substitution was never intended to address all of these difficulties. Instead, this pharmacotherapy was developed to reduce and eliminate heroin use and related criminal behavior. That it safely and effectively does so is no longer novel news. Data from national studies of drug abuse treatment outcome, such as the Treatment Outcome Prospective Study (Hubbard et al., 1989) and the Drug Abuse Reporting Program (Simpson & Sells, 1990), provide convincing evidence of the dramatic reduction of heroin use by patients treated in outpatient methadone programs. In a study of six methadone programs in the Northeast, Ball and Ross (1991) demonstrated that patients involved in more than 6 months of treatment evidenced a 79% reduction in criminal activity.

Yet the overall success of methadone substitution should not obscure the fact that many opioid-dependent individuals are not sufficiently helped by this intervention. Individuals who exhibit severe difficulties in many of the areas discussed above, such as polydrug use (Condelli, Fairbank, Dennis, & Rachal, 1991), psychiatric symptomatology (McLellan, Luborsky, Woody, O'Brien, & Druley, 1983), poor social support (Havassy, Hall, & Wasserman, 1991), and unemployment (McLellan, Ball, Rosen, & O'Brien, 1981), have poorer prognosis in standard methadone substitution therapy, as seen in higher rates of drug use and shorter length of treatment stay. We intend to show that the structure of methadone programs provides an ideal context to motivate substantial behavior change in many of these areas, thus increasing the likelihood that patients will respond favorably to methadone substitution. Before discussing how this may be accomplished, we must first examine the resources available from routine drug abuse treatment programs offering methadone substitution.

ROUTINE METHADONE TREATMENT

Methadone treatment can be loosely divided into two separate components: methadone delivery and ancillary services. The methadone delivery component is relatively consistent across treatment programs. Patients attend the clinic daily at scheduled times to ingest the drug orally. In essence, methadone attenuates the effects of short-term opioids (e.g., heroin) and prevents the development of withdrawal symptoms for 24–36 hr. The methadone dose is adjusted for each patient on the basis of side-effects and clinical efficacy; in general, treatment programs use stable methadone doses between 40 and 60 mg (Ball & Ross, 1991). Higher methadone doses are more effective for reducing heroin use, although individual variation in treatment response is common (Strain, Stitzer, Liebson, & Bigelow, 1993). Methadone take-home doses can be provided to reduce the number of days that patients must visit the clinic.

In addition to methadone delivery, clinics typically provide psychosocial, medical, and psychiatric services to address the multiple needs of the opioid-dependent population (Ball & Ross, 1991; Kauffman & Woody, 1995). All programs offer individual counseling, and some offer specialized education and skills-building groups. Counselors also make referrals to outside agencies (e.g., community psychiatry) to supplement work accomplished at the clinic. The availability of ancillary services, however, does not guarantee delivery of services. In fact, drug abuse patients often do not take advantage of the range of services offered in most methadone substitution programs. This is unfortunate because many psychosocial treatments show efficacy in reducing drug use and modifying other maladaptive behavior (Stanton & Todd, 1982; Woody et al., 1983).

IMPROVING TREATMENT EFFECTIVENESS WITH CONTINGENCY MANAGEMENT

Contingency management enhances the effectiveness of methadone substitution by arranging objective consequences to modify drug use or other maladaptive treatment behavior. Numerous well-controlled laboratory and outpatient studies provide unambiguous evidence that drug use behavior can be modified by its consequences (Stitzer, Bigelow, & McCaul, 1985).

It is interesting to note that many of the natural consequences experienced by drug abusers, such as job loss, social ostricization, and legal difficulties, often are surprisingly insufficient to motivate behavior change. In fact, persistent drug use in the face of these consequences helps define the syndrome of substance dependence (American Psychiatric Association, 1994). Yet the reinforcing value of these consequences tends to vary across patients and may interact with age. Younger patients, for example, may be more likely to change behavior following social consequences, whereas older patients may be more responsive to health concerns. Successful drug abuse treatment should always involve active assessment and optimal use of these contingencies. Clinical trials that have secured control of meaningful environmental consequences (i.e., community reinforcement) have been successful in modifying substance use (e.g., Azrin et al., 1994).

One advantage to working with patients receiving methadone substitution is that many aspects of routine care, including components of both methadone dosing practices and ancillary clinic services, can function as reinforcers and can be used contingently to affect meaningful behavior change. Reinforcers are most effective when they are modified by frequency or amount, administered repeatedly, and applied proximately to target behavior. Examples of clinic-based incentives within the domain of routine methadone-dosing practices that meet these criteria are take-home methadone doses and methadone dose alterations—incentives rated by methadone-treated patients as extremely valuable (Kidorf, Stitzer, & Griffiths, 1995; Stitzer & Bigelow, 1978) and subject to extensive scientific study. Potential reinforcers under the category ancillary clinic services, such as frequency of counseling attendance, frequency of urinalysis testing, reporting time at the clinic, and access to adjunct clinic services, have received less scientific study on their own but often are combined with other clinic-based incentives to affect behavior change. Contingent treatment availability, in which access to both methadone dosing and ancillary services is tied to compliance with target behavioral goals, has developed some empirical support, although it cannot be modified in frequency and amount or administered repeatedly.

CONTINGENT METHADONE TAKE-HOME DOSES

Methadone take homes are consistently rated by patients as the most valuable privilege offered in methadone treatment clinics (Kidorf et al., 1995; Stitzer & Bigelow, 1978). In this program, patients take home a sealed bottle of methadone from the dispensary window after consuming their usual daily dose. Patients are instructed to keep the bottle in a safe place (i.e., away from children) and to ingest the methadone at their usual dosing time the following day. This privilege is valuable because patients are not required to come to the clinic the next day. The obvious risk is that patients with a history of opioid abuse and criminal activity are given a narcotic to take outside the clinic without supervision. Patients may ingest the methadone on the same day they receive a dose in the clinic (i.e., double dosing) or divert the methadone by either giving it to an acquaintance or selling it at street value. Most clinics develop procedures to limit inappropriate use of methadone and diversion. For instance, a take-home recall policy is often used in which counselors call patients on a random basis and ask them to return their unopened take-home bottle on the following day. This policy is helpful for detecting diversion, yet patients are often willing to risk program consequences. It is also important to consider that the more stringent consequences are attached to diversion, the less valuable take homes may appear to patients.

Perhaps the earliest published experimental study evaluating the effects of contingent take-home reinforcement on drug use was conducted by Milby, Garrett, English, Fritschi, and Clarke (1978). These researchers randomly assigned 69 methadone maintenance patients to one of two groups. Following a 7-week baseline period, experimental patients ($n = 51$) were told that they would receive take home privileges if during a designated 7-week period they remained drug free and engaged in full-time productive activity (work or school). Take homes were withdrawn contingent on the submission of a drug-positive urine or the loss of productive activity.

It was implied (although not explicitly stated) that patients could re-earn take-home privileges immediately following return to abstinence or productive activity. Unfortunately, neither the total number of take homes administered nor the amount of time patients were observed following initiation of the intervention was reported. Control patients ($n = 18$) were informed that take-home privileges could not be earned for 2 months, after which time they could earn take homes in a manner consistent with the contingencies described above.

Patients in the contingent group evidenced a significant, albeit modest, increase in drug-negative urine samples submitted as compared with baseline rates (73% vs. 80%); patients in the control group did not evidence a significant change in drug-free urine samples submitted (87% vs. 88%). Further analyses revealed that a somewhat higher percentage of experimental patients submitted seven consecutive drug-free urine samples (36%) and were involved in productive activity (29%) than were control patients (25% and 22%, respectively). These results were not replicated, however, when patients in the control group were switched to the contingent intervention, perhaps because control patients were functioning much better at baseline than experimental patients and had little room for improvement. It is interesting to note that effects of the contingency were specific in that patients were satisfied to meet the minimum requirements of the contingency contract.

Ten years later, Magura, Casriel, Goldsmith, Strug, and Lipton (1988) extended the above study by reducing the duration of abstinence required to earn take homes. This decision was based on data published by Stitzer and colleagues (e.g., Stitzer, Bigelow, & Liebson, 1980; Stitzer, Bigelow, Liebson, & Hawthorne, 1982) showing that patients exhibited substantial changes in drug use (benzodiazepines, heroin) when monetary privileges were made contingent on shorter durations of abstinence. In addition to modifying the schedule of take-home reinforcement, these researchers worked with a different cohort of opioid abusers who were abusing cocaine at higher rates than previously observed. Thirty-three patients were observed for 3 months before being assigned to a series of 1-month contingency contracts specifying that they would receive one take home for each week a drug-free urine sample was submitted. Patients would not earn take homes on weeks they were drug positive. The monthly contracts were renewed as many as three times, although the conditions for renewal were not made clear.

A within-subjects analysis demonstrated that the mean percentage of drug-free urine samples submitted did not significantly differ from baseline (68%) to experimental (64%) conditions. Post hoc analyses, however, showed two discrete responses to the intervention: 34% completely abstained from drug use during the contingency period, and the remaining 66% submitted drug-positive urine samples at a rate equal to or greater than baseline. Cocaine abusers performed considerably worse than patients abusing other drugs, although no other individual difference variables differentiated treatment responders from failures.

More recently, Stitzer, Iguchi, and Felch (1992) used a well-controlled between-subjects design and a different reinforcement schedule to examine the effects of take homes on the drug use of new intakes to a methadone maintenance program. Fifty-three new intakes completed a 12-week baseline and were randomly assigned to one of two treatment conditions. Experimental patients ($n = 26$) earned one take home following each period of 2 consecutive weeks of drug-free urine samples submitted; one take home was withdrawn following each week with any drug-positive urine sample. A maximum of three take homes per week could be earned during the course of the study. Patients in the control condition ($n = 27$) received take homes on a random schedule independent of urinalysis results, permitting researchers to evaluate whether the contingent aspect of take-home administration (rather than the mere receipt of take homes) was responsible for changes in drug use. Control patients were transferred to the experimental intervention after 6 months.

The results were consistent with the above studies and showed only a modest increase in the overall mean percentage of drug-free urine samples submitted for patients in the experimental condition during the intervention as compared with the preintervention baseline (32% to 36%); patients in the control group evidenced a noticeable (although not significant) reduction in drug-free urine samples submitted (39% to 30%). Between-groups differences in drug-free urines submitted during the intervention also were not significant. However, post hoc analyses demonstrated that 32% of the patients in the experimental group showed improvement as defined by submitting at least 4 consecutive weeks of drug-free urine samples and increasing overall percentage of drug-free urines by a minimum of 10%. Only 8% of the patients in the control group met this success criteria. In addition, 28% of the patients in the control group met success criteria after switching to the experimental condition. A study of individual difference responding revealed that a relatively low rate of baseline drug use, as seen by at least occasional submission of a drug-free urine sample, best predicted success.

What can one learn from these studies? Each study evaluated slightly different reinforcement schedules for initiating and maintaining drug abstinence. Also the patient samples in these studies exhibited progressively higher rates of drug use throughout the decade, reflecting perhaps both the emerging influence of cocaine as the primary drug of choice in opioid-dependent outpatients (Ball & Ross, 1991; Condelli et al., 1991) and increased urinalysis surveillance. Nevertheless, the results across studies were remarkably consistent and demonstrated only modest aggregate changes in drug use from baseline to intervention. Yet a substantial number of patients (approximately 30–35%) appeared to significantly benefit from the take-home intervention, suggesting that this intervention holds promise as a useful adjunct to the treatment for a subgroup of opioid abusers.

It is important to note that these studies also identified patients most likely to succeed in a take-home incentive program. Magura et al. (1988) observed that contingent take homes were more effective for patients using illicit drugs other than cocaine, although Stitzer et al. (1992) showed that it was the rate of baseline drug use, rather than class of drug use, that best predicted treatment response. Kidorf, Stitzer, and Brooner (1994) engaged in a more detailed analysis of individual difference responding to a clinic-wide application of the contingent take-home intervention used by Stitzer et al. In addition to replicating the finding that lower baseline rates of drug use predicted successful treatment outcome, these researchers showed that variables such as full-time employment and a non-drug-using partner also predicted good outcome.

It is not surprising, of course, that patients with higher severity of drug or other psychosocial problems would be less responsive to the take-home intervention. How might take homes be used to affect this subset of resistant drug users? One possibility is to limit the take-home intervention to a single class of drugs. Although the studies reviewed above targeted all illicit-drug use, outcomes for some patients may be improved by intensifying the focus to the drug most frequently used. Stitzer and colleagues, for example, conducted a series of within-subjects studies (e.g., Stitzer et al., 1980, 1982) showing that patients reduced selected drug use (benzodiazepines, heroin) when reinforcement (money or take homes) was provided contingent on extended periods of drug abstinence. These studies also showed that abstinence achieved within one class of drugs did not cause a significant increase in the use of other classes of drugs.

It is also likely that at least a subset of patients in the above studies who did not respond favorably to the take-home incentive were sedative dependent and unable to safely reduce and stop use on their own. For these patients, it may be helpful to supplement clinic-based incentives with supervised inpatient or outpatient medical detoxification (Smith, Landry, & Wesson, 1989). Take homes may be used to extend treatment gains established during the detoxification.

A similar strategy may be used for cocaine abusers, although detoxification from cocaine does not pose the same medical risks. Another alternative is to increase the potency of the take-home incentive through integration with other clinic-based incentives. Kidorf and Stitzer (1996), for example, randomly assigned 16 methadone patients who had not responded to the clinic's usual take-home incentive program to one of two treatment conditions. In the experimental condition, patients received a take home for each drug-free urine sample submitted. For each drug-positive urine sample, however, patients received a splitdose of their methadone. Patients were required to come to the clinic on two separate occasions (during the morning and afternoon hours) to receive a complete daily dose of methadone. Patients exposed to this intervention submitted significantly more drug-free urine samples (29%) than patients assigned to a control condition who did not receive take homes or a split dose (9%), illustrating the potential benefits of a combined approach.

Up until now, we focused on studies evaluating the impact of contingent take homes on drug use. However, many patients may lack the skills necessary to initiate abstinence. An alternative means by which take homes may be used is to help patients build abstinence-related skills or to reinforce attendance to counseling sessions that teach these skills. In fact, studies that apply contingent take homes in this fashion demonstrate reliable and robust results. In perhaps the earliest controlled evaluation of take-home incentives, Stitzer et al. (1977) showed that patients attended scheduled routine counseling sessions much more frequently when they received take homes contingent on attendance (75–89% of the time) as compared with when they were not rewarded for counseling attendance (an approximately 45% compliance rate). Kidorf, Stitzer, Brooner, and Goldberg (1994) extended this finding by demonstrating that take homes could be used to reinforce attendance at special skills building sessions supplemental to routine counseling; patients who received take homes attended 75% of scheduled sessions, whereas those who did not receive take homes attended only 7% of scheduled sessions.

The question of whether take-home contingencies would be more effective in modifying drug use when applied to counseling attendance versus directly to drug use was addressed in a study by Iguchi et al. (1996). All patients were scheduled to attend eight psychoeducational group counseling sessions during a 24-week trial. Patients assigned to the contingent attendance condition could earn up to four take homes per week for attending scheduled group counseling sessions. Patients assigned to the contingent urine condition could earn up to four take homes per week for submitting drug-free urine samples, based on a reinforcement schedule used by Stitzer et al. (1992). As expected, patients in the contingent attendance condition attended a greater proportion of scheduled groups (60%) than did patients in the contingent urine condition (0%). In contrast, patients in the contingent urine condition exhibited an increase in drug-free urine samples submitted over the course of the study (from 28% to 48%), whereas patients in the contingent attendance condition exhibited a decrease in drug-free urine samples submitted (from 42% to 32%). Thus, reinforcing drug-free urine samples was the more effective intervention, although eight psychoeducational groups during a 24-week period could be an inadequate number of counseling sessions to modify drug use in patients with severe substance use disorder.

Finally, take homes also may be used to reinforce other adaptive behavior more directly. Milby et al. (1978) showed that contingent take homes enhanced performance of productive activity, defined as employment, vocational training, or education. However, because the take-home contingency was placed on both drug use and productive activity, it was not possible to evaluate the impact of this intervention separately for each outcome measure. Expanding the scope of clinic behaviors, Stitzer and Bigelow (1984) showed that contingent take homes reinforced payment of routine clinic fees. In addition, Magura, Casriel, Goldsmith, and Lipton (1987) presented descriptive data showing that contingent take homes reinforced such behaviors as complying with clinic regulations, pursuing vocational behavior, and even saving money. These studies provide evidence that the contingent use of take homes can affect a range of behaviors thought to influence the treatment response of opioid abusers receiving methadone substitution.

CONTINGENT METHADONE DOSE ALTERATIONS

Patients receiving methadone substitution are typically preoccupied with the quantity of methadone dose they receive. They may get higher doses of methadone if they are actively using heroin, experiencing opiate withdrawal, or reporting enhanced desire to use heroin, although the effects of this intervention in isolation on heroin use is not clear (Havassy & Tschann, 1984). But what if patients use drugs supplemental to heroin, which is frequently the case for patients receiving methadone substitution? The same studies that demonstrate the effectiveness of higher methadone doses on heroin use (e.g., Strain et al., 1993) also show that methadone dose has little to no effect on the use of other drugs, such as cocaine or benzodiazepines. The conservative approach may be to treat heroin use and other drug use separately and initiate methadone dose changes on the basis of heroin use but independent of other drug use or behaviors in which patients may be engaged.

An alternative strategy, however, is to provide methadone dose alterations in a contingent manner to affect all supplemental drug use. That methadone dose alterations can be used as reinforcement is supported by studies showing that patients cite control over methadone dose as a desirable incentive, although somewhat less valuable than take homes (Kidorf et al., 1995; Stitzer & Bigelow, 1978). Other studies show that methadone produces a measurable euphoric effect (McCaul, Bigelow, Stitzer, & Liebson, 1982), that patients receiving methadone substitution will choose to self-administer methadone supplemental to their stable dose (Stitzer, McCaul, Bigelow, & Liebson, 1983), and that patients typically prefer higher versus lower doses (Bickel, Higgins, & Stitzer, 1986). These studies suggest that methadone dose alterations can potentially operate as a positive reinforcer when dose is raised contingent on behavior change and as a negative reinforcer when dose is reduced contingent on behavior change.

An advantage to using methadone dose alterations as a reinforcer is that patients are not provided with a narcotic to take away from the clinic. Methadone dose changes can be safely administered and supervised at the clinic. In addition, some patients may find control of methadone dose more reinforcing than methadone take homes. Yet this intervention is also associated with potential drawbacks. For instance, there is an accepted limit to how much methadone patients can be administered, thus placing a ceiling on the potency of the reinforcer. When used as a negative reinforcer, there is a risk that patients will increase heroin use as methadone dose is reduced (Senay, Dorus, Golberg, & Thornton, 1977). Patients also may find it increasingly difficult to make required behavior changes when their dose is at a lower level, increasing the chance of poor treatment outcome and eventual detoxification.

Glosser (1983) used a token reinforcement program to evaluate the efficacy of contingent methadone dose alterations. Patients in the contingency management group ($n = 97$) earned up to 4 points per day by meeting a number of objective treatment goals, such as attending scheduled counseling sessions and submitting drug-free urine samples. Each day, patients presented their point total at the dispensary window: Patients who earned the full 4 points could increase their dose by up to 4 mg, and those who earned less than 4 points had their dose reduced by the deficiency in their point total (i.e., 3 points = 1-mg decrease). Because the methadone dose was adjusted each day, there was theoretically no cap on how high successful patients could eventually take their dose, and detoxification from the program was possible for those who failed. Contingent patients were compared with a much smaller group of patients ($n = 20$) who received usual-care methadone treatment and individual counseling without contingent dose alterations. The results across the 6-month assessment period showed that contingency management patients submitted significantly fewer drug-positive urine samples (14%) than did patients in the usual-care control condition (39%). In addition, the intervention did not promote treatment dropout; in fact patients in the contingent condition remained in treatment twice as long as patients in the control condition. It is somewhat difficult to draw definitive conclusions from this study because patients were not randomly assigned to treatment groups. Nevertheless, the study illustrates the potential benefits of a clinicwide application of this intervention.

Stitzer, Bickel, Bigelow, and Liebson (1986) used a within-subjects design and a different contingent methadone delivery system to examine the impact of dose increase and decrease contingencies on illicit-drug use. Twenty patients who had submitted more than 50% drug-positive urine samples during a baseline assessment period were assigned to one of two methadone dose alteration conditions. Patients assigned to the positive incentive condition earned dose increases of 5 mg for each drug-free urine sample submitted, up to a maximum dose 160% higher than their starting dose, but they returned to their starting dose if drug-positive samples were submitted. Patients assigned to the negative incentive condition were given 5-mg dose decreases for each drug-positive urine sample submitted, but their dose could not fall below 40% of their starting dose. They also returned to their starting dose if drug-free samples were submitted. Results demonstrated that patients in both conditions exhibited significant increases over time in drug-free urine samples submitted, from average rates of 12–14% drug-free urine samples at baseline to rates of 41–44% drug-free urine samples during the assessment period. Analyses of the individual data show a bipolar response: Approximately one half of the patients showed marked improvement, whereas the other half exhibited little or no change. It is important to note that the researchers also observed that patients in the negative incentive condition were more likely to leave treatment earlier.

The efficacy of contingent methadone dose alterations also has been demonstrated during methadone detoxification. Higgins, Stitzer, Bigelow, and Liebson (1986) assigned 39 patients on a 90-day methadone detoxification schedule to one of three treatment conditions. All patients received a gradual dose reduction from Week 4 to Week 11. Patients in the contingent group (n = 13) received methadone dose supplements of up to 20 mg during the dose reduction phase for each opiate-free urine sample. Noncontingent patients (n = 13) could request 20-mg dose supplements independent of urinalysis results during the dose reduction phase. Control patients (n = 13) were not given the opportunity to earn dose supplements. Results show that patients in the contingent group submitted significantly fewer opiate-positive urine samples during the final 3 weeks of the dose reduction phase (14%) than patients in either the noncontingent (38%) or control (50%) conditions. These researchers also noted that the 20-mg increases offered to both the contingent and noncontingent groups probably accounted for the finding that these groups achieved better treatment attendance and retention throughout the detoxification phase than did the control group.

Finally, Iguchi, Stitzer, Bigelow, and Liebson (1988) evaluated whether methadone dose alterations enhanced the effectiveness of a take-home reinforcement intervention. Following a 12-week baseline period, 16 patients were randomly assigned to one of two treatment groups. Patients in both groups earned one take home for each period of 2 consecutive weeks of drug-free urine samples (maximum of three per week). The only difference between the groups was that patients exposed to the combined intervention received a 10% dose decrease every week in which two to three urine samples tested drug positive. Results show that both groups evidenced significant increases in drug-free urine samples submitted from baseline (8%) to intervention (42%). However, no between-groups differences were found, and the majority of treatment dropouts were patients exposed to the combined incentive condition.

In summary, this series of studies provides support for the effectiveness of using contingent methadone dose alterations to modify illicit-drug use. As discussed in the take-home literature, a substantial number of patients appear to benefit from this intervention. Note that these studies were virtually all conducted before the explosion of cocaine use in the methadone-using population when patients were supplementing primarily with opiates or sedatives; whether this intervention is effective for cocaine abusers remains to be determined. In fact, there has been little study of individual differences responding to methadone dose alterations, and it is likely that this intervention, like take homes, is most effective for those who exhibit less severe drug use and for those who find control of methadone dose a valuable incentive.

In addition, methadone-dose increases and decreases appear to yield similar results; dose decreases, however, seem to be associated with greater risk of treatment dropout, thus reducing the desirability of this intervention for modifying drug use. The same conclusion was drawn by Nolimal and Crowley (1990), who conducted a chart review of 14 patients to evaluate the results of methadone dose contracting implemented in their own drug abuse clinic. These investigators observed that such contracting clearly reduced drug use, although the positive effects appeared to diminish over time. In addition, 36% of the patients chose to detoxify off the methadone program rather than stop illicit-drug use. Nolimal and Crowley argued that the risk of discharge to some patients outweighed the potential benefits of this intervention, and they outlined a treatment policy such that patients would continue to be maintained on methadone despite continued drug use.

Use of this intervention for targeting behaviors other than drug use may have less of a negative impact on retention. Studies that used methadone dose alterations in this manner show dramatic results. One effective strategy is the use of a methadone dose decrease as a negative reinforcer to encourage patients to participate in more intensive treatment. Liebson, Tommasello, and Bigelow (1978), for example, used a contingent methadone dose intervention to treat severe alcohol problems of methadone patients. Twenty-five alcoholic methadone patients were assigned to one of two treatment groups. Patients in the experimental group had the drug Antabuse (disulfiram) mixed into their daily dose of methadone. Antabuse induces physical sickness following alcohol consumption. Patients who refused Antabuse were placed on a 21-day methadone dose taper unless they agreed to take the methadone–Antabuse combination. Control patients were given their daily methadone dose independent of the Antabuse prescription. As expected, patients in the experimental group evidenced significantly and substantially less drinking and fewer arrests than did patients in the control group.

Kidorf, Brooner, and King (1997) provided another example of the potency of this approach for enhancing treatment involvement. These researchers wanted methadone patients to bring in a drug-free significant other as part of their treatment. The purpose of the intervention was to use the significant other to monitor the patient's compliance to their treatment plan outside of the clinic. Seventy-five patients who were actively abusing illicit drugs were informed that their methadone dose would be lowered if they did not bring a drug-free significant other into treatment to participate in 6 weeks of conjoint group counseling; the dose would be raised to baseline level, however, contingent on compliance with this intervention. Although most patients initially reported that they could not identify a drug-free support person, 85% of the patients brought in drug-free support. Patients who brought in a significant other attended 85% of their scheduled counseling sessions. A similar approach was used to encourage patients to seek and find employment (Kidorf, Hollander, King, & Brooner, 1998). Unemployed patients participating in methadone treatment for at least 1 year were given 2 months to secure 20 hr of paid or volunteer work. Those who remained unemployed were referred to more intensive counseling for up to 10 additional weeks. Following the counseling phase, patients were placed on a methadone dose taper until employment was verified. The results showed that 75% of the patients attained employment and that most of these patients (78%) continued working throughout the 6-month follow-up. In addition to demonstrating the power of contingent methadone dose decreases, these two studies provide good examples of how clinic-based contingencies can be used to influence aspects of the patient's natural environment toward therapeutic ends.

Overall, contingent methadone dose alterations can dramatically affect both drug use and participation in treatment. This intervention appears to have similar effects on drug use whether used as a positive or negative reinforcer, although its ability to enhance treatment involvement when used as a negative reinforcer (i.e., avoiding dose decrease) is particularly impressive. As with any intervention, this contingency also has potential to harm. Patients unable to sufficiently modify behavior may progressively lose methadone dose to the point that continuation of treatment is jeopardized. Treatment discharge is particularly undesirable because patients separated from treatment may increase their drug use and intensify involvement in high-risk activities, such as needle sharing and unsafe sexual behavior. It is important to consider whether the benefits to the program outweigh the risks to selected patients. In fact, this dilemma is raised again within the context of the next intervention discussed in this chapter: contingent treatment availability.

CONTINGENT TREATMENT AVAILABILITY

Perhaps the most popular intervention used in contemporary methadone clinics is contingent treatment availability (Kolar, Brown, Weddington, & Ball, 1990). Patients are informed that they will be discharged from treatment if they fail to meet certain treatment requirements (e.g., submitting drug-free urine samples). Many programs view this intervention as their only leverage to modify drug use or other maladaptive behavior. It remains popular because it often works; patients faced with the possibility of losing access to treatment often change behavior to meet program demands. This intervention may be even more powerful when other contingencies operating outside of the clinic (e.g., probation) mandate that the patient remain in treatment.

Yet this intervention, as typically applied, possesses many drawbacks. In many programs, contingent treatment availability is used as a last resort at times when both the patient and clinical staff have become demoralized about the patient's treatment progress. In addition, the intervention often is applied inconsistently, such that patients do not receive reliable feedback regarding program expectancies. It also may be unreasonable to require some patients to stop drug use when they are not concurrently taught skills needed to initiate and maintain abstinence. Finally, patients who do not succeed are inevitably discharged from treatment, which may result in an escalation of drug use and other high-risk behavior (Nolimal & Crowley, 1990).

Note that the decision to detoxify a patient from treatment is never an easy one. On the one hand, treatment providers have the duty to deliver effective treatment services to all patients who seek care. Treatment termination is often an acknowledgement by the program that their services are not sufficient to help the patient. On the other hand, drug abusers largely outnumber community treatment slots, and it may be more cost effective to concentrate treatment efforts on the subset of patients willing to comply with program policies. Continued drug use while enrolled in a treatment program is not without its own risks (especially intravenous use), and resistant drug users may eventually be discharged because of chronic intoxication and other disruptive behaviors.

Studies that provide clear instruction regarding behaviors that will terminate treatment demonstrate that contingent treatment availability remains a powerful intervention. In a study by McCarthy and Borders (1985), methadone patients were assigned to one of two treatment conditions. Patients in the experimental group ($n = 36$) were informed that they would be discharged following 4 consecutive months in which they submitted at least one drug-positive urine sample. To further help this group comply, experimenters sent letters to patients who submitted 2 consecutive months of drug-positive urine samples, reiterating the treatment contracts and encouraging attendance at scheduled counseling sessions. The control group ($n = 33$) did not have any contingencies on their drug use. Results show that patients in the experimental group demonstrated a slightly higher percentage of drug-free months (57%) than did patients in the control group (51%); these differences were much more prominent in patients who completed 1 year of treatment (71% vs. 50%). It is interesting to note and perhaps counterintuitive that a higher percentage of experimental patients completed 1 year of treatment (53%) than did control patients (30%).

Dolan, Black, Penk, Robinowitz, and DeFord (1985) used a contingent treatment availability contract to modify the drug use of 21 male polydrug-abusing methadone patients. Patients were informed that they would be discharged from treatment if they submitted any drug-positive urine samples during the 30-day contracts. Contracts were initiated after different treatment durations for different study patients. Results show that 11 of the 21 patients submitted the required 30 days of drug-free urine samples during their contracts; the contract failures were discharged from treatment and were not permitted to reapply for more than 30 days following discharge. A post hoc evaluation of the data (Dolan, Black, Penk, Robinowitz, & DeFord, 1986) reveals that those who succeeded were older ($M = 46$ vs. 36 years), had more treatment experience, exhibited less baseline drug use, and were less likely to use opiates and cocaine in combination.

Contingent treatment availability can also be used as a positive reinforcer. Kidorf and Stitzer (1993) assigned 44 new admissions to a 90-day premaintenance probationary period. Within the first 7 weeks, patients in the experimental condition ($n = 22$) were required to submit 2 consecutive weeks of drug-free urine samples to gain access to 2 additional years of methadone maintenance treatment. Control patients ($n = 22$) were yoked to experimental patients, such that their access to long-term methadone maintenance was unpredictable and unrelated to performance. Results show that 50% of the experimental group submitted 2 consecutive weeks of drug-free urine samples, compared with only 14% of the yoked control group.

Despite the consistency in results across studies, it is hard to feel good about an intervention that discharges half of the patients to whom it is applied. Yet data from a large-scale clinical trial at Johns Hopkins University School of Medicine (Brooner, Kidorf, King, & Bigelow, 1996) suggest that it is possible to retain the power of contingent treatment availability while minimizing the adverse outcome of treatment dropout. This novel approach is called *behaviorally contingent pharmacotherapy*, in which continued methadone administration is completely integrated as a consequence of attendance at scheduled counseling sessions and drug use versus abstinence. This intervention extends contingency management research by integrating well-defined contingencies with psychosocial support designed to help patients succeed.

Patients exposed to behaviorally contingent pharmacotherapy are referred to increasing intensity of counseling services contingent on drug use or missed counseling sessions. Patients may return to a less intensive level of care if they demonstrate abstinence and comply with counseling. Patients who continue to use drugs or miss counseling sessions at the highest level of care, however, are discharged from treatment through a 21–30-day methadone detoxification. Even these patients can be readmitted to treatment if they attend scheduled counseling sessions and comply with other aspects of their treatment plan (e.g., engage in volunteer activity, include drug-free social support) during the detoxification phase. Thus, the discharge policy may be viewed as therapeutic as it highlights to patients the severity of their drug use and provides powerful incentive (i.e., treatment readmission) for compliance to their treatment plan.

To test the efficacy of this intervention, researchers study patients randomly assigned to either behaviorally contingent pharmacotherapy treatment or to a control group that received methadone substitution independent of drug use or counseling attendance. Preliminary results based on the first 75 patients demonstrate that patients exposed to the contingent intervention attended a higher percentage of scheduled counseling sessions (85% vs. 35%) and submitted a lower percentage of drug-positive urine samples (43% vs. 67%) during the first 90 days of treatment than did control patients. No between-groups differences in treatment retention were identified.

In summary, this group of studies suggests that for many patients contingent treatment availability is an effective intervention for reducing drug use. For a substantial number of patients, however, drug use continues unabated followed by immediate loss of access to treatment. This disadvantage can be at least partly circumvented by the institution of a readmission policy; yet it remains possible that a subset of patients will choose to continue drug use rather than remain in treatment and comply with all elements of the treatment plan. Development of strategies to help even the most resistant of patients respond favorably to these clinic-based contingencies should be the focus of future research.

CONCLUSION

Daily methadone substitution and weekly to monthly counseling cannot be expected to sufficiently address the range of problems presented by contemporary opioid abusers in treatment. There is enough evidence at this point to recommend the use of contingency management strategies for enhancing the effectiveness of methadone substitution. We focused on three clinic-based interventions that possess the most empirical support: contingent take-home methadone doses, contingent methadone dose alterations, and contingent treatment delivery. Each of these interventions can be targeted directly on supplemental drug use to reduce this unwanted behavior or targeted on participation in treatment services to indirectly reduce drug use by teaching coping skills and addressing other barriers to abstinence.

The interventions described in this chapter can be applied in most community clinics with little to no additional cost; maximum use of resources is especially important when funding for treatment is low and the ratio of patients to treatment staff is high. Each of these interventions can be structured within the usual-care practices of the clinic (with the advantage of consistent application across all patients; see Calsyn & Saxon, 1987) or can be applied on a case-by-case basis to help patients adhere to recommendations specified by their individual treatment plan. Our experience is that contingency management procedures energize treatment staff and help restructure the therapist–patient relationship in a positive way, such that both parties work together to meet program expectancies and goals.

More important than the effect of contingency management on treatment providers, of course, is its effect on patient behavior. The objective evidence is clear: A substantial number of patients modify drug use and other maladaptive behavior in response to carefully implemented clinic-based contingencies. But the subjective impact of contingency management is no less important. Patients often look to treatment programs to provide structure and support, and they often are willing to work up to the expectations set by these programs. Contingency management clarifies these expectations and provides objective consequences on the basis of patient response. In other words, patients receive what they are told they will receive—a seemingly unremarkable event that is too rare in the lives of many drug abusers.

REFERENCES

American Psychiatric Association. (1994). *Diagnostic and statistical manual of mental disorders* (4th ed.). Washington, DC: Author.

Azrin, N. H., McMahon, P. T., Donohue, B., Besalel, V. A., Lapinski, K. J., Kogan, E. S., Acierno, R. E., & Galloway, E. (1994). Behavior therapy for drug abuse: A controlled treatment outcome study. *Behavior Research and Therapy, 32,* 857–866.

Ball, J. C., & Ross, A. (1991). *The effectiveness of methadone maintenance treatment.* New York: Springer-Verlag.

Bickel, W. K., Higgins, S. T., & Stitzer, M. L. (1986). Choice of blind methadone dose increases by methadone maintenance patients. *Drug and Alcohol Dependence, 18,* 165–171.

Brooner, R. K., King, V. L., Kidorf, M., Schmidt, C., & Bigelow, G. E. (1997). Psychiatric and substance use comorbidity among contemporary treatment-seeking opioid abusers. *Archives of General Psychiatry, 54,* 71–80.

Brooner, R. K., Kidorf, M., King, V. L., & Bigelow, G. E. (1996). Using behaviorally contingent pharmacotherapy in opioid abusers enhances treatment outcome [Abstract]. In L. S. Harris (Ed.), *Problems of drug dependence 1996: Proceedings of the 58th annual scientific meeting, the College on Problems of Drug Dependence* (NIDA Monograph Series 174, p. 305). Washington, DC: U.S. Government Printing Office.

Calsyn, D. A., & Saxon, A. J. (1987). A system for uniform application of contingencies for illicit drug use. *Journal of Substance Abuse Treatment, 4,* 41–47.

Condelli, W. S., Fairbank, J. A., Dennis, M. L., & Rachal, J. V. (1991). Cocaine use by clients in methadone programs: Significance, scope, and behavioral interventions. *Journal of Substance Abuse Treatment, 8,* 203–212.

Dolan, M. P., Black, J. L., Penk, W. E., Robinowitz, R., & DeFord, H. A. (1985). Contracting for treatment termination to reduce illicit drug use among methadone maintenance treatment failures. *Journal of Consulting and Clinical Psychology, 53,* 549–551.

Dolan, M. P., Black, J. L., Penk, W. E., Robinowitz, R., & DeFord, H. A. (1986). Predicting the outcome of contingency contracting for drug abuse. *Behavior Therapy, 17,* 470–474.

Glosser, D. S. (1983). The use of a token economy to reduce illicit drug use among methadone maintenance clients. *Addictive Behaviors, 8,* 247–252.

Havassy, B. E., Hall, S. M., & Wasserman, D. A. (1991). Social support and relapse: Commonalities among alcoholics, opiate users, and cigarette smokers. *Addictive Behaviors, 16,* 235–246.

Havassy, B. E., & Tschann, J. M. (1984). Chronic heroin use during methadone treatment: A test of the efficacy of high maintenance doses. *Addictive Behaviors, 9,* 57–65.

Higgins, S. T., Stitzer, M. L., Bigelow, G. E., & Liebson, I. A. (1986). Contingent methadone delivery: Effects on illicit opiate use. *Drug and Alcohol Dependence, 17,* 311–322.

Hubbard, R. L., Mardsen, M. D., Rachal, J. V., Harwood, H. J., Cacanaugh, E. R., & Ginzburg, H. M. (1989). *Drug abuse treatment: A national study of effectiveness.* Chapel Hill: University of North Carolina Press.

Iguchi, M. Y., Lamb, R. J., Belding, M. A., Platt, J. J., Husband, S. D., & Morral, A. R. (1996). Contingent reinforcement of group participation versus abstinence in a methadone maintenance program. *Experimental and Clinical Psychopharmacology, 4,* 315–321.

Iguchi, M. Y., Stitzer, M. L., Bigelow, G. E., & Liebson, I. A. (1988). Contingency management in methadone maintenance: Effects of reinforcing and aversive consequences on illicit polydrug use. *Drug and Alcohol Dependence, 22*, 1–7.

Kauffman, J. F., & Woody, G. E. (1995). *Matching treatment to patient needs in opioid substitution therapy* (DHHS Pub. No. SMA 95-3049). Washington, DC: U.S. Government Printing Office.

Kidorf, M., Brooner, R. K., & King, V. L. (1997). Motivating methadone patients to include drug-free significant others in treatment: A behavioral intervention. *Journal of Substance Abuse Treatment, 14*, 23–28.

Kidorf, M., Brooner, R. K., King, V. L., Stoller, K. B., & Wertz, J. (1998). Predictive validity of cocaine, sedative, and alcohol dependence diagnoses. *Journal of Consulting and Clinical Psychology, 66*, 168–173.

Kidorf, M., Hollander, J. R., King, V. L., & Brooner, R. K. (1998). Increasing employment of opioid dependent outpatients: An intensive behavioral intervention. *Drug and Alcohol Dependence, 50*, 73–80.

Kidorf, M., & Stitzer, M. L. (1993). Contingent access to methadone maintenance treatment: Effects on cocaine use of mixed opiate-cocaine abusers. *Experimental and Clinical Psychopharmacology, 1*, 200–206.

Kidorf, M., & Stitzer, M. L. (1996). Contingent use of take-homes and split-dosing to reduce illicit drug use of methadone patients. *Behavior Therapy, 27*, 41–51.

Kidorf, M., Stitzer, M. L., & Brooner, R. K. (1994). Characteristics of methadone patients responding to take-home incentives. *Behavior Therapy, 25*, 109–121.

Kidorf, M., Stitzer, M. L., Brooner, R. K., & Goldberg, J. (1994). Contingent methadone take-home doses reinforce adjunct therapy attendance of methadone maintenance patients. *Drug and Alcohol Dependence, 36*, 221–226.

Kidorf, M., Stitzer, M. L., & Griffiths, R. R. (1995). Evaluating the reinforcement value of clinic-based privileges through a multiple choice procedure. *Drug and Alcohol Dependence, 39*, 167–172.

Kolar, A. F., Brown, B. S., Weddington, W. W., & Ball, J. C. (1990). A treatment crisis: Cocaine use by clients in methadone maintenance programs. *Journal of Substance Abuse Treatment, 7*, 101–107.

Liebson, I. A., Tommaselo, A., & Bigelow, G. E. (1978). A behavioral treatment of alcoholic methadone patients. *Annals of Internal Medicine, 89*, 342–344.

Magura, S., Casriel, C., Goldsmith, D. S., & Lipton, D. S. (1987). Contracting with clients in methadone treatment. *Social Casework: The Journal of Contemporary Social Work, 68*, 485–494.

Magura, S., Casriel, C., Goldsmith, D. S., Strug, D. L., & Lipton, D. S. (1988). Contingency contracting with polydrug-abusing methadone patients. *Addictive Behaviors, 13*, 113–118.

McCarthy, J. J., & Borders, O. T. (1985). Limit setting on drug abuse in methadone maintenance patients. *American Journal of Psychiatry, 142* 1419–1423.

McCaul, M. E., Bigelow, G. E., Stitzer, M. L., & Liebson, I. (1982). Short-term effects of oral methadone in methadone maintenance subjects. *Clinical Pharmacology and Therapeutics, 31*, 753–761.

McLellan, A. T., Ball, J. C., Rosen, L., & O'Brien, C. P. (1981). Pretreatment source of income and response to methadone maintenance: A follow-up study. *American Journal of Psychiatry, 138*, 785–789.

McLellan, A. T., Luborsky, L. K., Woody, G. E., O'Brien, C. P., & Druley, K. A. (1983). Predicting response to alcohol and drug abuse treatments. *Archives of General Psychiatry, 40*, 620–625.

Milby, J. B., Garrett, C., English, C., Fritschi, O., & Clarke, C. (1978). Take-home methadone: Contingency effects on drug-seeking and productivity of narcotic addicts. *Addictive Behaviors, 3*, 215–220.

Nolimal, D., & Crowley, T. J. (1990). Difficulties in a clinical application of methadone-dose contingency contracting. *Journal of Substance Abuse Treatment, 7*, 219–224.

Rounsaville, B. J., Weissman, M. M., Crits-Christoph, K., Wilber, C., & Kleber, H. (1982). Diagnosis and symptoms of depression in opiate addicts: Course and relationship to treatment outcome. *Archives of General Psychiatry, 39*, 151–156.

Senay, E. C., Dorus, W., Goldberg, F., & Thornton, W. (1977). Withdrawal from methadone maintenance. *Archives of General Psychiatry, 34*, 361–367.

Simpson, D. D., & Sells, S. B. (Eds.). (1990). *Opioid addiction and treatment: A 12-year follow-up.* Malabar, FL: Krieger.

Smith, D. E., Landry, M. J., & Wesson, D. R. (1989). Barbiturate, sedative, hypnotic agents. In *Treatment of psychiatric disorders* (Vol. 2, pp. 1294–1308). Washington, DC: American Psychiatric Association.

Stanton, M. D., & Todd, T. C. (1982). *The family therapy of drug abuse and addiction.* New York: Guilford Press.

Stitzer, M. L., Bickel, W. K., Bigelow, G. E., & Liebson, I. A. (1986). Effect of methadone dose contingencies on urinalysis test results of polydrug-abusing methadone-maintenance patients. *Drug and Alcohol Dependence, 18*, 341–348.

Stitzer, M., & Bigelow, G. (1978). Contingency management in a methadone maintenance program: Availability of reinforcers. *International Journal of the Addictions, 13*, 737–746.

Stitzer, M. L., & Bigelow, G. E. (1984). Contingent methadone take-home privileges: Effects on compliance with fee payment schedules. *Drug and Alcohol Dependence, 13*, 395–399.

Stitzer, M., Bigelow, G. E., Lawrence, C., Cohen, J., D'Lugoff, B., & Hawthorne, J. (1977). Medication take-home as a reinforcer in a methadone maintenance program. *Addictive Behaviors, 2*, 9–14.

Stitzer, M. L., Bigelow, G. E., & Liebson, I. (1980). Reducing drug use among methadone maintenance clients: Contingent reinforcement for morphine-free urines. *Addictive Behaviors, 5*, 333–340.

Stitzer, M. L., Bigelow, G. E., Liebson, I. A., & Hawthorne, J. W. (1982). Contingent reinforcement for benzodiazepine-free urines: Evaluation of a drug abuse treatment intervention. *Journal of Applied Behavior Analysis, 15,* 493–503.

Stitzer, M. L., Bigelow, G. E., & McCaul, M. E. (1985). Behavior therapy in drug abuse treatment: Review and evaluation. In R. S. Ashery (Ed.), *Progress in the development of cost-effective treatment for drug abusers* (NIDA Research Monograph 58, DHHS Pub. No. ADM 88-1401, pp. 31–50) Washington, DC: U.S. Government Printing Office.

Stitzer, M. L., Iguchi, M. Y., & Felch, L. (1992). Contingent take-home incentive: Effects of drug use of methadone patients. *Journal of Consulting and Clinical Psychology, 60,* 927–934.

Stitzer, M. L., McCaul, M. E., Bigelow, G. E., & Liebson, I. A. (1983). Oral methadone self-administration: Effects of dose and alternative reinforcers. *Clinical Pharmacology and Therapeutics, 34,* 29–35.

Strain, E. C., Stitzer, M. L., Liebson, I. A., & Bigelow, G. E. (1993). Methadone dose and treatment outcome. *Drug and Alcohol Dependence, 33,* 105–117.

Vaillant, G. (1992). Is there a natural history of addiction? In C. P. O'Brien & J. H. Jaffe (Eds.), *Addictive states* (pp. 41–57). New York: Raven Press.

Woody, G. E., Luborsky, L., McLellan, A. T., O'Brien, C. P., Beck, A. T., Blaine, J., Herman, I., & Hole, A. (1983). Psychotherapy for opiate addicts: Does it help? *Archives of General Psychiatry, 40,* 639–645.

12

REDUCING CIGARETTE SMOKING IN METHADONE MAINTENANCE PATIENTS

STEVEN SHOPTAW, SANDY DOW, DOMINICK L. FROSCH,
WALTER LING, DAMIAN C. MADSEN,
AND MURRAY E. JARVIK

Despite increased awareness of the health risks and often the desire and repeated attempts to quit, nearly 60 million (29%) Americans smoke tobacco (Substance Abuse and Mental Health Services Administration, 1996), and cigarette smoking remains the leading cause of premature and preventable mortality in the United States (U.S. Department of Health and Human Services [DHHS], 1988). Twenty percent of all deaths in the United States are directly related to smoking, including 90% of all lung cancer deaths and 30% of all other cancer deaths. Forty-five percent of all

Preparation of this chapter was supported by National Institute on Drug Abuse Grants R01 DA09992-01 and P50 DA09260-02. Nicotine replacement therapy for the main study was graciously supplied by Smith Kline Beecham. We recognize the expert research assistance of Arthur Corrales, who understands the rigor of the behavioral technician and the complexities of gathering data from substance abusers.

smokers in the United States will die from a tobacco-induced disorder (Orleans, 1995). Lung cancer and cardiovascular diseases resulting from cigarette smoking represent the major preventable causes of death in the United States (U.S. DHHS, 1989).

Although the prevalence of smoking has declined substantially over the past 20 years, this decline has been much slower and less apparent in persons with comorbid drug addiction (American Psychiatric Association [APA], 1996). In fact, the incidence of tobacco smoking among people who abuse alcohol and drugs remains dramatically greater than among the general population (Burling & Ziff, 1988; Sees & Clark, 1993; Zimmerman, Warheit, Ulbrich, & Auth, 1990). Among opiate-dependent and methadone-maintained people, tobacco smoking is significantly associated with morbidity and mortality (Hser, McCarthy, & Anglin, 1994). Yet it is estimated that 85–98% of this addict population smoke cigarettes (Berger & Schweigler, 1972; Carmody, 1992; Sees & Clark, 1991) three times as much as among the general population.

Recent reports indicate that heavy smokers and those with comorbid addiction need more intensive smoking cessation interventions than standard pharmacotherapy alone (Rose, 1996). In this chapter, we briefly review standard smoking cessation treatments and discuss the use of contingency management as a new behavioral intervention for optimizing smoking cessation treatment outcome in methadone-maintained patients.

TOBACCO SMOKING AND ALCOHOL–OTHER DRUG DEPENDENCE

Tobacco smoking or nicotine dependence is classified as a substance abuse disorder (APA, 1994), yet addiction treatment specialists generally maintain that encouraging patients to quit smoking while in treatment for alcohol or other drug dependencies may interfere with their recovery from the primary drug of abuse (Burling, Marshall, & Seidner, 1991). Some substance abuse counselors have argued that it is more important to quit illicit-drug use than to quit smoking. Many counselors have also argued that because cigarette smoking is legal, it is different from other drug dependencies and should be treated differently. They contend that because it is as difficult to quit smoking as it is to achieve abstinence from alcohol–other drugs, concurrent treatment may be too stressful (Hurt et al., 1994). Still, nicotine dependence is the only substance dependence not generally addressed in substance abuse treatment programs (Sees & Clark, 1991).

CONCURRENT TREATMENT FOR SMOKING
AND SUBSTANCE ABUSE

Although clearly smokers with alcohol–drug abuse problems are not likely to stop smoking unless their primary dependence is resolved, it is less clear whether alcohol–drug abusers in treatment are likely to stop smoking (APA, 1996). Among illicit-drug users, the desire to stop smoking during treatment is only slightly less than among nondrug users who smoke (DiFranza & Guerrera, 1990). Recent studies indicate that 50% or more of those in treatment for substance dependence would participate in concurrent smoking cessation treatments if given the option (Frosch, Shoptaw, Jarvik, Rawson, & Ling, 1998a; Joseph, Nichol & Anderson, 1993; Kozlowski, Skinner, Kent, & Pope, 1989). Of 223 daily smokers surveyed while in treatment at the Substance Abuse Inpatient Unit of the San Francisco (California) Veterans Administration Medical Center, 50% of alcohol-, 52% of cocaine-, and 42% of heroin-dependent individuals indicated that they would be interested in quitting smoking while in drug treatment (Sees & Clark, 1993). Yet despite the amount of interest expressed by this group, few substance abuse treatment programs offer concurrent smoking cessation therapy.

Even though illicit-drug users in substance abuse treatment may be more recalcitrant to smoking cessation therapy than nondrug users, some investigators have obtained encouraging treatment results. When Hurt et al. (1994) randomly assigned alcohol–drug-dependent inpatients to a group that received concurrent smoking cessation treatment or to a control group that received no smoking cessation treatment, a similar number of patients in both groups (11 of 51 and 5 of 50, respectively) were not smoking at the end of their hospitalization. However, 6 of the 51 patients in the intervention group were not smoking at the 1-year follow-up compared with none in the control group. Abstinence rates from alcohol and other nonnicotine drugs of dependence were similar for both the intervention (68.6%) and control (66.0%) groups, refuting the notion that concurrent smoking cessation treatment jeopardizes outcomes for treatment of primary drugs of abuse.

Noncontrolled studies suggest that smoking cessation treatment when provided as an adjunct to treatment for other substance abuse actually helps patients attain and maintain sobriety from nonnicotine drugs (Bobo, 1989; Bobo, Gilchrist, Schilling, Noach, & Schinke, 1987; Sees & Clark, 1993). In one large-scale survey of patients in substance abuse treatment at a Veterans Administration medical center where smoke-free environment policies had been adopted, patients who attempted smoking cessation were generally more likely to be drug abstinent at follow-up than those who were treated at the facility before these policies were initiated (Joseph, Nichol, & Anderson, 1993). In a follow-up survey conducted by Sandor

(1991), smokers relapsed to their primary drug more frequently and sooner than nonsmokers.

These findings also are supported by controlled clinical investigation. When Burling, Marshall, and Seidner (1991) randomly assigned 39 veterans in a substance abuse program at the Palo Alto Veterans Administration Medical Center to either a stop-smoking treatment group or to a wait-list control group, not only did the experimental group stay in residential treatment longer, but their postdischarge drug and alcohol abstinence rates were consistently higher than those of the control group. Although no one in either group was abstinent from smoking at the 6-month follow-up, some patients in the treatment group did attain short-term smoking abstinence (about 10 days). Researchers concluded that patients in the treatment group developed a sense of accomplishment from achieving even a short period of nonsmoking, and this limited success may have generalized to their ability to abstain from other drugs.

Despite the advances in developing effective pharmacological and behavioral smoking cessation therapies, only about one fifth to one third of treated smokers are likely to remain abstinent at a 1-year follow-up (Fiore, Smith, Jorenby, & Baker, 1994). This chapter consists of an overview of pharmacological and behavioral treatments currently proposed or used for treatment of nicotine dependence, followed by a review of our work toward optimizing pharmacological smoking cessation therapies in a severely dependent group of cigarette smokers.

EFFECTIVE TOBACCO SMOKING TREATMENTS

Pharmacological Treatments

Pharmacological treatments have played an important role in smoking cessation therapy over the past 2 decades. The most widely used treatments include nicotine agonist (nicotine delivered through polacrilex gum, transdermal patch, nasal spray, etc.) and, more recently, nicotine antagonist (mecamylamine) medications. Other pharmacological treatments, with less demonstrated efficacy, include those that cause aversive reactions to smoking (silver salts), those that involve dopamine release (Zyban), and nonnicotine medications that duplicate nicotine effects (lobeline). Acupuncture and various devices also may be included in this category (APA, 1996). In this chapter, we discuss only those medications that act as nicotine agonists or antagonists.

Nicotine Agonists (Replacement Therapy)

Nicotine replacement therapies act on the nicotinic system directly and are generally used to relieve symptoms of nicotine withdrawal. Nicotine gum (nicotine polacrilex), developed in Sweden, was the first nicotine substitution product marketed for smoking cessation and has been on the market since the mid-1970s. Other methods for delivering nicotine replacement include the transdermal patch, which takes advantage of ready absorption of nicotine across the skin, and, most recently, a nicotine nasal spray. The patch approximates nicotine gum in efficacy (Daughton, Heatley, & Prendergast, 1991; Fiore, Smith, et al., 1994; Hughes & Glaser, 1993; Sachs, Sawe, & Leischow, 1993) and demonstrates good compliance and social acceptability (Transdermal Nicotine Study Group, 1991). Both the gum and patch are now sold over the counter. Nicotine delivery systems on the market in Europe include a nicotine inhaler (Hjalmarson, Franzon, Westin, & Wiklund, 1994), and new nicotine delivery formulations under development in the United States and Europe include a nicotine lozenge, nicotine aerosol (Eclipse), and a nicotine toothpick.

Smokers treated with nicotine replacement alone have demonstrated approximately a 21% success rate for achieving abstinence (Fiore, Smith, et al., 1994; Fiore, Kenford, et al., 1994). Nicotine gum and nicotine nasal spray appear helpful for heavy smokers (Heatherton, Kozlowski, Frecker, & Fagerstrom, 1991), but nicotine patches demonstrate efficacy with both heavy smokers and those who are less nicotine dependent (Sachs et al., 1993; see Rose, 1996, for a discussion). Although nicotine replacement appears most effective when provided in concert with behavioral therapy, the data indicate that replacement therapy alone is effective. However, for highly nicotine-dependent smokers (those craving a cigarette when they wake up) and those with dual dependencies, such as methadone-maintained opiate abusers, it may be necessary to integrate behavioral methods with pharmacological treatment to achieve the shorter and longer term smoking cessation rates comparable with those achieved with non-substance-dependent smokers (Carmody, 1992; Jarvik & Schneider, 1992; Story & Stark, 1991).

Nicotine Antagonists

Antagonist medications are used primarily to prevent the positive reinforcing and subjective effects of nicotine (APA, 1996). Mecamylamine, a nicotine antagonist that involves indirect blocking of both central nervous system and peripheral nicotinic receptors (Rose et al., 1994), is nearing approval for marketing. Although results of some early studies suggest at least short-term efficacy, high doses of mecamylamine produce significant dropout rates because of adverse side-effects (Tennant, Tarver, & Rawson, 1984). When combined nicotine patch and oral mecamylamine treatment was compared with nicotine patch plus placebo (Rose et al., 1994), the mecamylamine group had a three times higher rate of abstinence for 7 weeks than did the control group. Continuous abstinence at 6- and 12-month follow-ups also remained higher for the mecamylamine group (37.5% vs. 12.5% at 6 months, 37.5% vs. 4.2% at 12 months), indicating that a combined agonist–antagonist therapy could substantially improve current smoking cessation treatments.

Behavioral Treatments

Over the past 30 years, a range of behavior strategies has shown moderate success for treatment of tobacco smoking in the general population (Fiore, Smith, et al., 1994; Lando, 1991; Shiffman, 1993; Silagy, Mang, Fowler, & Lodge, 1994). These strategies generally attempt to change the antecedents to smoking (including mood and cognition), provide reinforcement for nonsmoking, and teach avoidance skills for high-risk situations. They are typically based on the theory that "learning processes operate in the development, maintenance, and cessation of smoking" (APA, 1996, p. 10). A number of behavioral therapies are used for smoking cessation treatment, including stimulus control and behavior modification (self-monitoring, identification, and avoidance of stimuli associated with smoking), aversion therapy (induction of mild nicotine intoxication to make smoking more aversive and less reinforcing), social support (buddy system or support groups), nicotine fading (gradual reduction of nicotine in cigarettes), and positive feedback (reinforcing nonsmoking behavior).

The success of behavioral treatments for smoking cessation varies widely. However, abstinence rates at 1 year following treatment are about 20%, which is similar to the results obtained from pharmacological treatments (Viswesvaran & Schmidt, 1992), compared with about 6% for controls (see Jarvik & Schneider, 1992, for review) and about 5% for self-quitters (Hughes et al., 1992).

Relapse Prevention

Relapse prevention, which has been extensively studied for treatment of tobacco smoking (see Carmody, 1992; and Mermelstein, Karnatz, & Reichmann, 1992, for reviews), uses the techniques originally developed to teach behavioral and coping skills for preventing relapse once smoking abstinence is achieved (Marlatt & Gordon, 1985). Patients are generally taught how to identify and manage high-risk situations and are instructed on coping skills, including slips, cognitive reframing, inoculation against the abstinence violation effect, and lifestyle balancing (Mermelstein et al., 1992; see Shiffman, 1993, for a review).

Although empirical evidence supporting the use of relapse prevention is equivocal (see Mermelstein et al., 1992, for a review), about 20% of non-substance-abusing smokers treated with relapse prevention maintain smoking abstinence for 12 months after seeking treatment (Carmody 1992); Davis & Glaros, 1986; Dooley & Halford, 1992; Lichtenstein, Glasgow, & Abrams, 1986). Hall, Rugg, Tunstall, and Jones (1984) randomly assigned smokers to either a relapse prevention condition, which emphasized cue-associated relaxation training, commitment enhancement, and relapse prevention skills training, or to a standard discussion condition. Twelve-month abstinence rates were significantly higher for relapse prevention patients (46%) compared with discussion patients (30%). Curry, Marlatt, Gordon, and Baer (1988) compared a relapse prevention approach with a standard behavioral counseling approach and found that neither demonstrated superior efficacy at the 12-month follow-up. Although patients assigned to the relapse prevention condition were more likely to be abstinent at follow-up compared with those in the standard condition, they also tended to relapse more quickly after treatment ended.

When combined with the nicotine patch or polacrilix gum, relapse prevention may boost smoking abstinence rates over either treatment alone (see Hughes, 1995, for a discussion). Killen, Macoby, and Taylor (1984) found that 7 weeks of relapse prevention treatment combined with nicotine gum resulted in a 50% abstinence rate at 10.5 months compared with a 23% abstinence rate for the gum-only condition and a 30% abstinence rate for a relapse-prevention-only condition. In a well-controlled empirical evaluation of relapse prevention in combination with different types of transdermal nicotine therapies (individual dose level vs. fixed dose), Buchkremer, Minneker, and Block (1991) reported a 35% abstinence rate at the 12-month follow-up for the 403 patients enrolled in their trial. By contrast, Hall, Tunstall, Ginsberg, Benowitz, and Jones (1987) reported that the gum plus a minimal contact condition produced significantly greater abstinence rates at 52 weeks (50%) compared with gum plus relapse prevention (34%). However, attrition at a 1-year follow-up may have affected these estimates.

Contingency Management

As discussed in many of the other chapters in this volume, contingency management has well-documented empirical support for use as an effective element in comprehensive cocaine treatment programs (see Higgins et al., 1991, 1993; Higgins, Budney, & Bickel, 1994; and Silverman et al., 1996) and in decreasing illicit-drug use among methadone-maintained patients (Hall, Bass, Hargreaves, & Loeb, 1979; McCaul, Stitzer, Bigelow, & Liebson, 1984; Stitzer, Bigelow, Liebson, & Hawthorne, 1982; Stitzer, Iguchi, & Felch, 1992).

Although contingency management is well accepted by patients as a behavioral intervention for treatment of cocaine and opiate abuse, it rarely is used for treatment of nicotine dependence. Early work by Stitzer and Bigelow (1982) indicates that expired air carbon monoxide (CO) readings were a reliable marker of recent smoking and could thus be used as an objective target for contingency management intervention to promote smoking reduction. Stitzer and Bigelow (1983) performed the initial trial of contingency management for tobacco smoking. They randomly assigned 60 hospital employee volunteers, whose initial CO levels were at least 18 ppm, to one of four contingency management treatment conditions that offered $0, $1, $5, or $10 daily for reducing their afternoon CO levels to 50% or less of baseline values. Although afternoon CO levels returned to baseline after withdrawal of contingencies, the average amount of behavioral change, as noted by self-report and 5 days per week CO levels, was directly proportional to the amount of money offered. For those who met CO targets, a typical smoking pattern was 4–6 daytime cigarettes followed by 5 hr abstinence prior to afternoon CO testing. When targets were not met, little change in smoking activity was observed. The investigators concluded that contingency management had specific behavioral effects that extended beyond positive feedback and instructional interventions.

Stitzer, Rand, Bigelow, and Mead (1986) extended this work by evaluating contingency management procedures for reducing tobacco smoking in a group of 34 research volunteers. During an initial 5-day cutdown period, volunteers were paid from $0 to $6 per day depending on the extent of reduction from their baseline CO levels. During the trial, breath samples were obtained three times daily, and volunteers were paid $4 for each CO reading less than or equal to 11 ppm. Researchers found that the majority of participants (68%) were able to temporarily stop smoking. Furthermore, those who earned greater amounts of money in the cutdown period were significantly more likely to achieve smoking abstinence.

In a later study (Rand, Stitzer, Bigelow, & Mead, 1989), researchers evaluated the relationship of contingency management and worksite CO monitoring to the long-term maintenance of smoking abstinence. Forty-seven hospital employees, after refraining from smoking for 5 days (confirmed by CO analysis), were randomly assigned to one of three conditions: (a) contingent payment and frequent CO monitoring (n = 17); (b) noncontingent, frequent monitoring (n = 16); or (c) noncontingent payment and nonfrequent monitoring (n = 14). Although there were no differences in quit rates at the 6-month follow-up, those assigned to the contingent payment and frequent monitoring condition documented smoking for a significantly longer period than those assigned to either of the other conditions and demonstrated a delayed return to cigarette smoking.

In an effort to reduce smoking among people with chronic obstructive pulmonary disease, Crowley, Macdonald, Zerbe, and Petty (1991) conducted a 3-month trial of contingency management procedures alone (lottery tickets in return for reduced CO levels). One group of patients earned

0–3 tickets per day depending on the extent of CO reduction below baseline, and a control group was given the same number of tickets regardless of CO levels. Neither group changed smoking behaviors after 3 months. In their report, the investigators incorporated pharmacotherapy with the contingency management procedures as one follow-up study. Patients were assigned a postbaseline quit date, were given nicotine gum, and were paid a maximum of 5 tickets per night for CO levels less than 10 ppm. Although CO levels dropped sharply during the early intervention period, levels gradually rose. A second follow-up study used a "richer" reinforcement schedule for nonquitters and relapsers (a maximum of 20 tickets per night for CO levels less than 10 ppm), resulting in a drop of daily CO concentrations during intervention, with rapid increases following intervention cessation. The investigators concluded that although few patients stopped smoking, CO levels and the number of cigarettes smoked per day were reduced.

CONTINGENCY MANAGEMENT FOR TREATMENT OF TOBACCO SMOKING IN METHADONE-MAINTAINED PATIENTS

Although methadone-maintenance patients often express interest in stopping smoking (Frosch et al., 1998a; Joseph et al., 1993; Kozlowski et al., 1989), they have much more difficulty quitting than nondrug users (DiFranza & Guerrera, 1990). This may be because of the increased smoking satisfaction derived from concurrent opioid, including methadone, use (Chait & Griffiths, 1984), or it may simply reflect a generalized increase in smoking activity following drug use or methadone dosing (Mello, Mendelson, Sellers, & Kuehnle, 1980).

Whatever the reason for the paucity of smoking cessation studies in this group of addicts, methadone-maintained patients provide a good sample for evaluating stop-smoking strategies in drug users. Because they have been stabilized on methadone, these patients do not experience the anxieties generally associated with opiate withdrawal and initial abstinence. Moreover, they generally attend clinic reliably, their treatment retention rates are high, and they often maintain close contact with clinic staff (Craig, Rogalski, & Veltri, 1982; Grey, Osborn, & Reznikoff, 1986; Simpson, Savage, & Lloyd, 1979). Given the high prevalence of cigarette smoking among methadone-maintained patients, they could also expect to derive significant health benefits from smoking cessation treatments.

Story and Stark (1991) examined the hypothesis that opioids block or attenuate the effects of nicotine withdrawal (Chait & Griffiths, 1984) by providing a behaviorally based stop-smoking program to 22 methadone maintenance patients. Patients earned $25 stipends for not smoking and, if desired, an increase in their methadone dose. No significant difference in abstinence rates was reported between the treatment group and a control group that was given a placebo 1-mg methadone dose increase and did not earn stipends. Patients in the treatment group reported significantly more nicotine craving and other withdrawal symptoms during the 1st week of treatment and demonstrated significantly more smoking activity during the entire 10 weeks of treatment than did patients in the control group. Increasing the methadone dose initially helped 65% of the patients to abstain from smoking, but most returned to smoking by the end of the study period. The investigators concluded that increasing the methadone dose probably increases the urge to smoke cigarettes and would thus be ineffective as a pharmacological adjunct to behavioral strategies for smoking cessation. They conjectured, however, that other pharmacological therapies such as nicotine substitution may be beneficial for smoking cessation in this group if provided in concert with behavioral treatments.

The other report on smoking cessation treatment in opiate abusers was conducted by Schmitz, Rhoades, and Grabowski (1995). The investigators used an A-B-A-B design to cycle 5 methadone-maintained patients through 2-week periods during which they received either contingent reinforcement (Period A: $5 for CO levels below noncontingent levels on two occasions per week) or no reinforcement for smoking abstinence (Period B). The investigators reported that contingent reinforcement corresponded to modest, nonsignificant decreases in cigarette smoking compared with smoking during noncontingent periods. They further suggested that increasing the size or timing of contingencies or augmenting contingencies with skills training and social reinforcement may increase contingency management efficacy among this difficult-to-treat group of smokers.

A MODEL PROGRAM

Interest Survey

The Los Angeles Addiction Research Consortium is developing a model program designed to use contingency management for the treatment of smoking in methadone maintenance patients. Prior to beginning the program, Frosch et al. (1998a) conducted a survey of 30 smokers receiving methadone maintenance at a mid-city methadone clinic to determine their interest in smoking cessation treatment. Respondents, who averaged 20.2 cigarettes daily ($SD = 13.4$), were asked to complete an 18-item questionnaire that assessed their attitudes toward smoking and health (Chapman, Wong, & Smith, 1993) and their interest in participating in a stop-smoking program. Responses to the questionnaire were recorded using a 5-point Likert scale ($1 = $ *strongly disagree* to $5 = $ *strongly agree*).

In general, patients disagreed ($M = 2.1$, $SD = 0.8$) with the statement "smoking less than 20 cigarettes per day is safe." Patients had similar attitudes about tobacco smoking and health whether they had quit smoking at some point in their lives and relapsed ($n = 20$) or had never quit smoking ($n = 10$). However, never quitters were significantly more likely to agree that "most lung cancer is caused by air pollution, gas fumes, etc." ($M = 3.8$, $SD = 0.8$) than relapsers ($M = 2.7$, $SD = 1.2$), separate variance $t(25.4) = 3.16$, $p < .01$. Never quitters also were more likely to agree that "you have to smoke a lot more than I do to put your health at risk" ($M = 3.4$, $SD = 1.1$) than relapsers ($M = 2.4$, $SD = 1.2$), separate $t(20.3) = -2.63$, $p < .05$. More important, 21 of 30 patients rated their interest in a stop-smoking program as 4 or greater on a 5-point scale ($1 = not at all interested$ to $5 = very interested$), with no differences in interest shown between quitters and relapsers.

To obviate any bias caused by the close affiliation of the investigators and the involved clinic, researchers replicated the survey at three Los Angeles methadone maintenance clinics that had no affiliation with the investigators and the same results were obtained (Frosch et al., 1998a). Results of the surveys indicate that methadone-maintained cigarette smokers accurately perceive the health risks associated with smoking and that a majority are interested in participating in a stop-smoking program.

Pilot Study

Shoptaw, Jarvik, Ling, and Rawson (1996) next conducted a preliminary pilot study to evaluate the feasibility of using contingency management alone as a smoking cessation intervention for methadone-maintained patients. Twenty patients initially agreed to participate in the treatment, but 1 patient was terminated early on because of a very light dependence on tobacco (less than five cigarettes per day), and 2 other patients underwent methadone detoxification after failure to pay clinic fees. Seventeen patients with at least 1 year of methadone maintenance treatment completed the 4-week pilot study.

To document smoking abstinence, Shoptaw et al. (1996) adopted an extremely conservative 4-ppm CO criterion. Three times a week, patients provided breath samples that were analyzed for CO levels and urine samples that were analyzed for metabolites of heroin and cocaine. Patients earned vouchers of increasing value for each consecutive no-smoking breath sample provided, so that those who completed the entire 4-week program without smoking could earn a total of $73. Patients who provided breath samples that indicated smoking received no voucher for that day but could begin earning vouchers again when a breath sample showed smoking abstinence. Vouchers were contingent only on smoking abstinence and were not withheld for urine samples that indicated illicit-drug use.

Although all patients had resumed smoking by the end of the trial, smoking levels were significantly reduced, as indicated by a reduction of average CO levels from 16.06 ppm (SD = 7.7, range = 7–38) at baseline to an average of 10.35 ppm (SD = 6.6, range = 1–22) by treatment end, matched $t(16)$ = 3.04, p < .01. Four patients (23.4%) produced three or more consecutive no-smoking samples (1 week of no smoking), and 9 patients (52.9%) provided at least one breath sample with ambient CO levels (1 to 2 days of no smoking). Post hoc analysis indicate that patients with less nicotine dependence at baseline (less than 16 ppm, n = 10) were significantly more likely to achieve smoking abstinence than those with greater (n = 7) nicotine dependence, $\chi^2(1)$ = 7.14, p < .01. The fact that smoking cessation outcomes were not maintained over time indicates that at the rate delivered in the pilot study, this contingency management procedure only modestly affects smoking outcomes. These results support the findings of other investigators that persons with lower levels of nicotine dependence exhibit a more positive response to smoking cessation interventions than those with higher levels of dependence (Jarvik & Schneider 1992; Story & Stark 1991). Shoptaw et al.'s (1996) analyses further indicate that patients who were able to maintain smoking abstinence were significantly less likely to use cocaine than those unable to maintain smoking abstinence, although no such relationship was identified regarding opiate use.

From these initial experiences, we conclude that (a) contingency management is an acceptable smoking cessation treatment for methadone-maintained opiate addicts; (b) contingency management can achieve modest smoking reductions when used alone, especially with less-dependent smokers; and (c) contingency management may be a viable behavioral strategy that could be integrated with other smoking cessation interventions, such as the transdermal nicotine patch, to optimize long-term outcomes. An interesting finding from the study is the significant correlation between reduction in smoking and reduction in cocaine use, but not illicit-opiate use, indicating that patients may generalize their ability to stop smoking to their use of cocaine but not to illicit opiates. If replicated, this finding could provide empirical evidence for associations between tobacco smoking and illicit-drug use.

RELEVANT ISSUES IN DETERMINING SMOKING ABSTINENCE FROM CARBON MONOXIDE IN BREATH

Criterion Levels for Establishing Smoking Abstinence

Several important issues relative to the criterion for determining smoking abstinence from breath samples emerge from these initial experiences with contingency management. First, the appropriate CO criterion for documenting recent smoking must be determined. Despite the fact that studies involving the general population of cigarette smokers consider CO levels in the range of 7 to 11 ppm as documenting smoking abstinence (see Fiore, Smith, et al., 1994), a more stringent 4-ppm criterion was adopted for the pilot to prevent opiate addicts from misrepresenting their smoking behaviors to earn money and to allow the researchers to discriminate those patients who "chipped" (i.e., smoked a few cigarettes) from those who were truly abstinent (Shoptaw et al., 1996).

To understand the importance of this criterion level, investigators plotted consecutive CO breath samples that would qualify for smoking abstinence at 4, 5, 6, and 7 ppm (see Table 12.1). As shown in Table 12.1, the criterion for determining smoking abstinence most greatly affected those who were generally successful at using contingency management to stop smoking. Patients 1, 2, and 3 accounted for most of the changes that resulted from raising the criterion for determining smoking abstinence. Only 1 additional patient met the criteria for achieving three or more consecutive samples by raising the CO threshold to 7 ppm. Careful questioning of these 4 patients revealed that they had, indeed, smoked a cigarette on the occasions when their breath samples were above 4 ppm.

TABLE 12.1
Numbers of Consecutive Smoking Cessation Breath
Samples That Indicate Tobacco Abstinence by Applying
Different Carbon Monoxide Criteria

Patient	Carbon monoxide level			
	4 ppm	5 ppm	6 ppm	7 ppm
1	3	6	10	12
2	3	4	9	12
3	4	4	6	10
4	0	1	1	1
5	0	0	0	0
6	3	4	4	4
7	0	0	0	0
8	0	1	1	1
9	2	2	2	4
10	1	1	1	1
11	0	0	0	0
12	2	2	2	2
13	1	1	1	1
14	0	0	0	0
15	1	1	2	2
16	0	0	0	0
17	0	0	0	0

Note. Consecutive smoking cessation breath samples refer to the largest number of carbon monoxide samples from a patient's expired breath taken on consecutive study visits over the 4-week treatment period, which indicated smoking abstinence by applying different levels of carbon monoxide as criteria. For example, for Patient 1, the value of 3 using the 4-ppm criterion indicates that the patient provided three consecutive expired breath samples with carbon monoxide levels at or below 4 ppm during treatment.

These results demonstrate that a more stringent criterion is appropriate when only complete smoking abstinence is acceptable, even though occasional false positives may occur. By contrast, if the goal is to distinguish those who have stopped smoking for the most part from those who continue to smoke, a less stringent criterion is appropriate. Still, the most striking conclusion from these data is that changing criteria for CO levels changes results.

Naturally Occurring Carbon Monoxide Levels in Los Angeles

Because Los Angeles is famous for its air pollution, it seemed reasonable to question whether ambient CO levels averaged near the 4-ppm level criterion used in the pilot. Further, in conducting the pilot we learned that additional information would help avoid false-positive and false-negative errors. When our pilot was conducted, we also were uncertain about the extent to which CO levels would vary within and between patients.

To empirically determine the expected level of CO in breath among nonsmokers in Los Angeles, Jarvik, Madsen, Shoptaw, and Frosch (1997) collected expired air CO samples from 9 staff members working inside our methadone clinic and from 38 individuals at an outdoor recreational area at the West Los Angeles Veterans Administration Medical Center, which is located near a major freeway. For comparison, CO samples were also collected from 58 smokers participating in other ongoing projects.

Expired CO levels were recorded from the indoor nonsmokers four times a week, between 10:00 a.m. and 12:00 p.m. for 5 weeks and from the indoor smokers and the outdoor nonsmokers on one occasion between 10:00 a.m. and 12:00 p.m. All participants were instructed to take three deep breaths and to hold the third breath for 20 s prior to exhaling through a Bedfont EC50 Micro Smokerlyzer CO meter (Innovative Medical Marketing, Medford, NJ). The highest levels shown on the meter were recorded.

CO breath samples from the indoor nonsmokers never exceeded 7 ppm ($M = 3.97$ ppm, $SE = 0.24$). The indoor nonsmokers demonstrated significantly higher and less variable CO levels than did the outside nonsmokers ($M = 3.16$ ppm, $SE = 0.27$), pooled $t(74) = 2.84$, $p < .01$. Expired breath CO levels for 95% of the outdoor (nonsmokers) sample were 6 ppm or less, with a range of 0–7 ppm. By contrast, active smokers averaged a CO level of 29.7 ppm ($SE = 1.70$).

The higher mean CO levels for the indoor group of nonsmokers can be explained by a corresponding low level of physical activity because expiration of alveolar CO is a function of activity level (Peterson & Stewart, 1970). Although ambient CO levels were higher at the outside freeway site than inside the office building, the variability of activity was sufficient to produce lower and more variant CO levels. Still, regardless of ambient

CO levels, these data indicate that it is unlikely that anyone with a CO above 7 ppm would be a nonsmoker. Thus, from both the pilot trial and the empirical CO data, we conclude that the most accurate method for verifying smoking abstinence should include some combination of CO levels in breath, a detailed 24-hr smoking history, and other biological measures of components of cigarette smoke.

CONCLUSION

Addiction to nicotine is both psychological and physiological (Benowitz, 1988). Trials of behavioral (nonpharmacological) smoking cessation treatments typically demonstrate less effectiveness than do nicotine replacement therapies, especially at posttreatment follow-ups (Jarvik & Schneider, 1992). A meta-analysis of several placebo-controlled studies of the nicotine patch indicates that although success rates at 6- and 12-month follow-ups are significantly better than those for a placebo, behavioral support is often (although not always) required (Fiore, Smith, et al., 1994; Fiore, Kenford, et al., 1994). Innovative smoking cessation treatments that integrate behavioral therapies with transdermal nicotine therapy would optimize outcomes, especially for treatment-resistant populations, such as alcohol and other substance abusers (Story & Stark, 1991).

These initial experiences support systematic evaluation of contingency management as a behavioral intervention for optimizing transdermal nicotine therapy. The application of contingency management procedures to methadone-maintained tobacco smokers indicates that because of their daily clinic attendance, this population provides an ordered data set that allows for the evaluation of smoking cessation treatments in the context of opiate substitution therapy.

In the fall of 1996, Shoptaw and colleagues began a project comparing the efficacy of relapse prevention and contingency management for reducing tobacco smoking in methadone-maintained opiate addicts (with a National Institute on Drug Abuse grant). Patients were randomly assigned to one of four conditions: (a) relapse prevention only, (b) contingency management only, (c) relapse prevention and contingency management combined, or (d) no behavioral therapy. To increase responsiveness to the behavioral treatments and to allow for more meaningful comparison between the two treatments, the investigators gave all patients standard transdermal nicotine patch therapy to ameliorate nicotine withdrawal symptoms and thereby reduce attrition. As of the fall of 1998, 162 patients have been randomized in this project, which will allow for careful evaluation of the short- and long-term efficacy of contingency management techniques in comparison with relapse prevention techniques for optimizing smoking cessation pharmacotherapy. By measuring urine toxicology at each assessment point (three times a week for 12 weeks) and at 6- and 12-month follow-ups, the investigators can evaluate the level at which tobacco smoking at baseline, during treatment, and at follow-up is associated with incidence of illicit-drug use. From the results of the work reported in this chapter regarding CO, two biological markers are used to document smoking abstinence in this study. CO readings are one aspect, and the contingencies available in this program are determined by CO in expired breath. To verify CO readings, a monthly serum thiocyanate sample is collected and analyzed. Serum thiocyanate represents a metabolite of cigarette smoke, but not nicotine, and can be used to document cigarette abstinence because all patients in this study receive nicotine replacement and hence have nicotine and metabolites of nicotine in their urine.

Study enrollment for this group of tenacious smokers continues through the end of 1998. Preliminary findings, however, offer opportunities for examining a number of questions that arose during its implementation. An initial evaluation of project data ($n = 22$) indicates that about 32% of the patients successfully used the treatments to stop smoking by the end of 12 weeks (Frosch, Shoptaw, Jarvik, Rawson, & Ling, 1998b). This quit rate remains relatively stable; the most recent data analysis ($n = 120$ patients) indicates that approximately 28% are nonsmokers by the end of 12 weeks of treatment (Shoptaw, Frosch, Jarvik, Rawson, & Ling, 1998). In a series of in-depth interviews with the first 20 participants across the four conditions, patients found nicotine replacement therapy to be the most valued aspect of their treatments (Nahom et al., in press). Additionally, women found the behavioral smoking cessation interventions more helpful than did the men. These initial reports support the rationale underlying this line of research. However, findings from the main study will provide important information about the relative efficacy of behavioral and pharmacological treatments in this difficult-to-treat group of cigarette smokers.

REFERENCES

American Psychiatric Association. (1994). *Diagnostic and statistical manual of mental disorders* (4th ed.). Washington, DC: American Psychiatric Association.

American Psychiatric Association. (1996). Practice guidelines for the treatment of patients with nicotine dependence. *American Journal of Psychiatry, 153,* 1–25.

Benowitz, N. L. (1988). Drug therapy: Pharmacologic aspects of cigarette smoking and nicotine addiction. *New England Journal of Medicine, 319,* 1318–1330.

Berger, H., & Schweigler, M. (1972). Smoking characteristics of methadone patients. *Journal of the American Medical Association, 222,* 705.

Bobo, J. K. (1989). Nicotine dependence and alcoholism epidemiology and treatment. *Journal of Psychoactive Drugs, 21,* 323–329.

Bobo, J. K., Gilchrist, L. D., Schilling, R. F., II, Noach, B., & Schinke, S. P. (1987).

Cigarette smoking cessation attempts by recovering alcoholics. *Addictive Behaviors, 12,* 209–215.

Buchkremer, G., Minneker, E., & Block, M. (1991). Smoking cessation treatment combining transdermal nicotine substitution with behavioral therapy. *Pharmacopsychiatry, 24*(3), 96–102.

Burling, T. A., Marshall, G. D., & Seidner, A. L. (1991). Smoking cessation for substance abuse inpatients. *Journal of Substance Abuse Treatment, 3,* 269–276.

Burling, T. A., & Ziff, D. C. (1988). Tobacco smoking: A comparison between alcohol and drug abuse inpatients. *Addictive Behaviors, 13,* 185–190.

Carmody, T. P. (1992). Preventing relapse in the treatment of nicotine addiction: Current issues and future directions. *Journal of Psychoactive Drugs, 22,* 211–238.

Chait, D., & Griffiths, R. R. (1984). Effects of methadone on human cigarette smoking and subjective ratings. *Journal of Pharmacological and Experimental Therapeutics, 229,* 636–640.

Chapman, S., Wong, W. L., & Smith, W. (1993). Self-exempting beliefs about smoking and health: Differences between smokers and ex-smokers. *American Journal of Public Health, 83,* 215–219.

Craig, R. J., Rogalski, C., & Veltri, D. (1982). Predicting treatment dropouts from a drug abuse rehabilitation program. *Journal of Addictions, 17,* 641–653.

Crowley, T. J., Macdonald, M. J., Zerbe, G. O., & Petty, T. L. (1991). Reinforcing breath carbon monoxide reductions in chronic obstructive pulmonary disease. *Drug and Alcohol Dependence, 29,* 47–62.

Curry, S., Marlatt, G. A., Gordon, J., & Baer, J. S. (1988). A comparison of alternative theoretical approaches to smoking cessation and relapse. *Health Psychology, 7,* 545–556.

Daughton, D. M., Heatley, S. A., & Prendergast, J. J. (1991). Effect of transdermal nicotine delivery as an adjunct to low-intervention smoking cessation therapy. *Archives of Internal Medicine, 151,* 749–752.

Davis, J. R., & Glaros, A. G. (1986). Relapse prevention and smoking cessation. *Addictive Behaviors, 11,* 105–114.

DiFranza, J. R., & Guerrera, M. P. (1990). Alcoholism and smoking. *Journal of Studies on Alcohol, 51,* 130–135.

Dooley, R. T., & Halford, W. K. (1992). A comparison of relapse prevention with nicotine gum or nicotine fading in modification of smoking. *Australian Psychologist, 27,* 186–191.

Fiore, M. C., Kenford, S. L., Jorenby, D. E., Wetter, D. W., Smith, S. S., & Baker, T. B. (1994). Two studies of the clinical effectiveness of the nicotine patch with different counseling treatments. *Chest, 105,* 524–533.

Fiore, M. C., Smith, S. S., Jorenby, D. E., & Baker, T. B. (1994). The effectiveness of the nicotine patch for smoking cessation: A meta-analysis. *Journal of the American Medical Association, 271,* 1940–1946.

Frosch, D., Shoptaw, S., Jarvik, M. E., Rawson, R. A., & Ling, W., (1998a). Interest in smoking cessation among methadone maintained outpatients. *Journal of Addictive Diseases, 17,* 9–19.

Frosch, D. L., Shoptaw, S., Jarvik, M. E., Rawson, R. A., & Ling, W. (1998b). Preliminary experiences with opiate abusers seeking smoking cessation treatment. In L. S. Harris (Ed.), *Problems of drug dependence 1997: Proceedings of the 59th annual scientific meeting, the College on Problems of Drug Dependence* (NIDA Research Monograph 178, p. 67). Washington, DC: U.S. Government Printing Office.

Grey, C., Osborn, E., & Reznikoff, M. (1986). Psychosocial factors in outcome of two opiate addiction treatments. *Journal of Clinical Psychology, 42,* 185–189.

Hall, S. M., Bass, A., Hargreaves, W. A., & Loeb, P. (1979). Contingency management and information feedback in outpatient heroin detoxification. *Behavioral Therapy, 10,* 443–451.

Hall, S. M., Rugg, D., Tunstall, C., & Jones, R. (1984). Preventing relapse to cigarette smoking by behavioral skill training. *Journal of Consulting and Clinical Psychology, 55,* 603–605.

Hall, S. M., Tunstall, C. D., Ginsberg, D., Benowitz, N. L., & Jones, R. T. (1987). Nicotine gum and behavioral treatment: A placebo controlled trial. *Journal of Consulting and Clinical Psychology, 55,* 603–605.

Heatherton, T. F., Kozlowski, L. T., Frecker, R. C., & Fagerstrom, K. O. (1991). The Fagerstrom Test for Nicotine Dependence: A revision of the Fagerstrom Tolerance Questionnaire. *British Journal of Addiction, 86,* 1119–1127.

Higgins, S. T., Budney, A. J., & Bickel, W. K. (1994). Applying behavioral concepts and principles to the treatment of cocaine dependence. *Drug and Alcohol Dependence, 34,* 87–97.

Higgins, S. T., Budney, A. J., Bickel, W. K., Hughes, J. R., Foerg, F., & Badger, G. (1993). Achieving cocaine abstinence with behavioral approach. *American Journal of Psychiatry, 150,* 763–769.

Higgins, S. T., Budney, A. J., Bickel, W. K., Hughes, J. R., Foerg, F., & Fenwick, J. W. (1991). A behavioral approach to achieving initial cocaine abstinence. *American Journal of Psychiatry, 148,* 1218–1224.

Hjalmarson, A., Franzon, M., Westin, A., & Wiklund, O. (1994). Effect of nicotine nasal spray on smoking cessation. *Archives of Internal Medicine, 154,* 2567–2572.

Hser, Y. I., McCarthy, W. J., & Anglin, M. D. (1994). Tobacco use as a distal predictor of mortality among long-term narcotics addicts. *Preventive Medicine, 23,* 61–69.

Hughes, J. R. (1995). Combining behavioral therapy and pharmacotherapy for smoking cessation: An update. In L. S. Onken, J. D. Blaine, & J. J. Boren (Eds.), *Integrating behavioral therapies with medications in the treatment of drug dependence* (NIDA Research Monograph 150, pp. 92–109). Washington, DC: U.S. Government Printing Office.

Hughes, J. R., & Glaser, M. (1993). Transdermal nicotine for smoking cessation. *Health Values, 17,* 24–31.

Hughes, J. R., Gulliver, S. B., Fenwick, J. W., Valliere, W. A., Cruser, K., Pepper, S., Shea, P., Solomon, L. J., & Flynn, B. S. (1992). Smoking cessation among self quitters. *Health Psychology, 11*, 331–334.

Hurt, R. D., Eberman, K. M., Croghan, I. T., Offord, K. P., Davis, L. J., Jr., Morse, R. M., Palmen, M. A., & Bruce, B. K. (1994). Nicotine dependence treatment during inpatient treatment for other addictions: A prospective intervention trial. *Alcoholism: Clinical and Experimental Research, 18*, 867–872.

Jarvik, M. E., Madsen, D., Shoptaw, S., & Frosch, D. (1997). Ambient and outdoor carbon monoxide levels among non-smokers in Los Angeles. In L. S. Harris (Ed.), *Problems of drug dependence 1996: Proceedings of the 58th annual scientific meeting, the College on Problems of Drug Dependence* (NIDA Research Monograph 174, p. 210). Washington, DC: U.S. Government Printing Office.

Jarvik, M. E., & Schneider, N. G. (1992). Nicotine. In J. H. Lowinson, P. Ruiz, & R. B. Millman (Eds.), *Substance abuse—A comprehensive textbook* (2nd ed., pp. 334–356). Baltimore: Williams & Wilkins.

Joseph, A. M., Nichol, K. L., & Anderson, H. (1993). Effect of treatment for nicotine dependence on alcohol and drug treatment outcomes. *Addictive Behaviors, 18*, 635–644.

Killen, J. D., Macoby, N., & Taylor, C. B. (1984). Nicotine gum and self-regulation training in smoking relapse prevention. *Behavior Therapy, 15*, 234–248.

Kozlowski, L. T., Skinner, W., Kent, C., & Pope, M. A. (1989). Prospects for smoking treatment in individuals seeking treatment for alcohol and other drug problems. *Addictive Behaviors, 14*, 273–278.

Lando, H. A. (1991). Toward a comprehensive strategy for reducing the health burden of tobacco. *British Journal of Addiction, 86*, 649–652.

Lichtenstein, E., Glasgow, R. E., & Abrams, D. B. (1986). Social support in smoking cessation: In search of effective interventions. *Behavioral Therapy, 17*, 607–619.

Marlatt, G. A., & Gordon, J. R. (Eds.). (1985) *Relapse prevention: Maintenance strategies in the treatment of addictive behaviors*. New York: Guilford.

McCaul, M. E., Stitzer, M. L., Bigelow, G. E., & Liebson, I. A. (1984). Contingency management interventions: Effects on treatment outcome during methadone detoxification. *Journal of Applied Behavioral Analysis, 17*, 35–43.

Mello, N. K., Mendelson, J. H., Sellers, M. L., & Kuehnle, J. C. (1980). Effects of heroin self-administration on cigarette smoking psychopharmacology. *Psychopharmacology, 27*, 45–52.

Mermelstein, R. J., Karnatz, T., & Reichmann, S. (1992). Smoking. In P. H. Wilson (Ed.), *Principles and practice of relapse prevention* (pp. 43–68). New York: Guilford Press.

Nahom, D., Shoptaw, S., Frosch, D. L., Jarvik, M. E., Rawson, R. A., & Ling, W. (in press). Factors associated with successful tobacco abstinence among methadone-maintained tobacco smokers. In L. S. Harris (Ed.), *Problems of drug dependence 1998: Proceedings of the 60th annual scientific meeting, the Col-*

lege on Problems of Drug Dependence. Washington, DC: U.S. Government Printing Office.

Orleans, C. T. (1995). Preventing tobacco-caused cancer: A call to action. *Environmental Health Perspective, 103*(Suppl. 8), 149–152.

Peterson, J. E., & Stewart, R. D. (1970). Absorption and elimination of carbon monoxide by inactive young men. *Archives of Environmental Health, 21*, 165–171.

Rand, C. S., Stitzer, M. L., Bigelow, G. E., & Mead, A. M. (1989). The effects of contingent payment and frequent workplace monitoring on smoking abstinence. *Addictive Behaviors, 14*, 121–128.

Rose, J. E. (1996). Nicotine addiction and treatment. *Annual Review of Medicine, 47*, 493–507.

Rose, J. E., Frederique, M. B., Westman, E. C., Levin, E. D., Stein, R. M., & Ripka, G. V. (1994). Mecamylamine combined with nicotine skin patch facilitates smoking cessation beyond nicotine patch treatment alone. *Clinical Trials and Therapeutics, 56*(1), 86–99.

Sachs, D. P., Sawe, U., & Leischow, S. J. (1993). Effectiveness of a 16-hour transdermal nicotine patch in a medical practice setting, without intensive group counseling. *Archives of Internal Medicine, 153*, 1881–1890.

Sandor, R. S. (1991). Relapse to drinking: Does cigarette smoking contribute? *California Society of Addiction Medicine News, 18*, 1–2.

Schmitz, J. M., Rhoades, H., & Grabowski, J. (1995). Contingent reinforcement for reduced carbon monoxide levels in methadone maintenance patients. *Addictive Behaviors, 20*, 171–179.

Sees, K. L., & Clark, H. W. (1991). Substance abusers want to stop smoking! [Abstract 16]. *Alcoholism: Clinical Experimental Research, 15*, 152.

Sees, K. L., & Clark, H. W. (1993). When to begin smoking cessation in substance abusers. *Journal of Substance Abuse Treatment, 10*, 189–195.

Shiffman, S. (1993). Smoking cessation treatment: Any progress? *Journal of Consulting and Clinical Psychology 61*, 718–722.

Shoptaw, S., Frosch, D., Jarvik, M. E., Rawson, R. A., & Ling, W. (1998). *Smoking cessation in methadone maintenance treatment: The evaluation of nicotine replacement and behavioral therapies*. Unpublished manuscript, Los Angeles Addiction Treatment Research Center, CA.

Shoptaw, S., Jarvik, M. E., Ling, W., & Rawson, R. A. (1996). Contingency management for tobacco smoking in methadone-maintained opiate addicts. *Addictive Behaviors, 21*, 409–412.

Silagy, C., Mang, D., Fowler, G., & Lodge, M. (1994). The effectiveness of nicotine replacement therapies in smoking cessation [110 paragraphs]. *Online Journal of Current Clinical Trials* [On-line serial]. Available: Doc. No. 113.

Silverman, K., Higgins, S. T., Brooner, R. K., Montoya, I. D., Cone, E. J., Schuster, C. R., & Preston, K. L. (1996). Sustained cocaine abstinence in methadone maintenance patients through voucher-based reinforcement therapy. *Archives of General Psychiatry, 53*, 409–415.

Simpson, D. D., Savage, L. J., & Lloyd, M. R. (1979). Follow-up evaluation of treatment of drug abuse during 1969 to 1972. *Archives of General Psychiatry, 36,* 772–780.

Stitzer, M. L., & Bigelow, G. E. (1982). Contingent reinforcement for reduced carbon monoxide levels in cigarette smokers. *Addictive Behaviors, 7,* 403–412.

Stitzer, M. L., & Bigelow, G. E. (1983). Contingent payment for carbon monoxide reduction: Effects of pay amount. *Behavior Therapy, 14,* 647–656.

Stitzer, M. L., & Bigelow, G. E. (1985). Contingent reinforcement for reduced breath carbon monoxide levels: Target-specific effects on cigarette smoking. *Addictive Behaviors, 10,* 345–349.

Stitzer, M. L., Bigelow, G. E., Liebson, I. A., & Hawthorne, J. W. (1982). Contingent reinforcement for benzodiazepine-free urines: Evaluation of a drug abuse treatment intervention. *Journal of Applied Behavioral Analysis, 15,* 493–503.

Stitzer, M. L., Iguchi, M. Y., & Felch, L. J. (1992). Contingent take-home incentive: Effects on drug use of methadone maintenance patients. *Journal of Consulting and Clinical Psychology, 60,* 927–934.

Stitzer, M. L., Rand, C. S., Bigelow, G. E., & Mead, A. M. (1986). Contingent payment procedures for smoking reduction and cessation. *Journal of Applied Behavior Analysis, 19,* 197–202.

Story, J., & Stark, M. J. (1991). Treating cigarette smoking in methadone maintenance clients. *Journal of Psychoactive Drugs, 23,* 203–215.

Substance Abuse and Mental Health Services Administration. (1996). *National Household Survey on Drug Abuse: Main findings 1994.* Rockville, MD: U.S. Department of Health and Human Services.

Tennant, F. S., Jr., Tarver, A. L., & Rawson, R. A. (1984). Clinical evaluation of mecamylamine for withdrawal from nicotine dependence. In L. S. Harris (Ed.), *Proceedings of the 45th annual scientific meeting, the Committee on Problems of Drug Dependence* (NIDA Research Monograph 49, pp. 239–246). Washington, DC: U.S. Government Printing Office.

Transdermal Nicotine Study Group. (1991). Transdermal nicotine for smoking cessation: Six month results from two multicenter controlled trials. *Journal of the American Medical Association, 266,* 3133–3138.

U.S. Department of Health and Human Services. (1988). *The health consequences of smoking: Nicotine addiction* (DHHS Pub. No. CDC 88-8406). Washington, DC: U.S. Government Printing Office.

U.S. Department of Health and Human Services. (1989). *Reducing the health consequences of smoking: 25 years of progress.* Rockville, MD: U.S. Department of Health and Human Services, Public Health Service, Centers for Disease Control, Center for Chronic Disease Prevention and Health Promotion, Office on Smoking and Health.

Viswesvaran, C., & Schmidt, F. L. (1992). A meta-analysis comparison of the effectiveness of smoking cessation methods. *Journal of Applied Psychology, 774*, 554–561.

Zimmerman, R. S., Warheit, G. J., Ulbrich, P. M., & Auth, J. B. (1990). The relationship between alcohol use and attempts and success at smoking cessation. *Addictive Behaviors, 15,* 197–207.

13

COMBINED BEHAVIORAL AND PHARMACOLOGICAL TREATMENT DURING OPIOID DETOXIFICATION: A REVIEW

WARREN K. BICKEL AND LISA A. MARSCH

Heroin and other opioid dependencies remain an important public health problem, which unfortunately appears to be increasing. The number of young heroin users has recently increased apparently because of both the decreased price and increased purity of heroin (Hartnoll, 1994). In addition, more emergency room visits have been reported that are heroin and morphine related (Swan, 1992). The public health consequences of this trend are magnified by the criminal activity and injection drug use endemic to this drug-using population (Ball & Ross, 1991). In particular, injection drug use increases the risk of contracting and spreading both hepatitis and HIV infection (Curran, Jaffe, & Hardy, 1988; Hser, Anglin, & Powers, 1993; Rice & Kelman, 1989).

Not surprisingly, these developments have led to calls for treatment services to be expanded (McLellan, Arndt, Metzger, Woody, & O'Brien, 1993). One treatment often available, although rarely discussed or recommended to opioid-dependent individuals, is outpatient detoxification with replacement medications such as methadone. Detoxification treatment may not be recommended because of its documented lack of efficacy (Milby, 1988). Typically, studies of outpatient detoxification treatment with methadone report high treatment retention and opioid abstinence when the dose of methadone is high but dramatically decreased retention and increased opioid use when the dose is tapered (Milby, 1988). Similar outcomes are reported when buprenorphine is used (Bickel et al., 1988). Buprenorphine is a partial morphine-like opioid agonist currently being investigated as a replacement medication for opioid dependence (see Bickel & Amass, 1995, for a review).

These poor outcomes raise an important question: Is the efficacy of opioid detoxification treatment strictly a function of the utility of the pharmacotherapy used during detoxification, or can efficacy be improved by combining pharmacotherapy with other nonpharmacological (i.e., psychosocial) interventions? The answer to this question could address the health policy issue of whether outpatient ambulatory detoxification treatments may be effective and should therefore be provided.

A similar question was addressed by McLellan et al. (1993), who examined methadone maintenance, a pharmacotherapy of documented efficacy that provides a constant daily dose of methadone for an indefinite period of time (see Ball & Ross, 1991). Specifically, McLellan et al. examined the effects of three levels of psychotherapeutic services during methadone maintenance. Minimum treatment consisted of daily methadone alone. Standard treatment was composed of methadone and counseling services. (Note that counseling involved applying rewarding and punishing contingencies to reduce illicit-drug and alcohol use.) In addition, take-home methadone was available for drug-free urine samples and verifiable employment. Enhanced treatment consisted of the same services provided in the standard treatment, with the addition of extended employment and family counseling as well as on-site medical and psychiatric services. Sixty-nine percent, 41%, and 19% of the patients assigned to minimum, standard, and enhanced treatment services, respectively, engaged in persistent use of opioids and cocaine. Thus, methadone maintenance as a pharmacotherapy produces results ranging from poor to superior, depending on the additional psychosocial services provided during treatment.

In this chapter, we review the existing empirical literature to ascertain whether the addition of behavioral treatments improves outcomes in outpatient opioid detoxification. First, we briefly describe the purpose, procedures, and the efficacy of opioid detoxification treatments that are provided without behavioral treatment, specifically focusing on ambulatory detoxifications conducted with opioid agonists. Second, we comprehensively review those studies that added contingency management procedures to opioid detoxification treatment. Finally, we review the single study as of this writing that examined the effects of adding a combination treatment consisting of contingency management and the community reinforcement approach (CRA) to opioid detoxification treatment.

DETOXIFICATION TREATMENTS: PURPOSE, PROCEDURES, AND OUTCOMES

The purpose and aim of outpatient opioid detoxification is to progressively attain an opioid-free state while successfully eliminating opioid withdrawal as one condition that leads to continuing opioid use (Best, Oliveto, & Kosten, 1996; Fishbain, Rosomoff, Cutler, & Rosomoff, 1993; see Milby, 1988, for a more detailed review of opioid detoxification). Withdrawal from heroin and other short-acting morphine-like agonists typically starts 8–10 hr after the last dose and generally lasts for approximately 7–10 days. The symptoms of opioid withdrawal include anxiety, craving opioids, dysphoria, perspiration, runny nose, restlessness, tearing, and yawning. More severe withdrawal is characterized by bone ache, diarrhea, hot and cold flashes, fever, gooseflesh, muscle aches, and weight loss. Opioid withdrawal is noxious to the opioid-dependent patient, and it is avoided or terminated by opioid use. Thus, opioid withdrawal is a sufficient condition for opioid use. By eliminating withdrawal then, researchers can avoid one important relapse factor.

Typically, detoxification as a treatment is preferred for patients who are entering treatment for the first time or for patients with a minor degree of physical dependence. Also detoxification is used for long-term maintenance patients who want to be drug free. The untested belief behind the use of detoxification during the first treatment episode is that opioid use in relatively new or low-level users is controlled more by withdrawal than by the other factors that lead to drug use (e.g., positive reinforcement). Certainly, the rationale behind this belief may be questioned. Nonetheless, some patients may prefer detoxification treatment as opposed to maintenance treatment of an unspecified duration. Moreover, if detoxification treatment were effective, it certainly would be a less costly treatment to provide relative to long-term maintenance therapy.

The two opioid-agonist treatments that are primarily used for opioid detoxification are methadone and buprenorphine. Both methadone and buprenorphine have effects similar to other opioids and thus can properly be called replacement therapies. Both medications are long acting and can be given once daily. Methadone is a full agonist, indicating that the higher the dose, the greater the effect observed. Buprenorphine is a partial agonist, indicating that there is a ceiling on the magnitude of its effects. More specifically, as the dose of buprenorphine increases, the magnitude of its effect increases, until a point at which further increases in dose produce no further increase in effect. Because of this ceiling, buprenorphine is safe across a range of doses. Also some researchers have speculated that because buprenorphine tightly binds to the opioid receptor and disassociates slowly from the receptor, it should produce a smaller degree of physiological withdrawal than that associated with a full agonist treatment such as methadone (see Bickel & Amass, 1995, for a review).

In detoxification treatment, the patient is first stabilized on a dose of the drug, followed by a gradual taper of the treatment agent. The shortterm detoxification period typically lasts 30 days or fewer in duration, and the long-term detoxification period usually ranges from 30 to 180 days. During the detoxification treatment, counseling is often provided but generally is limited.

As noted above, studies of outpatient detoxification typically report high treatment retention and opioid abstinence when the dose of methadone or buprenorphine is high. As the dose is tapered, retention dramatically decreases and opioid use increases (Bickel & Amass, 1995; Milby, 1988). These outcomes are illustrated in a study that compared methadone and buprenorphine in a double-blind, double-dummy, placebo-controlled detoxification trial, in which both groups received minimal counseling (Bickel et al., 1988). The active drug was tapered during the first 7 weeks, and a placebo was administered for the following 6 weeks.

As shown in Figure 13.1, retention was poor, with only 35% and 26% of the buprenorphine and methadone groups, respectively, remaining by the 8th week of treatment (the 1st week of placebo administration). More than 60% of the urine samples from both groups were opioid positive by the 6th week. Moreover, self-reports of withdrawal tended to increase as the dose decreased. These studies demonstrate the typical outcome of detoxification treatment and indicate that such results are obtained with both methadone and buprenorphine.

Whether different methods of dose reduction produce improved results has yet to be convincingly established. There is, however, one generalization regarding drug taper: Rapid detoxification produces inferior results relative to long-term detoxification for both methadone and buprenorphine. For example, Senay, Dorus, Goldberg, and Thorton (1977) compared two types of methadone detoxification: One treatment tapered

Figure 13.1. (Opposite page) A represents the effects of 2-mg buprenorphine administered sublingually (n = 17) and 30-mg methadone administered orally (n = 14) on treatment retention. B shows self-reported withdrawal symptoms from a 20-item adjective checklist. C represents opiate drug use during detoxification. Brackets indicate standard error. From "A Clinical Trial of Buprenorphine: Comparison With Methadone in the Detoxification of Heroin Addicts," by W. K. Bickel, M. L. Stitzer, G. E. Bigelow, I. A. Liebson, D. R. Jasinski, and R. E. Johnson, 1988, Clinical Pharmacology and Therapeutics, 43, p. 75. Copyright 1988 by Mosby-Year Book, Inc. Reprinted with permission.

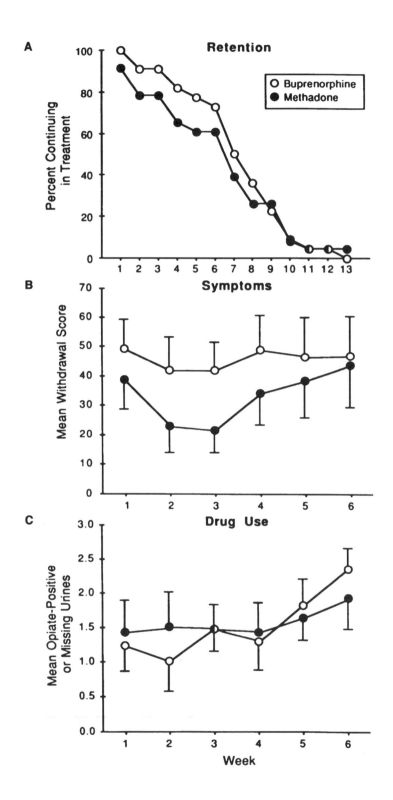

A **Retention**

B **Symptoms**

C **Drug Use**

the methadone dose over 10 weeks, and the other tapered methadone over 30 weeks. Twenty-four percent and 53% of the patients completed the treatment period in the rapid and gradual dose tapers, respectively. Moreover, the group receiving the rapid dose taper provided more urine samples positive for opioids. A small study using buprenorphine also compared rapid versus gradual dose taper (Amass, Bickel, Higgins, & Hughes, 1994) by tapering buprenorphine across 12 days (rapid taper) or across 36 days (gradual taper). Both groups received contingency management and CRA treatments. The rapid detoxification treatment resulted in fewer patients being retained, more opioid-positive urine samples, and greater self-reports of withdrawal relative to the group receiving the gradual buprenorphine dose reduction. These results suggest that the greater degree of opioid withdrawal experienced by the participants receiving the rapid dose taper led to their greater degree of relapse to opioid use.

Overall, the above studies indicate that although opioid detoxification treatments are reasonable treatment strategies, the results of typical pharmacotherapy-based, outpatient opioid detoxification protocols are less than desirable. The possibility of improving these results is one reason for considering supplementing detoxification treatments with additional behavioral therapies, such as contingency management procedures.

CONTINGENCY MANAGEMENT DURING OPIOID DETOXIFICATION

Behavioral contingency management procedures are used during outpatient opioid detoxification in an attempt to increase the success of detoxification protocols from that provided by traditional detoxification treatment systems. As discussed in many of the chapters in this volume (e.g., see Bigelow & Silverman, chapter 1; Kidorf & Stitzer, chapter 11; Morral et al., chapter 10; Piotrowski & Hall, chapter 9; Shoptaw et al., chapter 12; and Silverman et al., chapter 8), these procedures typically include the provision of scheduled nonpharmacological consequences (e.g., monetary payments) or pharmacologically based privileges (e.g., take-home methadone) contingent on opiate-free urine samples.

Studies of the efficacy of contingency management procedures during opioid detoxification show promising results; however, few such studies have been conducted. Indeed, a comprehensive literature search revealed only three studies conducted with humans and one preclinical study conducted with nonhuman animals that explored the effectiveness of these procedures during opioid detoxification (see Table 13.1 for a summary).

In 1977, Wurster, Griffiths, Findley, and Brady published the first study investigating the use of pharmacological and environmental manipulations during opioid detoxification. In this laboratory study, which pro-

TABLE 13.1
Summary of Studies on Efficacy of Contingency Management Procedures During Opioid Detoxification

Study	N	Gender (in %)	Mean age (in years)	Ethnicity (in %)	Length of detoxification	Intervention	Target drugs	Results
Hall et al. (1979)	81 (control, 41)	Men, 65; women, 35	28	White, 53; Black, 12; Latino, 24	16 days (3 weeks)	Multicomponent contingency management including payment for drug-free urine samples versus noncontingent control	Morphine, barbiturates	Contingent group showed significant improvement in number of drug-free urine samples and duration of abstinence; no treatment retention effect
McCaul et al. (1984)	20 (control, 10)	Men, 100	Experimental, 29.6; control, 29.4	Experimental, White, 30; Black, 70 (control: White, 50; Black, 50)	90 days (13 weeks)	Payment of methadone take home and clinic benefits were contingent on drug-free urine samples versus noncontingent control	Opiates	Contingent group showed significant improvement in number of opiate-free urine samples, duration of abstinence, and treatment retention
Higgins et al. (1986)	39 (13 per group)	Men, 100	Contingent, 32.6; noncontingent, 33.2; control, 31.4	Contingent: White, 38; Black, 62 Noncontingent: White, 62; Black, 38 Control: White, 54; Black, 46	90 days (13 weeks)	(a) Methadone dose increases were contingent, (b) noncontingent on drug use, or (c) no dose increase	Opiates	Contingent group had significantly lower percentage of opiate-positive urine samples; contingent and non-contingent had equivalent treatment retention
Wurster et al. (1977)	2 (baboons)	Male, 100	na	na	102 days	Food access contingent on progressive reduction in heroin self-administration versus noncontingent detoxification group	Heroin	Heroin intake was reduced to 15% of baseline levels; resumption of baseline levels of use in controls

vided an analogue to a clinical setting, the researchers used an animal model to investigate the rates of relapse to drug use that occurred during both standard detoxification procedures and detoxification procedures that included a contingency management component. Specifically, animals trained to self-administer heroin virtually eliminated their heroin intake when noncontingent morphine was administered and access to food reinforcement was provided (analogous to standard methadone maintenance). In addition, when the dose of noncontingent morphine was progressively decreased, animals increased their heroin administration to their baseline levels (analogous to relapse to drug use rates observed during standard methadone detoxification). However, when the noncontingent morphine dose was progressively decreased and access to food was made contingent on selection of increasingly lower doses of heroin, intake of heroin was reduced to approximately 15% of its original doses (analogous to detoxification that includes behavioral contingency management procedures).

The promising findings of this preclinical study, demonstrating the potential utility of behavioral therapies when included in detoxification procedures, were first replicated in humans by Hall, Bass, Hargreaves, and Loeb (1979), who reported a "surprising readiness on the part of detoxification clients to modify their heroin use when contingencies are presented" (p. 450). Hall et al. investigated the effectiveness of a multicomponent contingency management program that was used during the course of a 16-day methadone detoxification of 81 participants. Participants in the experimental group received (a) monetary reinforcement for the provision of morphine and barbiturate-free urine samples and on completion of the detoxification program (maximum potential earning of $56), (b) feedback from the experimenter about urine test results, (c) prompts designed to function as reminders of their opportunity to earn money, and (d) brief counseling regarding treatment progress. In comparison with a control group, which received noncontingent payment of $1 for each urine sample provided, participants in the experimental condition provided significantly more drug-free urine samples (approximately 20% more) and achieved a significantly longer period of abstinence (the experimental group experienced 5 days or more drug free with greater frequency than did controls), although no between-groups differences in treatment retention were evident.

McCaul, Stitzer, Bigelow, and Liebson (1984) extended Hall et al.'s (1979) findings by investigating (a) the effectiveness of behavioral contingency management procedures during a lengthier, 90-day (13-week) methadone detoxification and (b) the usefulness of providing varied incentives to participants contingent on their provision of opiate-free urine samples. Specifically, 20 participants who provided evidence that they had discontinued or reduced their use of illicit opiates during a methadone maintenance phase of the study were selected for inclusion in the detoxification phase of the study. Participants in the experimental condition received $10 and a single take-home medication privilege for each opiate-free urine specimen they provided, and they were required to participate in only the minimum level of clinic requirements during weeks in which they provided opiate-free urine samples. However, when these individuals provided opiate-positive urine specimens, they forfeited their $10 and take-home medication and were required to complete all clinic procedures, including counseling sessions in which they were questioned about their drug use and reminded of the immediate and long-term consequences of their drug use during detoxification. In contrast, the control group received $5 for each urine specimen they provided, independent of their opiate use. Results indicate that the use of contingency management procedures delayed the onset of relapse to illicit-opiate use during detoxification relative to standard detoxification procedures. Participants in the experimental group had significantly more opiate-free urine samples than control group participants during the methadone dose reduction phase but not the placebo phase of the detoxification program. Similarly, the group experiencing the contingencies during the detoxification had a significantly longer period of abstinence and longer treatment retention than control participants during the time that they were still receiving methadone but not after methadone administration was discontinued.

Higgins, Stitzer, Bigelow, and Liebson (1986) further explored the utility of behavioral contingencies during detoxification by investigating the relative effects of contingent and noncontingent supplemental methadone on relapse to drug use during methadone detoxification. In this study, participants who demonstrated evidence of reduced opiate use during maintenance randomly (a) received an increase in their daily dose of methadone (by 5, 10, 15, or 20 mg) during detoxification in a manner that was contingent on their provision of an opiate-free urine specimen (contingent dose-increase group), (b) received comparable dose increases independent of their urinalysis results (noncontingent dose-increase group), or (c) had no opportunity to receive dose increases (control group). In this study, the contingent group had a significantly lower percentage of opiate-positive urines than the noncontingent and control groups, with group differences most distinct when methadone dose fell below 10 mg and nonexistent when the intervention ended and methadone was no longer administered (see Figure 13.2). The improved outcomes for the contingent group cannot be attributed to the pharmacological properties of methadone because the noncontingent group received a greater amount of methadone on average than did the contingent group. Nevertheless, methadone appears to be an important variable in treatment retention because the contingent and noncontingent groups were retained in treatment for equivalent periods of time and for a significantly longer time than the control group.

As evidenced by these studies and suggested by Higgins et al. (1986),

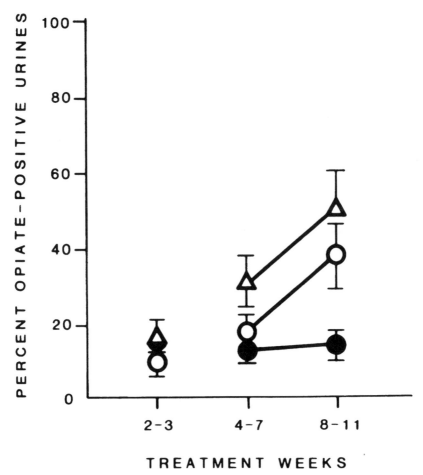

Figure 13.2. Percentage of opiate-positive urinanalysis results with all patients included as a function of treatment weeks. Results obtained during dose stabilization (Weeks 2–3) are presented as a 2-week block, and results during the intervention period (Weeks 4–11) are presented in two 4-week blocks. The contingent group is represented by closed circles, the noncontingent groups by open circles, and the control group by triangles. Brackets represent 1 standard error. From "Contingent Methadone Delivery: Effects on Illicit-Opiate Use," by S. T. Higgins, M. L. Stitzer, G. E. Bigelow, and I. A. Liebson, 1986, *Drug and Alcohol Dependence, 17,* p. 317. Copyright 1986 by Elsevier Science Ireland Ltd., Bay 15K, Shannon Industrial Estate, County Clare, Ireland. Reprinted with kind permission.

perhaps the most clinically significant use of behavioral contingencies during opiate detoxification is the delayed onset of relapse to illicit-opiate use that they promote (accompanied by a lack of symptom substitution or increased use of drugs other than those targeted by the contingency), thereby providing the opportunity to initiate more long-term preventive treatment strategies. That is, contingency-based interventions are shown to be most beneficial when used in conjunction with methadone, and high relapse rates are evident when methadone is no longer administered, despite available incentives for abstinence. To increase the efficacy of these promising interventions, researchers may need to provide postdetoxification treatment. This additional treatment could include the administration of the opiate antagonist, naltrexone, slower withdrawal of the available incentives, or a discontinuation of the incentives only after individuals have been maintained on a placebo. Furthermore, refining the behavioral intervention during opiate detoxification and thereby increasing its effectiveness may require identifying which incentives or treatment components (e.g., magnitude of incentives) are most effective with various subpopulations of opioid-dependent individuals, thereby customizing the intervention to increase the success of detoxification treatment strategies (Silverman, Chutuape, Bigelow, & Stitzer, 1997).

APPLICATION OF CONTINGENCY MANAGEMENT AND CRA TO DETOXIFICATION TREATMENT

A recent development in the field of contingency management is to combine it with CRA. To our knowledge, only one study has been conducted (Bickel et al., 1997) to compare the behavioral treatment approach developed by Higgins and colleagues (Higgins et al., 1991, 1993, 1994) with standard counseling in outpatient opioid detoxification. The behavioral treatment applied in that study consisted of two components. The first component consisted of a voucher incentive program for providing opioid-free urine samples and engaging in independently verifiable therapeutic activities: Vouchers were available for opioid-free urine samples taken three times a week and for engaging in three activities per week. The value of the vouchers for opioid-free urine samples increased in value with each consecutive urine sample provided. Similarly, the value of vouchers for engaging in verifiable, therapeutic activities increased in value on a weekly basis, assuming all three activities were completed each week. The second component consisted of the CRA, which incorporated employment, recreational, and relationship counseling, as well as instructions about the antecedents and consequences of opioid use. Standard treatment included lifestyle counseling typical of many methadone clinics. Thirty-nine opioid-dependent patients were randomly assigned to one of these two treatments.

Outcomes demonstrate that the behavioral treatment improved patient retention. More than twice as many patients receiving behavioral treatment (53%) as compared with standard treatment (20%) were retained beyond the last dose of buprenorphine for an additional 3 weeks of placebo administration. The retention in the behavioral treatment group exceeded results from the prior, strictly pharmacotherapeutic buprenorphine detoxification trial conducted by Bickel et al. (1988) that retained approximately 35% of the patients until the end of buprenorphine administration and fewer than 5% of the patients at the end of an additional 3 weeks of a placebo. Enhanced retention tends to be a consistent result of behavioral treatments, and it is an important outcome measure, given the association between longer retention and improvements on other treatment outcomes (Higgins et al., 1994).

Although several measures of abstinence in this study did not achieve statistical significance, the behavioral treatment group exhibited greater abstinence than the standard treatment group: Significantly more patients achieved 8 weeks of continuous opioid abstinence in the behavioral treatment than in the standard treatment group. To be accepted as a useful treatment approach, behavioral treatment's abstinence as well as retention results may have to be improved further; nonetheless, they demonstrate that results of opioid detoxification protocols do not need to be uniformly poor.

Finally in this study, a strong correlation was reported between the completion of activities and both opioid abstinence and retention. This result underscores the importance of competing sources of nondrug reinforcement in suppressing drug use (Bickel & DeGrandpre 1996; Vuchinich & Tucker 1988). This correlation is also consistent with the findings of basic human and animal research that demonstrate suppression of drug taking by making competing sources of nondrug reinforcement available (Bickel, DeGrandpre, Higgins, Hughes, & Badger, 1995; Carroll, Carmona, & May 1991; Higgins, Bickel, & Hughes 1994; Nader & Woolverton, 1992). Of course, this relationship may not be causal; therefore, other interpretations are possible. For example, these results also would be obtained if more patients complied with all aspects of their treatment, including abstinence, retention, and engagement in specified activities. Only prospective research can determine whether engaging in these activities independently contributes to improved treatment efficacy.

Thus, this single trial (Bickel et al., 1997) shows that a treatment package consisting of contingency management and CRA improves outcomes during outpatient buprenorphine detoxification. Although the magnitude of the effect is modest, the findings suggest that detoxification outcomes can be modified. Perhaps further additions to the treatment package could result in further improvement in detoxification outcome.

CONCLUSION

Combining behavioral and pharmacological interventions is an important pursuit for the development of a comprehensive approach to drug abuse treatment. Evidence from the studies reviewed above demonstrates that a pharmacotherapy's efficacy for maintenance and detoxification services can be rendered better or worse, depending on the additional psychosocial services provided (McLellan et al., 1993). Although outcomes following detoxification still may not be optimal, the behavioral treatments reviewed above demonstrate that results from that treatment are malleable. Moreover, this review supports the possibility of developing opioid detoxification as an efficacious treatment.

REFERENCES

Amass, L., Bickel, W. K., Higgins, S. T., & Hughes, J. R. (1994). A preliminary investigation of outcome following gradual or rapid buprenorphine detoxification. *Journal of Addictive Diseases, 13*, 35–47.

Ball, J. C., & Ross, A. (1991). *The effectiveness of methadone maintenance treatment.* New York: Springer-Verlag.

Best, S. E., Oliveto, A. H., & Kosten, T. R. (1996). Opioid addiction: Recent advances in detoxification and maintenance therapy. *CNS Drugs, 6*, 301–314.

Bickel, W. K., & Amass, L. (1995). Buprenorphine treatment of opioid dependence: A review. *Experimental and Clinical Psychopharmacology, 3*, 477–489.

Bickel, W. K., Amass, L., Higgins, S. T., Badger, G. J., & Esch, R. A. (1997). Effects of adding behavioral treatment to opioid detoxification with buprenorphine. *Journal of Consulting and Clinical Psychology, 65*, 803–810.

Bickel, W. K., & DeGrandpre, R. J. (1996). Basic psychological science speaks to drug policy: Drug cost and competing reinforcement. In W. K. Bickel & R. J. DeGrandpre (Eds.), *Drug policy and human nature: Psychological perspectives on the control, prevention, and treatment of illicit drug use* (pp. 31–52). New York: Plenum Press.

Bickel, W. K., DeGrandpre, R. J., Higgins, S. T., Hughes, J. R., & Badger, G. J. (1995). Effects of simulated employment and recreation on drug taking: A behavioral economic analysis. *Experimental and Clinical Psychopharmacology, 3*, 467–476.

Bickel, W. K., Stitzer, M. L., Bigelow, G. E., Liebson, I. A., Jasinski, D. R., & Johnson, R. E. (1988). A clinical trial of buprenorphine: Comparison with methadone in the detoxification of heroin addicts. *Clinical Pharmacology and Therapeutics, 43*, 72–78.

Carroll, M. E., Carmona, G. G., & May, S. A. (1991). Modifying drug-reinforced behavior by altering the economic conditions of the drug and nondrug reinforcer. *Journal of Experimental Analysis of Behavior, 56*, 361–376.

Curran, J. W., Jaffe, H. W., & Hardy, A. M. (1988). Epidemiology of HIV infection and AIDS in the United States. *Science, 33*, 15–26.

Fishbain, D. A., Rosomoff, H. L., Cutler, R., & Rosomoff, R. S. (1993). Opiate detoxification protocols: A clinical manual. *Annals of Clinical Psychiatry, 5,* 53–65.

Hall, S. M., Bass, A., Hargreaves, W. A., & Loeb, P. (1979). Contingency management and information feedback in outpatient heroin detoxification. *Behavior Therapy, 10,* 443–451.

Hartnoll, R. L. (1994). Opiates: Prevalence and demographic factors. *Addiction, 89,* 1377–1383.

Higgins, S. T., Bickel, W. K., & Hughes, J. R. (1994). Influence of an alternative reinforcer on human cocaine self-administration. *Life Sciences, 55,* 179–187.

Higgins, S. T., Budney, A. J., Bickel, W. K., Foerg, F. E., Donham, R., & Badger, G. J. (1994). Incentives improve outcome in outpatient behavioral treatment of cocaine dependence. *Archives of General Psychiatry, 51,* 568–576.

Higgins, S. T., Budney, A. J., Bickel, W. K., Hughes, J. R., Foerg, F., & Badger, G. (1993). Achieving cocaine abstinence with a behavioral approach. *American Journal of Psychiatry, 150,* 763–769.

Higgins, S. T., Delaney, D. D., Budney, A. J., Bickel, W. K., Hughes, J. R., Foerg, F., & Fenwick, J. (1991). A behavioral approach to achieving initial cocaine abstinence. *American Journal of Psychiatry, 148,* 1218–1224.

Higgins, S. T., Stitzer, M. L., Bigelow, G. E., & Liebson, I. A. (1986). Contingent methadone delivery: Effects on illicit-opiate use. *Drug and Alcohol Dependence, 17,* 311–322.

Hser, Y., Anglin, M. D., & Powers, K. (1993). A 24-year follow-up of California narcotic addicts. *Archives of General Psychiatry, 50,* 577–584.

McCaul, M. E., Stitzer, M. L., Bigelow, G. E., & Liebson, I. A. (1984). Contingency management interventions: Effects on treatment outcome during methadone detoxification. *Journal of Applied Behavior Analysis, 17,* 35–43.

McLellan, A. T., Arndt, I. O., Metzger, D. S., Woody, G. E., & O'Brien, C. P. (1993). The effects of psychosocial services in substance abuse treatment. *Journal of the American Medical Association, 269,* 1953–1959.

Milby, J. B. (1988). Methadone maintenance to abstinence. How many make it? *Journal of Nervous and Mental Diseases, 176,* 409–422.

Nader, M. A., & Woolverton, W. L. (1992). Choice between cocaine and food by rhesus monkeys: Effects of conditions of food availability. *Behavioral Pharmacology, 3,* 635–638.

Rice, D. P., & Kelman, S. (1989). Measuring comorbidity and overlap in the hospitalization cost for alcohol and drug abuse and mental illness. *Inquiry, 26,* 249–260.

Senay, E. C., Dorus, W., Goldberg, F., & Thorton, W. (1977). Withdrawal from methadone maintenance: Rate of withdrawal and expectation. *Archives of General Psychiatry, 34,* 361–367.

Silverman, K., Chutuape, M. A. D., Bigelow, G. E., & Stitzer, M. L. (1997). Reinforcement of cocaine abstinence in treatment-resistant patients: Effects of reinforcer magnitude. In *Problems of drug dependence: Proceedings of the 58th annual scientific meeting, the College on Problems of Drug Dependence* (NIDA

Research Monograph 174, p. 74). Washington, DC: U.S. Government Printing Office.

Swan, N. (1992). Heroin and cocaine-related visits to hospital emergency rooms continue to increase nationwide. *NIDA Notes 7*, 9–10.

Vuchinich, R. E., & Tucker, J. A. (1988). Contributions from behavioral theories of choices as a framework to an analysis of alcohol abuse. *Journal of Abnormal Psychology, 92*, 408–416.

Wurster, R. M., Griffiths, R. R., Findley, J. D., & Brady, J. V. (1977). Reduction of heroin self-administration in baboons by manipulations of behavioral and pharmacological conditions. *Pharmacology, Biochemistry, and Behavior, 7*, 519–528.

V

RESEARCH DEVELOPMENT
AND DISSEMINATION

14

MONITORING COCAINE USE DURING CONTINGENCY MANAGEMENT INTERVENTIONS

KENZIE L. PRESTON, KENNETH SILVERMAN, AND EDWARD J. CONE

Contingency management treatment for substance abuse has been proven an effective method for decreasing illicit-drug use and increasing drug abstinence in patients seeking treatment. A critical requirement for the application of contingency management is the capacity to determine whether drug use has occurred. Because illicit-drug use is a covert activity, drug use or drug abstinence is usually monitored indirectly through the testing of biological specimens, most frequently urine, for the presence or absence of a drug. Results of toxicology screens must be accurate and available quickly, so that contingencies can be applied appropriately and in a timely fashion.

The purpose of this chapter is to provide information relevant to monitoring drug use and interpreting toxicology screen results. We discuss factors affecting toxicology results, qualitative and quantitative urinalysis methods, and the use of other biological specimens for monitoring drug use. The general principles covered in this chapter apply to a range of drugs. However, because the vast majority of our empirical research focuses on cocaine abuse, monitoring cocaine use is the primary focus of our chapter.

WHY URINALYSIS TO MONITOR COCAINE USE?

The majority of clinical trials collect both self-reported use and urine specimens to monitor cocaine use. The principal advantage of self-reported drug use is that it can be collected easily, nonintrusively, and at a much lower cost compared with urinalysis. In addition, self-reports can cover a range of time periods. Respondents can be asked to report on use in the last 30 days, as in the widely used Addiction Severity Index (McLellan et al., 1985), or to report on use since the last visit, perhaps 1–7 days. In contrast, the time period over which urinalysis can detect drug use is limited by the pharmacokinetics of drug elimination and the sensitivity of the screening procedure. A significant disadvantage to relying on self-reported drug use, however, is that the validity of the reports is questionable (e.g., Magura, Goldsmith, Casriel, Goldstein, & Lipton, 1987; Sherman & Bigelow, 1992; Skog, 1992). In contingency management interventions, the pressure to minimize reported cocaine use is clear, and self-reported drug use cannot be relied on as a valid indicator of recent use.

METABOLISM AND ELIMINATION OF COCAINE

Cocaine has a relatively short plasma half-life of 1 to 2 hr. Only a small proportion of cocaine (1–5%) is eliminated in the urine as the parent compound (Jatlow, 1988) which is detectable for a only a short period of time (hours) after administration (Ambre, 1985). The principal route of elimination of cocaine is through metabolism primarily by esterase in blood and tissues. These water-soluble metabolites are then excreted in urine (Jatlow, 1988; Shuster, 1991). The major metabolite, benzoylecgonine, is inactive and is formed by hydrolysis of cocaine (Jatlow, 1988; Shuster, 1991). Because cocaine has a short half-life and only a small portion is excreted unchanged in urine, urine toxicology screens have been developed to detect the presence of the longer lasting metabolite benzoylecgonine. Benzoylecgonine has a urinary excretion half-life of 6–8 hr (Ambre, 1985) and can usually be detected for about 48 hr after cocaine administration (Saxon, Calsyn, Haver, & Delaney, 1988). The detection time of benzoylecgonine, however, is highly dependent on the amount of cocaine ingested, individual rates of excretion, and the sensitivity of the assay; there are reports of detection of benzoylecgonine well after 48 hr in patients in treatment (Kranzler, Dellafera, McLaughlin, & Wong, 1992; Peters et al., 1996).

URINALYSIS

Urine is produced continuously by the kidney as an ultrafiltrate of blood. During urine production, essential substances are reabsorbed by the kidney, and excess water and waste products such as urea, organic substances, and inorganic substances are eliminated from the body. The daily amount and composition of urine varies widely depending on many factors such as fluid intake, diet, health, drug effects, and environmental conditions. The volume of urine produced by a healthy adult in a 24-hr period ranges from 1 to 2 L, but normal values outside these limits are frequently encountered. Creatinine, a protein by-product of muscle metabolism, is present at a relatively constant concentration in blood and is excreted in urine. Consequently, the average 24-hr output of creatinine in urine is also constant. A comparison of creatinine concentration in urine to blood provides a means of assessing renal function. For most people, urine creatinine concentrations exceed 20 mg/dl, although concentrations lower than 20 mg/dl are occasionally encountered.

Urine specimens with creatinine concentrations below 20 mg/dl can be produced by excessive water intake. Drug users who are urine tested sometimes drink large amounts of water or herbal teas or add water to their specimens in an attempt to dilute the drug concentrations below the cutoff concentrations (Needleman, Porvaznik, & Ander, 1992). Consequently, many laboratories also test for creatinine and report specimens with creatinine concentrations below 20 mg/dl. Drug:creatinine ratios can be evaluated for evidence of an attempted dilution of the urine. A highly diluted specimen may test negative, but evaluation of the drug:creatinine ratio provides convincing evidence that the sample would have been positive if normal water intake had occurred. Specific gravity also can be used to detect dilute samples; the normal range of specific gravity is 1.007–1.035 (Edwards, Fyfe, Liu, & Walia, 1993).

When cocaine is administered by the intravenous or smoking route, absorption is nearly instantaneous and excretion in urine begins almost immediately. Absorption is slower when a drug is administered by the intranasal route, and excretion in urine may be delayed for several hours. Normally, specimens voided within 6 hr after cocaine administration contain the highest concentration of parent drug and metabolites. Because cocaine excretion in urine occurs at an exponential rate, the majority of the dose is eliminated within 48 hr after administration. Detection times vary slightly according to dose, frequency of administration, cutoff concentration, and numerous other factors. Despite a wide variance, it is helpful to know average detection times when interpreting urine test data. A list of average detection times and commonly used cutoff concentrations are shown in Table 14.1.

Most drugs of abuse have detection times of 2–4 days, unless accumulation has occurred as a result of frequent, multiple dosing over an extended period of time. In treatment studies, the relatively brief historical record of drug exposure provided by urinalysis must be considered when compared with retrospective self-report data. Urinalysis may cover only

TABLE 14.1
Typical Screening and Confirmation Cutoff Concentrations and Detection Times for Drugs of Abuse

Drug	Screening cutoff concentrations (ng/ml)	Analyte tested in confirmation	Confirmation cutoff concentrations (ng/ml)	Urine detection time
Amphetamine	1,000	Amphetamine	500	2–4 days
Barbiturates	200	Amobarbital, secobarbital, other barbiturates	200	2–4 days for short acting, up to 30 days for long acting
Benzodiazepines	200	Oxazepam, diazepam, other benzodiazepines	200	Up to 30 days
Cocaine	300	Benzoylecgonine	150	1–3 days
Codeine	300	Codeine, morphine	300, 300	1–3 days
Heroin	300	Morphine	300	1–3 days
		6-acetylmorphine	10	
Marijuana	100, 50, 20	11-nor-9-carboxy-Δ-9-tetra-hydrocannabinol	15	1–3 days for casual use, up to 30 days for chronic use
Methadone	300	Methadone	300	2–4 days
Methamphetamine	1,000	Methamphetamine, amphet-amine	500, 200	2–4 days
Phencyclidine	25	Phencyclidine	25	2–7 days for casual use, up to 30 days for chronic use

2–4 days, but self-report data may reference longer periods. Patients who accurately report drug use within the last month could easily have negative urine results. In this case, the urine result would not support the self-report data.

CHARACTERISTICS OF DRUG-TESTING METHODS

The usefulness of a drug test resides in its ability to accurately detect the presence of the parent drug or metabolite in a biological fluid or tissue following human drug administration. Individual differences in rate of absorption, metabolism, and excretion also are pharmacologic variables that may influence test outcome. In addition, analytic factors such as sensitivity, specificity, and accuracy are important.

Many commercial assays and published methodologies may be used for urine cocaine testing. For the most part, these methods can be grouped into two categories: screening assays and confirmation assays. The performance characteristics of these assays are listed in Table 14.2. These assays also can be adapted for measurement of drugs in other body fluids but must be properly validated before use. Generally, screening assays (immunoassays and thin-layer chromatography [TLC]) are commercial-based tests that are inexpensive and simple to perform. In contrast, confirmation assays (gas chromatography [GC] and gas chromatography/mass spectrometry [GC/MS]) are more expensive and more labor intensive, but sensitivity and specificity are usually higher than screening tests. Immunoassay-based screening tests may cross-react with a variety of similar chemical substances. For example,

TABLE 14.2
Performance Characteristics of Different Types of Assays
for Drugs of Abuse

Assay	Sensitivity	Specificity	Accuracy	Turnaround time	Cost (in $)
On-site	Moderate–high	Moderate	Qualitative[a]	Minutes	4–25
EMIT, FPIA, RIA, KIMS	Moderate–high	Moderate	Low–high	1–4 hr	1–5
TLC	Low–high	High	Qualitative[a]	1–4 hr	1–4
GC	High	High	High	Days	5–20
GC/MS	High	High	High	Days	10–100

Note. EMIT = enzyme multiplied immunoassay technique; FPIA = fluorescent polarization immunoassay; RIA = radioimmunoassay; KIMS = kinetic interaction of microparticles in solution; TLC = thin layer chromatography; GC = gas chromatography; GC/MS = gas chromatography/mass spectrometry.
[a]Results for on-site tests and TLC assays are generally expressed in qualitative terms (i.e., positive and negative); consequently, accuracy may be difficult to assess.

most commercial immunoassays for cocaine are designed to give positive test results for specimens containing benzoylecgonine, the major metabolite for cocaine, but some also cross-react with ecgonine methyl ester (a second cocaine metabolite in high abundance) and with cocaine. More specific methodology is needed if it is important to distinguish between cocaine and metabolites.

For treatment and research studies in which there are no punitive actions taken on the basis of positive test results, it becomes less important to use expensive, confirmation techniques, unless there are known interferences within a particular assay. Indeed, some screening assays have shown exceptionally high correlation with GC/MS methods. For example, Cone, Menchen, and Mitchell (1988) reported that urine test results from the TDx (Abbott Laboratories, Abbott Park, IL) assay for cocaine metabolite significantly correlated with results by GC/MS with no evidence of assay bias. Consequently in many cases, it may be more cost effective to use a highly selective immunoassay than to pay for the additional costs of confirmation. When immunoassays are used, turnaround time is often rapid. Results may be available immediately in some cases and almost always are provided within 24 hr of receipt at the laboratory. It is also important to select an assay system whose results can be compared with those from other studies. Many comparisons between different assay systems are not valid simply because the immunoassay antibodies used in the assay were not targeted toward the same drug or metabolite. Figure 14.1 illustrates the effects of two assays with different cutoff concentrations on detection time. It is important to select drug assays with equivalent performance characteristics if comparisons within and between studies are anticipated. Investigations of contingency management treatments generally use screening assays rather than confirmatory assays.

The frequency of urine collection in contingency management treatment should be based on the window of detection for the primary drug. Specimen collection intervals that are longer than the window of detection can result in underrepresentation of drug use, regardless of the analytic method used, although lowering cutoff concentrations can lengthen detection time as noted above. In contrast, short specimen collection intervals can result in an overrepresentation of drug use. Drug or metabolite from a single drug use may be detected in more than one urine specimen if the second specimen is collected before all drug or metabolite has been excreted. These multiple positives from a single use (*carryover positives*) artificially inflate the apparent rate of drug use by patients. Rates of carryover vary depending on the same factors that affect the window of detection listed above. The impact of sample collection frequency has been reviewed elsewhere (Jain, 1992).

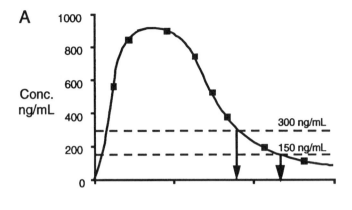

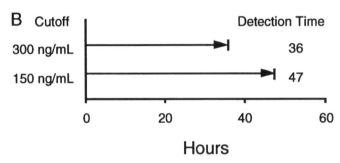

Figure 14.1. Influence of cutoff on detection time. (A) Illustration of drug excretion curve and (B) relationship of detection time to cutoff concentration (Conc.). From "New Developments in Biological Measures of Drug Prevalence" (p. 112), by E. J. Cone, 1997, in L. Harrison and A. Hughes (Eds.), *The Validity of Self-Reported Drug Use: Improving the Accuracy of Survey Estimates* (NIDA Research Monograph 167), Washington, DC: U.S. Government Printing Office. Copyright 1997 in the public domain.

URINALYSIS TESTS

Qualitative

Urine toxicology screening in substance abuse clinical trials is typically done with qualitative urinalysis. Qualitative tests give categorical results, either positive or negative, depending on whether the amount of drug or drug metabolite is above or below a set cutoff. The exact amount of drug is generally not determined. The standard cutoff concentration used in clinical trials to define positive and negative qualitative screens is 300 ng/ml of cocaine metabolite, the same as that set by the Department of Health and Human Services for workplace testing (Substance Abuse and Mental Health Administration, 1994). Standardization of cutoffs is extremely useful when results from separate studies are compared or when data from multiple small studies are combined to increase statistical power in meta-analyses (e.g., Levin & Lehman, 1991). Another advantage of qualitative tests is that they can be done quickly and are relatively simple to conduct. Some qualitative immunoassays can even be done on-site without any equipment and without extensive staff expertise or training (Cone, 1990; Cone, Darwin, Dickerson, & Mitchell, 1991). These characteristics have particular application in contingency management procedures because they enable immediate feedback to be given to patients, potentially even in the "field."

The primary disadvantage of qualitative urinalysis is that qualitative urine tests may be insensitive to moderate changes in drug use. Moderate decreases in frequency of use may not be detected if urine tests remain positive between uses because of carryover. Decreases in amount of drug per use without changes in frequency of use may similarly not be detected by qualitative tests if the amount of drug use is high enough to produce urine concentrations above the cutoff. In some clinical trials of cocaine treatments (e.g., Covi, Hess, Kreiter, & Haertzen, 1994; Kolar et al., 1992), researchers have found significant decreases in self-reported cocaine use without concomitant significant decreases in rates of cocaine-positive urine samples. Although discrepancies between self-report and qualitative urinalysis are usually ascribed to poor reporting of drug use by patients, they may be partially explained by carryover across multiple urine collections. Carryover positives may have a negative effect in contingency management treatment. When patients fail to receive a reinforcer when they are abstinent between treatment clinic visits, they may become discouraged with the treatment and even relapse before providing a negative urine specimen.

Quantitative

An alternative to qualitative urinalysis is the use of quantitative urine testing in clinical trials. In quantitative testing, the concentration of drug or metabolite in urine specimens is determined. Urine specimens are not reported as positive or negative, although cutoff values can be applied to concentration data to obtain results comparable to qualitative tests. Quantitative urinalysis is used in some clinical trials (e.g., Batki, Manfredi, Jacob, & Jones, 1993; Silverman et al., 1996) and is recommended for use in both treatment and clinical trial settings (McCarthy, 1994; Peters et al., 1996; Satel & Kosten, 1991).

A potential advantage is that changes in the pattern, frequency, and amount of use that are not apparent from qualitative urinalysis may be discernible from quantitative urinalysis. This is illustrated in Figure 14.2 with data for three measures of cocaine use (self-report, quantitative urinalysis results, and benzoylecgonine concentrations) from two representative patients participating in a contingency management clinical trial (Preston, Silverman, Schuster, & Cone, 1997a; Silverman et al., 1996). Fifty-one urine specimens were collected three times a week over 5 weeks of baseline treatment and 12 weeks of contingency management treatment. Results of qualitative urinalysis are shown as plus signs (+), indicating urine samples testing positive for cocaine metabolites at concentrations of 300 ng/ml or greater, and minus signs (−), indicating negative urine specimens; self-reported uses are indicated by arrows. Although both patients produced four cocaine-negative urine specimens during the baseline period based on a qualitative cutoff of 300 ng/ml, the concentration ranges differed markedly for the 2 patients over this interval. Quantitative urinalysis data suggest a cyclical pattern of use, even during times when urine benzoylecgonine concentrations never decreased below the 300 ng/ml cutoff. Self-reports of use tended to coincide with the longer periods of cocaine-positive urine specimens, and multiple self-reported uses were associated with longer periods during which consecutive urine specimen were above the 300 ng/ml positive–negative cutoff. In a larger sample of 37 patients (Preston et al., 1997b), the correlation coefficients were high between self-report and urinalysis results within patients: $r = .693$ for qualitative results and .798 for benzoylecgonine equivalents. Thus, patients who reported more cocaine use also tested positive for cocaine more frequently and had higher benzoylecgonine concentrations.

Quantitative urine testing also has some disadvantages. It is somewhat more expensive and requires more skilled staff to conduct the tests than qualitative urine screens. Urine drug–metabolite concentrations can be affected by many of the same variables, such as time between drug use and urine collection, fluid intake, and interindividual metabolic differences that affect qualitative tests. For example, a urine specimen collected just after self-administration of a small amount of the drug could have the same concentration as a specimen collected several days after self-administration of a large amount of the drug. Thus, the time of specimen collection could have greater impact on concentration than the total amount of drug used. Fluid intake also can affect urine drug–metabolite concentration, although corrections can be made using creatinine to adjust for water consumption. To take full advantage of the quantitative results requires the additional determination of creatinine concentrations, which may add to the cost of testing.

USES OF QUANTITATIVE URINALYSIS IN CONTINGENCY MANAGEMENT TREATMENT

Within the context of contingency management treatment, drug concentration data from quantitative urinalysis can be used in many ways.

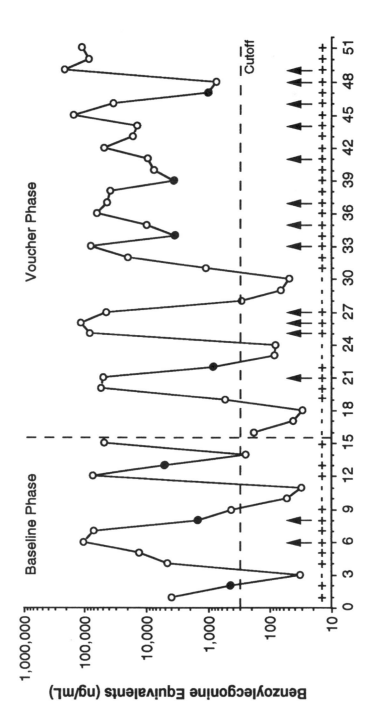

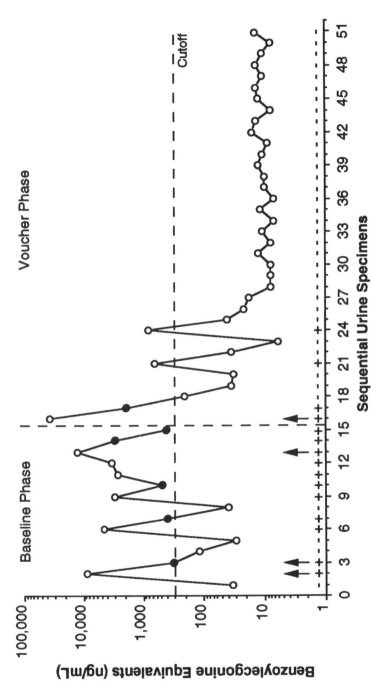

Figure 14.2. Urinalysis results and self-reported cocaine use across time from patients in the control (top panel) and contingency management (bottom panel) groups. Plus signs (+) indicate urine samples testing positive for cocaine metabolites at concentrations of 300 ng/ml or greater, and minus signs (−) indicate negative urine samples. Arrows indicate days on which the patient reported using cocaine within the previous 24 hr. Horizontal dashed line indicates 300 ng/ml; vertical dashed line indicates the end of the baseline phase. Filled circles indicate specimens identified as positive because of carryover according to the new use criteria.

First, contingencies can be placed on changes in urine drug concentration rather than reinforcing only negative urine specimens. Reinforcing decreases in concentration could allow for more frequent testing (e.g., every 24 hr) or earlier reinforcement of abstinence because urine does not reliably test negative at 48 hr after the last use of cocaine. In addition for some patients, abstinence may not be an attainable goal at the onset of treatment. These patients may benefit from identifying decreased use as an interim goal. Initial success, as measured by earning reinforcers for decreased urine concentration, may be an effective initial step toward total abstinence.

A second use of quantitative data is to prevent the inappropriate withholding of reinforcer delivery in cases where urine tests positive for cocaine because of carryover. Criteria have been developed to differentiate urine specimens that are positive because of new or recent use of cocaine from urine specimens that are positive because of carryover from prior use (Preston, Silverman, Schuster, & Cone, 1997a). The new use criteria are listed in Exhibit 14.1. These new use criteria can be systematically and objectively applied to clinical toxicology data, either on an ongoing basis or retrospectively, to samples collected 48–72 hr apart. The criteria are based on established pharmacokinetic parameters of cocaine and benzoylecgonine and include urine creatinine measures for the normalization of variations in water intake and excretion. Concentrations of cocaine metabolite in newly collected urine specimens are compared with those of

EXHIBIT 14.1
Criteria for Defining New Use and Carryover From Quantitative Urinalysis Results

Assume new use if the sample meets any of the following criteria:

Rule 1: An increase in cocaine metabolite concentration to any value over 300 ng/ml and the preceding urine specimen collected at an interval of more than 48 hr is negative (i.e., < 300 ng/ml).

Rule 2a (the one-half rule): Concentration is greater than 300 ng/ml and is more than one half that of the preceding urine specimen collected at an interval of more than 48 hr.

or Rule 2b (the one-quarter rule): Concentration is greater than 300 ng/ml and is more than one quarter that of the preceding urine specimen collected at an interval of more than 48 hr.

Rule 3: Cocaine metabolite is greater than 300 ng/ml in the first urine specimen.

Rule 4: If the preceding specimen is missing (not collected), then any urine specimen with cocaine metabolite greater than 300 ng/ml.

Rule 5: If cocaine metabolite is greater than 300 ng/ml and the cocaine metabolite:creatinine ratio is greater than the cocaine metabolite:creatinine ratio in the preceding specimen.

From "Assessment of Cocaine Use With Quantitative Urinalysis and Estimation of New Uses," by K. L. Preston, K. Silverman, C. R. Schuster, and E. J. Cone, 1997a, *Addiction, 92*, p. 721. Copyright 1997 by Carfax Publishing Ltd., P.O. Box 25, Abingdon, Oxfordshire OX14 3UE, United Kingdom. Adapted with permission.

previously collected specimens. The criteria take into account the possibility that even without additional use, benzoylecgonine concentrations may not decrease to below the standard cutoff with frequent testing schedules (i.e., Monday, Wednesday, Friday). Two different criteria for the required decrease in concentration from one specimen to the next were evaluated because of uncertainty about the exact amount of decrease one would expect to see under the natural conditions of outpatient treatment research with patients who self-administer large and varying amounts of cocaine (Preston et al., 1997a). Rule 2 applies if the concentration of benzoylecgonine in the new sample is greater than 300 ng/ml and has not decreased to less than one half (the one-half rule, Rule 2a) or to less than one quarter (the one-quarter rule, Rule 2b) that of the preceding urine specimen collected at an interval of 48 hr or more. Rules 2a and 2b assume that urine benzoylecgonine should be decreased by at least 50% or 75%, respectively, if no use of cocaine has occurred since the previous urine specimen collection at least 48 hr earlier. The application of the new use criteria is illustrated in Figure 14.2; specimens identified as positive because of carryover are indicated by filled circles.

The new use criteria were evaluated with data collected as part of two separate studies: a residential controlled dosing study in research volunteers and a cocaine abuse treatment study (Preston et al., 1997a). For validation, the new use criteria were tested with specimens collected from a cocaine dosing study (Cone, 1995) by comparing occasions in which urine benzoylecgonine concentrations were identified as new use on the basis of the new use criteria with known cocaine administrations. Five men participated in eight cocaine administration sessions over a period of 4–6 weeks while residing in a clinical research ward. Cocaine was administered by the intravenous, smoked, or intranasal route in doses of 0–32 mg. Urine specimens were collected as they were produced, not on a systematically controlled schedule. Cocaine metabolite concentrations (benzoylecgonine equivalents) were measured by fluorescence polarization immunoassay using TDx equipment and reagents. Rules 1, 2a (one-half rule), and 2b (one-quarter rule) were applied to urine specimens paired to simulate collections of 24-hr and 48-hr intervals, as illustrated in Figure 14.3. In particular, the results of the study gave information on the criteria for the required decrease in benzoylecgonine concentration (Rule 2) and the effects of urine collection interval.

Of the two criteria tested, the one-half rule was more accurate than the one-quarter rule. More specimens were correctly identified as carryover with the one-half than the one-quarter rule, and there were fewer incorrect identifications of new uses. The failures (incorrect identifications of new uses) were primarily attributable to the pairing of specimens with the 24-hr interval. Increasing the collection interval to 48 hr eliminated the incorrect identifications of new uses. The greater accuracy of the one-half

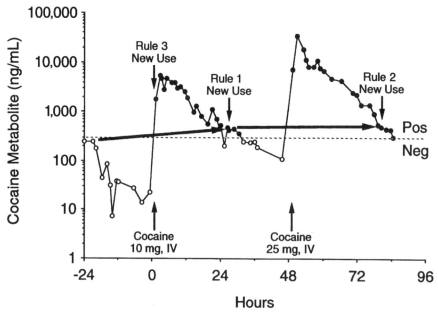

Figure 14.3. Application of new use rules to urine specimens collected from a volunteer administered cocaine (solid upward arrows) in the controlled dosing study. Positive (Pos) test results are identified by solid circles, and negative (Neg) test results are identified by open circles. The solid downward arrows illustrate the application of Rules 1 and 2 to specimens separated in time by a minimum of 48 hr (specimen pairs indicated by horizontal arrows). New use is predicted in both circumstances and for the first positive specimen (Rule 3: no specimen collected at least 48 hr earlier was available). From "Assessment of Cocaine Use With Quantitative Urinalysis and Estimation of New Uses," by K. L. Preston, K. Silverman, C. R. Schuster, and E. J. Cone, 1997a, *Addiction, 92,* p. 721. Copyright 1997 by Carfax Publishing Ltd., P.O. Box 25, Abingdon, Oxfordshire OX14 3UE, United Kingdom, Reprinted with permission.

rule cannot be explained on the basis of pharmacokinetic considerations of the excretion half-life of benzoylecgonine determined under laboratory conditions (Ambre, 1985) because both criteria are quite liberal. When a second specimen is obtained 48 hr following a positive specimen, the concentration of cocaine metabolite should be diminished to less than 2% of the original concentration, assuming a half-life of 8 hr. If the cocaine metabolite half-life is as long as 12 hr, the concentration in the second specimen should have diminished to less than 10% of the original concentration. The results suggest that there is large intersubject variability in the excretion half-life of cocaine metabolites, with some individuals excreting benzoylecgonine over a much longer period. In addition, the doses given in the study were much lower than those used by cocaine users on the street and may be detectable for shorter periods of time than patients in treatment. The results of this study supported the use of the less conservative one-half rule and urine collection intervals of no less than 48 hr.

The new use criteria have been further evaluated in a clinical trial of a contingency management treatment for cocaine abuse (Preston, Silverman, Schuster, & Cone, 1997a; Silverman et al., 1996). Thirty-seven patients received standard methadone maintenance drug abuse treatment throughout the study. At the end of a 5-week baseline period, participants were randomized to either a voucher-based abstinence reinforcement group that received vouchers for urine samples negative for cocaine metabolite or a control group in which patients received similarly valued vouchers independent of the urine test results for 12 weeks. Cocaine use was monitored 3 days per week by self-report and urine testing. Urine specimens were tested qualitatively and quantitatively for cocaine metabolite, and creatinine concentration was measured. Effects of the experimental treatment on self-reported drug use, qualitative urinalysis results, urine cocaine metabolite concentrations, and new uses calculated with the one-half and one-quarter new use criteria were analyzed.

The estimated new uses, as determined by the new use criteria, were informative in two primary areas. First, the new use criteria reconciled some differences between qualitative urinalysis data and self-report by eliminating positive specimens that were caused by carryover. The proportion of specimens identified as positive because of the new use of cocaine when the new use criteria were applied to urine benzoylecgonine concentrations was lower than the proportion of specimens testing positive in the qualitative assay. For example, in the control group the mean percentage of cocaine-positive specimens during baseline was approximately 85% by qualitative urinalysis, whereas the proportion of specimens indicated as new uses was about 65%. Patients reported using cocaine in the 24 hr before urine collection on only about 35% of these occasions. Second, new uses appeared to be a more sensitive measure for detecting differences in cocaine use than was the qualitative urinalysis measure (Preston et al., 1997a). Overall, the experimental contingency management treatment had significant effects on cocaine use, although different measures of cocaine use were differentially sensitive to the treatment effect when the data were analyzed as summary scores (means). Statistical analyses of new uses by both the one-half and one-quarter rules identified more significant differences between cocaine use in the treatment study populations than analyses of either the qualitative or quantitative data. For example, although decreases in cocaine use by the abstinence reinforcement group during the voucher phase were statistically significant compared with its own baseline use for both qualitative urinalysis and new uses, differences between the abstinence reinforcement group and the control group in cocaine use during the voucher phase were significant only for the new use measures, not for the qualitative urinalysis. Additional work to refine and validate the new use criteria is under way (Preston, Silverman, Goldberger, & Cone, 1997).

Robles, Silverman, Preston, Bigelow, and Stitzer (1998) in a pilot study applied the quantitative urinalysis and new use criteria to reinforce patients for abstinence from cocaine for a 2-day period. The patients earned a $100 voucher if they met criteria for having abstained from cocaine use for a brief period of time (between Monday and Wednesday) after being informed of the treatment goal on Monday. The criterion for abstinence was a 50% decrease in benzoylecgonine concentration in the urine specimens obtained on Wednesday compared with a specimen collected on Monday or a concentration below the standard 300 ng/ml cutoff on the Wednesday specimen. Urine benzoylecgonine concentrations were monitored for 1 week before and after the contingency was in place. Of the 38 patients tested, 87% met the abstinence criterion, approximately twice the number who met the criterion without the contingency. Furthermore, benzoylecgonine concentrations decreased in nearly all of the patients (95%); this is about twice the number of patients whose concentrations decreased in the weeks before and after the contingency was in place. Use of a qualitative test under the conditions of this study would have missed many of the patients who abstained from drug use over the 2-day period.

ALTERNATE BIOLOGICAL MATRICES FOR DRUG TESTING

The need for reliable, inexpensive urine-based drug tests has led to significant efforts in research and commercial development of such tests. At the same time, research has progressed on the evaluation of other biological fluids and tissues as useful matrices for drug detection. Presently, there is a growing interest in the use of alternate body fluids and tissues, such as saliva, sweat, and hair, for the diagnosis of drug use. The following discussion provides an overview of the validity of drug testing and the potential uses and limitations of urine, saliva, sweat, and hair testing for drugs of abuse as objective drug prevalence estimates in different populations. Table 14.3 summarizes the drug-detection time and major advantages and disadvantages of these biological matrices. Patterns of parent drug and metabolite distribution in the biological matrices are listed in Table 14.4.

Saliva

Saliva is secreted primarily by serous and mucousal cells in three glands: the parotid, submandibular, and sublingual. The flow of saliva is dependent on neurotransmitter stimulation and can vary widely from zero flow to rates as high as 10 ml/min. The pH of saliva generally is slightly acidic but increases with saliva flow rate, from a low of 5.5 pH to a high of 7.9 pH. Saliva composition is also dependent on flow but generally consists of approximately 90% water with the remainder being electrolytes,

TABLE 14.3
Comparison of Usefulness of Urine, Saliva, Sweat, and Hair as a Biological Matrix for Drug Detection

Biological matrix	Drug-detection time	Major advantages	Major disadvantages	Primary use
Urine	2–4 days	Mature technology, on-site methods available, established cutoffs	Only detects recent use	Detection of recent drug use
Saliva	12–24 hr	Easily obtainable, samples "free" drug fraction, parent drug presence	Short detection time, oral drug contamination, collection methods influence pH and saliva to plasma ratios, only detects recent use, new technology	Linking positive drug test to behavior and performance impairment
Sweat	1–4 weeks	Cumulative measure of drug use	High potential for environmental contamination, new technology	Detection of recent drug use
Hair	Months	Long-term measure of drug use, similar sample can be recollected	High potential for environmental contamination, new technology	Detection of drug use in recent past (1–6 months)

TABLE 14.4
Relative Occurrence of Parent Drug and Metabolite in Urine, Saliva, Sweat, and Hair

Drug	Urine	Saliva	Sweat	Hair
Amphetamine	Amphetamine	Amphetamine	Amphetamine	Amphetamine
Cocaine	BE > EME > cocaine	Cocaine > BE ≈ EME	Cocaine > EME > BE	Cocaine > BE > EME
Marijuana	Carboxy-metabolite	THC	THC	THC > carboxy-metabolite
Heroin	Morphine-glucuronide > morphine	Heroin ≈ 6-AM > morphine	Heroin ≈ 6-AM > morphine	6-AM > heroin ≈ morphine
Codeine	Codeine-glucuronide > codeine > nor-codeine	Codeine	Codeine	Codeine > morphine
Methamphetamine	Methamphetamine > amphetamine	Methamphetamine	Methamphetamine	Methamphetamine > amphetamine
Phencyclidine	Phencyclidine	Phencyclidine	Phencyclidine	Phencyclidine
Morphine	Morphine-glucuronide > morphine	Morphine	Morphine	Morphine

Note. BE = benzoylecgonine; EME = ecgonine methyl ester; THC = tetrahydrocannabinol; 6-AM = 6-acetylmorphine.

amylase, organics (glucose, urea, lipids), proteins (low concentrations), and hormones (cortisol, testosterone, estrogens, progesterone). Drugs may enter saliva by passive diffusion from blood, ultrafiltration, and active secretion, with passive diffusion being the most important route of entry for most drugs with the possible exception of ethanol, which has a molecule small enough to enter by ultrafiltration. Several reports and reviews have been published on the occurrence of drugs of abuse in saliva (Caddy 1984; Cone 1993; Schramm, Smith, Craig, & Kidwell, 1992).

Saliva offers a number of advantages and some disadvantages in comparison with urine testing for cocaine. The major advantages of saliva as a test media include its ready accessibility for collection, less objectionable nature (compared with urine), presence of parent drug in higher abundance than metabolites, and high correlation of saliva drug concentration that can be obtained with the free fraction of the drug in blood.

Despite the advantages of saliva, there are some disadvantages. The use of saliva cocaine concentrations to predict blood concentrations is limited because of the possibility of contamination of saliva from cocaine use by the oral, smoked, and intranasal routes of drug administration. When drugs are administered by these routes, contamination of the oral cavity and saliva can greatly distort saliva:plasma ratios, thereby distorting useful pharmacokinetic relationships. Even with this obvious limitation, saliva measurements can be used as evidence of recent drug use in some situations in which oral contamination is likely to be involved.

The short time course for detectability of drugs in saliva prevents this biological fluid from being used to detect long-term drug use. At the same time, this feature of saliva makes it useful for detection of very recent drug use. Most drugs disappear from saliva and blood within 12–24 hr after administration. There is often a temporal relationship between the disappearance of drugs in saliva and the duration of pharmacologic effects. Consequently, saliva may be most useful in the detection of recent drug use, such as in automobile drivers, accident victims, and employees prior to engaging in safety-sensitive activities (e.g., airline pilots). Its utility in contingency management treatment would depend on the ability to collect frequent saliva samples.

Sweat

Sweat is a watery fluid produced primarily by eccrine glands distributed widely across the skin surface of humans. The primary purpose of sweat production is heat regulation; consequently, the amount of sweat produced is highly dependent on environmental conditions. Sweat consists mostly of water (99%), with the greatest concentrated solute being sodium chloride (Robinson & Robinson, 1954). Routine sweat collection is difficult because of the large variations in the rate of sweat production and the lack of suitable collection devices.

A variety of drugs of abuse have been identified in sweat including amphetamine, cocaine, ethanol, methadone, methamphetamine, morphine, nicotine, and phencyclidine. The mechanism for drug entry into sweat is unclear but most likely occurs by passive diffusion from blood to the sweat gland. An alternate mechanism could involve drug diffusion through the stratum corneum to the skin surface where the drug would be dissolved in sweat.

Research on sweat testing for drugs is limited because of the difficulty in collecting sweat samples. Recently, a sweat collection device was developed that appears to offer promise for the collection of sweat for drug monitoring. The "sweat patch" resembles a Band-Aid that is applied to the skin and can be worn for several days to several weeks. The sweat patch consists of an adhesive layer on a thin transparent film of surgical dressing to which a rectangular absorbent cellulose pad (14 cm^2) is attached. Sweat is absorbed and concentrated on the cellulose pad. The transparent film allows oxygen, carbon dioxide, and water vapor to escape but prevents loss of drug constituents excreted in sweat. Over a period of several days, sweat should saturate the pad and the drug should slowly concentrate. The patch is then removed; the absorbent pad is detached from the device and analyzed for drug content.

Sweat testing for cocaine was evaluated by Cone, Hillsgrove, Jenkins, Keenan, and Darwin (1994). Cocaine was administered in doses of $1-25$ mg by the intravenous route to 4 cocaine-experienced, drug-free volunteers. Sweat patches were worn for 24–48 hr following drug administration. Following removal, the patches were extracted and analyzed for cocaine and metabolites by GC/MS. The primary analyte excreted in sweat was parent cocaine, followed by ecgonine methyl ester and benzoylecgonine. Generally, there appeared to be a dose–concentration relationship; however, there was wide intersubject variability.

Apparent advantages of the sweat patch for drug monitoring include the following: high patient acceptability of wearing the patch, low incidence of allergic reactions to the patch adhesive, and ability to monitor drug intake for a period of several weeks with a single patch. In addition, the patch appears to be relatively tamper proof (i.e., the patch adhesive is specially formulated, so that the patch can only be applied once and cannot be removed and successfully reapplied to the skin surface).

Disadvantages of the sweat patch include high intersubject variability, possibility of environmental contamination of the patch before application or after removal, and risk of accidental removal during a monitoring period. Extreme care must be taken when applying the patch to cleanse the skin surface and to avoid contamination of the cellulose pad. Similar care must be taken when removing the patch and handling for analysis. An additional disadvantage for use in contingency management treatment is that results from sweat samples as yet cannot be obtained rapidly enough to allow timely feedback and reinforcer delivery in most treatment settings.

Hair

Hair is composed primarily of a fibrous network of keratin strands intertwined to form elongated strands. The inner structure of hair is protected by a layer of cuticle cells that restrict or retard entry of environmental pollutants. As hair ages, the cuticle deteriorates from exposure to ultraviolet radiation, chemicals, and mechanical stresses. Head hair grows at an average rate of 1.3 cm/month, although there is some variation according to gender, age, and ethnicity (Saitoh, Uzuka, & Sakamoto, 1969). Collection of hair for testing is most often performed by cutting locks of hair near the scalp surface at the vertex of the head. During collection, the root and tip of the hair lock are identified for later use. Other types of hair such as pubic, axillary, and arm hair also can be used for drug testing.

Drug representatives from virtually all classes of abused drugs can be detected in hair, and hair testing for drugs of abuse is performed in numerous laboratories, some of which offer commercial drug-testing services. When hair is analyzed for drugs of abuse, the parent drug is often present in greater abundance than is found in urine. For example, the major analyte found in hair of cocaine users is parent cocaine. Benzoylecgonine, the primary urinary metabolite, is present in hair in amounts varying from trace concentrations to approximately one third of parent cocaine (Cone, Yousefnejad, Darwin, & Maguire, 1991). Heroin is found in hair in varying amounts together with 6-acetylmorphine and morphine (Goldberger, Caplan, Maguire, & Cone, 1991). 6-acetylmorphine is usually found in greatest abundance in hair, whereas conjugated morphine is the major metabolite in urine.

Although the technology of hair has progressed rapidly over the last decade, several highly controversial aspects of hair testing remain unresolved. It remains unclear how drugs enter hair. The most likely entry routes involve (a) diffusion from blood into the hair follicle and hair cells with subsequent binding to hair cell components, (b) excretion in sweat that bathes hair follicles and hair strands, (c) excretion in oily secretions into the hair follicle and onto the skin surface, and (d) entry from the environment. The possibility of drug entry from sweat and from the environment is particularly troubling because this allows the possibility of the production of false positives if an individual's hair absorbs drugs from the environment or from another person's drug-laden sweat. Another controversial issue in hair analysis is the interpretation of the dose–time relationship. Although it has been generally assumed that segmental analysis of hair provides a record of drug usage, studies with labeled cocaine do not support this interpretation.

Despite the controversial nature of some aspects of hair testing, this technique is used on an increasingly broad scale in a variety of circumstances. One of the most promising applications of hair testing appears to be its use in prevalence studies. The time record of drug use available from hair is considerably longer than any other biological specimen currently used. Self-reported drug use over a period of several months can be compared with hair test results from a hair strand (about 3.9 cm) representative of the same period. It is expected that this type of comparison would be more effective than urine testing because urine provides a historical record of only 2–4 days under most circumstances. Several research groups have compared self-reported cocaine use with hair and urine analysis and found that hair analysis was far more effective than either urinalysis or self-report in detecting a drug (Feucht, Stephens, & Walker, 1994; Mieczkowski, Barzelay, Gropper, & Wish, 1991), although others have shown somewhat higher concordance between hair assay and urinalysis or self-report (Magura, Freeman, Siddiqui, & Lipton, 1992).

Generally, hair analysis provides a longer estimate of drug use than either self-report measures or urinalysis. The wider window of detection is a clear advantage of hair testing as a drug use prevalence measure. Other advantages include ease of obtaining, storing, and shipping specimens; ability to obtain a second sample for reanalysis; low potential for evasion or manipulation of test results; and low risk of disease transmission in the handling of samples. A potential disadvantage of hair analysis, which has not been investigated, would be its inability to detect recent drug usage because of slow growth rate. Mounting evidence points to the likelihood that drug excretion in sweat is an important route of drug entry into hair. This allows the possibility of the drug appearing in hair within hours of drug administration. Another consideration regarding the use of hair analysis is the limited number of laboratories offering commercial hair-testing services. Both the inability to detect recent drug use and the limited availability of testing services may be serious disadvantages if used in contingency management treatment.

RESEARCH DIRECTIONS

The effective use of contingency management in the treatment of substance abuse depends in large part on the available methods to accurately monitor drug use. Collection and testing of urine specimens represent a significant cost in the implementation of this behavioral treatment. Wider use of contingency management in community treatment programs may depend not only on refinement of the behavioral technique but also on improvements in methods of monitoring drug use. Further improvements are needed to distinguish recent use from carryover, to increase the ease of specimen collection, and to decrease the cost of testing. Quantitative urinalysis and application of new use criteria are two methods suggested to improve measurement of cocaine use. Cocaine is ideal for quantitation because it is a single chemical entity with a specific metabolic profile. Some of the other classes of abused drugs, such as the opioids, have multiple substances with varying potencies and cross-reactivity in toxicology assays. Research into the use of quantitative urinalysis data for these more complex drugs is needed. The on-site urine tests have provided a means to get results rapidly and without highly trained staff and have increased the flexibility of where testing can be conducted. Further simplification of these tests, such as the development of "dipstick-type" tests, would be desirable. Development of techniques for monitoring drug use in biological specimens other than urine could decrease the cost and difficulty of specimen collection and increase the utility of contingency management techniques. For example, sweat and saliva samples, which unlike urine do not require same-sex staff, may be more convenient and less embarrassing for both staff and patients. Sweat and hair testing may be performed less frequently, which could decrease the cost of monitoring drug use. Testing of new monitoring methods can be performed as part of ongoing clinical trials of substance abuse treatments. Increased collaborations among chemists, pharmacokineticists, substance abuse research professionals, and the manufacturers of diagnostic devices could also facilitate development of better monitoring procedures.

REFERENCES

Ambre, J. (1985). The urinary excretion of cocaine and metabolites in humans: A kinetic analysis of published data. *Journal of Analytical Toxicology, 9,* 241–245.

Batki, S. L., Manfredi, L. B., Jacob, P., & Jones, R. T. (1993). Fluoxetine for cocaine dependence in methadone maintenance: Quantitative plasma and urine cocaine/benzoylecgonine concentrations. *Journal of Clinical Psychopharmacology, 12,* 243–250.

Caddy, B. (1984). Saliva as a specimen for drug analysis. In R. C. Baselt (Ed.), *Advances in analytical toxicology* (Vol. 1, pp. 198–254). Foster City, CA: Biomedical.

Cone, E. J. (1990). On-site drug testing expediency versus accuracy? *Employment Testing, 4,* 621–623.

Cone, E. J. (1993). Saliva testing for drugs of abuse. In D. Malamud & L. Tabak (Eds.), *Saliva as a diagnostic fluid* (Vol. 694, pp. 91–127). New York: New York Academy of Sciences.

Cone, E. J. (1995). The pharmacokinetics and pharmacodynamics of cocaine. *Journal of Analytical Toxicology, 19,* 459–478.

Cone, E. J. (1997). New developments in biological measures of drug prevalence. In L. Harrison & A. Hughes (Eds.), *The validity of self-reported drug use: Improving the accuracy of survey estimates* (NIDA Research Monograph 167, pp. 108–129). Washington, DC: U.S. Government Printing Office.

Cone, E. J., Darwin, W. D., Dickerson, S. L., & Mitchell, J. (1991, July). Evaluation of the Abuscreen ONTRAK assay for cocaine (metabolite). *Clinical Chemistry News,* p. 4.

Cone, E. J., Hillsgrove, M. J., Jenkins, A. J., Keenan, R. M., & Darwin, W. D. (1994). Sweat testing for heroin, cocaine, and metabolites. *Journal of Analytical Toxicology, 18,* 298–305.

Cone, E. J., Menchen, S. L., & Mitchell, J. (1988). Validity testing of the TDx cocaine metabolite assay with human specimens obtained after intravenous cocaine administration. *Forensic Science International, 37,* 265–275.

Cone, E. J., Yousefnejad, D., Darwin, W. D., & Maguire, T. (1991). Testing human hair for drugs of abuse: II. Identification of unique cocaine metabolites in hair of drug abusers and evaluation of decontamination procedures. *Journal of Analytical Toxicology, 15,* 250–255.

Covi, L., Hess, J. M., Kreiter, N. A., & Haertzen, C. A. (1994). Three models for the analysis of a fluoxetine placebo controlled treatment in cocaine abuse. In L. S. Harris (Ed.), *Problems of drug dependence, 1993: Proceedings of the 55th annual scientific meeting, the College on Problems of Drug Dependence* (NIDA Research Monograph 141, p. 138). Washington, DC: U.S. Government Printing Office.

Edwards, C., Fyfe, M. J., Liu, R. H., & Walia, A. A. (1993). Evaluation of common urine specimen adulteration indicators. *Journal of Analytical Toxicology, 17,* 251–252.

Feucht, T. E., Stephens, R. C., & Walker, M. L. (1994). Drug use among juvenile arrestees: A comparison of self-report, urinalysis and hair assay. *Journal of Drug Issues, 24,* 99–116.

Goldberger, B. A., Caplan, Y. H., Maguire, T., & Cone, E. J. (1991). Testing human hair for drugs of abuse: III. Identification of heroin and 6-acetylmorphine as indicators of heroin use. *Journal of Analytical Toxicology, 15,* 226–231.

Jain, R. B. (1992). Design of clinical trials for treatment of opiate dependence: What is missing? In R. B. Jain (Ed.), *Statistical issues in clinical trials for treatment of opiate dependence* (NIDA Research Monograph 128, pp. 29–36). Washington, DC: U.S. Government Printing Office.

Jatlow, P. (1988). Cocaine: Analysis, pharmacokinetics, and metabolic disposition. *Yale Journal of Biology and Medicine, 61,* 105–111.

Kolar, A. F., Brown, B. S., Weddington, W. W., Haertzen, C. C., Michaelson, B. S., & Jaffe, J. H. (1992). Treatment of cocaine dependence in methadone maintenance clients: A pilot study comparing the efficacy of desipramine and amantadine. *International Journal of the Addictions, 27,* 849–868.

Kranzler, H. R., Dellafera, S. S., McLaughlin, L., & Wong, S. H. Y. (1992). Persistent urinary benzoylecgonine following cocaine use. *American Journal of the Addictions, 1,* 265–271.

Levin, F. R., & Lehman, A. F. (1991). Meta-analysis of desipramine as an adjunct in the treatment of cocaine addiction. *Journal of Clinical Psychopharmacology, 11,* 374–378.

Magura, S., Freeman, R. C., Siddiqui, Q., & Lipton, D. S. (1992). The validity of hair analysis for detecting cocaine and heroin use among addicts. *International Journal of the Addictions, 27,* 51–69.

Magura, S., Goldsmith, D., Casriel, C., Goldstein, P. J., & Lipton, D. S. (1987). The validity of methadone clients' self-reported drug use. *International Journal of the Addictions, 22,* 727–749.

McCarthy, J. (1994). Quantitative urine drug monitoring in methadone programs: Potential clinical uses. *Journal of Psychoactive Drugs, 26,* 199–206.

McLellan, A. T., Luborsky, L., Cacciola, J., Griffith, G., Evans, F., Barr, H. L., & O'Brien, C. P. (1985). New data from the Addiction Severity Index: Reliability and validity in three centers. *Journal of Nervous and Mental Disease, 173,* 412–423.

Mieczkowski, T., Barzelay, D., Gropper, B., & Wish, E. (1991). Concordance of three measures of cocaine use in an arrestee population: Hair, urine, and self-report. *Journal of Psychoactive Drugs, 23,* 241–249.

Needleman, S. B., Porvaznik, M., & Ander, D. (1992). Creatinine analysis in single collection urine specimens. *Journal of Forensic Sciences, 37,* 1125–1133.

Peters, J. E., Chou, J. Z., Ho, A., Reid, K., Borg, L., & Kreek, M. J. (1996). Simplified quantitation of urinary benzoylecgonine in cocaine addiction research and for related pharmacotherapeutic trials. *Addiction, 91,* 1687–1697.

Preston, K. L., Silverman, K., Goldberger, B. A., & Cone, E. J. (1997). Criteria for identifying new cocaine use: Presence of cocaine in urine. *Clinical Pharmacology and Therapeutics, 61,* 191.

Preston, K. L., Silverman, K., Schuster, C. R., & Cone, E. J. (1997a). Assessment of cocaine use with quantitative urinalysis and estimation of new uses. *Addiction, 92,* 717–727.

Preston, K. L., Silverman, K., Schuster, C. R., & Cone, E. J. (1997b). Comparison of self-reported drug use with quantitative and qualitative urinalysis for assessment of drug use in treatment studies. In L. Harrison & A. Hughes (Eds.), *The validity of self-reported drug use: Improving the accuracy of survey estimates* (NIDA Research Monograph 167, pp. 130–145). Washington, DC: U.S. Government Printing Office.

Robinson, S., & Robinson, A. H. (1954). Chemical composition of sweat. *Annual Review of Physiology, 34,* 202–220.

Robles, E., Silverman, K., Preston, K. L., Bigelow, G. E., & Stitzer, M. L. (1998). Voucher-based reinforcement of brief cocaine abstinence in methadone patients. In L. S. Harris (Ed.), *Problems of drug dependence 1997: Proceedings of the 59th annual scientific meeting, the College on Problems of Drug Dependence* (NIDA Research Monograph 178, NIH Pub. No. 98-4305, p. 327). Washington, DC: U.S. Government Printing Office.

Saitoh, M., Uzuka, M., & Sakamoto, M. (1969). Rate of hair growth. In W. Montagna & R. L. Dobson (Eds.), *Advances in biology of skin* (Vol. 9, pp. 183–201). Oxford, England: Pergamon Press.

Satel, S. L., & Kosten, T. R. (1991). Designing drug efficacy trials in the treatment of cocaine abuse. *Journal of Nervous and Mental Disease, 179,* 89–96.

Saxon, A. J., Calsyn, D. A., Haver, V. M., & Delaney, C. J. (1988). Clinical evaluation of urine screening for drug abuse. *Western Journal of Medicine, 149,* 296–303.

Schramm, W., Smith, R. H., Craig, P. A., & Kidwell, D. A. (1992). Drugs of abuse in saliva: A review. *Journal of Forensic Science, 16,* 1–9.

Sherman, M. F., & Bigelow, G. E. (1992). Validity of patients' self-reported drug use as a function of treatment status. *Drug and Alcohol Dependence, 30,* 1–11.

Shuster, L. (1991). Pharmacokinetics, metabolism, and disposition of cocaine. In J. M. Lakoski, M. P. Galloway, & F. J. White (Eds.), *Cocaine pharmacology, physiology, and clinical strategies* (pp. 1–14). Boca Raton, FL: CRC Press.

Silverman, K., Higgins, S. T., Brooner, R. K., Montoya, I. D., Cone, E. J., Schuster, C. R., & Preston, K. L. (1996). An effective treatment for cocaine abuse: Reinforcement of sustained abstinence. *Archives of General Psychiatry, 53,* 409–415.

Skog, O. -J. (1992). The validity of self-reported drug use. *British Journal of Addiction, 87,* 539–548.

Substance Abuse and Mental Health Services Administration. (1994). Mandatory guidelines for federal workplace drug testing programs. *Federal Register, 59,* 29908–29931.

15

MONITORING THERAPIST AND PATIENT BEHAVIOR DURING BEHAVIORAL INTERVENTIONS FOR ILLICIT-DRUG USE: PROCESS RESEARCH PERSPECTIVES

MICHAEL V. PANTALON AND RICHARD S. SCHOTTENFELD

Behavioral interventions, including relapse prevention (Marlatt & Gordon, 1985), the community reinforcement approach (CRA; Higgins et al., 1991), and contingency management (Budney, Higgins, Delaney, Kent, & Bickel, 1991), show considerable promise for treating drug abuse. The multifaceted CRA, which includes all of the elements of relapse prevention and contingency management in the initial studies (Budney et al., 1991; Higgins et al., 1991, 1993, 1994), has led to the highest rate of patient retention in treatment and sustained abstinence of any behavioral or pharmacologic intervention for patients with cocaine dependence. Efforts to replicate these findings in other settings and patient populations are ongoing. For replication studies to be successful, however, the treatment interventions in the new settings must be comparable to those initially developed. If behavioral treatments do not fare as well in replication studies, it would be critical to determine if negative findings are caused by shortcomings of the treatment, the manner in which it was implemented, or differences in the patients treated and their response to the interventions.

To ensure that behavioral treatments are implemented as planned, first it is important to identify and specify the repertoire of therapist skills and interventions that are crucial components of the treatment and then to train the therapists in these skills and interventions and monitor treatment. However, measures of what is referred to as the *process* of treatment have not been systematically used in behavioral treatments of illicit-drug use as much as they have in other areas of psychotherapy research (Wright & Davis, 1994). Some notable exceptions are the work by Carroll et al. (1994), who developed process measures to assess the discriminability between two psychotherapies for the treatment of cocaine abuse (e.g., relapse prevention and clinical management), and by DiClemente, Carroll, Connors, and Kadden (1994), who presented four process domains (e.g., dose of treatment, within-session activities and interventions, therapeutic alliance, and extrasession activities) and suggested how they can be assessed in each of three treatments for alcoholism (e.g., cognitive–behavioral therapy, motivational enhancement, and 12-step facilitation) used in a multisite treatment matching study (Project MATCH Research Group, 1993).

In general, two major methodologies are used to evaluate psychotherapy. First, *outcome research* focuses on how effective a particular psychotherapy is in treating specific maladaptive behaviors or disorders in comparison with no treatment or another active treatment. Second, *process research* focuses on how these specific behaviors change and what behaviors on the part of the therapist and patient are crucial for establishing a context for this change. Recent advances in the drug abuse field are in part the result of methodological advances in the area of psychotherapy research in general (Goldfried & Wolfe, 1996). Methodologies for studying the outcome of behavioral treatments of drug abuse have become increasingly sophisticated, as noted by the use of dismantling strategies (to identify the effects of specific components of treatment), treatment-matching studies, empirically validated assessment tools, and detailed treatment manuals that clearly specify assessment and treatment procedures (Borkovec, 1993). As a result, outcomes have improved (Miller, 1992). The application of specific developments within the area of psychotherapy process research, expounded below, would further improve treatment outcomes of behavioral treatments for illicit-drug abuse, specifically CRA.

In this chapter, we present a model for applying psychotherapy process research methodologies to the behavioral treatment of cocaine and heroin dependence, with a particular emphasis on CRA. This is done to explicate the specific therapist and patient behaviors necessary for creating a context for positive change during CRA. In addition to ensuring the integrity of behavioral treatment research, a focus on treatment process facilitates therapist training and the dissemination of efficacious treatments. An evaluation of treatment process also can be used to refine and improve treatment interventions and inform patients about how best to achieve their goals. We first give a brief overview of CRA as well as the foundations of psychotherapy process research. Second, we detail how the specific practices of psychotherapy process research can be applied to CRA, with an emphasis on the identification and study of important therapist and patient behaviors.

THE COMMUNITY REINFORCEMENT APPROACH

CRA is based on a theoretical view that drug dependence is maintained by drug-related reinforcers (both positive and negative) and the relative lack of reinforcers unrelated to drug use. In this view, the development of alternative rewarding activities in the community that are incompatible with drug use (e.g., involvement in non-drug-related family, social, religious, vocational, and recreational activities) is essential to maintain abstinence. In addition to providing coping skills and relapse prevention counseling (e.g., instruction in recognizing antecedents and consequences of drug use, restructuring daily activities, avoiding antecedents or drug cues, and skills training such as relaxation training), CRA fosters the development of rewarding activities and social roles and networks that compete with continued drug use through structured behavioral techniques, educational and vocational counseling and assistance with practical needs, and reciprocal relationship counseling.

In the initial studies, CRA was combined with contingency management and a prescription of disulfiram for patients dually dependent on alcohol and cocaine; this led to significantly greater retention in treatment of cocaine dependence and higher rates of documented, sustained abstinence when compared with traditional drug counseling. Subsequent studies document that contingency management with a voucher procedure where each drug-free urine sample was rewarded with a voucher that had monetary value is an active ingredient of treatment and leads to improved outcomes when combined with other CRA components (Higgins et al., 1993, 1994) and methadone maintenance treatment (Silverman, Higgins & Brooner, 1996). The contingency management schedule of rewards provides repeated and frequent opportunities to reinforce abstinence as well as increasing incentives to stay abstinent for progressively longer periods. Providing vouchers, rather than money, also complements CRA because patients and therapists engage in discussions about how the vouchers can be used and the vouchers foster involvement in activities that serve as alternative, nondrug reinforcers. Although the specification and monitoring of the contingency management voucher procedures appears less complex than process evaluations of CRA, the development of process measures to evaluate the immediacy of reinforcement and the patient's response also are important, as are discussed in a later section. In the next section, we give a brief overview of psychotherapy process research, which is then applied to the specification of the core CRA components that are important to evaluate in replication studies.

PSYCHOTHERAPY PROCESS RESEARCH

Psychotherapy process research focuses on how particular maladaptive behaviors change within the therapeutic context and on how specific therapist behaviors and treatment components affect particular patient behaviors. Psychotherapy process research directs attention to both interpersonal variables (e.g., the relationship between the therapist and the patient) and "mechanism of action" variables that are closely tied to the theoretical and practical mechanisms that are thought to produce the change in the patient's maladaptive behavior (e.g., operant conditioning, cognitive coping skills). We illustrate the difference between these two types of process variables with the following: The number of non-drug-related activities, which compete with drug use, generated by the patient during a functional analysis of behavior is a mechanism variable; the therapist's empathic and supportive responses, including the number of times a therapist gives verbal praise (positive social reinforcement) to a patient for generating such alternative behaviors, are interpersonal variables.

Methodologies for assessing both interpersonal and mechanism of action variables usually involve the development and use of coding systems to rate video- or audiotapes of therapy sessions. The development of coding systems requires specification or operational definitions of the key behaviors to rate as well as the development of rating procedures, which might include frequency counts or data on the duration of certain behaviors, and methods for rating the consistency and appropriateness of the intervention. Therapist and patient behaviors may both be evaluated. For example, a checklist of critical behaviors could be devised for each component of CRA, and raters could tally the number of times a therapist or patient exhibits each behavior during a given session. The number of times a therapist responds with verbal praise when a patient practices a coping skill (e.g., relaxation) on his or her own is an example of a critical therapist behavior. The number of times a patient offers a trigger or consequence of drug abuse when prompted by the therapist is an example of a critical patient behavior that could be rated. Checklists of procedures from other behavioral and nonbehavioral treatments as well as miscellaneous comments also could be developed to facilitate training (e.g., increasing raters' ability to discriminate among treatments) and accuracy of ratings. Independent (e.g., unaware of condition) raters could then be trained to use the coding systems and rating procedures until they achieve good interrater reliability. Finally, randomly selected video sessions, from each therapist, patient, or both, could be rated.

APPLICATION OF PROCESS RESEARCH TO CRA

In the sections to follow, we suggest monitoring important therapist and patient behaviors (i.e., process variables) exhibited during the course of CRA for illicit-drug abusers, on the basis of existing psychotherapy process practices. First, we identify behaviors related to both mechanisms of action and interpersonal interactions in therapy for therapists and patients. Then, we propose specific research questions regarding the impact these process variables may have on CRA outcome.

Mechanism Variables

Although mechanism variables may be derived empirically by recording frequency counts during treatment on scales of potential process variables, they are likely to be more meaningful and clinically relevant when linked to key theoretical constructs underlying the treatment approach. Mechanism variables pertain to the degree to which the specific components of the treatment are implemented adequately or as directed in a detailed treatment manual. An evaluation of mechanism variables focuses on how consistently and how often a specific treatment component or technique is used, on how appropriately and competently it is used, and finally on whether the intervention leads to an anticipated and measurable outcome. In this section, we identify the specific core components or mechanisms of action of CRA that should be evaluated, considering issues related to the assessment of their frequency, appropriateness, quality, and impact. These mechanism variables defined in the CRA treatment manual are tightly linked to the theoretical base for the treatment.

Core CRA Components and Processes

On the basis of a review of the theoretical underpinnings of CRA, the CRA treatment manual, and our experience implementing CRA, we identified the following partial list of core elements or components of CRA: (a) an explanation of the theory underlying the treatment and interventions (e.g., rationales); (b) the "big picture" (long-term goals); (c) the functional analysis of behavior (FAB), including the identification of positive and negative consequences of behavior; (d) specific goals and objectives (e.g., homework), especially with regard to encouraging engagement in rewarding activities unrelated or incompatible with drug use and then tracking accomplishment of these goals or impediments to implementation (also includes goals and objectives refinement on the basis of accomplishments or impediments); and (e) skills training to assist in achieving specific goals and objectives, including the provision of cognitive and behavioral coping skills training to reduce risk of relapse (relapse prevention, self-monitoring). To rate whether, how often, or how adequately the core CRA components are used in treatment, counselors must define operationally the specific elements in each component. We provide some examples in the following descriptions of the CRA core components.

The use of rationales. The use of rationales to explain the helpfulness of specific treatment procedures improves the quality of the therapeutic relationship and may increase compliance with such procedures (Newman, 1994; Wright & Davis, 1994). Kazdin and Krause (1983) suggested that rationales that include statements about the research support for and the novelty and broad focus of the interventions result in greater expectations of positive change than other types of rationales. Additionally, rationales that include examples of patients who are successful in treatment are also rated favorably. CRA is based on a clear theory of drug dependence, and an explication of the theory and rationale for specific treatment interventions should be provided to patients throughout treatment.

The big picture. The big picture represents a vision of a patient's future life situation that both motivates the patient to change and sets the direction for change. The big picture consists of achievable shorter and longer range goals that are highly significant to the patient. To elicit the big picture, therapists challenge patients to be more specific if their initial response is global, vague, or nonspecific, such as "being happy," "having a lot of money," or "having a good family life." Once the big picture is established, therapists (and patients) should make reference to it in formulating or revising the specific goals, objectives, and activities that are planned or implemented. Thus, process measure ratings of therapist activity should include the assessment of therapist activities eliciting the big picture (e.g., whether, how often, and how effectively the therapist probes the patient's big picture and elicits specific, achievable, and salient shorter and longer range goals) and the therapist's use of the big picture during treatment (e.g., how often does the therapist relate the patient's activities and plans to the big picture?). Process measure ratings of the big picture could also focus on the patient's behavior. For example, does the patient formulate specific, achievable, and salient goals, and how often does the patient make use of or refer to the big picture in establishing goals, objectives, and plans?

Functional analysis of behavior. The FAB is one of the core skills taught in CRA. A FAB first identifies when, how often, and in what circumstances the behavior does and does not occur as well as the immediate and delayed rewarding (positive) or aversive (negative) consequences of the behavior. Second, a FAB identifies alternative activities, behaviors, or strategies that will affect the likelihood of its occurrence.

Although any given FAB may focus predominantly on only some aspects (e.g., the immediate mood state or some other context of drug use), process ratings of therapist activity need to assess whether, how often, and how consistently FABs are used, how often the therapist teaches the patient how to conduct a FAB, and whether temporal patterns (e.g., do behaviors occur predominantly at particular times of day or days of the week?) and the immediate antecedents or consequences of the behavior are evaluated. Process ratings must also assess the types of behavior patterns taught over the course of treatment (e.g., focusing on antecedents at the beginning of treatment and on consequences of various behaviors later in treatment) and the type, specificity, and strategic importance of the suggested behaviors. As with the big picture, it is also important to assess how persistently and effectively therapists probe the various components of the FAB. For example, does a therapist simply accept a patient's report that there were no benefits, positive or rewarding effects, of a recent episode of cocaine use? Or does the therapist probe to evaluate the immediate social and emotional reinforcers? Additionally, the importance of assessing the strategic importance of suggested alternative behaviors is illustrated by the example of a patient who repeatedly uses cocaine after finishing work at 1 a.m. Increasing recreational and social activities in general may be less advantageous than developing strategically more important recreational or social activities at 1 a.m. (e.g., watching videos with a non-drug-using family member) or planning highly rewarding activities early in the day (e.g., an 8 a.m. mountain bike expedition with a friend).

Homework assignments. CRA calls for a rather extensive use of homework assignments. Broadly conceived, homework assignments include work between sessions to accomplish all specific goals and objectives set for that interval, including, for example, working on goals regarding increasing engagement in social, recreational, family, or vocational activities. Research indicates that there is a significant and fairly robust positive correlation between the number of homework assignments given by the therapist and completed by the patient and the outcome among patients with depression (Burns & Nolen-Hoeksema, 1991). Similarly, the use of therapeutic contracts has been shown to enhance compliance with therapeutic activities and learning of specific skills (Kramer, Jeffery, Snell, & Forster, 1986; Levendusky, Berglas, Dooley, & Landau, 1983). Monitoring how often and with what results CRA therapists set specific goals and assign homework, offer contracts, assess patients' completion of goal-directed behaviors, and refine goals and objectives are important process variables to study.

Skills training. Other core skills training components of CRA include self-management training, social skills training, assertiveness training, drug refusal training, relaxation training, insomnia treatment, vocational counseling, reciprocal relationship counseling, and AIDS education. Although process variables particular to each of the skill components could be identified, in this chapter we consider process variables that are more generally related to skills training. Because CRA is a behavioral treatment relying on principles of learning to ensure the acquisition of new skills, the following more general process variables might be evaluated: (a) the number of times a therapist models the skills to learn, (b) the number of behavioral rehearsals and role-plays the therapist uses to teach the skill, (c) the number of times a therapist repeats each skill component throughout treatment, (d) the number of times the therapist contingently reinforces the patient for gradual approximations of the skills, and (e) competency of the training based on checklists of operationally defined critical procedures or skills to learn (e.g., whether the therapist assesses the level of relaxation following training or models appropriate eye contact when teaching patients to be assertive). Although this list is limited, it gives the reader a sense of the type of process variable that would be helpful in evaluating skills training and in refining or improving interventions.

In the remainder of this section, we cover other process (e.g., mechanism) variables relevant to CRA procedures: on- versus off-task therapist verbalizations, contingency management, the use of self-monitoring, and individualizing treatment.

On- versus off-task ratings of therapist verbal behavior. The amount of time per session focusing on CRA is another important process variable similar to medication dose in a pharmacologic clinical trial. Thus on-task (e.g., completing a FAB) versus off-task (e.g., discussing general, non-CRA issues) verbal behavior on the part of the therapist is important to assess. Such a process variable illustrates how much of the time therapist verbalizations during session are within the purview of CRA only versus another therapy or other miscellaneous comments.

Contingency management. Because contingency management is an integral component of CRA, it is important to devise process measures to assess the integrity of its administration. Critical aspects of voucher-based contingency management procedures can be implemented with varying levels of quality, and these variations can affect outcome. For example, the speed with which patients receive purchased items after they make a request to cash in their vouchers may be an important process variable to consider. If an experimenter tries to replicate a study that used vouchers but is slow in making requested purchases (e.g., it takes 2 weeks, on average, to buy the requested items), the result may not be as good as results obtained by one who makes purchases quickly (e.g., in less than 2 days). The effectiveness of the voucher system could also be altered by the nature and amount of restrictions placed on purchases as well as by the relevance of the items to a patient's target behavior or big picture (e.g., a tape player for a patient who wants to listen to recordings of a general education degree preparation class).

The social reinforcement given by the therapist during contingency management procedures is another important process variable to consider. For example, the number of verbalizations of praise for negative urine samples versus the number and type of verbalizations in response to positive urine samples may illuminate the degree to which positive urine results are inadvertently positively reinforced through supportive statements, suggesting the therapist's belief in the ability of the patient to give a negative urine sample at the next testing. Similarly, various patients' responses to receiving or not receiving vouchers (e.g., hopeful vs. negativistic statements) may differentially correlate outcome.

The use of self-monitoring. Self-monitoring is a fairly straightforward but very effective means of assessing the situational and patient variables that give rise to problematic behavior. Essentially, it involves a diarylike recording of when and under what conditions a particular behavior occurs as well as the patient's response to it. In fact, self-monitoring has become a mainstay of the behavioral therapist's armamentarium. On its own, self-monitoring is effective in producing initial but usually not sustained behavioral change. More important, it has been empirically validated as an essential tool in functionally assessing a target problem, deciding on what behaviors and situational factors should be targeted for change, and facilitating the teaching of self-control methods to the patient (Kanfer & Goldstein, 1991). Baker and Kirschenbaum (1993) have shown that self-monitoring is critical to weight control among obese individuals. Therefore, monitoring self-monitoring's application with drug abusers, who have similar deficits in self-regulatory skills (Budney & Higgins, 1995), could prove crucial to positive CRA outcomes. It is also important to evaluate how often the CRA therapist uses the information generated from self-monitoring in the treatment.

Individualizing treatment. Fishman (1981) suggested that attention to individual differences among patients can improve the efficacy of the treatment. Functionally analyzing the entire "clinical picture" of a patient, even if only a few behaviors are addressed, gives the therapist more information on which to base the selection, timing, and presentation of an intervention. Fishman provided the example of a patient for whom assertiveness training was indicated, based on a FAB that suggested that her requests of her boyfriend were frequently declined because of her passive behavior. These reactions from her boyfriend frequently led to drug use. However, when training did not seem to be effective in reducing drug use, it became apparent that a more salient drug trigger was the patient's anxiety about being responsible for honoring the requests her boyfriend would make of her. Subsequently, more appropriate interventions (e.g., a FAB of her anxiety, relaxation training) were used before assertion training was reintroduced. Thus, it appears that the successful implementation of a behavioral technique is compromised without a clear understanding of the functional relationships among problems, goals of therapy, and interventions. An example of a process measure of the degree to which CRA is individualized is the number of times a therapist uses functional analyses of various (vs. only drug use) patient behaviors to introduce the next treatment strategy.

Important Patient Behaviors

Most of the process variables discussed so far pertain mainly to therapist behaviors, but many could also be adapted to rate patient behaviors. Measuring patient process variables provides a means of evaluating the immediate impact of treatment, helps refine and improve interventions, and can be used to inform patients about what behaviors are most likely to lead to a successful outcome (e.g., reduced drug use). Ratings of patient behaviors also are important in evaluating whether the interventions lead to the intermediate activities or behaviors that are thought to be critically related to the major goals of treatment. For example, if CRA fails to reduce drug use, it will be important to evaluate whether the treatment failed to produce increased activities unrelated to drug use or increased engagement in these activities failed to reduce drug use. The former would suggest modifying the interventions, whereas the latter may occur if the activities are not as strategically important or relevant to the patient as possible or if CRA is not efficacious. Because behavioral treatments are designed to teach patients behavioral self-control techniques, ratings could be made of the patients' use of FABs or self-monitoring techniques. Additionally, because a major focus of CRA is on encouraging patients to engage in behaviors, activities, or social interactions unrelated or incompatible with drug use, assessment of changes in activity patterns of the patient also could be an important treatment process measure. We developed an activity rating scale for this purpose. The scale assesses the total number of hours spent each day, during the past week, in specific types of activities (e.g., work, recreational, social) and can be used to evaluate the relationship between changes in activity patterns and changes in drug use. We are also interested in exploring methods of rating the strategic importance of particular activities and activity patterns and how they affect outcome; however, obtaining good reliability and validity of the assessment of strategic importance of activity patterns has proved difficult.

Other patient behaviors that directly affect the mechanisms that are thought to make CRA an effective treatment are level of patient involvement in CRA activities, on- versus off-task verbal behavior, compliance with homework and self-monitoring assignments, and behavioral competencies.

Patient involvement in CRA activities. On the basis of their meta-analysis, Stiles, Shapiro, and Elliot (1986) suggested that a high degree of patient involvement may be a common ingredient in many psychotherapies and that it may, in part, account for positive outcomes among various treatments. Developing a process measure to assess whether this relationship is also found during CRA would require the identification of the behaviors that are thought to be the most indicative of positive involvement for each CRA component.

Patient on- versus off-task verbal behavior. As with therapists, the amount of time patients spend on CRA-relevant tasks should also be monitored during treatment. Because CRA relies on behavioral learning processes (e.g., role-playing, behavioral rehearsal, and active learning), it follows that a significant portion of the therapy session must be spent on CRA activities to lead to a positive outcome.

Compliance with homework and self-monitoring assignments. High levels of compliance with extrasession therapeutic assignments given by the therapist, such as homework to do a FAB or to self-monitor drug urges, have been shown to significantly improve psychotherapy outcome (Baker & Kirschenbaum, 1993; Burns & Nolen-Hoeksema, 1991). Monitoring of compliance with such assignments would inform the therapist about patient progress with particular CRA skills and would potentially alert them to areas with which the patient is having difficulty.

Behavioral competencies. Tests of behavioral competencies (see Marlatt & Gordon, 1985) involve naturalistic or imaginal (e.g., role-plays in the office) assessments of how well a patient can implement coping skills that have been taught during treatment in a high-risk situation (e.g., a neighborhood where the patient usually buys drugs). As with the tracking of homework compliance, assessing behavioral competencies during treatment informs the therapist about a problem the patient may have with a new skill early enough to attempt a different approach. One way we attempt to assess behavioral competencies is through a process called *shadowing*, in which a research assistant accompanies (i.e., shadows) a patient on his or her activities for an entire day (an 8-hr period). After the shadowing, the research assistant is videotaped while he or she gives a detailed account of the day (e.g., activities, stressors, coping responses) to the patient's therapist and supervisor, who can then plan new intervention strategies accordingly.

Interpersonal Variables

Although mechanism and interpersonal process variables are interrelated and often difficult to separate, they are conceptually distinct and thus addressed separately in this chapter for the sake of clarity. However, one should keep in mind that what affects the interpersonal interactions in therapy reciprocally affects whether the purported mechanisms of the treatment will actually lead to behavior change. We keep our discussion focused on interpersonal variables that have been empirically demonstrated to have a significant impact on the therapeutic relationship and subsequently on outcome. There is considerable overlap between interpersonal process variables that pertain to the therapist and those that pertain to the patient. For example, how warm and empathic the therapist is in therapy often is related to how involved the patient is in treatment and vice versa. Therefore, because the suggestions made for the use of process measures to study therapist behavior are very similar to those made for the study of patient behavior, in the following section we concurrently address both therapist and patient behaviors as they affect the interpersonal process of therapy.

A number of psychotherapy process researchers have suggested that the therapeutic relationship significantly affects the outcome of therapy in general (Beitman, Goldfried, & Norcross, 1989; Burns & Nolen-Hoeksema, 1992, Strupp, 1993, 1996) as well as the outcome of substance abuse treatment (McLellan, Woody, Luborsky, & Goehl, 1988). This also has been suggested for behavioral treatments, which are often mistakenly perceived as predominantly mechanistic (Kohlenberg & Tsai, 1991). However, relatively little has been done in the way of establishing empirical guidelines for the detailed and systematic study of how this relationship creates a context of positive change in the area of substance abuse treatment. Also researchers have had limited success determining how such interpersonal processes interact with the technical aspects of treatment (mechanisms of action) described above. The empirical question addressed here is, "What types of behaviors are effective in creating a successful therapeutic relationship, especially in the field of behavioral treatment of illicit-drug abuse?" For example, what behaviors are most effective in dealing with patient resistance, so that work on specific techniques (e.g., FAB) may move forward? In this section, we draw on clinical experience with CRA for cocaine- and heroin-dependent patients to suggest how drug abuse researchers may apply recent advancements in the field of process research to the empirical study of these therapeutic relationship issues. The research reviewed below suggests that the interactions between process and outcome are complex but illustrates that it is essential to investigate these processes to determine, even at a very basic level, which are most crucial to the successful implementation of CRA.

When one considers the therapeutic relationship as a process variable, the characteristic addressed is not static but changes from session to session, even moment by moment, depending on the responses of the patient. Thus, assessing the therapeutic relationship by asking whether the therapist exhibits unconditional positive regard or therapeutic empathy to the patient is not adequate. When and how much empathy is expressed to a patient and in response to which behaviors are the foci of interpersonal process measures. In the following sections, we briefly review the therapist and patient behaviors that have been shown to influence the therapeutic relationship, especially therapist and patient response to conflict.

Therapist and Patient Behaviors That Influence the Therapeutic Relationship

Psychotherapy researchers have identified crucial factors in the development of a therapeutic relationship that leads to a desired behavior change: (a) interactions considered flexible and positive in nature (Beck, Rush, Shaw, & Emery, 1979; Newman, 1994), (b) therapist warmth and empathy as perceived by the patient (Burns & Nolen-Hoeksema, 1992; Strupp, 1996), and (c) high levels of collaboration (Burns & Nolen-Hoeksema, 1991; Persons, 1989; Stiles, Shapiro, & Elliot, 1986). Similar therapist behaviors also have been empirically shown to positively impact on outcome in drug abuse treatment studies (e.g., reflective listening and empathy; Miller, Taylor, & West, 1980). Because we focus on identifying the process variables important to assess in CRA rather than the specific measures with which to assess them, we refer the reader to Wright and Davis (1994) for a review of the established methodologies for empirically studying these variables.

Therapist and Patient Responses to Conflict

Some researchers have found that the manner in which therapists and patients respond to conflict significantly predicts treatment outcome. Therapists who respond positively to conflict (e.g., resistance to homework) produce better outcomes than those who do not (Miller & Rollnick, 1991; Newman, 1994; Strupp, 1993). Examples of responding positively include expressing empathy or neutrally assessing the level of agreement on goals, tasks, and target behaviors between the therapist and the patient. This process variable is particularly relevant to the implementation of CRA for illicit-drug abusers because resistance is common in such patients (Monti, Abrams, Kadden, & Cooney, 1989) and because the successful implementation of CRA appears to depend on a high level of patient involvement in core activities.

Research Questions Regarding Process Variables

Once researchers assess the degree to which critical therapist and patient behaviors are exhibited during therapy sessions, they can investigate the relationship between process variables and the major outcome (e.g., number of negative urines) to refine and improve CRA. For example, investigating whether there is a significant correlation between the number of times a therapist encourages or explicitly assigns self-monitoring exercises to their patients and outcome could lead to specific recommendations regarding the use of that procedure.

Additionally, this strategy makes it possible to investigate whether better outcomes are significantly associated with (a) use of a wide variety of CRA interventions in a competent manner, (b) assignment and follow-up of homework, (c) relation of specific patient behaviors to the big picture, (d) use of FABs, (e) positive statements in response to resistance or a reported lapse in abstinence, (f) individualized intervention strategies (e.g., considering the relationship among problems), (g) an offer of a variety of rationales for interventions (e.g., including examples of successful cases), and (h) use of reflective listening skills.

Behaviors associated with better (or worse) outcomes may also be used to advise patients better during treatment. Thus, it is important to evaluate whether better outcomes are found for patients who generate triggers, consequences, and alternate non-drug-related behaviors to drug abuse during FABs; verbalize coping statements during role-playing of skills; acquire and use vouchers; respond to therapist efforts to resolve conflict with a positive, problem-solving attitude; report their therapist as warm and empathic; offer specific examples of and relate their present behavior to their big picture; engage in pleasant activities that are incompatible with drug use; and comply with homework, self-monitoring, and other therapy assignments.

CONCLUSION

In this chapter, we reviewed some of the therapist and patient behaviors that are thought to be critical to the successful implementation of CRA. Process variables by their nature are immediately relevant to a therapist's work because they address session-to-session therapist and patient behaviors rather than global measures of therapist or patient characteristics or outcome. An application of various practices and methodologies used in psychotherapy process research can lead to a better implementation of planned interventions in replication studies and clinical practice; it can also help elucidate the mechanisms and therapeutic relationship factors that are operative in CRA. Note that although the important therapist and patient behaviors reviewed above can be identified as "active ingredients," this does not mean that they are necessarily discrete units or traits of the therapist or patient. Many of the mechanisms of change in treatment result from a context or interaction between therapist and patient. Empirical study of process variables is critical for ensuring the integrity of behavioral treatments, facilitating therapist training and dissemination of effective treatments, refining and improving treatment interventions, and informing patients and therapist alike about how best to achieve their goals through timely data-based feedback on what processes are associated with the best outcomes. Process measures also can lead to improved communication of research findings on CRA to practitioners, which is needed to improve clinical practice (Schuster & Silverman, 1993).

REFERENCES

Baker, R. C., & Kirschenbaum, D. S. (1993). Self-monitoring may be necessary for successful weight control. *Behavior Therapy, 24,* 377–394.

Beck, A. T., Rush, A. J., Shaw, B. F., & Emery, G. (1979). *Cognitive therapy of depression.* New York: Guilford.

Beitman, B., Goldfried, M., & Norcross, J. (1989). The movement towards integrating the psychotherapies: An overview. *American Journal of Psychiatry, 146,* 138–147.

Borkovec, T. D. (1993). Between-group therapy outcome research: Design and methodology. In L. S. Onken, J. D. Blaine, & J. J. Boren (Eds.), *Behavioral treatments for drug abuse and dependence* (NIDA Research Monograph 137, NIH Pub. No. 93-3684, pp. 249–290). Washington, DC: U.S. Government Printing Office.

Budney, A. J., & Higgins, S. T. (1995). *A multicomponent behavioral intervention for cocaine dependence.* Manuscript in preparation, University of Vermont, Burlington.

Budney, A. J., Higgins, S. T., Delaney, D. D., Kent, L., & Bickel, W. K. (1991). Contingent reinforcement of abstinence with individuals abusing cocaine and marijuana. *Journal of Applied Behavior Analysis, 24,* 657–665.

Burns, D. D., & Nolen-Hoeksema, S. (1991). Coping styles, homework compliance, and the effectiveness of cognitive–behavioral therapy. *Journal of Consulting and Clinical Psychology, 59,* 305–311.

Burns, D. D., & Nolen-Hoeksema, S. (1992). Therapeutic empathy and recovery from depression in a cognitive–behavioral therapy: A structural equation model. *Journal of Consulting and Clinical Psychology, 60,* 441–449.

Carroll, K. M., Rounsaville, B. J., Gordon, L. T., Nich, C., Jatlow, P., Bisighini, R. M., & Gawin, F. H. (1994). Psychotherapy and pharmacotherapy for ambulatory cocaine abusers. *Archives of General Psychiatry, 51,* 177–187.

DiClemente, C. C., Carroll, K. M., Connors, G. J., & Kadden, R. M. (1994, December). Process assessment in treatment matching research. *Journal of Studies on Alcohol* (Suppl. 12), pp. 156–162.

Fishman, S. T. (1981). Narrowing the generalization gap in clinical research. *Behavioral Assessment, 3,* 243–248.

Goldfried, M. R., & Wolfe, B. E. (1996). Psychotherapy practice and research: Repairing a strained alliance. *American Psychologist, 51,* 1007–1016.

Higgins, S. T., Budney, A. J., Bickel, W. K., Hughes, J. R., Foerg, F., & Badger, G. (1993). Achieving cocaine abstinence with a behavioral approach. *American Journal of Psychiatry, 150,* 763–769.

Higgins, S. T., Budney, A. J., Bickel, W. K., Hughes, J. R., Foerg, F., Donham, R., & Badger, G. (1994). Incentives improve outcome in outpatient behavioral treatment of cocaine dependence. *Archives of General Psychiatry, 51,* 568–576.

Higgins, S. T., Delaney, D. D., Budney, A. J., Bickel, W. K., Hughes, J. R., Foerg, F., & Fenwick, J. (1991). A behavioral approach to achieving initial cocaine abstinence. *American Journal of Psychiatry, 148,* 1218–1224.

Kanfer, F. H., & Goldstein, A. P. (Eds.). (1991). *Helping people change* (4th ed.). New York: Pergamon Press.

Kazdin, A. E., & Krause, R. (1983). The impact of variations in treatment rationales on expectancies for therapeutic change. *Behavior Therapy, 14,* 657–671.

Kohlenberg, R. J., & Tsai, M. (1991). *Functional analytic psychotherapy: Creating intense and curative therapeutic relationships.* New York: Plenum Press.

Kramer, M. F., Jeffery, R. W., Snell, M. K., & Forster, J. L. (1986). Maintenance of successful weight loss over one year: Effects of financial contracts for weight maintenance or participation in skills training. *Behavior Therapy, 17,* 295–301.

Levendusky, P. G., Berglas, S., Dooley, C. P., & Landau, R. J. (1983). Therapeutic contract program: Preliminary report on a behavioral alternative to the token economy. *Behavior Research and Therapy, 21,* 137–142.

Marlatt, G. A., & Gordon, J. R. (Eds.). (1985). *Relapse prevention: Maintenance strategies in the treatment of addictive behaviors.* New York: Guilford.

McLellan, A. T., Woody, G. E., Luborsky, L., & Goehl, L. (1988). Is the counselor an "active ingredient" in substance abuse rehabilitation? An examination of treatment success among four counselors. *Journal of Nervous and Mental Disease, 176,* 423–430.

Miller, W. R. (1992). Client/treatment matching in addictive behaviors. *The Behavior Therapist, 15,* 7–8.

Miller, W. R., & Rollnick, S. (1991). *Motivational interviewing: Preparing people to change addictive behavior.* New York: Guilford Press.

Miller, W. R., Taylor, C. A., & West, J. C. (1980). Focused versus broad spectrum behavior therapy for problem drinkers. *Journal of Consulting and Clinical Psychology, 48,* 590–601.

Monti, P. M., Abrams, D. B., Kadden, R. M., & Cooney, N. L. (1989). *Treating alcohol dependence: A coping skills training guide.* New York: Guilford.

Newman, F. (1994). Understanding client resistance: Methods for enhancing motivation to change. *Cognitive and Behavioral Practice, 1,* 47–70.

Persons, J. B. (1989). *Cognitive therapy in practice: A case formulation approach.* New York: Norton.

Project MATCH Research Group. (1993). Project MATCH: Rationale and methods for a multisite clinical trial matching patients to alcoholism treatment. *Alcohol: Clinical and Experimental Research, 17,* 1130–1145.

Schuster, C. R., & Silverman, K. (1993). Advancing the application of behavioral treatment approaches for drug dependence. In L. S. Onken, J. D. Blaine, & J. J. Boren (Eds.), *Behavioral treatments for drug abuse and dependence* (NIDA Research Monograph 137, NIH Pub. No. 93-3684, pp. 5–18). Washington, DC: U.S. Government Printing Office.

Silverman, K., Higgins, S. T., & Brooner, R. K. (1996). Sustained cocaine abstinence in methadone maintenance patients through voucher-based reinforcement therapy. *Archives of General Psychiatry, 53,* 409–415.

Stiles, W. B., Shapiro, D. A., & Elliot, R. (1986). Are all psychotherapies equivalent? *American Psychologist, 41,* 165–180.

Strupp, H. (1993). The Vanderbilt Psychotherapy Studies: Synopsis. *Journal of Consulting and Clinical Psychology, 61,* 431–433.

Strupp, H. (1996). The tripartite model and the *Consumer Reports* Study. *American Psychologist, 51,* 1017–1024.

Wright, J. H., & Davis, D. D. (1994). The therapeutic relationship in cognitive–behavioral therapy: Patient perceptions and therapist responses. *Cognitive and Behavioral Practice, 1,* 25–45.

16

DISSEMINATING CONTINGENCY MANAGEMENT RESEARCH TO DRUG ABUSE TREATMENT PRACTITIONERS

KIMBERLY C. KIRBY, LESLIE AMASS, AND
A. THOMAS McLELLAN

The preceding chapters demonstrated the many ways in which contingency management procedures can improve the effectiveness of drug abuse treatment. Despite the growing body of research demonstrating effectiveness of these procedures, very few of these findings have been disseminated or adopted into general clinical practice. Indeed, among the most significant challenges confronting the area of drug abuse treatment is how to transfer research-based techniques to clinics in local communities. Too often drug abuse researchers operate independently from the treatment community. Although this is appropriate for the development and testing of new interventions, it can limit the external validity of the work because of inherent limitations and constraints on most community practices. Furthermore, this separation of research and clinical practice does not promote the dissemination of potentially applicable findings. In this chapter, we review this problem as it pertains to contingency management, discussing some of the challenges researchers (ourselves included) face, strategies for addressing these challenges, and ways to make the robust findings from contingency management research practical enough to withstand wider testing and adoption by a broader range of clinical situations.

ADAPTING AND PRESENTING CONTINGENCY MANAGEMENT PROGRAMS TO THE COMMUNITY

Contingency management programs have at least three general challenges to broader clinical application: (a) Contingency management interventions can be costly and labor intensive, (b) most clinicians are not trained in contingency management, and (c) philosophical and political opinions create barriers to applying contingency management techniques.

Cost and Labor Intensity

Both program and personnel costs necessary to support a contingency management program are likely to limit broad clinical application. Contingency management programs developed in research settings can be both costly and labor intensive. For example, reinforcers (e.g., vouchers) can be relatively expensive, at times costing hundreds of dollars per client. Furthermore, the frequency and cost of urine testing on which the contingency is usually based are also greater than in most community settings. In research settings, urine testing often occurs three to four times per week, as opposed to weekly or monthly testing that occurs in the majority of community clinics. Personnel resources to implement the contingency management program also are often far greater in research clinics than in community treatment programs. Because most community programs do not have the resources to implement contingency management interventions in the same manner as research programs, careful attention to the structure of community programs will be necessary if researchers want to successfully transfer contingency management principles into general clinical practice.

Reducing Cost of Reinforcers

We are aware of at least five strategies to reduce the cost of reinforcers used in contingency management programs. Perhaps the most direct method is to modify voucher programs, lowering their cost by reducing the magnitude of reinforcement available, modifying the schedule of reinforcement, or both. For example, variable schedules of reinforcement can be introduced (rather than maintaining fixed schedules) in ways that do not reduce the overall effectiveness of the contingency management program. A second strategy is to replace voucher reinforcers with contingently allocated clinic privileges. This strategy was first implemented in methadone maintenance clinics 2 decades ago (Stitzer et al., 1977; Yen, 1974; see also

Kidorf & Stitzer, chapter 11, this volume) and demonstrates that methadone take-home doses (Stitzer, Bigelow, Liebson, & Hawthorne, 1982) and medication dose adjustments (Stitzer, Bickel, Bigelow, & Liebson, 1986) function effectively as reinforcers. Other possibilities may include fee rebates (Amass, Ennis, Mikulich, & Kamien, 1998), letters to probation or parole officers, access to special services, or increased control over other aspects of treatment (e.g., reduced frequency of urine testing, increased or decreased counseling). In residential or confined populations, conjugal visits, release time, and increased access to recreation are possibilities to explore. A third strategy is to replace vouchers with privileges that are available and external to the clinic, such as housing, or entitlements, such as social security disability payments. These strategies already have been demonstrated to be manageable as consequences for drug abstinence and effective reinforcers (Milby et al., 1996; Schumacher et al., chapter 4, this volume; Shaner et al., 1995, chapter 5, this volume). A fourth approach, as described later in this chapter, is to recruit donations of retail items, gift certificates, and other services from the community for use as reinforcers in the program (Amass, 1997; Amass, Collins, Meffe, & Snelgrove, 1998). A fifth approach is to design a "best fit" reinforcement schedule likely to optimize clinical outcomes for a particular client. For example, a client with intermittent drug use may respond satisfactorily to a relatively lean and variable schedule of reinforcement, whereas a client with continuous drug use may respond better if the initial schedule of reinforcement is dense and fixed. Evidence suggests that several different schedules of reinforcement can be effective (e.g., Higgins et al., 1993; Kirby, Marlowe, Festinger, Lamb, & Platt, 1998; Stitzer et al., 1977). Systematic research is needed to determine the schedule that produces the best clinical outcomes at the least expense.

Another strategy sometimes suggested for reducing the cost of reinforcers is to replace the reinforcement contingency with a punishment or response-cost contingency. Delivering aversive consequences (e.g., sending clients to jail, requiring inpatient stays or increased clinic visits, writing letters reporting clients' drug use to their employers) or withdrawing assets or privileges (e.g., termination from methadone treatment, loss of down payments, loss of driving license, dose reductions) certainly removes or greatly reduces the expense of reinforcers. The use of punishment contingencies has been demonstrated as effective in reducing drug use (e.g., Anker & Crowley, 1982; Crowley, 1984; Dolan, Black, Penk, Robinowitz, & DeFord, 1985); indeed, they are about equally effective as reinforcement contingencies (Stitzer et al., 1986).

Unfortunately, outcomes from these studies also suggest that punishment contingencies have drawbacks. First, they can be unpleasant to implement; second, clients enrolled in voluntary programs tend to leave treatments involving punishment contingencies. When the punishing consequence for drug use is treatment termination, it is obvious that some clients will leave treatment. However, many leave before the clinic ever administers the consequence; even when treatment termination is not the punisher, many clients opt out of treatment. Crowley's early work using punishers in contingency contracts with clients shows that as many as half of the clients refused these contingency contracts (Anker & Crowley, 1982). A controlled comparison of a reinforcement and punishment contingency (Iguchi, Stitzer, Bigelow, & Liebson, 1988; Stitzer et al., 1986) reports that clients in the reinforcement contingency stayed in treatment and those in the punishment condition did not. These results are consistent with basic and applied research in behavior analysis that suggests that negative side-effects from punishment contingencies include behavioral suppression, fear, anger, and aggression in addition to escape and avoidance (i.e., treatment termination; e.g., Martin & Pear, 1992; Sidman, 1989). Furthermore, the effects of punishment are temporary, in that the punished behavior returns when the contingency is terminated (e.g., Ferster & Skinner, 1957) and sometimes even when the contingency remains in effect (Sidman, 1989). Of course, maintaining behavior change also is a challenge when positive reinforcement is used, but strategies for maintaining behavior under intermittent schedules of reinforcement are better developed than strategies for maintaining behavior under punishment schedules. Behavior analysts generally agree that punishment contingencies are not the first treatment of choice. Disagreement remains regarding whether these procedures can be justified under some circumstances.

Adapting Urine Testing Schedules

Urinalysis results commonly provide the basis for contingently delivered reinforcers. In research settings, contingency management programs typically use a fixed, monitored, three to four times per week urine sample collection and testing schedule. In contrast, most community-based programs collect and test urine samples much less frequently, with collection unmonitored and schedules ranging from a maximum of once a week to once a month or even less frequently. Thus, the labor and cost required for urinalysis in research and clinical settings can be vastly different.

Unfortunately, researchers have not explored the minimum urine sample analysis requirements of successful urinalysis-based contingency management. Some research demonstrates that analyzing one sample per week from samples collected three times a week yields the same information as analysis of all three weekly urine samples (Compton, Ling, Wesson, Charuvastra, & Wilkins, 1996). However, providing the same information is not the same as providing an equally effective contingency. Randomized schedules of urine monitoring as low as once every month have been demonstrated to reduce drug use (e.g., Calsyn & Saxon, 1987). This of course does not argue that very lean schedules would be appropriate for every clinical contingency management application. However, this experience does suggest that very lean schedules of testing can lead to behavior changes in some populations.

Random schedules of sample collection also have been successfully used in research (Anker & Crowley, 1982; Crowley, 1984). Further study of random schedules is important because these schedules are practical to implement and a potential cost savings for community-based treatments. Unfortunately, to our knowledge, no researchers have systematically varied frequency of sample analysis in ways that permit definitive conclusions regarding the most effective clinically manageable schedule to use in contingency management applications. This information is necessary to successfully transfer contingency management technology to community settings. However, note that in all of the above examples of random testing where consequences were applied, the consequences involved punishment. Although punishing consequences may be easier to arrange with random testing, they may have disadvantages. Applying an effective positive reinforcement contingency to a random sampling schedule is probably more complicated. Although random sampling may be an effective strategy for clients who already have achieved a period of abstinence, it would be less likely to be useful in initiating abstinence (e.g., Kirby et al., 1998).

We can think of four strategies for reducing the frequency of urinalysis that would be useful to examine experimentally to determine the minimum frequency of sample analysis. First, it would be useful to know if regular sample collection with a random sample analysis is any more effective than random sample collection alone. Second, a combination of self-report and urine testing could be explored. For example, on urine test days, clients could first be asked whether the urine sample is positive for any of the drugs tested. If the patient responds *yes*, the sample would be counted as positive and no reinforcer would be delivered; however, no response cost or only a small response cost would be administered (e.g., resetting an escalating schedule part way). If the client responds *no*, then testing would be conducted to confirm abstinence. If abstinence were confirmed by the test, a reinforcer would be delivered; however if the sample tested positive for drugs, a substantial response cost would be levied (e.g., resetting an escalating schedule all the way). This combination of self-report and urine testing could be systematically compared with standard urine testing contingency procedures. A third strategy for reducing urinalysis may be to identify times when the client is at lowest risk for using substances and minimize surveillance during these times and increase it when the client is at greater risk. For example, a client who is employed full time and tends to confine use to weekends may need more frequent testing on weekends and only occasional random sampling during weekdays. Clients who are at high risk after receiving a paycheck or welfare benefit may need increased sampling during these times. A fourth strategy for reducing costs may be to vary the frequency of testing by drug (e.g., marijuana may be tested less frequently than cocaine because marijuana's metabolites remain detectable in urine for longer periods after use) or to vary testing frequency by therapeutic progress. The latter strategy is most likely to work in the context of a good contingency management program.

Clients who have not yet initiated abstinence or who have relapsed may be tested three times a week until a sustained period of verified abstinence has been established. Then testing may be reduced to twice a week, then once a week, and eventually to very infrequent random tests for clients with extended periods of abstinence. Again some adjustment of reinforcement contingencies would be required, but the basic understanding of reinforcement schedules suggests that if reducing the schedule of urine testing and delivery of contingencies were performance based, it should be possible to maintain behavior changes (e.g., Ferster & Skinner, 1957; Skinner, 1956/1972). To date, most of the research in contingency management of drug use has focused on establishing abstinence, not on programming for long-term effects (but see Higgins et al., 1995). Although it is reasonable to delay consideration of long-term effects until researchers have established methods for initiating the desired behavior, it is probably time for researchers to examine the important clinical question of maintenance.

In addition to frequency of urine testing, other differences between research and clinical settings are the latency and specificity of urinalysis procedures. Most research programs use on-site testing technologies that provide immediate feedback on urinalysis results—and usually for several drugs. In contrast, practitioners seldom have on-site testing technology and usually send samples out to certified laboratories for analysis, rarely receiving urinalysis results sooner than within 3–4 days. Rowan-Szal, Joe, Chatham, and Simpson (1994) provided evidence that delays in contingency management interventions reduce the efficacy of the intervention. This finding is consistent with basic research showing that temporal delays between performance of the target behavior (e.g., providing a drug-negative urine sample) and delivery of the reinforcer weaken the effectiveness of the reinforcer (e.g., Chung, 1965; Perin, 1943; also see Bigelow, Stitzer, Griffiths, & Liebson, 1981). Strategies need to be developed to minimize or counteract the effects of such delays.

Of course, an alternative strategy to adapting urine testing schedules is to deliver reinforcers contingent on a behavior other than urine results. This strategy completely eliminates the increased expenses incurred when drug-free urine samples are reinforced and has been tried with some success (Iguchi, Belding, Morral, Lamb, & Husband, 1997; see also Morral et al., chapter 10, this volume). Further research on this approach is needed to ascertain its generality.

Use of Personnel Resources

Concerns about practitioners' workloads are typically at the forefront when any new procedure is introduced to community clinics. Clinic administrators and service delivery personnel typically feel overextended and have reservations about introducing any new procedure that places additional demands on them. Research programs do not address this problem, typically hiring special staff to implement the contingency management program. Iguchi and colleagues suggested a contingency management intervention that fully incorporates procedures into the counseling session and therefore may reduce this problem (Iguchi et al., 1997; see also Morral et al., chapter 10, this volume). In this intervention, clients earn vouchers by completing tasks that are part of their treatment plan. All tasks are negotiated in the counseling session, and the completion is tracked during the counseling session. However, this procedure has been tested only in research clinics where caseloads are usually less in number than those found in the community.

Another approach may be to implement a contingency management program on a limited basis to only a few clients at a time, allowing clinic staff to experience the benefits of contingency management before investing their resources. Researchers have done little to document the amount of time and effort involved in implementing contingency management programs and the benefits in terms of clinic resources saved. If an effective contingency management program reduces the amount of counseling time spent in unproductive struggles, allows effective switching from individual to group counseling, and shortens the amount of time in intensive treatment interventions, the net result may actually be a reduction in staff resources. Some of this information could be gathered by adopting the technologies outlined by Pantalon and Schottenfeld (chapter 15, this volume) regarding monitoring of therapist and patient behavior during psychotherapy.

Finally, we want to caution readers that the costs and labor intensity of contingency management interventions should be evaluated in the context of the costs and labor intensity for other interventions. Vouchers and contingency management interventions are relatively novel interventions, which probably recruit greater scrutiny regarding costs than more familiar or conventional interventions. Professionally delivered individual and group counseling sessions, for example, can be equally or more costly and labor intensive than most contingency management interventions; in addition, less is known about their efficacy. Costs and efficacy of interventions need to be examined across the board. When considered in this larger context, contingency management interventions may appear comparable or favorable, especially if they are delivered in lieu of more conventional interventions.

Training Practitioners to Implement Contingency Management Programs

The second challenge that we identify for dissemination of contingency management technologies is that practitioners generally are not trained in behavior analysis or contingency management and, therefore, are unaware of the basic principles for successfully implementing a contingency management program. Many aspects of contingency management can be misapplied by well-intentioned but inexperienced practitioners. Some common mistakes include offering items that do not function as reinforcers (e.g., appointment books, pencils, or abstinence literature), requiring initial behavior changes that are too large (e.g., a month of abstinence), or applying irregular or delayed contingencies. We also encountered less common mistakes, such as delivering the reinforcer before the target behavior has occurred. These mistakes suggest that a minimum set of principles must be clearly communicated when presenting and training practitioners in the use of contingency management procedures. These principles would include (a) choosing a well-specified and clearly observable behavior, (b) knowing the pitfalls of relying on unverified verbal reports or unverified urine samples, (c) choosing a variety of reinforcers that are likely to be effective and allowing clients to select reinforcers, (d) delivering reinforcers after the target behavior has occurred, (e) reducing delays between the behavior and reinforcer delivery as much as possible, (f) understanding that a reinforcer does not need to be delivered every time but should be delivered consistently and frequently as the desirable behavior is initially established, and (g) dealing with unusual circumstances in ways that are humane without inadvertently rewarding attempts to short-circuit contingencies (e.g., how and when to allow an exception to a contingency, so that a client can attend a loved one's funeral). The National Institute on Drug Abuse has released training manuals for clinicians and policy makers on the use of contingency management interventions (e.g., Budney & Higgins, 1998). These resources may prove helpful in guiding the training of practitioners. Even with these guidelines and manuals, we must emphasize that researchers do not always know a priori how to arrange an effective contingency management program. Practitioners should be prepared to evaluate and modify their program as necessary to create an effective one.

A Caution About Changes

Even minor changes in a contingency management program can significantly increase or decrease its effectiveness. Kirby et al. (1998) demonstrated that alterations in the schedule of voucher delivery made the difference between a program that was effective in reducing cocaine abuse and one that was completely ineffective. Similarly, Silverman et al. (1996) demonstrated that the addition of bonus payments to an escalating pay schedule of reinforcement significantly reduced mean weeks of cocaine abstinence achieved by methadone maintenance patients relative to the escalating schedule without the bonuses. Thus, researchers should be cautioned that even minor changes can alter the effectiveness of contingency management procedures, sometimes in ways that are counterintuitive. It is likely that this applies not only to planned changes in contingency management procedures but also to unplanned changes or the "procedural drift" that arises from the natural tendency for staff to become inconsistent or imprecise in following the protocol across time.

Managing Philosophical and Political Barriers

The third challenge in disseminating contingency management procedures are the philosophical and political problems associated with the idea of providing reinforcers to drug-abusing clients. To give drug abusers special rewards for not using drugs is seen as inappropriate; why should drug addicts receive special privileges for avoiding drugs when this is something they should be doing anyway? Even if the clinic staff can be convinced that contingency management is an appropriate intervention, how can the clinic gain community and political support for such a program?

Some of the barriers to implementing contingency management programs in community settings may dissolve as the technology becomes more available at a reduced cost. For example, developing programs that use contingent housing or contingency-based entitlements may be helpful in increasing the acceptability of incentive programs (e.g., Milby et al., 1996; Shaner et al., chapter 5, this volume). Philosophical barriers may be reduced by using reinforcers that clients have already received noncontingently and developing guidelines for delivering these same privileges contingently. This approach may foster incorporating contingency management into situations such as welfare, social security, or employee assistance programs. Delivering preexisting privileges contingently is less likely to be seen as providing offensive special treatments than when new reinforcers are introduced.

Another method of negotiating philosophical and political barriers may be to further develop contingency management programs such as the one described by Iguchi (Iguchi et al., 1997; see also Morral et al., chapter 10, this volume). Rewarding drug abusers for cooperating with their counselors and following their treatment plans is more likely to be perceived as socially acceptable than rewarding them for not using drugs. This approach is most likely to be preferred by counseling staff, especially if the counselor perceives that these procedures reduce client resistance. Finally, it may be wise to begin transferring the technology of contingency management to special populations that are viewed more sympathetically. The work described by Elk (chapter 6, this volume; Elk et al., 1995, 1997) with pregnant drug abusers is an example of such a population. This approach was taken a step further by Amass (1997; Amass et al., 1998), who not only initiated the contingency management program with pregnant drug abusers but also generated considerable community support for the contingency-based program, as discussed in the next section.

STRATEGIES FOR ACQUIRING REINFORCERS AND FUNDING COMMUNITY-BASED CONTINGENCY MANAGEMENT PROGRAMS

An obvious obstacle to the dissemination of contingency management programs to the treatment community is the development of practical, generalizable, and cost-effective strategies that can provide the supports essential to maintaining a successful behavioral management program. A primary concern is how to acquire nondrug reinforcers within community clinics that (a) can effectively compete with drug taking or other problem behavior, (b) are readily available in the client's community after treatment is completed, and (c) are affordable by the program. Certainly, contingency management procedures using drug reinforcers available in the clinic, such as methadone, have been explored extensively with methadone maintenance patients (Higgins, Stitzer, Bigelow, & Liebson, 1986; Stitzer et al., 1977, 1982, 1986; Stitzer, Bigelow, & Liebson, 1980; Stitzer, Bigelow, & Iguchi, 1993; Stitzer, Iguchi, & Felch, 1992) and can enhance treatment outcomes. However, drug reinforcers may not be available or relevant to the populations treated in many clinic settings. Moreover, to the extent that non-drug-alternative reinforcers readily available in the community can be used during routine treatment, the probability of their functioning as effective reinforcers after treatment is completed may be improved (Amass, Bickel, Crean, & Higgins, 1996). Increasing the range of potential reinforcers available to patients may also be helpful because clinicians would be better able to customize treatment to the individual patient or program site and increase the probability of positive treatment outcome (Amass et al., 1996).

At least two processes are important in acquiring reinforcers for use in community-based contingency management programs. First, practitioners should be encouraged to survey their clientele on a variety of activities or events occurring within their community as well as on a variety of retail items for their putative capacity to function as a reinforcer. Surveying the clients (the "consumer" of treatment services) may help provide clinicians with better insight as to what types of nondrug alternatives are likely to be effective reinforcers during treatment. Several surveys of substance-abusing patients receiving treatment for opioid dependence are illustrative (Amass et al., 1996; Schmitz, Rhoades, & Grabowski, 1994; Stitzer & Bigelow, 1978; Yen, 1974). Researchers have demonstrated a positive relationship regarding those privileges rated as preferred in surveys and those that are effective reinforcers for maintaining behavior change (Iguchi et al., 1988; Milby, Garrett, English, Fritschi, & Clarke, 1978; Stitzer et al., 1982, 1992, 1993).

In an effort to identify potential nondrug reinforcers for use in a contingency management program, Amass et al. (1996) evaluated clients' preferences for various clinic privileges, retail items, and social activities. Fifty-three opioid-dependent patients rank ordered 11 clinic privileges, 19 retail items, and 8 social activities from the most desirable (a rank of 1) to the least desirable (a rank equal to the number of items in that category). Consistent with findings from methadone treatment, cash payments for opioid-negative urine samples and take-home medication were the highest ranked clinic privileges. However, the results suggest that various retail items (e.g., restaurant gift certificates, movie passes) and social activities (e.g., going to the movies and client barbecues) may be useful for reinforcing positive treatment outcomes during outpatient drug treatment. In this regard, although many of the putative nondrug reinforcers assessed in the above study have not been evaluated empirically in controlled studies, those items identified by patients as most preferable are consistent with items typically requested by patients participating in some of the voucher programs described elsewhere in this volume (Bickel, Amass, Higgins, Badger, & Esch, 1997; Higgins et al., 1991, 1993, 1994). Thus, surveying clientele appears to be a valid mechanism for determining which items may actually function as reinforcers for behavior change. It would be useful to know whether a patient's ranking of reinforcers changes as he or she establishes abstinence and progresses in treatment. To our knowledge, no reinforcer survey has examined treatment tenure and length of abstinence to see if these factors predict reinforcer ranking. It is possible that socially acceptable activities (e.g., restaurant coupons, theater tickets) increase in ranking as patients reach later stages of rehabilitation. This type of analysis could be conducted with large surveys that include a variety of patients in different stages of rehabilitation.

After a range of putative reinforcers has been identified, the second step is to devise cost-effective strategies for acquiring these goods or services for use in the program. One strategy is to solicit donations from the local community (Amass, 1997; Amass et al., 1998). Donations can be solicited through a variety of techniques, including event fundraisers, direct-mail campaigns, and telemarketing. Local community volunteers also can assist with fundraising efforts and help create goods (e.g., sewing clothes) and manage the product donation inventory. The feasibility of securing donations to support a contingency management program and creating an on-site voucher store containing donated items has been demonstrated with a program for pregnant drug abusers (Amass, 1997; Amass et al., 1998). In this program, pregnant patients received vouchers contingent on the demonstration of drug abstinence by urinalysis. Vouchers were redeemable at an on-site store carrying a variety of products and services acquired through community donations.

In the above study, the product inventory was secured by a direct-mail fundraising campaign, and donations were solicited from 198 corporations, manufacturers, and local retailers. Local volunteers also were solicited through posters, word-of-mouth, and electronic-mail advertising. Potential donors were offered charitable receipts for taxation purposes as well as public acknowledgment in any radio or television interviews, program brochures, and quarterly mailings. Components of the campaign included selecting population-specific goods and services to stock in the voucher store, identifying and targeting potential sources of community sponsorship using the local yellow pages and marketing guides, constructing an effective donation request package, and carefully planning follow-up to the direct-mail campaign. Seven categories of goods and services were targeted for donations: baby accessories, baby clothes, toys, maternity wear and products, diapers, entertainment and recreation, and equipment. A positive response rate for corporate sponsorship of 19% was obtained over an 8-month period. More than half (53%) of the positive respondents were manufacturers, 34% were local attractions and restaurants, and 13% were local retailers. In addition, 120 women volunteered to produce and donate handmade baby and maternity items. Approximately $8,000 in goods and services were donated to the program, 49% of which were from the entertainment and recreation category. Another 19% of donations were toys, 13% baby clothes, 9% maternity wear and products, 4% equipment, 3% baby accessories, and 3% diapers. That nearly half of the goods donated to this program were in the entertainment and recreation category (i.e., restaurant gift certificates, movie passes, books) is particularly encouraging because these types of donations are not specific to pregnant women and could obviously be used with a range of clientele.

Although we do not currently have systematic data comparing community-sponsored on-site voucher stores with clinic or program purchased reinforcers, creating community-sponsored on-site stores may offer several advantages (Amass et al., 1998). First, the exchange of vouchers for goods can closely follow presentation of clean urine samples or other target behavior, increasing temporal contiguity between the behavior and reinforcer. Second, staff effort for supporting the voucher program may be reduced because travel to purchase goods for patients is no longer required. Third, patients have an opportunity to preview goods in the on-site store, exposing them to available reinforcers on a regular basis, which may have a "priming" effect. Fourth, establishing a community-sponsored voucher program reinforces the role of the local community in substance abuse treatment programming and potentially offers a long-term solution to funding community-based substance abuse treatment. Fifth, involving the local community is consistent with the philosophy of the community reinforcement approach (Azrin, 1976; Hunt & Azrin, 1973), which has proven efficacy for the treatment of drug abuse (e.g., Higgins et al., 1991, 1993).

Although community-based substance abuse programs may not have adequate personnel resources to dedicate to fundraising, the willingness of community volunteers to help support such programs suggests that these same volunteers may be willing to conduct and supervise the actual fundraising effort (Amass et al., 1998). Certainly, the above study offers only one solution to offset the cost of voucher programs and involve the local community in substance abuse programming efforts.

Other approaches, as reviewed earlier in this and other chapters, also may be useful for increasing the cost effectiveness of contingency management. For example, redirecting the use of state-subsidized disability or housing entitlements not only provides programs with funds needed to support monetary-based reinforcement strategies (see chapters 4, 5, and 6) but also appears to be a reasonable and effective strategy for reducing illicit-drug use in some drug-abusing populations. Finally, another avenue for generating reinforcers in a cost-effective manner currently under study is to examine existing revenue streams within the clinic (e.g., treatment fees) and determine the availability and feasibility of redistributing portions of this revenue to clients contingent on their performance in treatment (Amass et al., 1998). In summary, demonstrating the effectiveness of practical, creative, and affordable strategies such as those discussed above is essential for transferring contingency management technology into general clinical practice.

DEVELOPING AVENUES FOR DISSEMINATION

Clearly researchers have made some progress toward disseminating contingency management technologies. Several chapters in this volume suggest innovative methods for adapting contingency management technologies to the pragmatic constraints of community-based programs (Morral et al., chapter 10; Schumacher et al., chapter 4; Shaner et al., chapter 5; Kidorf & Stitzer, chapter 11). Some of these programs also have made the important step of integrating the intervention into the community and gaining community support (Amass, 1997; Amass et al., 1998; Milby et al., 1996). However, broad dissemination of contingency management interventions will likely require additional steps.

To better understand and develop the necessary modifications to make contingency management programs more practitioner friendly, researchers need to find community settings in which to modify and evaluate their contingency management programs. This requires identifying and cultivating community contacts. To develop a network of community contacts, researchers need to keep the method of successive approximations in mind. A good starting point may be to establish contacts that have some ties and experience working with a research institution. For example, researchers initially may want to develop contingency management programs in practices with medical schools or other academic institutions and then gradually move to an independent facility with experience serving as a research site. Only after establishing a positive reputation should researchers tackle using community-based or state systems as sites for new programming efforts. Of course, the important feature is not the institutional affiliation per se. The basic idea is to begin adapting contingency management interventions in community settings where staff and administration are familiar with experimental approaches, open to new ideas, likely to trust individuals with a research background, and likely to be patient and forgiving if the program is not immediately successful.

If dissemination is to be successful, researchers must gain the trust of community-based facilities. This may involve not only listening carefully and responding to agency concerns regarding the contingency management system but also assisting with unrelated concerns. For example, most state agencies are just now coming under pressure by legislatures to provide empirical documentation and demonstration of the effectiveness of their programs. Assisting state systems with the development and analysis of outcome data provides an excellent opportunity to establish a relationship that may lead to other collaborative efforts (Bickel & McLellan, 1996).

Another factor to consider is the way new ideas such as contingency management programs are presented to community-based facilities. Often enthusiasm for new programs and other changes come from program administrators, not from the counselors and other direct care staff who will be responsible for implementing the changes. It is important to be aware of these distinctions and to understand that even with clinics willing to adopt a contingency management program, trust and cooperation from all the relevant parties are unlikely. If dissemination is to be successful, researchers must be prepared to present compelling arguments and respond diplomatically to clinic administration and staff who will be responsible for implementing the program. One strategy is using contingency management to motivate the service delivery staff. Contingency management of treatment staff has been used successfully in other contexts (e.g., Parsons, Cash, & Reid, 1989; Parsons & Reid, 1995).

Success is the best tool for developing trust and selling contingency management programs. As such, researchers should be cautious about progressing too quickly. Starting small in contexts that appear most cooperative would allow for the opportunity to develop not only a successful program but also a community-based staff that supports contingency management and recommends it to others. This, in turn, can make the next agency more cooperative as the intervention is disseminated to additional programs.

The ultimate challenge of developing community relations will be adapting to contexts in which researchers have less control than they do in their research clinics without compromising the efficacy of contingency management interventions. Researchers will need to make sure that they have clearly communicated and documented their concerns but allow agencies to maintain control of the collaboration. A continued commitment by researchers to foster positive relationships with community treatment providers and a willingness to tailor their knowledge to the specific needs and resources of each community program will maintain contingency management's efficacy while it becomes more widely disseminated and acceptable to community-based treatment programs.

REFERENCES

Amass, L. (1997). Financing voucher programs for pregnant substance abusers through community donations. In L. S. Harris (Ed.), *Problems of drug dependence 1996: Proceedings of the 58th annual scientific meeting, the College on Problems of Drug Dependence* (NIDA Research Monograph 174, p. 59) Washington, DC: U.S. Government Printing Office.

Amass, L., Bickel, W. K., Crean, J., & Higgins, S. T. (1996). Preferences for clinic privileges, retail items and social activities in an outpatient buprenorphine treatment program. *Journal of Substance Abuse Treatment, 13*, 43–49.

Amass, L., Collins, J. C., Meffe, P., & Snelgrove, J. L. (1998). *Building community support for addiction treatment: Financing voucher programs for pregnant substance abusers through community donations.* Manuscript submitted for publication, University of Colorado.

Amass, L., Ennis, E., Mikulich, S. K., & Kamien, J. B. (1998). Using fee rebates to reinforce abstinence and counseling attendance in cocaine abusers. In L. S. Harris (Ed.), *Problems of drug dependence 1997: Proceedings of the 59th annual scientific meeting, the College on Problems of Drug Dependence* (NIDA Research Monograph 178, NIH Pub. No. 432-965-6003, p. 99) Washington, DC: U.S. Government Printing Office.

Anker, A. L., & Crowley, T. J. (1982). Use of contingency contracts in speciality clinics for cocaine abuse. In L. S. Harris (Ed.), *Problems of drug dependence 1981: Proceedings of the 43rd annual scientific meeting, the Committee on Problems of Drug Dependence* (NIDA Research Monograph 41, pp. 452–459). Washington, DC: U.S. Government Printing Office.

Azrin, N. H. (1976). Improvements in the community-reinforcement approach to alcoholism. *Behavior Research and Therapy, 11*, 365–382.

Bickel, W. K., Amass, L., Higgins, S. T., Badger, G. J., & Esch, R. A. (1997).

Effects of adding behavioral treatment to opioid detoxification with buprenorphine. *Journal of Consulting and Clinical Psychology, 65,* 803–810.

Bickel, W. K., & McLellan, A. T. (1996). Can management by outcome invigorate substance abuse treatment? *American Journal on Addictions, 5,* 281–291.

Bigelow, G. E., Stitzer, M. L., Griffiths, R. R., & Liebson, I. A. (1981). Contingency management approaches to drug self-administration and drug abuse: Efficacy and limitations. *Addictive Behaviors, 6,* 241–252.

Budney, A. J., & Higgins, S. T. (1998). *A community reinforcement plus vouchers approach: Treating cocaine addiction* (NIDA Therapy Manuals 2, NIH Pub. No. 98-4309). Washington, DC: U.S. Government Printing Office.

Calsyn, D. A., & Saxon, A. J. (1987). A system for uniform application of contingencies for illicit drug use. *Journal of Substance Abuse Treatment, 4,* 41–47.

Chung, S. H. (1965). Effects of delayed reinforcement in a concurrent situation. *Journal of the Experimental Analysis of Behavior, 8,* 439–444.

Compton, P. A., Ling, W., Wesson, D. R., Charuvastra, V. C., & Wilkins, J. (1996). Urine toxicology as an outcome measure in drug abuse clinical trials: Must every sample be analyzed? *Journal of Addictive Diseases, 15,* 85–92.

Crowley, T. J. (1984). Contingency contracting treatment of drug-abusing physicians, nurses, and dentists. In J. Grabowski, M. Stitzer, & J. Henningfield (Eds.), *Behavioral intervention techniques in drug abuse treatment* (NIDA Research Monograph 46, pp. 68–83). Washington, DC: U.S. Government Printing Office.

Dolan, M. P., Black, J. L., Penk, W. E., Robinowitz, R., & DeFord, H. A. (1985). Contracting for treatment termination to reduce illicit drug use among methadone maintenance treatment failures. *Journal of Consulting and Clinical Psychology, 53,* 549–551.

Elk, R., Mangus, L., LaSoya, R., Rhoades, H., Andres, R., & Grabowski, J. (1997). Behavioral interventions: Effective and adaptable for the treatment of pregnant cocaine-dependent women. *Journal of Drug Issues, 27,* 625–658.

Elk, R., Schmitz, J., Spiga, R., Rhoades, H., Andres, R., & Grabowski, J. (1995). Behavioral treatments of cocaine-dependent women and TB-exposed patients. *Addictive Behaviors, 20,* 533–542.

Ferster, C. B., & Skinner, B. F. (1957). *Schedules of reinforcement.* Englewood Cliffs, NJ: Prentice-Hall.

Higgins, S. T., Budney, A. J., Bickel, W. K., Badger, G. J., Foerg, F. E., & Ogden, D. (1995). Outpatient behavioral treatment for cocaine dependence: One-year outcome. *Experimental and Clinical Psychopharmacology, 3,* 205–212.

Higgins, S. T., Budney, A. J., Bickel, W. K., Foerg, F., Donham, R., & Badger, G. (1994). Incentives improve outcome in outpatient behavioral treatment of cocaine dependence. *Archives of General Psychiatry, 51,* 568–576.

Higgins, S. T., Budney, A. J., Bickel, W. K., Hughes, J. R., Foerg, F., & Badger, G. (1993). Achieving cocaine abstinence with a behavioral approach. *American Journal of Psychiatry, 150,* 763–769.

Higgins, S. T., Delaney, D. D., Budney, A. J., Bickel, W. K., Hughes, J. R., Foerg,

F., & Fenwick, J. W. (1991). A behavioral approach to achieving initial cocaine abstinence. *American Journal of Psychiatry, 148,* 1218–1224.

Higgins, S. T., Stitzer, M. L., Bigelow, G. E., & Liebson, I. A. (1986). Contingent methadone delivery: Effects on illicit-opiate use. *Drug and Alcohol Dependence, 17,* 311–322.

Hunt, G. M., & Azrin, N. H. (1973). A community-reinforcement approach to alcoholism. *Behavior Research and Therapy, 11,* 91–104.

Iguchi, M. Y., Belding, M. A., Morral, A. R., Lamb, R. J., & Husband, S. D. (1997). Reinforcing operants other than abstinence in drug abuse treatment: An effective alternative for reducing drug use. *Journal of Consulting and Clinical Psychology, 65,* 421–428.

Iguchi, M. Y., Stitzer, M. L., Bigelow, G. E., & Liebson, I. A. (1988). Contingency management in methadone maintenance: Effects of reinforcing and aversive consequences on illicit polydrug use. *Drug and Alcohol Dependence, 22,* 1–7.

Kirby, K. C., Marlowe, D. B., Festinger, D. S., Lamb, R. J., & Platt, J. J. (1998). Schedule of voucher delivery influences initiation of cocaine abstinence. *Journal of Consulting and Clinical Psychology, 66,* 761–767.

Martin, G., & Pear, J. (1992). *Behavior modification: What it is and how to do it* (4th ed.). Englewood Cliffs, NJ: Prentice-Hall.

Milby, J. B., Garrett, C., English, C., Fritschi, O., & Clarke, C. (1978). Take-home methadone: Contingency effects on drug-seeking and productivity of narcotic addicts. *Addictive Behaviors, 3,* 215–220.

Milby, J. B., Schumacher, J. E., Raczynski, J. M., Caldwell, E., Engle, M., Michael, M., & Carr, J. (1996). Sufficient conditions for effective treatment of substance abusing homeless persons. *Drug and Alcohol Dependence, 43,* 39–47.

Parsons, M. B., Cash, V. B., & Reid, D. H. (1989). Improving residential treatment services: Implementation and norm-referenced evaluation of a comprehensive management system. *Journal of Applied Behavior Analysis, 22,* 143–156.

Parsons, M. B., & Reid, D. H. (1995). Training residential supervisors to provide feedback for maintaining staff teaching skills with people who have severe disabilities. *Journal of Applied Behavior Analysis, 28,* 317–322.

Perin, C. T. (1943). The effect of delayed reinforcement upon the differentiation of bar responses in white rats. *Journal of Experimental Psychology, 32,* 95–109.

Rowan-Szal, G., Joe, G. W., Chatham, L. R., & Simpson, D. D. (1994). A simple reinforcement system for methadone clients in a community-based treatment program. *Journal of Substance Abuse Treatment, 11,* 217–223.

Schmitz, J. M., Rhoades, H., & Grabowski, J. (1994). A menu of potential reinforcers in a methadone maintenance program. *Journal of Substance Abuse Treatment, 11,* 425–431.

Shaner, A. E., Eckman, T. T., Roberts, L. J., Wilkins, J. N., Tucker, D. E., Tsuang, J. W., & Mintz, J. (1995). Disability income, cocaine use, and repeated hospitalization among schizophrenic cocaine abusers. *New England Journal of Medicine, 333,* 777–783.

Sidman, M. (1989). *Coercion and its fallout.* Boston: Authors Cooperative.

Silverman, K., Wong, C. J., Umbricht-Schneiter, A., Montoya, I. D., Schuster,

C. R., & Preston, K. L. (1996). Voucher-based reinforcement of cocaine abstinence: Effects of reinforcement schedule. In L. Harris (Ed.), *Problems of drug dependence 1995: Proceedings of the 57th annual scientific meeting, the College on Problems of Drug Dependence* (NIDA Research Monograph 162, p. 97). Washington, DC: U.S. Government Printing Office.

Skinner, B. F. (1972). A case history in scientific method. *American Psychologist, 11,* 221–233. (Original work published 1956)

Stitzer, M. L., Bickel, W. K., Bigelow, G. E., & Liebson, I. A. (1986). Effect of methadone dose contingencies on urinalysis test results of polydrug-abusing methadone-maintenance patients. *Drug and Alcohol Dependence, 18,* 341–348.

Stitzer, M. L., & Bigelow, G. E. (1978). Contingency management in a methadone maintenance program: Availability of reinforcers. *International Journal of the Addictions, 13,* 737–746.

Stitzer, M. L., Bigelow, G. E., & Iguchi, M. Y. (1993). Behavioral interventions in the methadone clinic: Contingent methadone take-home incentives. In L. S. Harris (Ed.), *Problems of drug dependence 1992: Proceedings of the 57th annual scientific meeting, the College on Problems of Drug Dependence* (NIDA Research Monograph 132, NIH Pub. No. 93-3505, p. 66). Washington, DC: U.S. Government Printing Office.

Stitzer, M. L., Bigelow, G. E., Lawrence, C., Cohen, J., D'Lugoff, B., & Hawthorne, J. (1977). Medication take-home as a reinforcer in a methadone maintenance program. *Addictive Behaviors, 2,* 9–14.

Stitzer, M. L., Bigelow, G. E., & Liebson, I. A. (1980). Reducing drug use among methadone maintenance clients: Contingent reinforcement for morphine-free urines. *Addictive Behaviors, 5,* 333–340.

Stitzer, M. L., Bigelow, G. E., Liebson, I. A., & Hawthorne, J. W. (1982). Contingent reinforcement for benzodiazepine-free urines: Evaluation of a drug abuse treatment intervention. *Journal of Applied Behavior Analysis, 15,* 493–503.

Stitzer, M. L., Iguchi, M. Y., & Felch, L. J. (1992). Contingent take-home incentive: Effects on drug use of methadone maintenance patients. *Journal of Consulting and Clinical Psychology, 60,* 927–934.

Yen, S. (1974). Availability of activity reinforcers in a drug abuse clinic: A preliminary report. *Psychological Reports, 34,* 1021–1022.

17

RESEARCH ON CONTINGENCY MANAGEMENT TREATMENT OF DRUG DEPENDENCE: CLINICAL IMPLICATIONS AND FUTURE DIRECTIONS

THOMAS J. CROWLEY

The chapters in this book show that contingency management procedures may now take their place among the most effective of treatments for substance use disorders, joining other well-studied treatments, such as methadone maintenance (Ball & Ross, 1991) and cognitive–behavioral interventions (Project MATCH Research Group, 1997). The well-controlled trials presented here are an applied clinical culmination of 35 years of basic and clinical research showing that drugs serve as reinforcers for drug-taking behavior. That long history of research, first highlighted in the seminal text of Thompson and Schuster (1968), also shows that well-established principles of operant learning are highly applicable to the initiation, maintenance, and termination of drug self-administration.

Preparation of this chapter was supported in part by Grants DA 09482 and DA 11015 from the National Institute on Drug Abuse.

It is appropriate that among the authors represented here are two who have contributed especially to the development of contingency management for the treatment of drug dependence. First, for many years Maxine Stitzer has quietly generated a large body of research showing that reinforcing abstinence could lead people to decrease or stop drug use. She steadily added to the evidence for that thesis, usually in studies with younger associates—many of whom (Higgins, Iguchi, Kidorf, and Preston) now present their own work in this volume. Second, building on Stitzer's parametric studies of reinforcing abstinence, Stephen Higgins dramatically moved the contingency management field forward with solid, recovery-directed randomized clinical trials, the sine qua non of clinical research (e.g., Higgins et al., 1994).

A BALANCE OF REINFORCEMENTS AND PUNISHMENTS

A drug-dependent person experiences many influences that reinforce or punish drug involvement. In Figure 17.1, these influences are shown as pressing on a balanced pointer, the left end of which tips up toward less (or no) drug use or down toward more drug use. Pressing down on the left end is the pharmacologic reinforcement of the drug itself—the powerful, behavior-driving influence of the drug on brain mechanisms (Koob & Le Moal, 1997; Nesse & Berridge, 1997). Also pressing the left end of the pointer toward more drug use are societal reinforcers for drug use, such as the companionship of other users. Pushing the left end up toward less drug use are societal reinforcers for abstinence, including greater job stability, a happier home life, and the company of drug-free friends. Also pushing the left end of the balance up toward less drug use are clinical reinforcers for abstinence, which are arranged by treatment staff. Such reinforcing consequences are the focus of this volume.

Pushing down on the right end of the balance, thus shifting the left end toward less use, are punishments for drug use (see Figure 17.1) "Natural" punishments may include the loss of friends, jailing, depression, anxiety, hepatitis, AIDS, a waste of personal savings, and job loss. In addition, at a patient's request, treatment staff may arrange clinical punishments to discourage relapse. Those may include formal reports of drug-containing urine samples to the patient's employer. Patients in treatment also may use disulfiram, causing them to become sick immediately after drinking alcohol, as a punishment to discourage drinking relapses. Users also may be punished by co-users for abstaining. For example, an alcoholic husband may berate and demean his alcoholic wife when she stops drinking and seeks treatment. This would raise the right end of the balance, moving the left end toward more use (see Figure 17.1).

Reinforcements and punishments arise outside the user, but the user's

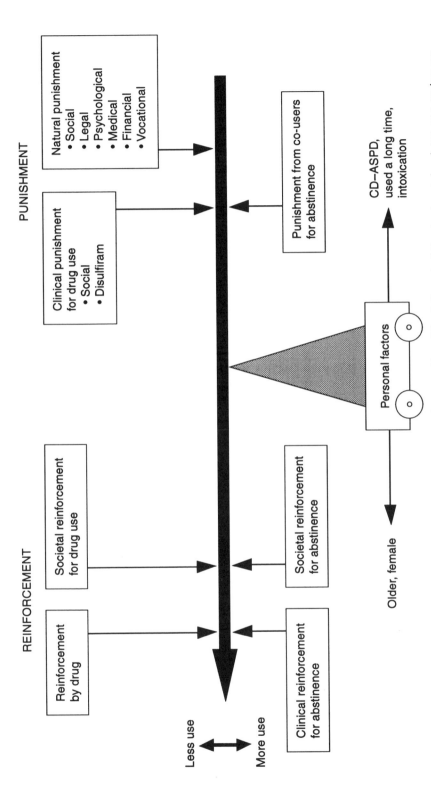

Figure 17.1. The balance of reinforcements and punishments of drug taking. The left end of the horizontal pointer can swing up toward less drug use or down toward more drug use. Reinforcers work at the left side of the pointer, some pushing it up and some pushing it down. Punishments push up or down on the right side. Personal factors, represented as a movable fulcrum for the pointer, can shift the balance to the right (more use) or left (left use). CD–ASPD = conduct disorder or antisocial personality disorder.

response to them may be influenced by personal characteristics. Figure 17.1 represents "personal factors" as a cart that slides the fulcrum along the balanced pointer. Being older or female usually predicts less involvement with drugs (Substance Abuse and Mental Health Services Administration, 1996)—factors that shift the fulcrum leftward, changing the balance and swinging the left end of the pointer upward. A long history of drug use, current intoxication (see Higgins et al., chapter 2, this volume), or a conduct disorder or antisocial personality disorder (ASPD) shift the fulcrum to the right, swinging the left end of the pointer down toward more use.

SPECIALIZED CONTINGENCY MANAGEMENT

As a means to influence behavior through rewards and punishments, contingency management is ubiquitous and hardly new. Your grandmother used it when she set the pie on the table and said "you can have dessert if you finish your broccoli" (a contract for positive reinforcement) and when she whisked the pie away and said "you can't have dessert today because you didn't finish your broccoli" (punishment). Similarly, the employers of all of the contributors of this book use contingency management when they tell them that their salaries depend on their productivity.

The legal system uses contingency management when it says "unless you stay clean and complete this treatment program, you will go to prison." The child-protection system uses contingency management when it says to drug-dependent parents that they can keep their children only if the parents' weekly urine samples remain drug free. Public-housing authorities use contingency management when they exclude drug users from such housing. The military uses it, collecting random urine samples from personnel and showing in surveys that many abstain out of concern that drugs in a sample could end their careers (Cohen, 1986). Similarly, many employers use contingency management by denying employment to applicants with drug-containing urine samples (National Institute on Drug Abuse [NIDA], 1988).

However, interventions by grandmothers, probation officers, military authorities, and others often lack behavioral precision. Figure 17.1 suggests that relapse in a drug-dependent patient is influenced by complex consequences—only a few of which are controlled by therapists. Fortunately, principles well established in the laboratory guide the work reported in this volume, almost certainly magnifying the therapists' impact. Explanations of five of these principles follow.

Make the Program and Schedule of Consequences Very Clear

The contributors in this volume provide their patients with clear, usually written agreements or contracts (see also Crowley, 1984). By comparison, many courts and probation officers are much less clear about, for example, how many drug-positive samples will be tolerated before the probationer is dispatched to prison.

Use a Foolproof System to Detect Drug Use

Although drug users are reasonably honest about their use when there is no advantage to lying (e.g., Winters, Stinchfield, Henly, & Schwartz, 1990–1991), the situation is different with contingency management. In contingency management, the drug user is motivated to get the arranged consequence of a voucher, a take-home dose of methadone, and so forth, so validity of self-reports is less certain. The clinical researchers represented in this volume test urine, breath, or other biological samples to assess abstinence. Moreover, contingency management researchers and therapists use schedules of either very frequent or random and unpredictable urine collection. Obviously, if urine samples are collected on random days, it is much more difficult to regulate one's cocaine taking to avoid detection. Such schedules also take into account the half-life of the target drugs because evanescent drugs like alcohol or fentanyl can be detected only briefly after use. Preston, Silverman, and Cone (chapter 14) provide useful new data on these issues.

Aim at Reasonably Brief Periods Between Consequences

A parent may tell a drug-using adolescent that he or she will be rewarded with a new car after the coming school year if he or she does not use drugs during that time. However, reinforcement is more effective if given more frequently. In the studies described in this volume, typically researchers collect urine or other biological samples at least three times a week. Patients in prolonged treatments eventually may switch to random schedules in which they call the clinic, for example, each Monday, Wednesday, and Friday and a recorded message advises them whether they need to provide a urine sample on that day (Crowley, 1987). They then remain at frequent risk for detection of drugs but can attend the clinic less often.

Use a Consequence Controlled by the Therapist

In this volume, the researchers used vouchers redeemable for commercial goods (e.g., Bickel & Marsch, chapter 13; Higgins et al., 1994), special privileges at a clinic (Kidorf & Stitzer, chapter 11), money (Elk, chapter 6), or goods donated by the community (Kirby, Amass, & McLellan, chapter 16). It is attractive to consider natural reinforcers from the patient's environment, such as a spouse preparing a favorite meal when the patient's urine is free of drugs. However, if the spouse is angry at the patient that day or out of town, the behavior may go unreinforced; even an occasional lapse in reinforcement schedules can disrupt behavior change.

Make Consequences Numerous, Initially Small, and Predictable

These clinicians reinforce behavior change with frequent and relatively small consequences. By comparison, the criminal justice system sometimes punishes with massive and almost irreversible consequences. A probationer may be warned about five drug-containing urine samples and receive a 5-year sentence for the sixth positive sample. Fortunately, drug courts are beginning to use more incremental punishments, with brief jailings for each drug-positive sample (National Association of Drug Court Professionals, 1997).

Recommendations

Continue Refining Contingency Management Schedules and Consequences

Although related to your grandmother's wisdom, contingency management actually is a complex psychological treatment. Its success is highly dependent on the type, magnitude, and delivery schedule of arranged behavioral consequences. In the simplest example, if paying people to stop using cocaine causes some patients to become abstinent, will more patients abstain if the payments increase? Then considering the limited budgets of public treatment programs, how small can payments be yet still remain effective? The contributors of these chapters examine these issues vigorously.

For example, Kidorf and Stitzer (chapter 11) thoughtfully review the literature on scheduling reinforcers and on using methadone dose adjustments and access to treatment as reinforcers or punishers. Kirby et al. (chapter 16) offer a valuable list of low-cost reinforcers that could be used in contingency management treatment. Morral et al. (chapter 10) propose reinforcing not drug-free urine samples but other behaviors considered incompatible with drug use, suggesting practical steps for selecting such behavior. Pantalon and Schottenfeld (chapter 15) also address behaviors incompatible with drug use.

In studying the pattern and amount of cocaine metabolite in successive urine samples, Preston et al. (chapter 14) provide useful guidance about the strength of the response that should be reinforced or punished in contingency management treatments: the urinary concentration of metabolite excreted by the patient. Similarly, Shoptaw et al. (chapter 12) consider (as did Crowley, Macdonald, & Walter, 1995) the level of breath carbon monoxide that should be used to reinforce patients for tobacco abstinence. Higgins et al. (chapter 2) discuss progressively increasing versus fixed-amount reinforcement schedules.

Study Contingency Management in Combination With Other Treatments

In chapter 2, Higgins et al. note that their pioneering study of contingency management for cocaine dependence used the community reinforcement approach (CRA) as the background treatment. Silverman et al. (chapter 8) show that their study of contingency management for cocaine dependence did not offer CRA but that patients received methadone maintenance treatment for their concurrent opioid dependence. Meanwhile, Rawson et al. (chapter 3) describe an ongoing cocaine-treatment trial in which one group receives contingency management with no other treatment. The resulting data could illuminate the question of contingency management's cost. Many clinics find contingency management too expensive to offer, but they consider it a supplement to standard counseling. If future research shows that contingency management alone, standard counseling alone, or the two combined are equally effective, then there is no need for combined treatment. Clinics could offer the cheapest treatment, and that may be contingency management alone. For such reasons, it is extremely important to assess the role of concurrent psychosocial treatments in the efficacy of contingency management.

Research also should address the interaction of contingency management with pharmacologic treatments for substance dependence. Methadone, acetylmethadol, naltrexone, disulfiram, nicotine replacement, and bupropion are all currently approved treatments for dependence on various substances. In one approach, contingency management is used to encourage the taking of disulfiram (Liebson, Bigelow, & Flamer, 1973) or naltrexone (Metzger et al., 1989), whereas in another approach medication taking is not reinforced, but contingency management and medication treatments are offered concurrently (see Silverman et al., chapter 8, this volume). It is important to know whether the effects of contingency management and these medications are additive, are synergistic, or interfere with one another.

LIMITS OF CONTINGENCY MANAGEMENT TREATMENTS

Relapse

Many of these chapters show clear evidence of patients relapsing to drug use after contingency management treatment (Piotrowski & Hall, chapter 9; Rawson et al., chapter 3; Schumacher et al., chapter 4; Silverman et al. chapter 8). I have maintained intermittent contact with one patient, a doctor, for 16 years. This patient wrote a letter to his licensing board stating that he had relapsed to drug use and was surrendering his license. He left the letter with me and directed me in a written contract to collect urine specimens from him. I was to mail the letter if any sample were positive for drugs of abuse. On several occasions over a number of years, the contract expired, and each time the patient quickly relapsed. His family would then return him to treatment, a new contract would be written, and he would remain abstinent again for the duration of that contract. Eventually the contract was terminated because he moved away. He again relapsed very quickly, came to administrative review, and lost his license. While holding a license to order drugs, he remained abstinent whenever the contract was in effect but relapsed whenever it was not.

Substance dependence often is a chronic relapsing disorder. The disorder tends to relapse, for example, among patients leaving methadone maintenance treatment (Ball & Ross, 1991) and among delinquents following residential treatment (Crowley, Mikulich, Macdonald, Young, & Zerbe, 1998). A drug-dependent person has experienced intense, frequent reinforcement from the drug. That experience is never forgotten, and the person always is at risk of relapse. Because of that, therapists aim to involve patients in alternatives to drugs that therapists hope will become more attractive than further drug use. Contingency management thus may be viewed as a temporary means to secure a period of abstinence, during which the patient learns to pursue and obtain reinforcers from work, family, and elsewhere—reinforcers incompatible with a return to drug use. Indeed, Morral, Iguchi, and Belding (chapter 10, this volume) directly reinforce those drug-incompatible behaviors.

This volume shows that contingency management does secure relatively long periods of abstinence. However, there is scant evidence that an episode of contingency management is any more effective than other treatments in reducing relapse across many months or years. Unfortunately, there is little evidence that any psychological treatment is more effective than another in that regard, but contingency management sometimes is criticized because its patients may relapse when abstinence no longer earns the reinforcers available during treatment.

Does relapse after contingency management treatment mean that it is ineffective? Oddly enough, in another chronic relapsing disorder, relapse after treatment is seen as evidence that the treatment is effective. Patients with schizophrenia receiving neuroleptic drugs tend to relapse when the drugs are withdrawn in double-blind studies (Klett, Point, & Caffey, 1972), leading to the recommendation that neuroleptics should be prescribed continually for patients with schizophrenia. Similarly, in drug dependence, medical treatments such as methadone are used long term, and life-long involvement in 12-step programs is encouraged although often not accomplished (Emrick, 1987). Many patients with drug dependence may need effective, reasonably priced, long-term maintenance treatments, but ongoing, formal psychological treatments seldom are offered. The ubiquity of contingency management interventions discussed above and their power when precisely applied suggest that contingency management should be examined as a long-term treatment for some patients.

Cost

Unfortunately, despite the effectiveness of voucher programs, their application in nonresearch community clinics is limited by cost. Some patients of Higgins et al. and Silverman et al. (chapters 2 and 8, this volume) received items worth almost $1,000 over a period of a few months. My clinic, for example, has about 400 adult outpatients, and spending more than $100,000 on contingency management in a few months is not possible. Kirby et al. (chapter 16, this volume) discuss numerous, innovative, and less expensive alternatives.

In summary, contingency management appears to be among the most effective treatments available for drug dependence. Like most short-term treatments for this chronic condition, however, contingency management's efficacy is limited by posttreatment relapse. Moreover, contingency management's application is limited by the cost of reinforcing patients for abstinence, and that cost would increase with longer courses of treatment. In the next section of this chapter, I recommend research that if fruitful could prolong treatment with little extra cost.

PUBLIC BENEFITS, LEGAL SANCTIONS, AND LONG-TERM CONTINGENCY MANAGEMENT

Contingency Management in Addicts Who Have a Lot to Lose

Anker and Crowley (1982) described middle- and upper-class cocaine addicts who were slowly losing their businesses, professions, homes, or life savings because of cocaine dependence. In treatment, they were offered contingency contracts in which that uncertain and stepwise loss would occur more quickly and more certainly after cocaine use. For example, one patient had put his life savings into a house that he was remodeling for a later sale, but he was having trouble meeting his mortgage payments because of cocaine purchases. He expected to lose the house eventually if he did not stop using cocaine. In treatment, he prepared a deed giving the property to a person he despised, and he deposited the deed with his therapist. In a written contract, he directed the therapist to collect urine samples, test them for cocaine, and mail the deed to the despised person if a urine sample contained the drug.

This procedure was extended to health care professionals who used a variety of drugs. They deposited with therapists letters surrendering their licenses, and in contracts they directed the therapists to send the letter to the licensing board if a urine sample contained drugs (Crowley, 1984). All these patients clearly but slowly were losing something important because of drug use. However, on any occasion of temptation, they had been able to tell themselves that they probably could "get away with" one more dose without losing the valued item. Indeed, they probably could. However, the contracts and frequent random urine samples changed that balance. Many patients volunteered for this treatment because they felt that the ultimate prospect of keeping a house or license was better with the contract and the clear consequence than without them (Crowley, 1987; Crowley, Krill-Smith, Atkinson, & Selgestad, 1987). These patients volunteered for possible punishment under the contracts because they believed that the contract actually reduced the likelihood of punishment (or loss).

Contingency Management in Addicts Who Have Nothing to Lose

Unfortunately, many persons with severe drug dependence do not volunteer for treatments involving possible punishment. They fear losing few concrete items as a result of drug use. Jobs, legal incomes, and properties usually are long gone when these patients seek treatment. What little they have (e.g., minor personal possessions and relationships with other drug users) is probably not threatened by further drug use. A physician may place his license on the line in a contingency contract because he believes the contract actually decreases his chance of losing his license. However, a street cocaine addict will not place his old car on the line because he expects to keep it even if he continues using cocaine.

In this volume, Elk (chapter 6) shows that automatic methadone-dose decreases, as punishment for drug use, result in the discharge of many patients. Alternatively, most of the clinical researchers in this volume used positive reinforcement (rather than punishment) to motivate abstinence among patients who had little to lose. There is a long history of such studies. Addicts in methadone maintenance received take-home doses of methadone (Milby, Garrett, English, Fritschi, & Clarke, 1978; Stitzer, Bigelow, & Liebson, 1982) or methadone dose increases (Higgins, Stitzer, Bigelow, & Liebson, 1986) for drug-free urine samples. Boudin et al. (1977) offered as reinforcers record albums, theater passes, free meals, and gift certificates, all donated by local merchants. Higgins et al. (1994) formalized and extended Boudin et al.'s use of commercial items into the most effective treatment currently available for cocaine dependence. Vouchers redeemable for commercial items also significantly reduced drug use among inner-city methadone maintenance patients (Silverman et al., 1995).

But can a patient's substance use be controlled by changing the balance of reinforcers and punishers with stimuli existing naturally in the user's environment? In this volume, Shaner et al. (chapter 5) review, for example, the use of Supplemental Security Income benefits as an incentive for abstinence in patients with schizophrenia and substance dependence.

Schumacher et al. (chapter 4, this volume) also address this problem. They provided access to public housing and supervised work as positive reinforcers for abstinence in homeless cocaine addicts. Half of their patients were assigned randomly to an experimental group who for 2 months got free housing and placement in supervised jobs when they were abstinent. If urine samples revealed drug use, these patients had to move to homeless shelters and could not go to their jobs. However, they could return to the house and job by again producing drug-free urine samples. The experimental patients' abstinence rate significantly exceeded that of control patients who did not have the housing–job contingency.

Of course, housing and job supervision are not cheap. In this pioneering work, Schumacher et al. relied on a research grant to pay these costs. However, many addicts already receive or are eligible for a bewildering array of valuable social benefits and privileges. They vary in different jurisdictions and for different patients, but in Denver (Colorado), they may include Social Security Income benefits, food stamps, homeless shelters, detoxification facilities, Medicaid care, city hospital medical services, low-income housing, vocational rehabilitation and placement, and veterans' benefits. Addicts with children may receive Temporary Assistance to Needy Families benefits and child-care services. In addition, adolescents with drug dependence may receive foster care, family preservation services, special education, and certain transportation services. Private agencies, such as skid row missions, Goodwill, shelters for runaway youths, and the Salvation Army offer food, clothing, shelter, and specially supervised jobs.

Unfortunately, these services are rarely offered contingent on drug abstinence. Indeed, they often are applied in a purposely noncontingent manner, in the good-hearted belief that unconditional assistance to addicts will help them abstain. The success of contingency management procedures reported in this volume suggests, however, that making social benefits contingent on abstinence may improve substance dependence in many recipients. Indeed, Miller (1975; also see Miller, Hersen, Eisler, & Watts, 1974) studied 20 deteriorated skid row alcoholic volunteers. Ten were randomly chosen to be eligible for social benefits when blood alcohol levels were under 10 mg/dl. Ten others received noncontingent services. Blood alcohol levels and employment improved dramatically in experimental participants in comparison with baseline measures and with controls. Contingent benefits swung the balance (see Figure 17.1) toward less use. Miller (1975) noted that such measures "can be implemented with minimal expenditures of time, effort, and money, and [can be] incorporated into existing community agencies" (p. 917).

Some clinicians may argue that making addicts' benefits contingent on abstinence endangers addicts' families for whom these benefits may be life saving. Food stamps, for example, may supply necessary nutrition to addicts' children. However, food stamps also are sold in the black market. Society does not discharge its responsibility to children by dispensing food stamps to addicted parents who trade them for drugs. Indeed, the drugs obtained by selling those food stamps actually may make the lives of those children worse. Child protection services must be active whenever parents are addicted whether benefits are contingent on abstinence or not. Thus, the argument is for protecting addicts' families rather than against contingent social benefits.

Mostly absent from the chapters in this volume are discussions of punitive consequences. In their thoughtful chapter (chapter 16), Kirby et al. correctly point out the advantages of treatment based on positive reinforcement, but most clinicians have treated patients who do not improve until a probation officer seriously threatens to revoke probation. Kirby et al. state that some academic treatment researchers will not use punishing contingencies for drug use. That view, however, seems remote from the reality of a world in which drug-containing urine samples do result in discharges from the military, refusals of employment, firing from jobs, loss of professional licenses, termination of parental custody, revocation of probation, loss of drivers' licenses, exclusion from athletic contests and teams, school expulsions, and marriage break-ups. Addicts face many punitive sanctions for drug use. The issue of whether society should use punishing contingencies was settled long ago. The relevant question now is whether punishment can be used to benefit addicts, not simply as retribution. The five contingency management principles, enumerated above and used by the contributors in this volume, may provide a basis for studying aversion contingencies to alter addictive behavior to the benefit of addicts.

For example, probation or parole may be revoked for drug-positive urine tests. However, sound behavioral principles seldom are followed by complex criminal justice systems. Courts and probation officers often do not punish one or a few drug-positive urine samples. They instead warn, lecture, and order more treatment, hoping thereby to avoid using scarce jail space for a nonviolent offender. Finally, after several or many drug-positive samples, they jail the offender, often for months or years. A probationer may need only 3 days in jail to convince him to stop using drugs; however, if he has a 3-year deferred sentence, revocation gets him 3 years, not 3 days. Fortunately, drug courts are changing this practice, applying brief incisive jailing for any drug-containing urine samples (Harrell & Cavanagh, 1996). Drug courts show that social systems can evolve to use sound contingency management procedures.

When the five principles given above are followed, the contributors suggest that contingency management can alter the course of substance dependence. However, contingency management is criticized for its cost and (like many substance-dependence treatments) its rather high posttreatment relapse rates. Society, meanwhile, currently applies big appetitive and aversive stimuli to addicts for long periods, usually without following the five key principles. Future contingency management research may assess the harnessing of currently available appetitive and aversive stimuli to the humane clinical and social aims of suppressing addicts' drug use, helping addicts and their families, and achieving a more stable society.

However, conducting contingency management research in social and criminal justice agencies is not easy. The heavy workloads of probation officers and child-protection workers are complicated by overcrowded jails and shortages of foster placements. Because these agencies must attend most carefully to violent situations, monitoring and responding to mere drug relapses are low priorities. There is little overall coordination of the web of social service and criminal justice agencies. Many workers in those systems have little knowledge of or interest in research. They are stressed by huge caseloads, funding cuts, and uncertainties of program survival. Still, contributors in this volume suggest that it may be possible to develop and test procedures to make social benefits contingent on drug abstinence and social sanctions contingent on drug use.

Recommendations

Study Contingent Management of Public Benefits for Drug Abstinence

Schumacher et al. and Shaner et al. report reinforcing abstinence through the contingent use of public benefits (chapters 4 and 5, respectively). Prolonged contingency management treatment may be especially important for Shaner et al.'s substance-dependent patients with schizophrenia as well as for the special populations examined by Elk (chapter 6) and certain adolescent patients (e.g., Whitmore et al., 1997) who receive public benefits. These patients in particular may need long-term "prosthetic environments" with clear consequences for abstinence or relapse.

Contingency management principles now appear in federal laws, mandating that welfare recipients must have "performance contracts" that require progress toward employment. The recipients, formerly "entitled" to welfare benefits, now must perform as specified or the benefits may be discontinued. If drug use interferes with progress toward employment, welfare agencies can require in these contracts abstinence and participation in treatment. Failure to provide drug-free urine samples could lead to a reduction or withholding of benefits. Will agencies apply precise, sound contingency management principles like those enumerated at the beginning of this chapter, aiming at behavior change? Or will they simply dispense retribution by withdrawing benefits completely? Can researchers work with agencies to identify the most effective contingency management procedures for producing behavior change? Schumacher et al. and Shaner et al. provide affirmative answers in their pioneering work.

Study Contingent Management of Social Punishments for Drug Use

The real world outside of clinics and laboratories often applies aversive consequences to drug use. Unfortunately, such consequences may only serve to exact retribution, with little regard to changing behavior. Behavior changes only when punishing or reinforcing consequences are applied with precise attention to schedule, type, and magnitude, as outlined in the five principles above. Agencies empowered to punish drug use seldom follow these principles.

Fortunately, drug courts are beginning to use punishment in behaviorally sound ways (National Association of Drug Court Professionals, 1997). They may ask contingency management researchers practical questions such as the following: "Could we safely and more quickly parole some convicts from prison by permitting them to volunteer for community naltrexone or disulfiram treatment, requiring brief jail time for each missed dose?" "If a probationer relapses, can we initiate another remission by briefly jailing him or her for each drug-containing urine sample?" "How long should such jailings be (1 day, 3 days, 1 week)?" "Would it be better to use escalating consequences (e.g., 1 jail day for the first positive sample, two for the second)?" "How big should those steps be (1 or 2 jail days for the first sample, 2 or 4 for the second, etc.)?" There are now only a few answers to such questions, and only research can provide those answers.

More broadly, American society now widely, but unsystematically, applies powerful and expensive aversive consequences to drug-use behavior. Research can show whether society's aim of reducing substance-related morbidity and mortality is better achieved when aversive stimuli are applied systematically (using the five principles) or nonsystematically.

Unfortunately, research in criminal justice agencies may be complicated, for example, by legally mandated jail terms and the need to ensure that control groups receive "equal treatment before the law." However, despite such problems, future research on contingency management therapy increasingly should address better scheduling of society's numerous and expensive punishers for drug use. In such studies, *better* must mean better for the individual and for society. Because those two targets at times conflict, ethical considerations are especially important in studies of punishment-based contingency management.

An effort to bring treatment researchers into criminal justice agencies needs support from the top. NIDA and the Institute of Justice should issue joint requests for applications for contingency management research in courts, probation offices, and other criminal justice agencies. These requests should offer funds for rigorously controlled studies to test innovative, contingency management-based procedures for better application of criminal justice sanctions in the handling of drug-dependent offenders. Collaboration must be reinforced; only teams including experienced contingency management researchers and criminal justice officials should receive funds.

DIFFERENCES IN BEHAVIOR REQUIRE
DIFFERENCES IN APPROACH

People differ, and there is growing evidence that behavioral differences are heavily influenced by genetics (Grove et al., 1990). The antisocial conditions of conduct disorder (CD) and ASPD are highly comorbid with substance dependence and appear to be under genetic control. They influence learning on the basis of reinforcement and punishment. In this section, I review how CD–ASPD influence learning from reinforcement and punishment, relevant to contingency management treatment for substance dependence, and offer two research recommendations. As background, I first review the diagnostic characteristics of CD–ASPD, the comorbidity of those conditions with substance problems, and the genetic underpinnings of the disorders.

Conduct Disorder and Antisocial Personality Disorder

CD is a persistent pattern of behavior in children and adolescents in which the basic rights of others or societal norms or rules are violated (American Psychiatric Association [APA], 1994). The diagnosis requires at least 3 of 15 symptoms, such as fighting, stealing, or bullying. Most seriously delinquent, antisocial youths probably have CD (Offord, 1990). Adult ASPD is a pervasive pattern of disregard for and violation of the rights of others that begins in childhood or early adolescence and continues into adulthood (APA, 1994). This diagnosis requires evidence of childhood CD and at least 3 of 7 symptoms, such as unlawful acts, repeated lying, and reckless disregard for safety of self and others.

Human behavior tends to be stable across time. Behavior ratings in 3-year-old children significantly predict impulsivity, danger seeking, and aggression in early adulthood (Caspi & Silva, 1995). Although the antisocial behavior of many adolescents does not evolve into adult ASPD (Moffitt, 1993; Robins, Tipp, & Przybeck, 1991), for many others antisocial problems begin early in childhood and persist through life (Farrington, 1973; Henn, Bardwell, & Jenkins, 1980; Mitchell & Rosa, 1981; Olweus, 1979; Robins, 1978; Tremblay, Pihl, Vitaro, & Dobkin, 1994).

These disorders are common. CD occurs in 10% of adolescent boys and 4% of adolescent girls (Boyle & Offord, 1991; Crowley & Riggs, 1995). ASPD exists in about 2.5–3.5% of adults (Kessler et al., 1994; Regier et al., 1990; Robins, Tipp, & Przybeck, 1991).

CD–ASPD and Substance Comorbidity

CD is highly comorbid with substance involvement in adolescence and later in life (Crowley & Riggs, 1995; Young et al., 1995). Numerous studies show a relationship among conduct disorder, delinquency, and youthful substance problems—a relationship not caused by social class (Boyle & Offord, 1991; Clark, Jacob, & Mezzich, 1994; Harford & Parker, 1994; Windle, 1994). Furthermore, the more CD symptoms a child has, the greater the risk for substance problems in adulthood (Robins & McEvoy, 1990). Among adults with ASPD, substance abuse or dependence occurs at a rate almost five times greater than in the general population (Regier et al., 1990). Thus, substance use disorders are major comorbid problems in CD and ASPD. Moreover, evidence suggests that ASPD in drug-using patients is not simply an antisocial lifestyle forced on persons by their addiction to illegal drugs (Compton, Cottler, Shillington, & Price, 1995; Dinwiddie & Reich, 1993; Young et al., 1995).

CD–ASPD are heavily overrepresented in drug-abuse treatment programs. CD exists in about 80% of adolescents in my substance treatment programs (Whitmore et al., 1997; Young et al., 1995), and ASPD occurs in 25–60% of adult patients in drug clinics (Brooner, Greenfield, Schmidt, & Bigelow, 1993; Compton et al., 1995; Darke, Hall, & Swift, 1994; Gill, Nolimal, & Crowley, 1992; Rounsaville & Kleber, 1986). This comorbidity affects response to substance treatment (Woody, McLellan, Luborsky, & O'Brien, 1985) because "most therapists agree that [ASPD's] presence is indicative of a poor treatment outcome" (Gerstley et al., 1989, p. 508).

Genetic Influence on Comorbid Substance Dependence and CD–ASPD

Much evidence suggests that both the antisocial behavior and the comorbid drug dependence of patients with CD–ASPD are partly under some common genetic control. Antisocial disorders and alcoholism run together in families (Hesselbrock, Meyer, & Hesselbrock, 1992; Lewis & Bucholz, 1991; Mathew, Wilson, Blazer, & George, 1993). Goldman's (1995) review states that "four large, methodologically sound twin studies published in the 1990's have substantiated the conclusion that alcoholism is heritable (>50%) . . . and that the heritability of early-onset alcoholism tends to be greater than late-onset alcoholism" (p. 824). Early-onset alcoholism usually indicates comorbidity with ASPD (Cloninger, Bohman, & Sigvardsson, 1981; Hesselbrock, Hesselbrock, & Workman-Daniels, 1986; Liskow, Powell, Nickel, & Penick, 1991). Alcoholics with onset before age 20 have "high genetic loading . . . , start abusing alcohol early . . . , [have] a severe course, and . . . aggressive tendencies, impulsivity, antisocial tendencies, or criminality" (Buydens-Branchey, Branchey, & Noumair, 1989).

Adoption studies also suggest that genes contribute to early-onset alcohol dependence (Cloninger et al., 1981). Indeed, common genetic factors appear to influence the development of ASPD and alcohol dependence (Pickens, Svikis, McGue, & LaBuda, 1995) as well as the nonalcohol

360   THOMAS J. CROWLEY

drug dependence of antisocial people (Cadoret, Troughton, O'Gorman, & Heywood, 1986; Chassin, Rogosch, & Barrera, 1991; Luthar, Merikangas, & Rounsaville, 1993; Rounsaville et al., 1991; Sher, Walitzer, Wood, & Brent, 1991). In a twin study, Grove et al. (1990) found that monozygotic twins raised apart were likely to be concordant for antisocial behavior, excessive drinking, and drug use, both in childhood and later. The researchers suggested that genes jointly influence antisocial behavior, excessive drinking, and drug use. Of course, environment also is important, and adoptees with genetic disposition to CD–ASPD displayed more symptoms if raised by adoptive parents with substance dependence, legal difficulties, or marital or psychiatric problems. However, without the genetic disposition, CD–ASPD was unlikely to appear, regardless of the adoptive environment (Cadoret, Yates, Troughton, Woodworth, & Stewart, 1995).

CD–ASPD and Learning by Reinforcement and Punishment

Contingency management treatment depends on learning through reinforcement and punishment, and genetically based disruptions of such learning may impede contingency management treatment in persons with CD–ASPD. Unfortunately, "the link between neuropsychological impairment and antisocial outcomes is one of the most robust effects in the study of antisocial behavior" (Moffitt, 1993, p. 680). Neuropsychological impairment is common in criminals; frontal and temporal regions usually are involved (Yeudall, 1980). There also is considerable evidence for "executive" deficits in delinquent youths (Moffitt & Silva, 1988). Antisocial people pursue rewarding ends with little regard for possible punishing consequences, taking risks that others would eschew. This is one of the executive deficits in ASPD that have been linked to frontal-septal abnormalities (Patterson & Newman, 1993). This risk-taking characteristic sharply differentiates antisocial people from controls in mixed-motivation (approach–avoidance or combined reward–punishment) tests (Daugherty & Quay, 1991; Giancola, Peterson, & Pihl, 1993; Newman, Widom, & Nathan, 1985). Considerable evidence suggests that as punishing consequences increase, antisocial people (unlike others) fail to suppress previously reinforced behavior (Greenwald, Booner, Schuster, & Johanson, 1997; Newman, Patterson, & Kosson, 1987; Newman et al., 1985; Patterson & Newman, 1993; Shapiro, Quay, Hogan, & Schwartz, 1988).

This impairment of approach–avoidance learning may explain the remarkable comorbidity of drug dependence and CD–ASPD. Drugs are rewarding, but excessive use leads to punishing consequences. People with CD–ASPD are especially likely to pursue drug reinforcement while disregarding probable adverse consequences. After an initial series of drug-reward experiences, these people may fail to inhibit drug use as punishing consequences mount. As diagrammed in Figure 17.1, CD–ASPD shifts the fulcrum, so that with any given set of reinforcers and punishers, persons with those conditions are more likely than others to use drugs. This behavioral mechanism, under partial genetic control, may underlie the substance problems so common in CD–ASPD.

Recommendations

Study Nonresponders

All drug-dependent patients experience some balance of rewards and punishments for their drug use (see Figure 17.1 and Crowley, 1972, 1988), and contingency management therapy attempts to alter that balance. The chapters in this volume show that many substance-dependent patients do not respond to contingency management procedures and that many patients who do, relapse. How do they differ from those responding favorably? Are there predictors of response? If so, it is important to study different contingency management treatment approaches to get better responses from different groups of patients. For example, Higgins et al. (chapter 2, this volume) and Piotrowski and Hall (chapter 9, this volume) suggest that parameters of contingency management treatment may need to be different for patients abusing different drugs. As another example, in this volume Pantalon and Schottenfeld (chapter 15) and Higgins et al. (chapter 2) disagree about whether there are gender differences in contingency management responding. Although Piotrowski and Hall (chapter 9) did not find patient differences that predicted nonresponse, they emphasize that further studies are needed.

An important and empirically answerable question is whether a nonresponse to contingency management represents in some patients with CD–ASPD an insensitivity to the normally punishing consequences of drug dependence. As shown in Figure 17.1, being less sensitive to the natural punishing consequences of drug use would tend to tip the pointer down toward more use, even when clinicians offered special reinforcements for abstinence. Persons with CD–ASPD may require especially effective clinical reinforcement for abstinence or especially effective clinical punishments for drug use to swing the pointer back toward less use; devising such reinforcements and punishments is a future research challenge. Indeed, if CD–ASPD and their associated insensitivity to punishment are in part genetically controlled, is it all immutable and hopeless? Or can contingency management procedures improve outcomes even for persons with a deficit in learning from consequences?

Fortunately, clinical experience indicates that persons with CD–ASPD are constrained by consequences (either rewarding or punishing) that are especially well structured, that is, unusually strong in predictability, immediacy, and perhaps magnitude. Such constraint may occur, for example, during the monitoring of intensive probation. Thus, apparently this deficit is not a complete inability to learn from consequences, suggesting a need to find special consequences and schedules effective for these patients.

If patients with CD–ASPD have a permanent executive deficit, will they need treatment indefinitely? With a better understanding of what behavioral dispositions these patients inherit, researchers may be able to design and test long-term "prosthetic" psychosocial environments to enhance abstinence and prosocial behavior while minimizing the adverse influence of the antisocial disposition. With ongoing contingency management, the genes and the behavioral disposition presumably would remain, but the environment would exert a sustained and strong constraining influence. Presumably, such environments would need to be sufficiently attractive that patients voluntarily would remain with them.

Develop Nonpharmacologic Representations of Learning and Terminating Drug Self-Administration

Laboratory studies of how people learn to take and to stop taking drugs could help in the design of more effective contingency management procedures. However, ethics prohibit studies that initiate drug taking in drug-naive persons, and ethics severely limit studies of drug taking by addicts. Mixed-motivation, go–no-go laboratory tests apparently do assess a risk-taking disposition that may underlie a vulnerability to drug problems, and they do so without the administration of drugs. These laboratory models could help clarify, first, whether drug-dependent people experience more reinforcement from drugs than others do ("reward dependence"; Cloninger, 1987), or whether they are less sensitive to drugs' behavior-suppressing aversive consequences ("harm avoidance"; Cloninger, 1987). Second, because the tests appear relevant to but do not require drug taking, they could be used with drug-naive people or abstinent addicts in treatment, perhaps illuminating behavioral processes in initiating, relapsing to, and terminating drug taking. Third, such tests may become clinical assessments, showing when treatment had reduced the risk-taking propensity that may predict relapse. Fourth, such tests could facilitate studies in twins aimed at uncovering a genetically based insensitivity to punishment that may underlie some cases of drug dependence. Fifth, these tests if conducted during brain imaging could localize human cerebral mechanisms mediating reward and punishment, revealing individual differences and abnormalities in those systems. As a sixth issue, among animals, alcohol and depressant drugs increase responding in approach–avoidance tests by reducing the response-suppressing effect of punishment (Cook & Davidson, 1973). For a drug-dependent person, drug taking is an approach–avoidance situation with chances for both reinforcement and punishment. If those animal data apply to humans, taking some alcohol may increase the likelihood of responding further (i.e., taking more drug) because the first doses may weaken the ability of future punishments to suppress use. Folk wisdom states that "one drink is too many and 50 is not enough," implying that one drink may facilitate a binge. Higgins et al. (chapter 2, this volume) show that alcohol, which enhances approach–avoidance responding, does increase cocaine taking in the laboratory. Studies using go–no-go procedures with priming doses of drugs could clarify the role of "the first drink" (or other drugs) in binges and relapses.

Multicenter Trials of Contingency Management Treatment

Eventually, when the best schedules and contingencies have been clarified, when the contingency management treatment needs of patient subgroups like CD–ASPD are known, when interactions with other treatments are understood, and when naturally available benefits and sanctions have been harnessed contingently in treatment, one or more multicenter trials will be needed to establish finally contingency management's efficacy. Such trials should occur in realistic community clinics operating with realistic budgets and aiming at long-term recovery. They should compare contingency management with standard psychological treatments, like those derived from Project MATCH (Carroll et al., 1994; Project MATCH Research Group, 1997) or NIDA's recommended protocols (Zackon, McAuliffe, & Ch'ien, 1993). If the result shows an advantage for contingency management, then NIDA and the Substance Abuse and Mental Health Services Administration should develop consensus conferences aimed at widespread implementation of contingency management procedures by state agencies responsible for regulating the treatment of substance dependence.

CONCLUSION

Contingency management procedures are ubiquitous in society but have been refined through research into invaluable treatment techniques. Further research is needed to develop more precise schedules and consequences, to clarify interactions with other treatments, to use "natural" consequences available in patients' environments, to uncover reasons for nonresponse, to exploit nonpharmacological models of drug taking, and to conduct multicenter trials of contingency management treatments.

REFERENCES

American Psychiatric Association. (1994). *Diagnostic and statistical manual of mental disorders* (4th ed.). Washington, DC: Author.

Anker, A. L., & Crowley, T. J. (1982). *Use of contingency contracts in specialty clinics for cocaine abuse* (NIDA Research Monograph 41, pp. 452–459). Washington, DC: U.S. Government Printing Office.

Ball, J. C., & Ross, A. (1991). *The effectiveness of methadone maintenance treatment.* New York: Springer-Verlag.

Boudin, H. M., Valentine, V. E., Inghram, R. D., Brantley, J. M., Ruiz, M. R., Smith, G. G., Catlin, R. P., & Regan, E. J. (1977). Contingency contracting with drug abusers in the natural environment. *International Journal of Addictions, 12,* 1–16.

Boyle, M. H., & Offord, D. R. (1991). Psychiatric disorder and substance use in adolescence. *Canadian Journal of Psychiatry, 36,* 699–705.

Brooner, R. K., Greenfield, L., Schmidt, C. W., & Bigelow, G. E. (1993). Antisocial personality disorder and HIV infection among intravenous drug abusers. *American Journal of Psychiatry, 150,* 53–58.

Buydens-Branchey, L., Branchey, M. H., & Noumair, D. (1989). Age of alcoholism onset: I. Relationship to psychopathology. *Archives of General Psychiatry, 46,* 225–230.

Cadoret, R. J., Troughton, E., O'Gorman, T., & Heywood, E. (1986). An adoption study of genetic and environmental factors in drug abuse. *Archives of General Psychiatry, 43,* 1131–1136.

Cadoret, R. J., Yates, W. R., Troughton, E., Woodworth, G., & Stewart, M. A. (1995). Genetic–environmental interactions in the genesis of aggressivity and conduct disorders. *Archives of General Psychiatry, 52,* 916–924.

Carroll, K. M., Rounsaville, B. J., Gordon, L. T., Nich, C., Jatlow, P., Bisighini, R. M., & Gawin, F. H. (1994). Psychotherapy and pharmacotherapy for ambulatory cocaine abusers. *Archives of General Psychiatry, 51,* 177–187.

Caspi, A., & Silva, P. A. (1995). Temperamental qualities at age three predict personality traits in young adulthood: Longitudinal evidence from a birth cohort. *Child Development, 66,* 486–498.

Chassin, L., Rogosch, F., & Barrera, M. (1991). Substance use and symptomatology among adolescent children of alcoholics. *Journal of Abnormal Psychology, 100,* 449–463.

Clark, D. B., Jacob, R. G., & Mezzich, A. (1994). Anxiety and conduct disorders in early onset alcoholism. *Annals of the New York Academy of Sciences, 708,* 181–186.

Cloninger, C. R. (1987). A systematic method for clinical description and classification of personality variants. *Archives of General Psychiatry, 44,* 573–588.

Cloninger, C. R., Bohman, M., & Sigvardsson, S. (1981). Inheritance of alcohol abuse: Cross-fostering analysis of adopted men. *Archives of General Psychiatry, 38,* 861–868.

Cohen, S. (1986). The Military Worldwide Surveys: Deterrent effects of urine testing on drug use. *Drug Abuse & Alcoholism Newsletter, 15*(9).

Compton, W. M., Cottler, L. B., Shillington, A. M., & Price, R. K. (1995). Is antisocial personality disorder associated with increased HIV risk behaviors in cocaine users? *Drug and Alcohol Dependence, 37*, 37–43.

Cook, L., & Davidson, A. B. (1973). Effects of behaviorally active drugs in a conflict–punishment procedure in rats. In S. Garattini, E. Mussini, & L. O. Randall (Eds.), *The benzodiazepines* (pp. 327–345). New York: Raven Press.

Crowley, T. J. (1972). The reinforcers for drug abuse: Why people take drugs. *Comprehensive Psychiatry, 13*, 51–62.

Crowley, T. J. (1984). *Contingency contracting treatment of drug-abusing physicians, nurses, and dentists* (NIDA Research Monograph 46, pp. 68–83). Washington, DC: U.S. Government Printing Office.

Crowley, T. J. (1987). Clinical issues in cocaine abuse. In S. Fisher, A. Raskin, & E. H. Uhlenhuth (Eds.), *Cocaine: Clinical and biobehavioral aspects* (pp. 193–211). New York: Oxford University Press.

Crowley, T. J. (1988). *Learning and unlearning drug abuse in the real world: Clinical treatment and public policy* (NIDA Research Monograph 84, pp. 100–121). Washington, DC: U.S. Government Printing Office.

Crowley, T. J., Krill-Smith, S., Atkinson, C., & Selgestad, B. (1987). A treatment for cocaine-abusing health care professionals. In A. M. Washton & M. S. Gold (Eds.), *Cocaine–A clinician's handbook* (pp. 152–172). New York: Guilford Press.

Crowley, T. J., Macdonald, M. J., & Walter, M. I. (1995). Behavioral antismoking trial in chronic obstructive pulmonary disease patients. *Psychopharmacology, 119*, 193–204.

Crowley, T. J., Mikulich, S. K., Macdonald, M., Young, S. E., & Zerbe, G. O. (1998). Substance-dependent, conduct-disordered adolescent males: Severity of diagnosis predicts two-year outcome. *Drug and Alcohol Dependence, 49*, 225–237.

Crowley, T. J., & Riggs, P. D. (1995). *Adolescent substance use disorder with conduct disorder and comorbid conditions* (NIDA Research Monograph 156, pp. 49–111). Washington, DC: U.S. Government Printing Office.

Darke, S., Hall, W., & Swift, W. (1994). Prevalence, symptoms and correlates of antisocial personality disorder among methadone maintenance clients. *Drug and Alcohol Dependence, 34*, 253–257.

Daugherty, T. K., & Quay, H. C. (1991). Response perseveration and delayed responding in childhood behavior disorders. *Journal of Child Psychology and Psychiatry, 32*, 453–461.

Dinwiddie, S. H., & Reich, T. (1993). Attribution of antisocial symptoms in co-existent antisocial personality disorder and substance abuse. *Comprehensive Psychiatry, 34*, 235–242.

Emrick, C. D. (1987). Alcoholics Anonymous: Affiliation processes and effectiveness as treatment. *Alcoholism: Clinical and Experimental Research, 11*, 416–423.

Farrington, D. P. (1973). Self-reports of deviant behavior: Predictive and stable? *Journal of Criminal Law and Criminology, 64*(1), 99–110.

Gerstley, L., McLellan, A. T., Alterman, A. I., Woody, G. E., Luborsky, L., & Prout, M. (1989). Ability to form an alliance with the therapist: A possible marker of prognosis for patients with antisocial personality disorder. *American Journal of Psychiatry, 146*, 508–512.

Giancola, P. R., Peterson, J. B., & Pihl, R. O. (1993). Risk for alcoholism, antisocial behavior, and response perseveration. *Journal of Clinical Psychology, 49*, 423–428.

Gill, K., Nolimal, D., & Crowley, T. J. (1992). Antisocial personality disorder, HIV risk behavior and retention in methadone maintenance therapy. *Drug and Alcohol Dependence, 30*, 247–252.

Goldman, D. (1995). Identifying alcoholism vulnerability alleles. *Alcoholism: Clinical and Experimental Research, 19*, 824–831.

Greenwald, M. K., Brooner, R. K., Schuster, C. R., & Johanson, C. E. (1997, June). *Effects of antisocial personality disorder and provocation on aggressive responding.* Paper presented at the meeting of the College on Problems of Drug Dependence, Nashville, TN.

Grove, W. M., Eckert, E. D., Heston, L., Bouchard, T. J., Segal, N., & Lykken, D. T. (1990). Heritability of substance abuse and antisocial behavior: A study of monozygotic twins reared apart. *Biological Psychiatry, 27*, 1293–1304.

Harford, T. C., & Parker, D. A. (1994). Antisocial behavior, family history, and alcohol dependence syndromes. *Alcoholism: Clinical and Experimental Research, 18*, 265–268.

Harrell, A., & Cavanagh, S. (1996, July 17). *Preliminary results from the evaluation of the D.C. Superior Court Drug Intervention Program for drug felony defendants.* Paper presented at the National Institute of Justice Research in Progress Seminar, Washington, DC.

Henn, F. A., Bardwell, R., & Jenkins, R. L. (1980). Juvenile delinquents revisited: Adult criminal activity. *Archives of General Psychiatry, 37*, 1160–1163.

Hesselbrock, V. M., Hesselbrock, M. N., & Workman-Daniels, K. L. (1986). Effects of major depression and antisocial personality on alcoholism: Course and motivational patterns. *Journal of Studies on Alcohol, 47*, 207–212.

Hesselbrock, V., Meyer, R., & Hesselbrock, M. (1992). Psychopathology and addictive disorders: The specific case of antisocial personality disorder. *Research Publications Association for Research in Nervous and Mental Disease, 70*, 179–191.

Higgins, S. T., Budney, A. J., Bickel, W. K., Foerg, F. E., Donham, R., & Badger, G. J. (1994). Incentives improve outcome in outpatient behavioral treatment of cocaine dependence. *Archives of General Psychiatry, 51*, 568–576.

Higgins, S. T., Stitzer, M., Bigelow, G., & Liebson, I. (1986). Contingent methandone delivery: Effects in illicit opioid use. *Drug and Alcohol Dependence, 17*, 311–322.

Kessler, R. C., McGonagle, K. A., Zhao, S., Nelson, C. B., Hughes, M., Eshleman, S., Wittchen, H., & Kendler, K. S. (1994). Lifetime and 12-month prevalence of *DSM-III-R* psychiatric disorders in the United States: Results from the National Comorbidity Study. *Archives of General Psychiatry, 51,* 8–19.

Klett, C. J., Point, P., & Caffey, E. (1972). Evaluating the long-term need for antiparkinson drugs by chronic schizophrenics. *Archives of General Psychiatry, 26,* 374–379.

Koob, G. F., & Le Moal, M. (1997). Drug abuse: Hedonic homeostatic dysregulation. *Science, 278,* 52–58.

Lewis, C. E., & Bucholz, K. K. (1991). Alcoholism, antisocial behavior and family history. *British Journal of Addiction, 86,* 177–194.

Liebson, I., Bigelow, G., & Flamer, R. (1973). Alcoholism among methadone patients: A specific treatment method. *American Journal of Psychiatry, 130,* 483–485.

Liskow, B., Powell, B. J., Nickel, E., & Penick, E. (1991). Antisocial alcoholics: Are there clinically significant diagnostic subtypes? *Journal on Studies on Alcohol, 52,* 62–69.

Luthar, S. S., Merikangas, K. R., & Rounsaville, B. J. (1993). Parental psychopathology and disorders in offspring: A study of relatives and drug abusers. *Journal of Nervous and Mental Disease, 181,* 351–357.

Mathew, R. J., Wilson, W. H., Blazer, D. G., & George, L. K. (1993). Psychiatric disorders in adult children of alcoholics: Data from the Epidemiologic Catchment Area Project. *American Journal of Psychiatry, 150,* 793–800.

Metzger, D. S., Cornish, J., Woody, G. E., McLellan, A. T., Druley, P., & O'Brien, C. P. (1989). *Naltrexone in federal probationers* (NIDA Research Monograph 95, pp. 465–466). Washington, DC: U.S. Government Printing Office.

Milby, J. B., Garrett, C., English, C., Fritschi, O., & Clarke, C. (1978). Take-home methadone: Contingency effects on drug-seeking and productivity of narcotic addicts. *Addictive Behaviors, 3,* 215–220.

Miller, P. M. (1975). A behavioral intervention program for chronic public drunkenness offenders. *Archives of General Psychiatry, 32,* 915–918.

Miller, P. M., Hersen, M., Eisler, R. M., & Watts, J. G. (1974). Contingent reinforcement of lowered blood alcohol levels in an outpatient chronic alcoholic. *Behavioral Research and Therapy, 12,* 261–263.

Mitchell, S., & Rosa, P. (1981). Boyhood behavior problems as precursors of criminality: A fifteen-year follow-up study. *Journal of Child Psychology and Psychiatry, 22,* 19–33.

Moffitt, T. E. (1993). Adolescence-limited and life-course-persistent antisocial behavior: A developmental taxonomy. *Psychological Review, 100,* 674–701.

Moffitt, T. E., & Silva, P. A. (1988). Neuropsychological deficit and self-reported delinquency in an unselected birth cohort. *Journal of the American Academy of Child and Adolescent Psychiatry, 27,* 233–240.

National Association of Drug Court Professionals. (1997). *Defining drug courts: The key components.* Washington, DC: U.S. Department of Justice Programs.

National Institute on Drug Abuse. (1988). *Medical review officer manual: A guide to evaluating urine drug analysis* (DHHS Pub. No. ADM 88-1526). Washington, DC: U.S. Government Printing Office.

Nesse, R. M., & Berridge, K. C. (1997). Psychoactive drug use in evolutionary perspective. *Science, 278,* 63–66.

Newman, J. P., Patterson, C. M., & Kosson, D. S. (1987). Response perseveration in psychopaths. *Journal of Abnormal Psychology, 2,* 145–148.

Newman, J. P., Widom, C. S., & Nathan, S. (1985). Passive avoidance in syndromes of disinhibition: Psychopathy and extraversion. *Journal of Personality and Social Psychology, 48,* 1316–1327.

Offord, D. R. (1990). Conduct disorder: Risk factors and prevention. In D. Shaffer, I. Phillips, & N. D. Enzer (Eds.), *Prevention of mental disorders, alcohol and other drug use in children and adolescents* (OSAP Prevention Monograph 2, pp. 273–297). Rockville, MD: U.S. Department of Health and Human Services.

Olweus, D. (1979). Stability of aggressive reaction patterns in males: A review. *Psychological Bulletin, 86,* 852–875.

Patterson, C. M., & Newman, J. P. (1993). Reflectivity and learning from aversive events: Toward a psychological mechanism for the syndromes of disinhibition. *Psychological Review, 100,* 716–736.

Pickens, R. W., Svikis, D. S., McGue, M., & LaBuda, M. C. (1995). Common genetic mechanisms in alcohol, drug, and mental disorder comorbidity. *Drug and Alcohol Dependence, 39,* 129–138.

Project MATCH Research Group. (1997). Matching alcoholism treatments to client heterogeneity: Project MATCH posttreatment drinking outcomes. *Journal of Studies on Alcohol, 58,* 7–29.

Regier, D. A., Farmer, M. E., Rae, D. S., Locke, B. Z., Keith, S. J., Judd, L. L., & Goodwin, F. K. (1990). Comorbidity of mental disorders with alcohol and other drug abuse: Results from the Epidemiologic Catchment Area (ECA) Study. *Journal of the American Medical Association, 264,* 2511–2518.

Robins, L. N. (1978). Sturdy childhood predictors of adult antisocial behavior: Replications from longitudinal studies. *Psychological Medicine, 8,* 611–622.

Robins, L. N., & McEvoy, L. (1990). Conduct problems as predictors of substance abuse. In L. N. Robins & M. Rutter (Eds.), *Straight and devious pathways from childhood to adulthood* (pp. 182–204). New York: Cambridge University Press.

Robins, L. N., Tipp, J., & Przybeck, T. (1991). Antisocial personality. In L. N. Robins & D. A. Regier (Eds.), *Psychiatric disorders in America: The Epidemiologic Catchment Area Study* (pp. 258–290). New York: Free Press.

Rounsaville, B. J., & Kleber, H. D. (1986). Psychiatric disorders in opiate addicts: Preliminary findings on the course and interaction with program type. In R. E. Meyer (Ed.), *Psychopathology and addictive disorders* (pp. 140–168). New York: Guilford Press.

Rounsaville, B. J., Kosten, T. R., Weissman, M. M., Prusoff, B., Pauls, D. Anton, S. F., & Merikangas, K. (1991). Psychiatric disorders in relatives of probands with opiate addition. *Archives of General Psychiatry, 48,* 33–42.

Shapiro, S. K., Quay, H. C., Hogan, A. E., & Schwartz, K. P. (1988). Response perseveration and delayed responding in undersocialized aggressive conduct disorder. *Journal of Abnormal Psychology, 97*, 371–373.

Sher, K. J., Walitzer, K. S., Wood, P. K., & Brent, E. E. (1991). Characteristics of children of alcoholics: Putative risk factors, substance use and abuse, and psychopathology. *Journal of Abnormal Psychology, 100*, 427–448.

Silverman, K., Higgins, S. T., Brooner, R. K., Montoya, I. D., Schuster, C. R., & Preston, K. L. (1995). *Differential reinforcement of sustained cocaine abstinence in intravenous polydrug abusers* (NIDA Research Monograph 153, p. 212). Washington, DC: U.S. Government Printing Office.

Stitzer, M., Bigelow, G., & Liebson, I. (1982, April). Contingent reinforcement of benzodiazepine-free urines from methadone maintenance patients. In L. S. Harris (Ed.), *Problems of drug dependence 1981: Proceedings of the 43rd annual scientific meeting, the Committee on Problems of Drug Abuse* (NIDA Research Monograph, pp. 282–287). Washington, DC: U.S. Government Printing Office.

Substance Abuse and Mental Health Services Administration. (1996). *National Household Survey on Drug Abuse: Population estimates 1995* (DHHS Pub. No. SMA 96-3095). Washington, DC: U.S. Government Printing Office.

Thompson, T., & Schuster, C. R. (1968). *Behavioral pharmacology.* Englewood Cliffs, NJ: Prentice-Hall.

Tremblay, R. E., Pihl, R. O., Vitaro, F., & Dobkin, P. L. (1994). Predicting early onset of male antisocial behavior from preschool behavior. *Archives of General Psychiatry, 51*, 732–739.

Whitmore, E. A., Mikulich, S. K., Thompson, L. L., Riggs, P. D., Aarons, G. A., & Crowley, T. J. (1997). Influences on adolescent substance dependence: Conduct disorder, depression, attention deficit hyperactivity disorder, and gender. *Drug and Alcohol Dependence, 47*, 87–97.

Windle, M. (1994). Coexisting problems and alcoholic family risk among adolescents. *Annals of the New York Academy of Sciences, 708*, 157–164.

Winters, K. C., Stinchfield, R. D., Henly, G. A., & Schwartz, R. H. (1990–1991). Validity of adolescent self-report of alcohol and other drug involvement. *International Journal of Addictions, 25*, 1379–1395.

Woody, G. E., McLellan, A. T., Luborsky, L., & O'Brien, C. P. (1985). Sociopathy and psychotherapy outcome. *Archives of General Psychiatry, 42*, 1081–1086.

Yeudall, L. T. (1980). A neuropsychosocial perspective of persistent juvenile delinquency and criminal behavior: Discussion. *Annals of the New York Academy of Sciences, 347*, 349–355.

Young, S. E., Mikulich, S. K., Goodwin, M. B., Hardy, J., Martin, C. L., Zoccolillo, M. S., & Crowley, T. J. (1995). Treated delinquent boys' substance use: Onset, pattern, relationship to conduct and mood disorders. *Drug and Alcohol Dependence, 37*, 149–162.

Zackon, F., McAuliffe, W. E., & Ch'ien, J. M. N. (1993). *Recovery training and self-help: Relapse prevention and aftercare for drug addicts* (NIH Pub. No. 93-3521). Washington, DC: U.S. Government Printing Office.

AUTHOR INDEX

Baxter, R. C., 154, *159*
Beatty, D., 206, *217*
Bebout, R. R., 97, 99, *116, 117*
Beck, A. T., *241*, 321, *323*
Begin, A. M., 106, *117*
Beitman, B., 320, *323*
Belding, M. A., 209, 211, *218, 219, 238,*
    332, 343
Bell, D. S., 98, *115*
Bellack, A. S., 99, *115*
Bellavia, C. W., *94*
Benda, B., 96, *115*
Benowitz, N. L., 249, 257, *258, 260*
Berger, H., 244, *258*
Berglas, S., 315, *324*
Berman, K. F., 98, *120*
Berridge, K. C., 346, *369*
Bertera, R. L., 150, *158*
Besalel, V. A., *237*
Best, S. E., 267, *277*
Bickel, W., 19, 20, 27, 35, 36–39, *41–*
    45, 50, 53, 54, 56, 72, 79, 93,
    117, 129, 144, 159, 179, 184,
    199, 201, 218, 230, 240, 249,
    260, 266, 268–270, 275, 276,
    277, 278, 309, 323, 324, 329,
    336, 337, 340, 341, 208, 213,
    217, 229, 238, 342, 344, 367
Bien, T. H., *11*
Biernacki, P., 158, *161*
Bigelow, G., 5, 8, *11, 12,* 17, 19, 20, 26,
    27–29, 46, 56, 58, 59, 72–74,
    129, 131, 142, 144, 166, 171,
    174, 176, *178, 180, 181,* 184,
    195, *199, 201,* 204, 206, 207,
    212, 213, *218–220, 221–225,*
    229, 230–232, 235, 238–241,
    249, 250, 261–263, 268, 272–
    275, 277, 284, 298, 307, 308,
    329, 330, 332, 336, 337, 342–
    344, 351, 354, 360, 365, 367,
    368, 370
Birkhead, G. S., 150, *158*
Bisighini, R. M., *71, 323, 365*
Black, J. L., 214, *217, 235, 238,* 329,
    342
Blaine, J., *241*
Blaine, J. D., 4, 7, *12*
Blair, S. N., *159*
Blazer, D. G., 360, *368*
Blitz, C. C., 150, *159*
Block, D., 68–69, *72*

Block, M., 249, *259*
Bloom, B. R., 124, *141*
Bly, J. L., 150, *158*
Bobo, J. K., 245, *258*
Bohman, M., 360, *365*
Bond, G. R., 99, *115*
Bonk, S., *143*
Borders, O. T., 234, *239*
Boren, J. J., 8, *12, 18, 30*
Borg, L., *307*
Borkovec, T. D., 310, *323*
Boronow, J. J., *120*
Bostow, D. E., *18, 28*
Bouchard, T. J., *367*
Boudin, H. M., *365*
Bowers, M. B., Jr., 96, *117*
Bowser, B., *160*
Boyle, M. H., 359, 360, *365*
Brabau, J. C., *158*
Brady, C., 125, *143*
Brady, J. V., *18, 30, 279*
Brady, K., 96, 100, *115*
Braff, D., *115, 118, 121*
Branchey, M. H., 360, *365*
Brantley, J. M., *365*
Brawley, E. R., *19, 29*
Breakey, W. R., 6, *10, 78, 92*
Brenner, G. F., 8, *11*
Brent, E. E., 361, *370*
Breslow, L., 150, *158*
Brethen, P., *72, 74*
Brewington, V., 174, *178*
Brodie, B., *58, 71*
Brodsky, M. D., *58, 72*
Bromberg, A., *143*
Bromberg, R., *143*
Brooks, S., *158*
Broomer, R., 8, *10*
Brooner, R. K., 17, *27, 55, 79, 94,* 168,
    169, *172, 180, 201, 208, 213,*
    214, 218, 219, 221, 227, 228,
    233, 235, 238, 239, 262, 308,
    311, 325, 360, 361, 365, 367,
    370
Brotman, R., 125, *144*
Brown, B. S., 151, *159,* 234, *239,* 306
Brown, J. M., *11*
Brown, S. S., 125, *141*
Bruce, B. K., *261*
Bryant, K. J., 42, *53*
Buchkremer, G., 249, *259*
Bucholz, K. K., 360, *368*

Corrigan, E. M., 78, 92
Corrigan, P. W., 49, 54
Corty, E., 99, 118
Costantini, M. F., 149, 152, 160
Cottler, L., 189, 201, 360, 365
Coughey, K., 147, 159
Council on Scientific Affairs, 78, 93
Coursey, R., 111, 118
Covi, L., 290, 306
Craig, P. A., 301, 308
Craig, R. J., 251, 259
Craig, T. J., 96, 97, 118
Crapanzano, M. S., 96, 114
Crean, J., 336, 341
Crits-Christoph, K., 221, 240
Croghan, I. T., 261
Crowley, T. J., 232, 234, 240, 250, 259,
    329–331, 341, 342, 348–350,
    352–354, 359, 360, 362, 365–
    367, 370
Cruser, K., 55, 261
Cuffel, B., 96, 97, 116
Cummings, K. M., 150, 159
Curran, J. W., 265, 277
Curry, S., 249, 259
Curtis, R., 124, 141
Cushman, P., 58, 72
Cutler, R., 206, 218, 267, 277

Daeschler, C. V., 94
Dahlgren, L. A., 7, 11
Dallabetta, G., 148, 160
Darke, S., 183, 184, 191, 199, 202, 360,
    366
Darwin, W. D., 290, 302, 303, 306
Datallo, P., 96, 115
Daugherty, T. K., 361, 366
Daughton, D. M., 247, 259
Davenny, K., 179
Davidson, A. B., 363, 366
Davidson, P. T., 124, 142
Davis, D. D., 310, 314, 321, 325
Davis, H., 148, 158
Davis, J. M., 98, 117
Davis, J. R., 249, 259
Davis, K., 159
Davis, L. J., Jr., 261
Davis, W. H., 148, 158
Davis, W. R., 150, 159
Dayhoff, D. A., 186, 199
De La Rosa, M., 58, 72

Decker, K. P., 100, 116
DeFord, H. A., 214, 217, 235, 238, 329,
    342
DeGrandpre, R. J., 19, 27, 276, 277
DeJesus, A., 180
Delaney, C. J., 284, 308
Delaney, D., 54, 72, 93, 107, 115, 159,
    179, 199, 218, 278, 309, 323
Delis, D. C., 118
Dellafera, S. S., 284, 307
Delucchi, K., 12, 55, 187, 199, 200, 201
Dennis, M. L., 174, 179, 222, 238
Deren, S., 150, 159, 174, 178
DeRisi, W., 106, 118
Dern, R. S., 117
Des Jarlais, D., 141, 143
Devaul, R., 96, 117
Devlin, C. J., 124, 142
Dews, P. B., 18, 28
Diamond, R., 112, 116
Dickerson, S. L., 290, 306
Dickson, S., 119
DiClemente, C. C., 310, 323
DiFranza, J. R., 245, 251, 259
Dimeff, L. A., 58, 72
Dinwiddie, S. H., 360, 366
Dixon, J., 184, 199
Dixon, L., 98, 114, 116
D'Lugoff, B., 181, 219, 240, 344
Dobkin, P. L., 359, 370
Dobson, D. J., 99, 116
Docherty, J. P., 120
Dolan, M. P., 214, 217, 235, 238, 329,
    342
Donham, R., 37, 38, 39, 54, 117, 324,
    342, 367
Donohue, B., 237
Dooley, C. P., 315, 324
Dooley, R. T., 249, 259
Dorus, W., 230, 240, 268, 278
Drake, R. E., 78, 93, 96, 97, 99, 115–
    117
Drossman, A. K., 96, 121
Drucker, E., 58, 72
Druley, K. A., 222, 240
Druley, P., 368
Dukes, W., 107, 116
Dunmeyer, S., 4, 12
Dyck, D., 106, 119

Eberman, K. M., 261

Fyfe, M. J., 285, 306

Gainey, R. R., 62, 74
Galanter, M., 97, 116
Galloway, E., 237
Ganju, V. K., 96, 120
Garrett, C., 59, 73, 164, 179, 197, 200, 206, 219, 224, 240, 337, 343, 354, 368
Gastfriend, D. R., 100, 117
Gawin, F. H., 62, 71, 98, 119, 323, 365
Gazaway, P., 125, 143
Gearon, J. S., 99, 115
Gelberg, L., 78, 93
Geller, J., 112, 117
General Accounting Office, 125, 142
Genser, S., 4, 12
Gentile, M. A., 197, 199
George, L. K., 360, 368
Geringer, W. M., 150, 159
Gershon, S., 98, 114
Gerstein, D., 125, 142
Gerstley, L., 360, 367
Gerwitz, G., 96, 117
Giancola, P. R., 361, 367
Gibson, D. R., 149, 152, 160
Gilchrist, L. D., 245, 258
Gill, K., 360, 367
Gimarc, J. D., 159
Ginsberg, D., 249, 260
Ginzburg, H. M., 238
Glaros, A. G., 249, 259
Glaser, M., 247, 260
Glasgow, R. E., 249, 261
Glicksman, M., 206, 218
Glosser, D. S., 212, 218, 230, 238
Goehl, L., 320, 324
Gold, J. M., 98, 117
Gold, M. S., 96, 117
Gold, V. J., 18, 29
Goldberg, F., 230, 240, 268, 278
Goldberg, J., 208, 213, 218, 228, 239
Goldberg, S. R., 19, 28
Goldberg, T. E., 98, 117
Goldberger, B. A., 297, 303, 306, 307
Goldfried, M., 310, 320, 323
Goldman, D., 367
Goldman, H. H., 97, 118
Goldsmith, D., 59, 72, 206, 218, 225, 229, 239, 284, 307
Goldstein, A. P., 317, 324

Goldstein, M., 141
Goldstein, M. B., 186, 199
Goldstein, P. J., 284, 307
Goodwin, F. K., 12, 55, 118, 369
Goodwin, M. B., 370
Gordon, J., 58, 60, 73, 185, 186, 193, 200, 248, 249, 259, 261, 309, 319, 324
Gordon, L. T., 62, 63, 71, 323, 365
Gossop, M., 184, 201
Götestam, K. G., 206, 219
Gould, J., 155, 160
Grabowski, J., 116, 125, 128, 129, 131, 137, 138, 142, 217, 252, 262, 337, 342, 343
Graham, J. M., 40, 53
Grant, B. F., 42, 54
Green, M. F., 98–100, 117, 118
Greenfield, L., 360, 365
Greenwald, M. K., 361, 367
Grey, C., 251, 260
Griffith, G., 307
Griffiths, R. R., 5, 11, 17, 19, 20, 28, 224, 239, 251, 259, 279, 332, 342
Groerer, J. C., 58, 72
Gropper, B., 58, 72, 307
Gross, B., 94
Gross, J., 58, 74
Grove, W. M., 359, 367
Guerrera, M. P., 245, 251, 259
Guess, D., 19, 28
Gulati, V., 72
Gulliver, S. B., 55, 261
Gur, R. C., 119
Gur, R. E., 119
Gurwitch, R. H., 197, 200
Guydish, J., 160

Haas, G., 98, 114, 116
Hadler, S. C., 158
Haertzen, C. A., 290, 306
Haertzen, C. C., 306
Hagan, T., 125, 142
Halford, W. K., 249, 259
Halikas, J. A., 4, 11
Hall, R. C. W., 96, 117
Hall, S. M., 4, 11, 12, 55, 59, 72, 165, 179, 184–186, 197, 199–202, 205, 212, 218, 222, 249, 260, 271, 272, 278

Hall, W., 183, 202, 360, 366

Han, D., 160

Handelsman, L., 72

Handmaker, N. S., 11

Hangford, P. V., 18, 30

Hanna, B. A., 143

Hardesty, A. S., 96, 121

Hardy, A. M., 265, 277

Hardy, J., 370

Harford, T. C., 42, 54, 360, 367

Hargreaves, W. A., 59, 72, 96, 120, 165,
179, 249, 260, 272, 278

Harrell, A., 356, 367

Harris, F. R., 19, 29

Harris, M., 97, 99, 116, 117

Harris, W. C., 17

Harris-Adeeyo, T., 161

Harrison, L., 58, 72, 289

Hart, B. M., 19, 29

Hartel, D. M., 58, 72, 171, 179

Hartley, D., 102, 119

Hartnoll, R. L., 265, 278

Hartwell, N., 13

Harvey, P. D., 98, 117

Harwood, H., 125, 142, 238

Hasson, A., 70, 73, 74

Hatsukami, D. K., 7, 11

Haugland, G., 96, 97, 118

Havassy, B. E., 4, 11, 184, 185, 197, 199,
202, 222, 229, 238

Haver, V. M., 284, 308

Haverkos, H. W., 142

Hawkins, J. D., 62, 74

Hawkins, T. D., 171, 179

Hawthorne, J., 59, 74, 181, 204, 219,
220, 225, 240, 249, 263, 329,
344

Headlee, C. P., 17, 29, 30

Heather, N., 184, 186, 199

Heatherton, T. F., 247, 260

Heatley, S. A., 247, 259

Heaton, R., 118, 121

Hefferline, R. F., 18, 29

Heintz, G. C., 96, 114

Hellerstein, D. J., 117

Henly, G. A., 349, 370

Henn, F. A., 359, 367

Henningfield, J. E., 5, 11, 17–19, 28

Herman, A. A., 124, 143

Herman, I., 241

Herrman, A. A., 150, 158

Herrnstein, R., 29

Hersen, M., 355, 368

Hersen, M. Z., 131, 142

Heselbrock, M., 367

Hess, J. M., 290, 306

Hesselbrock, M., 360, 367

Hesselbrock, V., 360, 367

Hester, R. K., 11, 106, 117

Heston, L., 367

Heywood, E., 361, 365

Higgins, S., 4–6, 11, 13, 19, 20, 27, 29,
35–46, 48–50, 53–56, 57, 59,
60, 72, 74, 78, 79, 93, 94, 106,
107, 112, 115, 117, 150, 159,
165, 166, 168–170, 172, 173,
177, 179, 180, 184, 193, 195,
199, 201, 212, 214, 216, 218,
219, 229, 231, 238, 249, 260,
262, 270, 271, 273–276, 277,
278, 308, 309, 311, 323–325,
329, 332, 334, 336, 337, 339,
341–343, 346, 354, 367, 370

Hillsgrove, M. J., 302, 306

Hinton, M., 150, 159

Hirsch, C. S., 13

Hjalmarson, A., 247, 260

Ho, A., 307

Hodos, W., 18, 29, 171, 179

Hoffman, J. S., 78, 93

Hoffman, R. G., 4, 11

Hogan, A. E., 361, 369

Hole, A., 241

Holland, J. G., 18, 30

Hollander, J. R., 233, 239

Holt, C. S., 40, 53

Holz, W. C., 18, 27

Holzer, C. E., 96, 120

Honer, W., 96, 117

Hopkins, B. L., 19, 29

Horger, B. A., 44, 55

Horton, A. M., 4, 12

Howanitz, E., 115

Hser, Y., 244, 260, 265, 278

Hua, S., 147, 159

Hubbard, R. L., 174, 179, 222, 238

Huber, A., 61, 72

Huber, J. H., 186, 199

Huggins, G., 125, 143

Huggins, N., 197, 201

Hughes, A., 289

Hughes, J. R., 7, 11, 35, 41–44, 46, 53–
55, 72, 93, 159, 179, 199, 218,

Ofstead, C., 150, *160*
Ogden, D., *54, 342*
O'Gorman, T., 361, 365
Oliveto, A. H., 267, 277
Olsen, G. D., 4, *11*
Olweus, D., 359, 369
Onken, L. S., 4, 7, *12*
Opler, L. A., 96, *119*
Oppenheimer, E., 184, *201*
Orleans, C. T., 150, *160, 244, 262*
Osborn, E., 251, 260
Ottomanelli, G., 206, *218*
Ownes, B. J., *94*

Pakes, J., 125, *143*
Palmen, M. A., *261*
Paluzzi, P. A., 125, *143*
Pangiosonlis, P., *217*
Paone, D., *143*
Paradise, M. J., 186, *201*
Parker, D. A., 360, 367
Parson, P., *158*
Parsons, M. B., 340, *343*
Passannante, M. R., 150, *159*
Passero, J. M., *94*
Patch, V. D., 206, *219*
Patterson, C. M., 361, 369
Pauls, D., *369*
Paulsen, J. S., 98, *118*
Pear, J., 330, *343*
Penick, E., 186, 187, 200, 360, 368
Peniston, E., 106, *118*
Penk, W. E., 214, *217, 235, 238, 329, 342*
Pensec, M., 99, *115*
Pepper, B., *94*
Pepper, S., *55, 261*
Perin, C. T., 332, *343*
Perkins, M. P., *143*
Perlman, D. C., 124, *143*
Perry, P. J., 96, *118*
Perry, W., *118*
Persons, J. B., 321, *324*
Peters, J. E., 284, 290, 307
Petersen, R. C., *148*
Peterson, J. B., 361, 367
Peterson, J. E., *262*
Peterson, K. A., 186, *201*
Peterson, P. L., 62, *74*
Peterson, R. C., *159*
Peterson, R. F., 19, *27*

Petty, T. L., 250, *259*
Phibbs, C. S., 125, *143*
Phillips, E. L., *30*
Pickens, R., 17, 19, *30, 360, 369*
Pierce, C. H., 18, *30*
Pihl, R. O., 359, 361, 367, 370
Piotrowski, N. A., *12, 55*, 184, 185, 195, 198, 200, *201*
Piserchia, P. V., 150, *160*
Platt, J. J., 154, 159, 165, 174, *179, 180, 186, 200, 218, 238, 329, 343*
Pliskoff, S. S., 171, *179*
Plutchik, R., *115*
Point, P., 352, 368
Polk, A., 205, *218*
Pope, G. C., 186, *199*
Pope, M. A., 245, *261*
Popkin, M. K., 96, *117*
Popkin, S. J., *93*
Portera, L., *13*
Porvaznik, M., 285, 307
Powell, B. J., 200, 360, 368
Powers, K., 265, *278*
Premack, D., 18, *29*
Prendergast, J. J., 247, *259*
Preston, K. L., *55*, 168, 169, 172, 173, *180, 181, 201, 219, 262*, 291, 294, 295–298, 307, 308, 344, 370
Price, R. K., 360, 365
Primm, B. J., 206, *217*
Project MATCH Research Group, 25, 30, 310, 324, 345, 364, 369
Prout, M., 367
Prusoff, B., *369*
Przybeck, T., 359, 369
Pust, R. E., *143*

Quay, H. C., 361, 366, 369
Quigley, L. A., 186, *200*
Quinones, M. A., 150, *159*
Quoc Le, H., 124, *142*

Racenstein, J. M., *119*
Rachal, J. V., 174, *179, 222, 238*
Rachel, J. V., 58, *71*
Raczynski, J. M., 77–79, 93, *94, 197, 200, 343*
Rae, D. S., *12, 55, 118, 369*

Saitoh, M., 303, *308*
Sakamoto, M., 303, *308*
Salem, D. A., 78, *94*
Salisbury, Z., *159*
Salomon, N., *143*
Salzinger, K., 18, *30*
Sande, M. A., 58, *71*
Sandor, R. S., 245, *262*
Satel, S., 98, 102, *119*, 290, *308*
Savage, L., 125, *144*, 251, *263*
Sawe, U., 247, *262*
Saxon, A. J., 214, *219*, 237, *238*, 284, *308*, 330, *342*
Saykin, A. J., 98, *119*
Scarpelli, E. M., 58, *72*
Schenk, S., 44, *55*
Schilling, R. F., II, 245, *258*
Schinke, S. P., 245, *258*
Schmidt, C., 221, *238*, 360, *365*
Schmidt, F. L., 248, *264*
Schmitz, J., *116*, 128, 129, 131, 137, *142*, 217, 252, *262*, 337, *342*, *343*
Schneider, N. G., 247, 248, 254, 257, *261*
Schnitz, J., 129, *142*
Schoenbaum, E. E., 58, *72*, *144*, *179*
Schottenfeld, R. S., 125, *143*
Schramm, W., 301, *308*
Schroeder, S. R., 18, *30*
Schulman, A., 18, *30*
Schultz, S. K., 98, *116*
Schumacher, J. E., 77, 79, 82, 83, 89, 93, 94, 197, *201*, *343*
Schuster, C. R., 17, *31*, *55*, 147, *160*, 168, 169, 172, *180*, *201*, *219*, 262, 291, 294, 296, 297, *307*, *308*, 323, *325*, *343*, 345, 361, *367*, *370*
Schwartz, K. P., 361, *369*
Schwartz, R. H., 349, *370*
Schwartz, R. M., 125, *143*
Schweigler, M., 244, *258*
Sckell, B. M., *144*
Sees, K., *12*, *55*, 186, 187, 195, *199–201*, 244, 245, *262*
Segal, N., *367*
Seibyl, J. P., 96, *119*
Seidman, S. N., 149, *160*
Seidner, A. L., 8, *11*, 244, 246, *259*
Selander, J., *115*
Selgestad, B., 354, *366*

Sellers, M. L., 251, *261*
Sells, S. B., 222, *240*
Selwyn, P. A., 58, *72*, 124, *144*, *179*
Senay, E. C., 230, *240*, 268, *278*
Serper, M. R., 96, *119*
Sevy, S., 96, *119*
Shaffer, H. J., 186, *201*
Shaner, A., 48, 49, *55*, 96, 98, 99, 102, 105, 106, 109, *117*, *119*, *120*, 165, *180*, 329, *343*
Shapiro, D. A., 319, 321, *325*
Shapiro, M., 107, *120*
Shapiro, S. K., 361, *369*
Shaw, B. F., 321, *323*
Shea, P., *55*, *261*
Sheehan, M., 184, *201*
Sher, K. J., 361, *370*
Sherer, M. A., 98, *120*
Sherman, J. A., 19, *27*
Sherman, M. F., 284, *308*
Shiffman, S., 248, *262*
Shillington, A. M., 360, *365*
Shipley, R. H., 150, *160*
Shopshire, M. S., *12*, *55*, 200
Shoptaw, S., 61, *72*, 74, 245, 253–256, *258*, 260–262
Shumway, M., 96, 97, *116*, *120*
Shuster, L., 284, *308*
Sibthorpe, B., 151, 155, 156, 157, *160*
Siddiqui, Q., 58, *73*, 304, *307*
Sidman, M., 18, *30*, 330, *343*
Sigvardsson, S., 360, *365*
Silagy, C., 248, *262*
Silva, P. A., 359, 361, *365*, *368*
Silverman, K., 8, *12*, 17, *27*, 37, 39, *55*, 79, *94*, 166, 168–174, 176–178, *180*, 184, 193, 195–197, *201*, 204, 212, 214, *219*, 249, *262*, 275, *278*, 290, 291, 294, 296–298, *307*, *308*, 311, 323, *325*, 335, *343*, 354, *370*
Simon, S., 70, *74*
Simpson, D., 125, *144*, 207, *219*, 222, 240, 251, *263*, 332, *343*
Simpson, E. E., 4, *13*, 58, *74*
Simpson, T. L., *11*
Skinner, B. F., 16, 18, 28, *30*, 164, 168, *179*, 330, 332, *342*, *344*
Skinner, W., 245, *261*
Skog, O.-J., 284, *308*
Slesinger, D. P., 150, *160*
Smith, D. E., 227, *240*

Thorton, W., 268, 278
Tidey, J., 44, 50, 52, 55, 56
Tipp, J., 359, 369
Todd, T. C., 206, 219, 223, 240
Tommasello, A., 29, 131, 142, 207, 218, 232, 239
Tonigan, J. S., 11
Toro, P. A., 78, 94
Tortu, S., 150, 159
Transderman Nicotine Study Group, 263
Tremblay, R. E., 359, 370
Trickett, E. J., 78, 94
Troughton, E., 361, 365
Trumble, J. G., 148, 159
Tsai, M., 320, 324
Tschann, J. M., 229, 238
Tsuang, J., 55, 105, 109, 119, 120, 180, 343
Tucker, D. E., 55, 98, 105, 106, 109, 119, 120, 180, 343
Tucker, J. A., 164, 171, 181, 203, 220, 276, 279
Tunis, S., 142
Tunstall, C., 249, 260
Turey, M., 96, 117
Tusel, D., 12, 55, 187, 195, 199–201

Ulbrich, P. M., 244, 264
Umbricht-Schneiter, A., 55, 172, 180, 219, 343
Unnithan, S., 184, 201
U.S. Department of Health and Human Services, 243, 244, 263
U.S. General Accounting Office, 58, 74
Usdan, S., 83, 93
Uzuka, M., 303, 308

Vaccaro, J. V., 98, 119
Vaillant, G., 221, 241
Valadez, A., 44, 55
Valentine, V. E., 365
Valliere, W. A., 55, 261
Van Deusen, J. M., 206, 219
van Kammen, D. P., 98, 120
Van Pragg, H. M., 96, 119
Velten, E., 151, 160
Veltri, D., 251, 259
Viswesvaran, C., 248, 264
Vitaro, F., 359, 370

Vollmer, T. R., 205, 219
Vuchinich, R. E., 164, 171, 181, 203, 220, 276, 279

Wait, R. B., 149, 160
Walia, A. A., 285, 306
Walitzer, K. S., 361, 370
Walker, M. L., 304, 306
Wall, D. D., 78, 94
Wall, T. L., 149, 152, 160
Wallace, D., 83, 93
Wallach, M. A., 78, 93, 96, 118
Wallen, M. C., 97, 120
Waller, M. B., 18, 30
Walter, M. I., 350, 366
Wang, J. C., 96, 117
Wapner, R., 142
Warburton, D. M., 186, 202
Ward, J., 183, 184, 202
Warheit, G. J., 244, 264
Wasserman, D. A., 4, 11, 184, 185, 197, 199, 202, 222
Watters, J. K., 157, 161
Watts, J. G., 355, 368
Way, L., 100, 115
Webster, D., 142
Wechsberg, W. M., 152, 155, 156, 161
Weddington, W. W., 184–186, 202, 234, 239, 306
Weeks, J. R., 17, 31
Weiden, P. I., 98, 114, 116
Weinberger, D. R., 98, 117, 120
Weiner, H. D., 97, 120
Weinman, M. L., 149, 160
Weinstein, M., 184, 202
Weiss, B., 18, 31
Weissman, M. M., 221, 240, 369
Weller, R. A., 4, 11
Wellman, P. J., 44, 55
Wells, E. A., 62, 63, 74
Werner, A., 119
Wertz, J., 221, 239
Wesson, D. R., 227, 240, 330, 342
West, J. C., 321, 324
Westin, A., 247, 260
Westman, E. C., 262
Wetter, D. W., 259
Wexler, D., 113, 120
Whitaker, D. L., 58, 74
Whitmore, E. A., 357, 360, 370
Widom, C. S., 361, 369

SUBJECT INDEX

Methadone maintenance (*continued*)
  reinforcing treatment plan behaviors, 205–207, 210–217
  relapse definition, 185
  relapse risk, 103–104, 183–184
  smoking-cessation program, 251–254, 257–258
  support from drug-free significant other, 233
  take-home doses, 164, 224–229, 272–273, 328–329
  tobacco use among clients, 8–9
  treatment approaches, 8
  treatment plan behaviors, 205
  voucher incentives for opiate abstinence, 171–173
Methadone transition treatment, 194
  baseline stabilization in, 195–196
  clinical trial design, 188–190
  clinical trial outcomes, 194–195
  contingency contracting in, 188, 191–194, 196
  course, 187
  effectiveness, 195–198
  goals, 187
  methadone regimen, 190
  monetary reinforcement, 191–194
  performance feedback, 194
  psychosocial intervention, 190–191
  research opportunities, 198
Methamphetamine abuse
  behavior therapy, 65
  behavior therapy with medication, 65–66, 68–69
  cognitive impairment in, 66, 70
  trends, 58–59
Monetary reinforcement
  cash payments, 109
  cocaine preference vs., 41–42, 52
  contingent disbursement of disability payments, 103–106, 110–115
  flexibility of procedures, 164–165
  interventions with cocaine-abusing pregnant women, 138–140
  limitations, 165
  in multiple drug abstinence interventions, 191–194
  in opioid detoxification, 272–273
  patient financial circumstances and response to, 107–109
  smoking-cessation programs, 46–47, 250

tuberculosis treatment incentives, 126, 131–133
Monitoring for drug use, 5–6, 283
  effective use of, 349
  hair analysis, 303–304
  methadone take-home dosing, 164
  new use vs. carryover effects, 294–298
  research directions, 304–305
  saliva analysis, 298–301
  self-reported data, 284
  smoking abstinence measures, 250, 253, 254–257, 258
  sweat testing, 301–303
  urinalysis-based vs. other contingencies, 212–213, 214, 216–217
  See also Urine testing
Multiple drug use
  contingency management efficacy in, 52–53
  contingent methadone dosing, 229–234
  in methadone maintenance patients, 183–184
  methadone transition treatment, 187–198
  rationale for targeting, 184–187
  single drug targets, 227
  tobacco, 244–246

Naltrexone, 173–174
Negative punishment, 5
Negative reinforcement
  contingent methadone dosing, 232–233
  as cost-reduction strategy, 329–330
  definition, 5
Neurobehavioral treatment model, 61

Operant psychology
  clinical applications, 18–19
  conceptual basis, 16
  conceptualization of drug use, 16–17
  laboratory foundations, 17–18, 19–20
  origins of contingency management, 15–16
  treatment implications, 19
Opioid abuse
  buprenorphine therapy, 266
  characteristics of dependence, 221, 223

detoxification agents, 267–268
detoxification effectiveness, 268–270
detoxification goals, 267
detoxification indications, 267
detoxification programs, 9, 231
detoxification with behavioral intervention, 266–267, 276–277
detoxification with contingency management, 270–275
naltrexone therapy, 173–174
role of behavioral intervention, 7–8
social consequences of addiction, 223
voucher systems for medication compliance in abusers, 173–174
withdrawal symptoms, 267
See also Methadone maintenance; specific drug
Outcomes research, 310
community reinforcement approach, 36–42, 310–311
methadone maintenance, detoxification effects, 265–267
methadone transition treatment, 194–195

Patterns of drug use, 3
among seriously mental ill, 7
Pharmacotherapy
antipsychotic, 99–100
with behavior therapy for methamphetamine abusers, 65–66, 68–69
behaviorally contingent, 235–236
for opioid dependence, 266
schizophrenia with substance abuse, 99–100
smoking-cessation treatments, 246–248
stimulant abuse, 59
vouchers for naltrexone compliance, 173–174
See also Methadone maintenance; specific medication
Positive punishment, 5
Positive reinforcement
abstinence, 203
client motivation and, 354
definition, 5
social benefits, 355–356, 357
Pregnant women, 7
cocaine relapse prevention, 137–138
cocaine use problems, 124–125

design of contingency management intervention, 140
effectiveness of contingency management for treatment compliance, 140
interventions with cocaine-dependent women, 133–137
prenatal care, 125
rationale for drug abuse intervention, 125
Preventive intervention
tuberculosis, 124
See also Relapse prevention
Process research, 310, 312–313
community reinforcement approach, 312–323
contingent management analysis, 316–317
for improving therapy, 321–322
Prostitution, 125
Psychosocial intervention
abstinence-related skills, 228
methadone clinic ancillary services, 222–223, 266
in methadone transition treatment, 190–191
outcomes research, 310
process research, 310, 312–313
psychoeducational, 60, 228
Punishment contingencies
client motivation and, 354
in contingency management, 5
contingency management conceptualization of drug use, 346–348
as cost-reduction strategy, 329–330
criminal justice system, 356
effective use of, 348–349, 356, 357
effectiveness, 330
random urine testing and, 331
research opportunities, 358
social benefits, 358

Rate effects. See Schedule of reinforcement
Recruitment into treatment
contingency management strategies, 148–150
detoxification design, 156–157
gender considerations, 156
previous treatment experience as factor in, 157

intervention with methadone patients, 8–9, 251–254, 257

measures of abstinence, 250, 253, 254–257, 258

multiple drug intervention, 197

in multiple drug use treatment, 244–246

nicotine agonists, 247

nicotine antagonists, 247–248

pharmacological interventions, 246

relapse prevention, 248–249

schedule of reinforcement for abstinence, 46–47

Social incentives, 9–91, 80–81, 84, 216, 354–355, 357

motivation to seek treatment, 223

punishment contingencies, 358

Social learning intervention, 58

Social reinforcement, 317

Social Security payments, 100–101

Special populations, 6–7. See also *population of interest*

Stimulant abuse

see Cocaine use–abuse; Methamphetamine abuse

See also *specific drug*

Sweat analysis, 301–303

Therapeutic relationship

in community reinforcement approach, 320–321

conflict resolution in, 321

as mechanism of change, 321

as outcome factor, 320

Therapist skills

community reinforcement approach, 313–318

process research, 312–313

training, 310

Training of therapists, 310, 334

Treatment, generally

benefits, 4

challenges, 4

enrollment incentives, 8

for injection drug users, 147–148

operant conditioning rationale, 19

operant environmental manipulations, 20

social factors in goal setting, 186–187

technology transfer, 327–328

Treatment plan behaviors

definition, 205

promoting abstinence by reinforcing, 206–207

reducing drug use by reinforcing, 207–217

reinforcing, 205–206

research opportunities, 215–216

task formulation, 209–210

Tuberculosis infection

compliance with treatment, 124

effectiveness of contingency management for treatment compliance, 140

methadone dose contingencies for treatment compliance, 127–129

monetary incentives for cocaine-abusing TB patients, 126, 131–133

preventive therapy, 124

rationale for drug abuse intervention, 125

risks in cocaine dependency, 123–124

screening, 126

treatment for, 126–127

treatment incentives, 126

Urine testing

alternative tests, 298

analytic factors, 287

biological basis, 284–285

during client high-risk periods, 331–332

in clinical trials, 289

confirmation assays, 287

in contingency management, 291–298

cost-reduction strategies, 331–332

delay in analysis, 332

dilution of sample, 285

drug concentration targets, 294

effectiveness of urinalysis-based contingencies, 212–213, 214, 216–217

frequency, 288

methods, 287–288

minimum schedule, 330–331

new use vs. carryover effects, 294–298

qualitative, 289–290

ABOUT THE EDITORS

Stephen T. Higgins earned his PhD from the University of Kansas in 1983 and completed postdoctoral training at the Johns Hopkins University School of Medicine and the National Institute on Drug Abuse (NIDA). In 1986, he joined the faculty of the University of Vermont, where he is now a professor of psychiatry and psychology. Dr. Higgins has received several national scientific awards, including the Joseph Cochin Award from the College on Problems of Drug Dependence and the Dan Anderson Award from the Hazelden Foundation. He is currently president of the Division of Psychopharmacology and Substance Abuse of APA. He is principal and co-investigator on numerous grants from NIDA and has published more than 150 scientific reports, chapters, and books. His research is a blend of laboratory and treatment–outcome research, with the common goal of furthering scientific understanding of the behavioral and pharmacological processes involved in cocaine abuse.

Kenneth Silverman received his PhD from the University of Kansas in 1984. His doctoral training and research focused on the areas of operant conditioning and behavior analysis. He completed a postdoctoral research fellowship in behavioral pharmacology at the Johns Hopkins University School of Medicine in 1991 and served as a staff fellow for the Clinical Trials Section of NIDA's Intramural Research Program in Baltimore, MD, from 1991 to 1993. He also joined the faculty of the department of psychiatry and behavioral sciences at the Johns Hopkins University School of Medicine in 1991, where he is currently an associate professor of behavioral biology. Funded by NIDA, his research focuses on the development and evaluation of abstinence reinforcement interventions for heroin and cocaine abuse in poor, inner-city adults and the integration of those abstinence reinforcement contingencies into model employment settings.